The WineProject

WASHINGTON STATE'S WINEMAKING HISTORY

Enjoy

RONALD IRVINE
WITH WALTER J. CLORE

Sketch Publications

Library of Congress Cataloging-in-Publication Data:
Irvine, Ronald, 1949–
The Wine Project: Washington State's Winemaking History / by Ronald Irvine with Walter J. Clore.—1st Sketch Publications ed.
p. cm.
Includes bibliographical references and index
ISBN 0-9650834-9-7
1. Wine and winemaking—Washington state—History.   2. Washington state—History.   3. Washington state—Industry.
I. Title
            96-092401
            Library of Congress Pre-Assigned Card

Editors: Miriam Bulmer, Kris Fulsaas
Cover design, interior design and composition: Cameron Mason
Cover art: Tim Girvin Design
Map artist: Marge Mueller
Sketch Publications logo: Tim Girvin Design

The author is grateful for permission to reprint the following material:
"The Washington Wine History," an original presentation made by Howard Somers to the Enological Society of the Pacific Northwest.
"History of the Northwest Grape 1825–1958," by Noel V. Bourasaw, Publisher of the *Northwest Wine Almanac.*
"Planting Dreams," by Ron Irvine January/February 1993 Vol. 6, No. 6. *NW Palate Magazine.*
"Planting Dreams, Part II: The Washington Wine Industry 1934–1970," by Ron Irvine March/April 1993 Vol. 7, No. 1. *NW Palate Magazine.*

Sketch Publications
P.O. Box 833
Vashon, WA 98070
206-463-5538
800-430-7843
e-mail: sketchpub@aol.com

Printed in the United States of America

To Virginia, for patience, and to Andrew and Claire, for the future.
Ronald Irvine

To my wife, Irene, after over 62 years of marriage, who persevered
while I visited all of those vineyards.
Walter J. Clore

CONTENTS

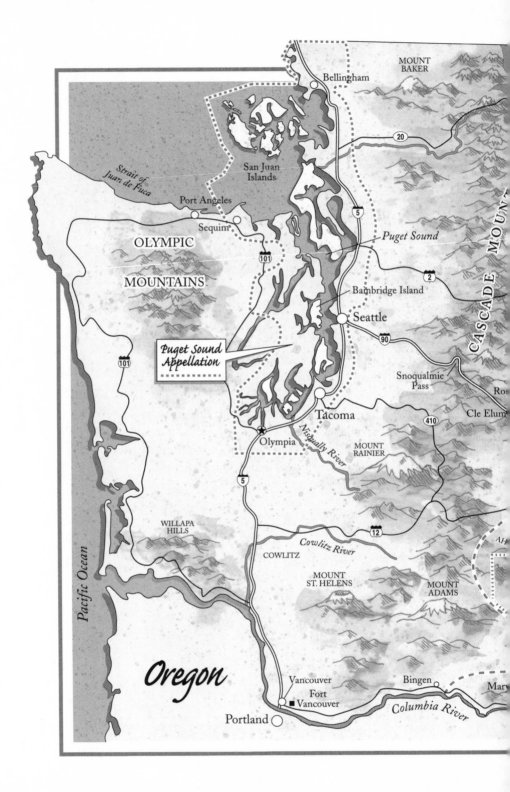

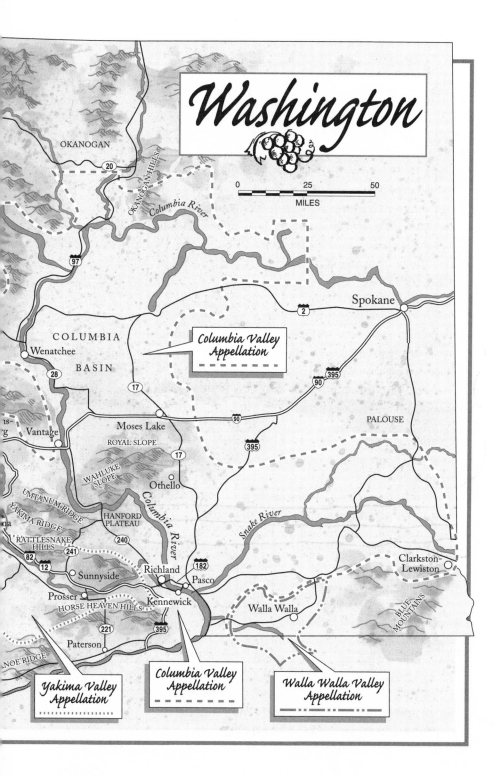

PREFACE

I grew up during Prohibition in a teetotaler, nonsmoking Methodist family. My mother was a staunch WCTUer (Woman's Christian Temperance Union). My first alcoholic drink was a taste of a sweet blackberry wine obtained from a local farmer and snuck into my Oklahoma A&M College fraternity house, where the thirty-five members shared a taste from the gallon jug.

One and a half months after getting married, I found myself a graduate student at Washington State College in Pullman, Washington. This was just six months after Repeal. Alcohol of any kind was the furthest thing from my mind. My wife, Irene, and I were young adults during the Great Depression and we were determined to make the best of this schooling opportunity.

Gradually, through successive steps, I was encouraged to consider the cultural problems of the *vinifera* wine grape. In 1964, with the developing interest in fine table wines, the Washington Wine and Grape Growers Council provided funding to Washington State University to determine the best adaptable varieties of grapes for making premium wines. I was intrigued. I then discovered wine's power: its historical significance; its use as a civilizing drink, both as a food beverage and as a social beverage; its political influence; its investment opportunities; and as a subject for lengthy and interesting discussions.

As a horticulturist I was mostly concerned with growing grapes, so I had to solicit other researchers and specialists in different disciplines involving grape culture, winemaking, marketing, and the economics of it all. This was not a difficult task for I found the interest of co-workers high, involving not only those in Washington but those of like interests in Oregon, Idaho, and British Columbia.

I was glad to retire on July 1, 1976. I wanted to be more directly involved with the wine industry, as my enthusiasm for grapes had intensified with the increase in large and small plantings made in the lower Yakima Valley, the Columbia Basin, and along the Columbia River as far down as White Salmon. For the past twenty years I have had the pleasure of consulting for over fifty clients about the culture of grapes, and I have witnessed a phenomenal interest and growth in both grape growing and winery development.

It has been exhilarating to participate in the sustained growth of the wine industry in Washington state, despite frost and winter cold damage, and even the occasional glut of too many grapes. The Columbia Basin viticultural appellation is approximately 18,000 square miles, larger than the combined area of New Jersey and New Hampshire, and encompasses the smaller appellations of the Yakima Valley and the Walla Walla Valley. With so large an area, the frost and winter cold problems wine growers face are never total. This is because of differences in the hardiness of varieties, latitudes, topography, macro- and micro-climates, sites, soils, slopes, and elevations, and the influence of the Columbia River and its tributaries.

The recently approved 7,500-square-mile Puget Sound viticultural appellation, west of the Cascade Mountains, is a moderate and temperate area which produces less than 1 percent of Washington's wine grape yield. Because of limited macro-climatic areas and urbanization, the potential of grape production expansion west of the Cascades is not great.

In the Columbia Basin, when good cultural practices are followed, every year is a vintage year. I envision no limitations to the continued growth of the premium wine industry, especially with the vast area of good vineyard sites. All that is necessary is a minimum of water, good viticultural practices, and maintaining high standards of wine quality.

I finally got my mother to taste Washington state premium table wines, but she preferred the sweet Concord. Anyway, I am still a Methodist.

Walter J. Clore
Prosser, Washington

ACKNOWLEDGMENTS

Writing a book is very much like growing a grapevine. Not just planting a grapevine but, rather, pulling together all the materials that make a grapevine.

The Wine Project: Washington State's Winemaking History, like a grapevine, required sustenance and a foundation. It required a root structure, and material to be built, word by word. It grew shoot by shoot, leaf by leaf, and cluster by cluster—vignettes in the true sense of the word. It required pruning and shaping, cutting, slashing, and rebuilding. Still, that wasn't enough: it needed a design, a form; then it needed to be printed, distributed, and sold. And it needed an audience.

The most essential component to this book is Dr. Walter Clore. He has been my personal archivist, editor, proofreader—and, finally, friend. He has been unbelievably patient and supportive. My hope is that someday you, too, will meet this type of giving, caring person.

This has been a cooperative venture, and although the narrative is written from my viewpoint, I have incorporated as much of Walt's thoughts and concerns as possible. Walt was with me, always. And he was always updating and fidgeting with an almost perfect chronology, which appears at the back of the book.

Now that the book is completed, I and my contributing author, Dr. Walter Clore, can let out an enormous sigh of relief, as we are truly grateful to all who have helped grow this book.

We would like to especially thank our families for their unceasing support, and occasional prodding. They have been our sustenance.

In the beginning of our venture we asked people to pre-purchase a book, to become either "Project Partners," "Project (and Commercial) Sponsors," or "Project Donors," through various levels of financial support. The response was heartwarming and reassuring. We wish to publicly thank all of our generous patrons, over 170 contributors, especially the "Donors": Wayne and Anne Gittinger, Jack and Harriet Bagdade, Stimson Lane Vineyards and Estates (and Jack Kelly), Fred Artz, Mr. and Mrs. Julian Steenbergen, John Salvini, and the Enological Society of the Pacific Northwest. Also, thanks to Dan Mitchell of Mitchelli's Family Restaurants, Queen Anne Thriftway in Seattle, and Norm Mathews at my local Thriftway on Vashon Island.

During the process of writing, I called on a number of people for advice and counsel, which was always given freely and generously.

Thanks to Dan Chasan, Elliott Wolfe of Peanut Butter Publishing, Ann Spiers, Kathy Nichols and Bob Allen, Pat Lawler, and Nina Bakeman.

I received plenty of editorial help from experienced editors: Miriam Bulmer and Kris Fulsaas; sometimes I wonder who really wrote this book. I got a final editorial boost from Noel Bourasaw. Of Noel I must say that this is the book that he could have, and maybe should have, written, but I am indebted to him for his help and for material that he made available from his own interest in history.

Thanks to Howard Somers, a quiet, modest visionary, who so obviously shared the desire to record this history, and who has been a remarkable resource. He recorded the first chronology of Washington's wine history. And to Bill Somers for making available the region's only wine museum, the Olde Ste. Charles Winery on Stretch Island.

Walt and I relied mightily on many of the small museums and historical societies throughout the state. The granddaddy of them all is the Washington State Historical Society in Tacoma, home to the astounding Asahel Curtis photograph collection.

And libraries: Especially my local branch of the King County Library and its always attentive staff, and their seemingly magical ability to make available obscure resource material. And thanks to two remarkable resource centers (goldmines, really): the University of Washington Special Collections and the Northwest Room at the central Tacoma Library.

We must pay tribute to those who told their stories; over seventy-five audio interviews and hundreds of telephone and personal conversations provided the root structure to our book.

Before the text was finished, I received munificent help from Tim Girvin and Sheila Klokkevold, of Tim Girvin Design in Seattle, whose bold design graces the cover. And finally, Cameron Mason carefully designed the layout of the book, shaping it with a decorative flourish.

This is not a typical history book. I adapted a scholarly methodology to a narrative, and very personal, style. I have tried to immerse the reader in a sense of place and history by telling the past through the present, as near as I experienced it.

Walt and I hope that you enjoy the rich harvest of this grapevine, our book.

Ronald Irvine
Vashon Island, Washington

GENESIS VINEYARD

"To understand the story of Washington wine you've got to learn how great the story is. It's a miracle!"

Leon Adams, *The Wines of America*

—*PROSSER, APRIL 1992*—

Dr. Walt Clore and I waited at tiny Prosser Airport, located just outside the business district of Prosser, Washington. Suddenly a white Chevy pickup pulled up alongside us. Out jumped Mike Hogue of Hogue Cellars. Hogue, stocky and energetic, shook our hands and welcomed us.

We were about to fly in his airplane over the Yakima Valley. Mike hopped on a small John Deere tractor and used it to pull his Cessna 310 onto the hangar's apron. The plane had been recently painted silver and metallic-blue, the sleek corporate colors of Hogue Cellars' distinctive wine label.

We boarded the four-seat airplane. As Mike fired up the propeller's engine, we adjusted our headphones so we could communicate with each other over the noise of the airplane.

Walt sat in the back seat. Then eighty years old, he is a sprightly figure, wearing his wavy white hair combed back. His slightly stooped posture is misleading: he is a tall man, but because he is hard of hearing, he often must bend down to better hear whomever he is conversing with. A recurring and bothersome tumor makes talking a chore—it twists his face to resemble a stroke victim. Beyond these outward discomforts, Walt is a fit, strong man. His mind is active and bright. He has difficulty recalling minute details, but who wouldn't, with a mind so full of information?

The spring sky was overcast and dramatic, and huge gray and black clouds billowed over the surrounding hills. At the end of the runway, to the west, white Mount Adams glistened, surrounded by a small round opening of blue sky.

As we lifted off I was excited to be flying above the Yakima Valley. I expected to gain a new perspective and appreciation for this valley that I had come to know so well. Hogue was taking us over his Genesis Vineyard, 20 acres that border the Irrigated Agriculture Research Extension Center (IAREC), about five miles northeast of Prosser. Dr. Clore began working at the center in 1937, retiring in 1976. I was flying above the valley with two of its most enthusiastic residents, one a successful farmer, the other a relentless scientist.

Below, the land curved up toward us, and the horizon shot past like a horizontal line on a television screen. A checkered quilt of brown and green lay draped beneath us. The farmland below, about a thousand feet down, appeared animated and unreal; the cars along Interstate 82 seemed suspended. The land looked fertile, with the promise of spring slowly unfolding: apple trees in bloom, rows of uniform grapevines, and brown fields of asparagus.

Walt's voice crackled into my headphone: "There's George Carter's home." The sound of the intercom was metallic and foreign, as if we were flying through space on a journey. I felt that we were breaking through some kind of time barrier and going back through the years.

Carter's home is located right next to the Genesis Vineyard. The Carters and Clores are close friends. George Carter was the winemaker at the research center, making wines from grapes that Walt and his associates had planted at the varietal test site in the center's vineyard.

Then Mike pointed down to Genesis Vineyard, saying, "There it is. It's twenty acres planted to Cabernet Sauvignon, Merlot, and Cabernet Franc." Hogue also pointed out his home on the north side of the research center and said that this was the area that spawned the beginnings of the Hogue Cellars back in 1983.

Mike recalled how he chose the name Genesis for this vineyard. He felt that Washington's premium wine industry really got its start here at the research center. This is where Clore, Carter, Charles Nagel, and a host of other scientists, economists, and field workers associated with Washington State University proved to the farmers and the wine industry that premium wine grapes could be grown successfully in eastern Washington.

Walt was touched to hear that Mike chose the name Genesis because of the vineyard's location next to the research center. But he also knew that the Washington wine industry did not start here. Its story is much, much broader and longer, going back to the first settlements in the Oregon Country—before there was even a state of Washington.

Mike pulled back on the yoke, and the plane's nose lifted into the gray Northwest sky. Rain lashed at the windshield. We were headed due north, flying over the Rattlesnake Hills. Farther north we could see the Yakima Ridge and the Umtanum Ridge, which are a series of dramatic east-west uplifts that rise to over 2,000 feet and shelter the Yakima Valley. The Rattlesnake Hills, especially, slope ever so slowly to the south as they dip down to the curving Yakima River, about twenty miles away.

Passing the Rattlesnake Hills, we flew over the Cold Creek Vineyard, owned by Stimson Lane Vineyards and Estates, owners of Chateau Ste. Michelle, Washington's largest winery operation. The gently sloping hills of the Cold Creek valley rise just past the Rattlesnake Ridge and at the tail end of the Yakima Ridge. Walt helped select that site in 1973 and is convinced it is one of the best in the valley. The vineyard site affords superb air drainage, the best protection against frosts and subzero temperatures. To the east and north are the broad valleys of the Columbia Basin; to the east and south, the Hanford Site, a broad plateau made inaccessible by the federal government, home to nuclear plants and government-sponsored research facilities. Also to the north is the Wahluke Slope, an area of great agricultural promise that slopes south toward the Columbia River and takes a slight east-west jog at this point. Most of the area is covered with fine sandy-loam soil of varying depths.

Flying over these ridges, I became disoriented. I knew the lay of the land well. I had driven on many of the roads, searching out vineyards and wineries, over the last twenty years. Viewed from high above, the land tended to flatten. Far off I could see the brilliance of Mount Adams. I knew it lay to the west, but it seemed to have moved to the north. I tried to re-orient myself. Then the Yakima River came back into view. Close by, running roughly parallel to the river, are the Sunnyside and Roza irrigation canals, which retrieve water from the snowmelt of the Cascade Mountains and bring sustenance to this

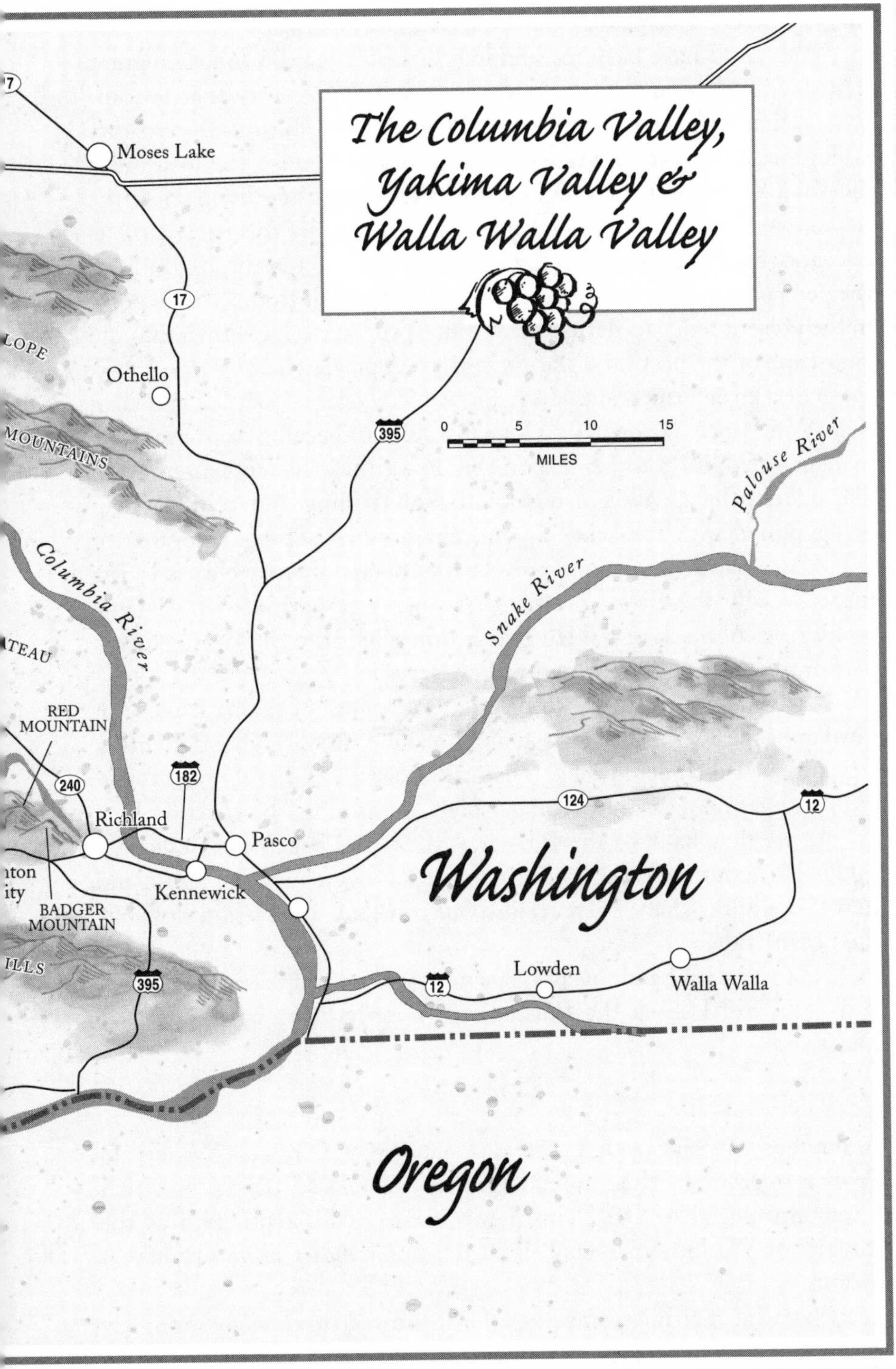

The Columbia Valley, Yakima Valley & Walla Walla Valley

Moses Lake

17

LOPE

MOUNTAINS

Othello

395

0   5   10   15
MILES

Palouse River

Columbia River

Snake River

TEAU

RED
MOUNTAIN

240

Richland

182

Pasco

124

12

Washington

Kennewick

BADGER
MOUNTAIN

nton
ity

ILLS

395

12

Lowden

Walla Walla

Oregon

magical desert. Everything was back where it belonged.

Walt and I have been researching the history of the wine and grape industry in Washington for several years. It is a history that encompasses the lush and magnificent Puget Sound Basin, the mighty Columbia River, the rolling wheat fields of the Palouse, the lush valley of Walla Walla, and the unique river valleys carved by floods over the millennia. We have come to recognize the richness of this past—and its relevance as a foundation for the industry's present and future. But, like the perspective from an airplane, looking at the past from a single point in the present tends to flatten the terrain. You have to get down into the landscape of the past (and the present) to appreciate it.

Mike turned the plane south and we flew over a vineyard and farm that Walt once co-owned. Unfortunately it became too much to manage in addition to his responsibilities at the research center. Walt, like many others, saw the possibilities of farming and couldn't help being pulled into the wine dream, envisioning sloping vineyards of grapevines twisting up out of the earth to hang on wire trellises. In the fall, especially, there is no prettier sight than a grapevine, with triangular bunches of black or golden grapes drooping from the vine against a backdrop of delicate green and yellow leaves.

Mike says he loves the challenge of farming, of taking a piece of raw land covered with sagebrush and breaking up the soil and planting a crop that will someday yield a bountiful harvest.

"You get hooked on it. You get high on farming," he exclaims.

As we flew back to the Prosser Airport and began our descent, I told Mike about the earliest efforts to produce wine in Washington and how those efforts have been cyclical but constant: an ebb and flow like the ocean's tide.

He turned his head toward us, with a serious and determined look, and said, "But I think the Washington wine industry is here to stay. Don't you?"

A number of years back I attended a party at Chinook Winery in Prosser, to celebrate their annual Merlot wine release. It was there that I was introduced to Dr. Clore. I was aware of his reputation as the "father" of Washington's wine industry, but I didn't know what that meant.

I knew at that initial meeting that I wanted to someday interview him and record his history.

About two years later, I decided to sell my share in Pike and Western Wine Shop. Pike and Western had begun in 1975 as a small storefront on the northern ramp down to the lower levels of Seattle's Pike Place Market. Through the years it continued to grow and expand, twice moving into a larger retail space. From the beginning, Pike and Western featured the wines of the Pacific Northwest, including wines from Idaho, Oregon, and Washington. I can still look back and see the shelves of that first store and the small selection of Northwest wines: Ste. Michelle, Tualatin, Knudsen-Erath (and Erath separately), Puyallup Valley Wine Cellars, Veredon, Timmens' Landing (Salishan), Associated Vintners, and Boordy.

We nurtured those wines. Our motive was simple. The wines were good and they showed great promise. We at Pike and Western saw ourselves as wine specialists and merchants serving our customers by providing them with the best of the Northwest. Being in the Pike Place Market meant we were surrounded by the best food products available—an abundance of seafood and meats, fresh fruits and vegetables, and gourmet items that at the time were found mainly in the small shops in the market. We aspired to be, and became, the wine store of the Pike Place Market.

After fifteen years of selling wine from all over the world, I decided to sell my shares to Michael Teer and said goodbye to my original partner, Dr. Jack Bagdade. One of the first things I did was to call Dr. Clore and arrange an interview with him. We met at his home in Prosser. It is a nice, solid, old-fashioned home, decorated with numerous Japanese furnishings and works of art. His interest in Japan goes back to a one-year sabbatical in 1961, when he and his wife lived in Kyoto.

Walt was eighty years old when I interviewed him. He begged me to sit in the comfortable chair under the light next to the picture window. He himself sat straddle-legged on an ottoman. He wasn't wearing his glasses, though he often does. Behind his right ear he wore his hearing aid. Without it, he says, he would be lost.

As Walt spoke, his recounting sounded stiff, almost a recitation of a logical chain of events. He knew his history, and I could tell this was not his first interview. As I listened I tried to pinpoint highlights we could explore later. He made his career and his life seem so cut and dried, so ordinary. Listening to him, one would think that anyone could have done what he has done in his lifetime. I don't think he appreciates his ability to have continually progressed in his life, always adding something to the foundation.

At the time, I was still fairly ignorant about Dr. Clore's contributions to agriculture in eastern Washington. I know today what I didn't know at that first interview: I was sitting across from a man whose contributions to agriculture could be measured in millons of dollars.

I asked Walt if he had a scrapbook to record events in his life. It turned out he is also an extraordinary archivist. He had a whole library of newspaper clippings, photo albums, books, and papers concerning everything that had happened in grape culture in Washington for the last half century.

But I didn't know that then. And I listened as Walt told me his story.

—MEETING DR. CLORE—

Walter Clore was born in Tecumseh, Oklahoma, in 1911. Eventually his family moved to Tulsa, where, along with two brothers, he lived a pretty normal mid-American life. Visits to his grandparents' farm instilled in him an interest in agriculture that followed him his entire life.

After studying botany and agriculture in high school, Walt attended Oklahoma Agricultural and Mechanical College (today called Oklahoma State University), where he majored in horticulture with a special interest in floriculture and landscape gardening. During the summer between his sophomore and junior years, he did survey work in Ohio and Indiana for the United States Department of Agriculture. He also turned out for football all four years of college and lettered the last two years as a lineman. During all four years, his team never lost to the more famous University of Oklahoma Sooners. Walt was also the president of Alpha Gamma Rho, an agricultural fraternity, and was elected to another, honorary agricultural fraternity, Alpha Zeta.

Walt's life developed a pattern. He was not afraid to take charge of an organization, and he was aware of his interest in agriculture early on. This insight guided him during the tough years of the Depression. He knew he wasn't interested in the oil refining business, one of the main employers in Tulsa. Hard hours spent cleaning out huge oil tanks convinced him that he should go back to college and get an advanced degree. He applied for a horticultural fellowship and was accepted at Washington State College in Pullman for a half fellowship that paid $500 a year.

He married Irene Welsh, his hometown sweetheart, and moved to the Pacific Northwest in 1934. His initial studies involved a project that measured the effect of Bordeaux sprays (a mixture of lime and sulfur) on the photosynthesis of Delicious apples.

Irene helped pay the rent by cooking in the boardinghouse where they lived. After one year, the fellowship turned full-time and Walt's salary went to $1,000 per year. He was assigned to work on orchard studies in Grandview and the Naches Heights above Yakima. Walt and Irene lived in Prosser during the summer, then returned to Pullman during the school year.

In 1937, Walt accepted the position of assistant horticulturist at the Irrigation Branch Experiment Station (today called the Irrigated Agriculture Research and Extension Center) just a few miles outside of Prosser, beginning an association that would last until his retirement in 1976, just short of forty years. He was then one of only three faculty members.

The research center had been carved out of 200 acres of sagebrush desert in 1919, the result of a state legislative act that had been signed into law in 1917. The initial crops were potatoes, corn, millet, wheat, rye, and sweet clover. The first horticultural crop, 6 acres of apples, was planted in 1922 for an irrigation study. When Walt arrived fifteen years later, his job was to help develop crops that could be successfully used by the agricultural community. He was put in charge of evaluating the apple irrigation project and the tree-fruit variety plantings, and also oversaw the planting of other fruits, including grapes, red and purple raspberries, strawberries, blackberries, and dewberries.

"When I first arrived at the Experiment Station in Prosser, I felt like a pioneer," Walt says. "With 1 million acres of the Columbia Basin to be irrigated, and the prospects of 72,000 acres on the Roza, I felt that I had to learn about the adaptability of many horticultural crops." Most important, he helped plant 20 American type grapes, mostly *Vitis labrusca* hybrids as well as seven *Vitis vinifera* grape varieties. It was the beginning of his long association with grapes and their culture.

This trial block of grapevines would expand over the years, in numbers and in importance. In the following six years a total of 45 American hybrids, 71 *vinifera,* and 10 interspecific *Vitis* hybrids of rootstock species were planted. Additional varieties were added when the Wine Project started in 1964, including over 16 French hybrids. By 1974, over 312 varieties had been established in the Foundation Block at the research center. Stock for this trial block came from a variety of sources. Most came from California, the USDA Plant Introduction

Service, but some came from local sources. William B. Bridgman's vineyard in Sunnyside contributed *vinifera* stock in 1940. Thirteen *vinifera* varieties, including Limberger, a grape that Walt would later relish as an adopted child, came from the Tunbridge Nursery in British Columbia in 1941.

Walt can look back on a distinguished career. In 1967 he was awarded the title "Mr. Asparagus" by the Washington Asparagus Growers Association for his pioneering work in harvest management and variety work. Ten years later he was crowned "Man of the Year" by the Washington State Grape Society. In 1988 he received the Governor's Award for service to the premium wine industry. In 1990, he received the Gamma Sigma Delta Honor Society of Agriculture Award of Service to Washington Agriculture and Home Economics. In 1992, he received the Alec Bayless Prize Award for viticultural contributions to the wine industry. In 1993, Washington State University established the Walter J. Clore Scholarship for students in agriculture and home economics. More recently, in 1995, he received the American Society for Enology and Viticulture's Merit Award. He has also been recognized by numerous organizations for his contributions to the community as well as to the agriculture industry.

Throughout, Walt remained very much a family man. He and Irene raised two daughters and a son. They also assisted a great many people by giving them a place in their home to help them get back on their feet. This caring comes from the wellspring of Walt's and Irene's kindness, nurtured by their commitment to church and community.

This sense of community has been an important element in Walt's ability to bring people together, despite their diverse and often conflicting agendas and views. He has brought together juice grape people and wine grape people, scholars and farmers, and different branches of academia. The sense of family within the wine and grape community persists to this day. That, above all else, is Walt's crowning achievement.

—PROSSER, MAY 1992—

I drove north out of Prosser to the research center, about five miles northeast. The temperature was in the mid-seventies.

I had contacted Dr. Sara Spayd to see if it would be possible to taste wines that had been made by the research center and were still in storage there. She readily agreed and suggested that we include Dr. Clore and some of his former associates.

In some ways, Dr. Spayd is Walt's modern counterpart. A food technologist, also with a bachelor of science in horticulture, she heads up the grape and wine areas at the research center. She is, however, more narrowly defined in her work than Walt was, mainly because the industry that he helped to nurture is much larger and more complex today.

Dr. Spayd speaks directly and clearly. She has to. Her job, like Walt's, is to work with the growers. Walt is her link to the past, a close phone call away if Sara has a question, or just wants to talk. It is a role he appreciates.

The entrance road to the research center is shaded by beautiful tall oak trees planted under the supervision of Dr. Clore, who had been asked by Harold Singleton, then the superintendent at the station, to landscape the grounds of the center. On the right is a rose garden. Nearby is the former site of Dr. Clore's experimental chrysanthemum garden, which was maintained until his retirement. The 1-acre garden harbored All-American roses, chrysanthemums, and Japanese peonies. He once told me, "These flowers attracted more total visitors to the grounds of the center than all the other research programs."

I parked in front of the West Building, the site of our wine tasting. I was very excited. In attendance, besides myself, were close associates of Dr. Clore's who worked with him during the '60s and '70s: George Carter, Dr. Charles Nagel, Vere Brummund, Mike Wallace, and Bob Fay, the core group of early-day researchers; Dr. Spayd and Dr. Bob Wample, both current researchers at the research center; Kay Simon, enologist at Chinook Winery; Dr. Wade Wolfe, owner of Thurston-Wolfe Winery and a viticulturist, and general manager of Hogue Cellars; and Helen Willard, a longtime writer for the *Prosser Record Bulletin* and other publications. Attending but not tasting were Mrs. Bea Nagel and IAREC workers Barbara Seymour and Alan Kawakami.

The tasting took place in a standard lecture room on the top floor of the West Building. At the head of the room was a table with all the wines lined up. In the middle of the room was a long table with place settings and empty wine glasses. It was quite a gathering.

I recognized George Carter, the winemaker at the research center from 1967 to 1977. Dr. Charles "Chas" Nagel, food technologist, was looking at the cluster of unlabeled dark green wine bottles. Dr. Nagel recently retired from Washington State University. He was the winemaker for the research center's first two vintages, in '64 and '65.

Clore, Carter, and Nagel were the starting lineup of an elite group of scientists who threw themselves into proving that Washington state could grow European wine grapes and produce quality wines from them. This challenge, which became known as the Wine Project, was a direct result of frantic requests from the Washington wine industry for help.

Almost thirty years later, in the company of these early wine pioneers, we were about to taste some of the wines made at the research center by George Carter and later by Joe Powers, who followed Carter.

Dr. Spayd explained the tasting: We would be given five groups (or flights) of wines. Information about each wine, including harvest data, must data, and wine analysis, would be given on a sheet of paper, along with a list of the wines in each flight.

The first flight was three different Cabernet Sauvignons from the 1968 vintage. Two of the wines were from the varietal block at the center, one of which had been treated with American oak chips. The third wine was from grapes received from the Alhambra Winery, grown in the Otis Vineyard near Grandview.

The wines were in great shape. Mike Wallace commented that they all had a pronounced raspberry quality to them. On the palate, the wines varied. The wine that showed best was the one made from the varietal block grapes without oak. For the technical minded, the numbers on the wine were: pH, 3.42 (pH is a measure of the hydrogen ion concentration of acidity to alkalinity of a solution); T.A., .795 (T.A. is the total acidity measured in grams per 100 milliliters); alcohol, 11.9%; V.A., .027 (V.A. is a measure of the percentage of volatile acids); and tannin level, .180 (tannins are the astringent compounds found mostly in red wines, measured in milligrams per liter).

The next flight was five Merlots from the 1978 vintage, made by Joe Powers following Carter's retirement. These Merlots represented some of the first Merlots made in the state—today one of Washington's signature wines. The grapes came from five different sites: Preston Vineyards, the research center, Sagemoor Farms, and two vineyards owned by Chateau Ste. Michelle. The best wine of this group was one made from grapes grown at Chateau Ste. Michelle's Cold Creek Vineyard. The flavors were ripe, and the wine was fruity and pretty.

The third flight of wines was again Merlot. This time the wines were vertically arranged from five successive vintages: '76, '77, '78, '79, and '80. As a group these wines were all very good, capturing the inherent fruitiness of the grapes—not a sweet fruitiness, but rather a tactile

Tasters at IAREC-Prosser wine tasting. May, 1992. Pictured back row from left: Dr. Charles Nagel, Vere Brummund, George Carter , Dr. Robert Wample, Dr. Walter Clore, Bob Fay. Front row from left: Dr. Wade Wolfe, Ronald Irvine, Kay Simon, Mike Wallace, and Dr. Sara Spayd. —*Photo by Alan Kawakami. Courtesy of WSU-IAREC.*

fruitiness that filled the mouth with flavors of the grape. All of these grapes came from the experimental vineyards located on the Roza Project. The best of the group was the '79 vintage; the concentrated flavors exploded on the palate. Suggestions of ripe plums and cherries enhanced the telltale softness of the Merlot grape.

The fourth flight of wines featured Cabernet Sauvignon from the '67, '68, and '69 vintages. The '67 and the '69 were treated with American oak chips; the '68 was treated with French oak chips. The '69 wine was beautiful. It captured completely the concentrated flavors of the Cabernet Sauvignon grape with a smooth, soft mouth feel. This was really a delicious, world-class wine, despite being made in a standard procedure with few frills. What if the wine had been allowed to undergo malolactic fermentation (a second fermentation that softens the acids slightly), or had been treated in oak barrels, or had been fined with egg whites? It was very exciting to taste this wine, twenty-three years old and still full of power and vigor. It spoke so loudly: wines being made today by Washington's trained winemakers should have even greater potential.

The last flight of wines was another vertical tasting of Cabernet

Sauvignon made from grapes grown at the research center. Five vintages were tasted: '72, '73, '74, '79, and '80. As a group these wines were generally more tart, but behind the tartness lay a fruity, berrylike flavor.

There was a lot of festive laughing at the conclusion of the tasting. Participants were feeling the convivial effects of the wine, and friendly barbs were exchanged around the table. Behind this frivolity was a sense of community. I was among cherished friends who respected and loved one another. Dr. Spayd said, "We couldn't find any Cabernet Sauvignons from the '75, '76, or '77 vintages." Mike Wallace chimed in merrily, "They were probably used for George's retirement."

At the beginning of the tasting, I had presented a slide show of pictures Dr. Clore and I had obtained during our research. I unexpectedly realized that this group was part of a larger effort in our state's history to grow and make wines, that they were part of a multigenerational phenomenon, and that the effort to produce quality wines has been going on for well over a hundred years in Washington state.

Part I

ROOTS, SHOOTS, CANES, AND SUCKERS

"The cultivation of the grape in this country is no longer an experiment. Indeed, the success is so great that the more sanguine claim that our climate is as favorable to the growth of the grape as that of California. This being the case, our grape growers are already considering the question: Whence can they find a market for the surplus crop?"

Walla Walla Statesman, 1876

Chapter One

CANOE RIDGE

Walt and I began our morning typically. I was the last to awaken, and when I arrived downstairs in the kitchen for breakfast, Walt had already made the coffee, set out the cereal and a bowl for me, and arranged slices of melon on a plate.

As usual, I brought my notebook to breakfast, as I never knew when Walt would begin talking about the grape or wine industry. He pointed out two stories written by Bob Woehler that appeared in that morning's *Tri-Cities Herald*. One was a survey of various wineries and their plans for expansion; the other was about Stimson Lane's development of the Canoe Ridge vineyards. A picture accompanying the articles showed large stainless steel tanks being readied for the new winery.

Walt has a particular affinity for Stimson Lane. Stimson Lane Vineyards and Estates is the corporate name of what most Northwesterners call, simply, Ste. Michelle, the abbreviated form of Chateau Ste. Michelle. Chateau Ste. Michelle, the dominant winery in Washington, began as two separate wineries—the National Wine Company (Nawico) and Pommerelle Winery—in 1934, when Prohibition was repealed. The companies later merged as American Wine Growers, in 1954, then changed into Ste. Michelle Vintners, then Chateau Ste. Michelle Vineyards, and now Stimson Lane Vineyards and Estates. Walt has watched this company grow from its infancy. In fact, he still works for them as a consultant.

Our plan for the day was to head up to Canoe Ridge, the site of new vineyard development and a new winery by Stimson Lane. The morning was crisp and clear. The thermometer in Walt's study showed the outside temperature was 59° F, with a low reading of 40° F during the night. Walt always knows the temperature and is aware of any changes in the weather pattern.

We drove Walt's faded red-orange Chevrolet Luv pickup. He wouldn't let me take my car because he was afraid we might get stuck in the sand in some vineyard. His well-used pickup was equipped with cement blocks in the back for ballast, and a shovel in case we needed to dig ourseves out. Lying next to the shovel were some old grapevines.

From Prosser we headed west along State Highway 22, which runs along the south side of the Yakima Valley near the base of the Horse Heaven Hills. We turned left at a nondescript dirt and gravel road and started climbing the hills. It was the back way, one of those dirt paths that run up the Horse Heaven Hills that one sees from the interstate. I was a little nervous with Walt's driving. For some reason he was driving on the wrong side of the road. Going around sharp corners, I thought about how we might end up down a bank or, worse, I imagined, crash into an oncoming truck. This road was barely wide enough for two cars. Walt told me that he sees better if he drives on the left side of the road, due to the glare from the bright morning sun. A magpie, like a jester in comic relief, flew across the road, its distinctive black-and-white markings a stark contrast to the yellow and brown of the hillsides.

As we reached the peak, a covey of quail, maybe a dozen or more, shot across the road. "I haven't seen a covey of quail that large for a long time," exclaims Walt.

We were at about 1,200 feet in elevation, heading directly south. The road had become paved and well marked. The sagebrush gave way to rolling wheat fields, and the tops of the hills flattened out. On the open road, Walt still tended to drive on the left side, especially around corners, and I wondered how he had survived driving in this manner.

"I hope this weather prevails," Walt says. "If we have three weeks more, the wine grapes will make it."

It had been an unusual year. Because of the early coolness and wetness of spring, the bloom set on the vines was very irregular, but very heavy. Cool, overcast weather was the rule up until late June, except for a spurt of heat in mid-May. July and August were both cooler than usual, followed by a warm, dry September. The grapes ripened at a very uneven rate, due to the heaviest set on record. Walt pointed out that grapes that had ripened normally had been either closely pruned or thinned heavily shortly after berry set. Normally, Chardonnay grapes are the first to be harvested, followed by Semillon, Sauvignon Blanc, Merlot, and then Cabernet Sauvignon. This year, in some vineyards, Merlot grapes ripened about the same time as the Chardonnay grapes, and Semillon was harvested with Cabernet Sauvignon.

In the vineyard, the grapes had been slow to accumulate sugar, hovering around 19° and 20° Brix, a measurement used to calibrate the available sugars in the fruit. Ideally winemakers like to see white grapes harvested at 22° Brix and red grapes at 24° Brix. Walt said that the grape growers were on pins and needles waiting to see if the sugars would increase. The Concord growers were especially anxious because their crop was most excessive.

Concord vineyards were particularly hard hit by a physiological disease called black leaf, a kind of incipient potassium deficiency. Black leaf causes leaves to turn purplish and then black, with a loss of chlorophyll, their basic unit for transmitting sugar to the grape. The top leaves dry up and fall to the ground. From a distance, black leaf makes the vineyard look quite dark, almost as if it has been frosted. Because there had been less evidence of black leaf in the wine grape vineyards than in the juice grape areas, the contrast was stark when the two types of vineyards were viewed next to each other.

Walt says that the National Grape Cooperative Association (a large juice processor) had already declared a disaster for some vineyards in this year's harvest. The association does not buy Concord grapes below 14° Brix, and many growers were hoping that enough live leaves remained on the vine to convert the sun's rays into sugar.

Farming. I think about how tough it is. The grower is always challenged by the environment; the climate, diseases, insects, soil nutrition, and the availability of water conspire to reward or ruin the grower's gamble.

As we drove toward the Columbia River, with vast wheat fields stretching out beside us on the Horse Heaven Hills, my mind went back in time to the pioneers' first lonely efforts to establish themselves in this vastness. Sure, they could grow crops in this land, but how could they hope to sell their production when they were so far removed from the marketplace?

We passed through Alderdale, an area at the edge of the hills just before the drop down to the Columbia River. Alderdale is the home of the Mercer homestead. Don Mercer used to farm the Alderdale Vineyards as part of his winery. Mercer was a casualty of the weather and the marketplace. His brother, Bud, was then in the process of taking over the vineyards, which he bought back from the insurance company. [I have since learned that a syndicate of winemakers, including Rick Small, Alex Golitzen, Chris Camarda, and others, have purchased this vineyard.]

I remember visiting Don and Linda Mercer at their winery about eight years before. Don and I drove out over the land around his winery, passing through the sagebrush to a point overlooking the Columbia. It was spectacular. To the south across the river, Oregon's landscape, because of the perspective, rose like a checkered wall. Don, a soft-spoken and gentle man, showed me the beauty of the land, pointing out the wildflowers—mustard and lupine. Up close, sagebrush was beautiful, its trunk twisting and knotted like a grapevine. The grass, yellowed but strong, resisted the pull of the persistent wind and held down the soil.

Mercer told me about the early settlers who had poured into this area, lured by cheap land and promises of riches. During the late 1800s, he said, the weather pattern was particularly wet for a period of about ten years. Wet enough, apparently, for pioneer farmers to grow crops without irrigation. Then, suddenly, the normal weather pattern reasserted itself and the farmers were left high and dry.

I'm sorry Don Mercer is no longer in the wine business. I can still taste his Limberger wines—bold, ripe and soft, with a kiss of oak. The taste memory lingered as Walt says, "There's the back side of Canoe Ridge." The soil on the ridge is dotted in places with basalt, the hard rock remaining from volcanic uplifts from below the earth's surface.

The Columbia, blue like the vast sky above us, is a peaceful river at this point. It is maybe a mile across, plenty large enough for barges to make their way up to Lewiston, Idaho. The blue ribbon of water cuts through the golden hills. To the east the river basin spreads out, with numerous trees along its bank.

A new sign at the entrance to the Canoe Ridge vineyard boldly proclaimed this as Vineyard #12, established in 1991. The road was dusty. We drove up about 200 feet to the new winery Stimson Lane was installing. It was a cement shell. Lying on their sides were the massive stainless steel tanks that had been featured in Bob Woehler's newspaper column. Up close, reflecting the sun, they were bright and imposing.

Jack Kelly met us just outside of his small construction trailer and extended a hand to Walt, then myself. He asked Walt how he was doing. Although Kelly looks like a tough guy, the man has a heart of gold. Over the years he has been responsible for maintaining contact with the old-timers, the people who have worked for the various companies in Stimson Lane's history.

Kelly has been with the company for more than twenty years. He arrived from Connecticut in 1975 and drew the original plans for Chateau Ste. Michelle in Woodinville. Trained as an engineer, he has overseen the design and construction of all of Stimson Lane's additions, including the spectacular Columbia Crest Winery at Paterson, about ten miles east of Canoe Ridge. He said he planned to retire after this year, but first, as vice-president of operations, he was in charge of getting the new Canoe Ridge winery built and operating.

Kelly readily gave us a tour of the structure. We walked through fine dust six to eight inches thick; little puffs rose around our footsteps. I was amazed at how fine the soil was; it is the wonder of this region, the accrual of fine volcanic dust.

Inside, Kelly showed us the new fermenting room. Workers were readying the pads, almost three feet high, that will elevate the stainless steel tanks off the winery floor. Along the walls were horizontal rows of large plastic and steel pipes, the beginnings of a refrigeration system that will allow perfect temperature control for the wine and allow quick transport of the wine between tanks and barrels.

Kelly said that Canoe Ridge Estate will be devoted strictly to the production of high-quality red wines, especially Cabernet Sauvignon and Merlot. One part of the winery will house a separate experimental winery that will be overseen by Bob Betz, Stimson Lane's vice-president of enology and education. Betz plans to oversee experiments with new varieties and new techniques.

The cement walls rose nearly fifty feet in the air. Kelly pointed to the barrel room that will eventually house 14,000 barrels. It was awe-inspiring. He also talked about the 6,000-gallon fermenting tanks that will allow control over individual lots of wines (6,000-gallon fermenters can hold a truck's worth of crushed juice) and the 13,000-gallon tanks for storage and blending. I could hear the soft, guttural sounds of forklifts moving barrels of wine, men and women quietly attending to the detail of transferring wine. Soft sunshine shone through vaulted windows, casting light into the shadows of the winery.

After our winery tour, Walt and I drove to the top of Canoe Ridge, more than 900 feet in elevation. The vines, planted three years before, were now in their first year of production. We saw workers in the various vineyard blocks hand-picking the grapes. There was very little sound except for the tractor crawling along the vineyard row next to the pickers. All the workers were Hispanic. Many wore white aprons; some covered their mouths with handkerchiefs to protect against the dust. The view was astounding. To the north were the rich farmlands of the Horse Heaven Hills' long slope; the area directly below our hillside viewpoint was made up of large circle irrigation units and called the 100 Circles. These circles were close to a half-mile in diameter, I guessed. The landscape, dotted by huge circles of green and gold, flattened out in front of us.

To the south, the Columbia River flows to the Pacific Ocean, 250 miles to the west. Directly east, right next door, we could see the Canoe Ridge Vineyards planted by the Chalone Group, from California, in 1989. Walt noted that the vineyards appeared to drain north, away from the river. He wondered why they chose to orient the vineyard to the north.

—CANOE RIDGE VINEYARD, SEPTEMBER 1993—
After leaving Stimson Lane's vineyard, we drove over to the Chalone vineyard. Walt drove directly into the vineyard. Inside the vineyard, the orientation seemed slightly different. While the slope definitely faced north, plenty of vines were exposed to the east as well. The orderly rows cascaded down the sides of Canoe Ridge. Walt was slightly concerned: the base of the vineyard appeared to be in a frost pocket. Twenty feet away, a circular planting of corn showed evidence of frost, but the nearby vineyards seemed fine. The vines looked healthy.

The winter of 1990 was exceptionally severe, hardly a kind welcome to the Californians. It was a particularly bad year for wine grapes in eastern Washington. Yields were down nearly 50 percent from the previous year. Hardest hit were the new Merlot plantings in most of the vineyards in eastern Washington. This is not friendly country. But neither is it usually as severe as in 1990. Walt and others have shown that, about every six years, cold snaps occur that devastate vineyards, especially those planted in the wrong place and those with less mature vines. It's nature's way of pruning both the vines and the producers.

Walt has harped for decades on the need to plant in an open, well-drained area, preferably slightly sloped to the south. His rule: "If you can't see out, it is probably not a good place to plant wine grapes."

We got back on Highway 14 and drove east toward Paterson.

Along the way we stopped and looked back, trying to get a view of Canoe Ridge. Finally, about three miles away, it became more apparent. The ridge, about five miles long, looked like an upside-down canoe, and was viewed by Lewis and Clark as they journeyed down the Columbia during their famous scouting tour of the far west, passing this area at the same time of year, but in 1805. Walt had found that it was officially named in published maps by the U.S. Department of Interior Geology Survey in 1908. From this distance we saw the rounded point of the canoe, but the vineyards were beyond our view. I marveled at how little the landscape has changed since it was seen by those unbelievably brave explorers and the native Umatillas who guided them.

—JEFFERSON'S WINE DREAM—

This is where the history of wine in Washington began. President Thomas Jefferson had sent Meriwether Lewis and William Clark west to explore the vast new territory known as the Louisiana Purchase. Jefferson wanted to know what the U.S. government had acquired and he also wanted to establish an American presence in the Oregon Country to deter the advances of the English.

Ironically, Jefferson had attempted all his life to establish European wine grapes in his native Virginia, but without success. Early colonists had marveled at the ease with which native grapes grew on the Atlantic coast. They were amused (as Leif Eriksson had been when he visited the North American continent and called it Vinland) that the vines grew on and over the trees.

What the colonists (and Vikings) saw were native vines, primarily *Vitis labrusca* and *Vitis raparia*, tough species adapted to the cold, moist climate of the East Coast. The colonists and Jefferson were used to *Vitis vinifera*, European grapes that have been cultivated for centuries to produce wines. Unfortunately, despite many noble experiments, their efforts to establish European wine grapes met with little or no success.

Gradually, as manifest destiny moved our nation's boundary westward, *vinifera* vines were planted with great hope and expectation in New York, then Pennsylvania, then Ohio. In each instance they eventually succumbed to cold or disease.

Jefferson wasn't thinking about wine when he sent Lewis and Clark west, but his explorers, by charting this vast area, helped establish the very beginnings of western agriculture that would someday include the planting of *vinifera* vines. The vast inland area explored by Lewis and Clark became known as the Columbia Country because of the dominance of the Columbia River and its tributaries. The river is the heart of the Columbia Basin, a remarkable valley surrounded by mountains on all sides that extends south into Oregon state and east into Idaho state.

Lewis and Clark understood instantly the significance of a river so large. It wasn't the Northwest Passage, but it could be the next best thing. When they reported back to President Jefferson, they convinced him that the United States should begin looking west for commerce rather than east. They felt that trade could be developed between the Columbia region and the Far East. Items received in trade could be transported back across the American continent. It was a bold idea.

The years between 1810 and 1812 saw remarkable growth in the Columbia Country. By 1812, three transcontinental overland routes—the Saskatchewan Route, the Missouri Route, and the Platte Route—had been established; all three went through the Columbia Basin.

The first to arrive in the Columbia region were Americans led by Wilson Prince Hunt, sent by John Jacob Astor of New York City, and organized as the Pacific Fur Company. Meanwhile, the British were pushing south from the Canadian interior at about the same time; their fur trade was dominated by the North West Company. The North West Company established a fort at Spokane, while the Astorians established forts at Astoria, Oregon; at the mouth of the Okanogan River in Canada; and at the mouth of the Clearwater River in Idaho. The War of 1812, between Britain and the United States, led to a settlement when the Astorians realized that they were isolated and in a weakened position. The North West Company purchased the forts from the Pacific Fur Company shortly thereafter.

By 1818, the North West Company had monopolized the entire region, from upper Canada south to the California border, and built a strategic trading post on the Walla Walla River called Fort Nez Perce. It was now a major center of commerce that connected the vast trading region of North America with markets in the Far East, whose purchased goods were then shipped to London. Supplies for the interior could be delivered via the Pacific Coast as ships arrived at the former Astoria, renamed Fort George.

During this period, French Canadians worked the Columbia region. They were fearless trappers, and they were particularly adept at gaining the trust of the Native tribes. It was very common for French Canadian trappers to marry Native women.

There is little doubt that this is when European agriculture began in the Columbia Basin. It is likely, though undocumented, that the French Canadians tried to establish grape cuttings in the area, maybe as early as 1810. Vines could have been brought west either overland or by boat to the mouth of the Columbia.

In 1821 the North West Company was purchased by the Hudson's Bay Company. It was a daring move, because it wasn't clear that the Columbia region was as important to the Hudson's Bay Company as it had been to the North West Company. At the time, many of the French Canadians who had been employed by the North West Company settled in this region. Their initial settlements became more permanent.

By 1825, the Hudson's Bay Company had recognized the importance of the Columbia River to its trade and established a fort at Vancouver, Washington. Fort Vancouver became the trading center of their entire North American enterprise. Lines of communication were well in place, settlers were beginning to venture into the country along with the French Canadians, and new forms of trade were being sought to replace the vanishing fur trade.

—FIRST KNOWN PLANTING—

The first known planting of grapevines in what is today Washington state occurred at Fort Vancouver in 1825, when the fort was established by the Hudson's Bay Company. The first vineyard was planted from seeds brought from England to Vancouver by ship. One of the more entertaining stories of how the seeds made their way here is that during a dinner party in London, a couple of young women slipped apple and grape seeds into the vest pockets of two young men getting ready to ship out to the New World. The women promised that if the seeds sprouted and gave fruit, the officers could return and claim the women as wives.

More likely, these first seeds were brought by George Simpson, the governor of the American operations of the Hudson's Bay Company, who came to Fort George, the former Fort Astoria, during an inspection tour of 1824. Fort Vancouver was then established, in recognition of its agricultural advantages over Fort George. Possibly the seeds were sent by Governor Simpson with instructions to the founders of Fort Vancouver to become self-reliant.

1854 sketch of Fort Vancouver by G. Sohon. Includes St. James Catholic church on
center left and Hudson's Bay Company's stockade, upper right.
—*Photo courtesy of Fort Vancouver National Historic Site.*

Because the vines were grown from seed, it is difficult to know what variety the grapes could have been. Unless vines are propagated as cuttings, there is no way to know what the grape's type is, because it would almost definitely be a seedling, as unrecognizable as a volunteer squash in a compost pile. Because the seeds came from Europe, they were most likely *Vitis vinifera.* Walt has recently postulated that these first vines could have been either the Black Hamburg or the Black Prince varieties, both popular glasshouse varieties grown at that time in England. The Mission grape also may have been available, as it was grown extensively in California. In a letter to Dr. Clore, Professor Emeritus Harold Olmo of the University of California Davis writes that the Black Prince "is one of the few *vinifera* varieties that will produce vigorous and fruitful offspring from seed."

Drawings of old Fort Vancouver show a number of orchards upon a hill overlooking the Columbia River and the fort. With some license, it is possible to recognize what looks like grapevines. Dr. Clore believes vines would have been planted around the orchards, as was typical of that time. Importation records of corks and bottles seem to indicate that the company bottled its own wines, perhaps from grapes grown at the fort. This would have been in keeping with Simpson's directive to be self-reliant. On the other hand, this was not really necessary. The Hudson's Bay Company was one of the great merchants of the time: supplier, seller, and procurer to all the great markets of the world. There wasn't anything that couldn't be had.

Hudson's Bay Company records indicate that wine was a cherished commodity enjoyed by the general community employed by the company. Wine was shipped directly to the fort from suppliers in England, in bulk or bottled. There are indications that the finest wines of the world were available, including fine ports, sherries, Madeiras, hocks, and Bordeaux.

It was customary for the chief factor, Dr. John McLoughlin, to serve wine with all of his meals. Early records of meals served to visitors describe lavish feasts, with most or all of the ingredients supplied by the large farm surrounding the fort, accompanied by wines from such notable chateaux as Chateau Margaux and Chateau Cantenac-Brown. McLoughlin proudly served the products of his farm; it is likely that he would have reveled in pouring an estate-grown and -made wine. In September 1836, missionary Narcissa Whitman wrote in her journal:

> After chatting a little we were invited to a walk in the garden. And what a delightful place this. What a contrast this to the barren sand plains through which we had so recently passed. Here we find fruit of every description. Apples peaches grapes. Pear plum & Fig trees in abundance. Cucumbers melons beans peas beats cabbage, taumatoes, & every kind of vegitable, to numerous to be mentioned. Every part is very neat & tastefully arranged fine walks, eich side lined with strawberry vines. On the opposite end of the garden is a good Summer house covered with grape vines.

Continuing, Mrs. Whitman spoke of the great variety of foods available at the table, concluding with a description of a typical meal:

> After this melons next make their appearance, some times grapes & last of all cheese, bread or biscuit & butter is produced to complet the whole. But there is one article on the table I have not yet mentioned & of which I never partake, That is wine The gentlemen frequently drink toasts to each other but never give us the opportunity of refusing for they know we belong to the tetotal Society. We have many talks about drinking wine, but no one joins our society. They have a *Temprance* Society herre & at the Wallamut, formed by Mr. Lee. Our tea is plain, bread and butter, good tea plenty of milk & sugar.

Finally:

The grapes are just ripe & I am feasting on them finely. There is a bunch now on the table before me, they are very fine. I save all the seeds of those I eat for planting & apples also. This is a rule of Vancouver. I have got collected before me an assortment of garden seeds which I take up with me, also I intend taking some young sprouts of apple peach & grapes & some strawberry vines &c from the nursery here.

It is noteworthy that Whitman mentions in her journal three different locations of grapes. First she mentions them in the garden, in conjunction with the apple and peach trees. Then she makes note of grapevines at the summer house. And lastly she places grapes, or grapevines, as being located in the nursery. This suggests that the nursery activities at the fort were well intended to propagate fruit in the Columbia Department.

Among the Hudson's Bay Company's customers were the Russian-Americans who were trading along the Pacific Coast north of the Columbia River. They depended on Fort Vancouver for fresh foods of all kinds: fruits, vegetables, grains, and meat. To supply their needs and to strengthen the British claim to the Oregon Country north of the Columbia, the Hudson's Bay Company created, in 1833, a wholly new subsidiary called the Puget's Sound Agricultural Company, with the idea of encouraging British, French Canadian, and Scottish citizens who were retired from the Hudson's Bay Company to settle, with their families, in what today is southwestern Washington.

This ambitious project spread north through the Cowlitz and Nisqually River valleys to the shores of southern Puget Sound. Unfortunately, the scheme had two drawbacks. First, because the Hudson's Bay Company wanted to keep close control of the new corporation, they restricted solicitation for land purchases, through share options, to former employees of the company. It was a bad business arrangement, because settlers could purchase land cheaply and without restraint in the Willamette Valley to the south.

Second, according to an agreement between the British and American governments, the Oregon Country was to be jointly managed. Each had substantial claims to the area. Between 1833 and 1850, Americans began arriving in this area, ignoring the land claims of the Puget's Sound Agricultural Company's settlers. The clever corporate takeover of the land ignored the fact that the British did not own the land they were subscribing.

Meanwhile, it is likely that at least a few French Canadians would have attempted to plant grapes on their farms, mainly for their own needs, but possibly as a test of their commercial use. Between 1826 and 1835, grapes were being planted successfully in California, especially in what is now the Los Angeles area. The most important planting at this time was by the aptly named Jean Louis Vignes ("vines"). Vignes may have been the first to recognize the limitations of the local Mission grape and imported French cuttings for his vineyard and winery, indicating the ability to secure European vines with relative ease.

By the late 1830s, vineyards were a commercial reality in California. The discovery that *Vitis vinifera* could be grown on the Pacific slope brought excitement to California's new arrivals. It also meant that wine grapes were readily available from sources in California as well as the nursery and garden at Fort Vancouver.

Chapter Two

LA CENTER
"THE GRAPE AND I"

It was midafternoon on a beautiful fall day when Walt and I drove down to Salishan Vineyards, a winery owned by Joan and Lincoln Wolverton. It is situated on a hill above the tiny hamlet of La Center, less than twenty miles north of Fort Vancouver on the Columbia River.

Along the way, we drove through the Nisqually Delta, a major estuary that drains into the upper reaches of Puget Sound. The delta is a significant wonder—home to great numbers of migrating birds. The basin that runs south from the mouth of the river is covered with rich river-bottom soil, and gentle hillsides rise on the east and west to form a collage of deep green, golden orange, and brown, highlighted by the dreamy blue sky overhead and the deep blue waters of the Sound to the north.

Geologically, the area was carved out by huge ice fields that descended from the north to a point close to the Nisqually plains. As the ice fields melted in retreat, they left the vast network of land and water that we call Puget Sound. Puget Sound represents about half of the landmass of western Washington north of the Columbia River up to the Canadian border. It abounds in islands and water passages; one finger of water, Hood Canal, runs more than fifty miles.

To the west of Puget Sound are the dynamic and picturesque Olympic Mountains, which provide a rain shadow for much of the Sound north of Seattle. The Olympics also significantly disturb the weather pattern by causing unique conversion and weather trough systems throughout the Sound. To the south, lowland hills provide a gentle buttress to the main weather systems that roll in off the Pacific

Ocean about sixty miles south of Olympia. They are similar to the Coast Range, which protects and moderates much of the Willamette Valley in Oregon. To the east, the rugged Cascade Mountain Range separates western Washington from eastern Washington. The Cascades are the great water thieves of Washington, causing the clouds to drop their loads before heading east. A great series of rivers and lakes within the Cascades drains their bounty both east and west. Snowcapped volcanic mountains stand like sentries over the landscape.

As we passed through these river valleys, I thought of the early settlers, settling a rugged new land, dealing with Native peoples, and battling to clear the land of tall Douglas firs. Walt and I wondered at their industry and native talents.

The early settlers came up north out of the Vancouver area. They could follow the Columbia River in its northern bend toward the Pacific until they reached the mouth of the Cowlitz River at today's Longview-Kelso. The Cowlitz River runs nearly due north, and early travelers would follow the river about twenty-five miles before arriving at the Cowlitz Prairie, a broad expanse of fertile soil and open space. From the Cowlitz Prairie, the rest of the trip north required overland travel through dense forest and brush. Intricate river systems run through this area; many of them channel into the Chehalis River, allowing for passage to the Nisqually prairies thirty-five miles to the north.

The area is lush and undeveloped, even to this day. The soils are rich and fertile, and the hills and valleys provide protection from the marine ocean air. It is a forgotten area; most of the development went north to the Puget Sound region. The area was settled by French Canadians and retired Hudson's Bay employees, and is similar to the settlements of French Canadians who found their way to the Walla Walla Valley, at Frenchtown (what is today called Lowden), as well as the Moxee Valley near Yakima. To a Frenchman, the upper Puget Sound region might have seemed like a primordial Burgundy.

Early plantings could have occurred with grape cuttings from Fort Vancouver or California. Grapevines could have been sent from Europe as well, either overland or by sea. Dr. Clore has told me that a grapevine cutting, kept slightly moist and cool, can easily last up to a year before it needs to be planted.

Walt and I arrived at Salishan Vineyards in the early evening. The sun had set, but there was enough light to see the vineyards behind the Wolvertons' home.

Walt headed directly into the vineyard. I went to the front door. Joan Wolverton greeted me and asked me in. She apologized and said she needed to sit down because she had been picking Chardonnay and lugging large plastic boxes of grapes most of the day. Lincoln came into the kitchen from his office, and he and I walked outside to find Walt, who was just emerging from the vineyard, carrying three or four grape leaves and a couple of clusters of dark grapes. Linc seemed slightly embarrassed, probably because the vineyard was in such disarray.

Back inside, Joan was up and moving around. She told us she did not prune the vineyard this year—the first time in twenty-three years—because she didn't want a crop. The winery vats and barrels were full. A wet and poor early summer meant that the vineyards were hard hit by mildew as well as overcropping. To have Dr. Clore walk through the vineyard when it was in this state must be like having a home designer walk through your home after your kids have just had a rousing sleep-over in your living room.

We sat down at their kitchen table. Lincoln opened a bottle of the 1979 Salishan Vineyards Pinot Noir and offered us a glass. It smelled of Pinot Noir with hints of raspberry and vanilla but, at fourteen years old, it was beginning to fade. It had developed a smoky quality characteristic of other Salishan Vineyard Pinot Noirs I have tasted.

Later Linc opened an '87 Pinot Noir and an '89. The '89 seemed young and tight-knit. The body was lean and nicely weighted, but the flavors were undeveloped. The aroma was starting to show that unique smoky quality. I would like to try this wine in about five years. The '87 was just beginning to show the beauty of Pinot Noir, with that contradictory combination of complex flavors, at once fruity yet mature, like the smell of autumn leaves; this layered on a light, delicate body.

I asked where their grapevines came from. Joan says, "A third is a Pommard strain that we got from Oregon, a third is that 'old A.V. [Associated Vintners] clone' that came from Sunnyside, and a third of it is a Wente clone."

Pinot Noir is the darling of Oregon, especially the Willamette Valley. Oregon wine producers have done exemplary marketing to put Oregon on the international map for producing first-rate Pinot Noirs. Unfortunately, Pinot Noir is a very temperamental wine. Its flavors seem to change monthly, and can be affected by the food it is served with. Appreciating Pinot Noir requires knowledge of how it changes and how it can vary. But the patient search and wait can be worthwhile. When Pinot Noir is "on," it is one of the world's great wines.

And Pinot Noirs can age so gracefully. Their flavors and aromas expand and broaden; hints of raspberry are often layered with barnyard smells, a wild mix of hay, barnwood, and—yes—manure. The palate impression is soft and silky.

The Wolvertons have never been able to market their Pinot Noirs with the Oregon Pinots, even though their growing conditions have more in common with the Willamette Valley of Oregon than with the Puget Sound region. They are in a no-man's land, ignored by the Washington industry and beyond the pale of the Oregon industry.

"When we first got started, back in 1969, we went to the old-timers down in Oregon," Linc says. At that time only a few commercial wines were available from Oregon; among them were the wines produced by Richard Sommers of Hillcrest Vineyards and by David Lett of the Eyrie Vineyards. Linc and Joan recalled that Dick Erath and Dick Ponzi were just then making wines at home from grapes off three- and four-year-old vines. It was inspirational.

Joan says, with a broad smile and a twinkle in her eye, "Lincoln conned me into this, actually. He conned me into trying the Hillcrest wines. Then he conned me into visiting all these wineries. He wanted to have a vineyard, and a winery, and a restaurant. All I got out of it was a restaurant."

Lincoln denies this: "That's not true."

"It is too," shoots back Joan. "And he wanted geese. He was going to organically grow these dumb grapes and he was going to have all these monster geese coming in and attacking everything."

Excited by tasting the wines of these pioneer Oregon winemakers, Lincoln began to search for a location in western Washington that would be close enough to their Seattle home to allow them to commute to the vineyard on weekends. (Lincoln was studying economics at the University of Washington; Joan was a writer for the lifestyle section of the *Seattle Times.*) His sister provided him with fifty years of weather data from Burgundy. Armed with this information, he began a sophisticated search for a comparable climate in western Washington.

"We looked at Concrete; that's a warm spot, though wet. We looked down at Grapeview. Then we went down to Centralia and looked around there. Then we looked down here around La Center and

Battleground," he recalls. His computer-assisted search led him to La Center, a two-and-a-half-hour drive from Seattle. He found that the weather pattern was similar to but kinder than the weather in Burgundy.

With youthful idealism, the Wolvertons set out to plant their vineyards with the help of friends and investors. That first year, 1971, was wet, and they sloshed through mud and rain, planting their vineyard. It was a situation that would continue to dog them. Even though the rainfall is not a problem for harvest, because generally August, September, and October are especially dry, rainfall is common the rest of the year. Winter pruning is tough, wet work. And vineyard culture is difficult when it is physically nearly impossible to cut the weeds and grass in the rain.

Linc recalls, "It was either Walt or Chas Nagel who told us we couldn't grow grapes here."

It definitely has not been easy. But the couple have persevered. Lincoln eventually landed a job in Portland, working with Portland General Electric.

This left most of the winery work up to Joan. She calls it her "Grape and I" story, and laughs her hearty laugh. Still, she looks worn by the unrelenting demands made upon a grower. Her short brown hair frames piercing blue eyes. Sun wrinkles play at the edges of her mouth and eyes. Dirt under her fingernails proclaims her occupation.

Neither Joan nor Linc had ever had a garden before they planted their vineyard, nor had Joan ever driven any vehicle other than a car with an automatic transmission. But soon their vineyard grew to 10 acres. And Joan, besides caring for their two infant sons, had to learn viticulture and winemaking by the seat of her pants.

She also had to sell their wines.

When they started, there were only a handful of wineries in Washington state. Lincoln and Joan tried to remember them: Ste. Michelle Vintners, Associated Vintners, Boordy Vineyards, Alhambra Winery, and a few others just starting out. It was a struggle to get people to buy Salishan's first wines.

The struggle hasn't grown any easier. Joan sighs, "There are simply too many wineries and too much wine."

The Wolvertons' children are grown. Joan and Linc are left with an empty nest, a winery full of unsold wine, and a vineyard in neglect.

Joan comments caustically, "When you are in your thirties, it's fun. When you're in your fifties, it's not." But she and her husband have lived a dream. Few of us have that kind of tenacity.

As I listened to them, I wondered what they could have improved or how they might still make the winery work. They have been burdened with winemaking and vineyard chores. They need to get out and sell their wine and tell their story to restaurants and retailers.

Lincoln served me a glass of Chardonnay from the 1989 vintage. There was no need to tell me which vineyard it came from, as all of their grapes are estate grown. The bouquet was magnificent. It smelled exactly like Chablis from France, which also uses the Chardonnay grape. And the taste confirmed the smells. Its weight was perfect. The flavors were neither heavy nor brooding. It was not overwrought with oak. Beautiful piercing acids carried the flavor throughout the wine. I thought to myself, "This wine may be one of the very finest made in America." It was concentrated in flavors, nutty and buttery, but not at all cloying and sweet. This wine was so beautiful. Europeans would appreciate it greatly.

I was amazed. Grapes have been grown in Washington state since the very beginnings of early settlement, and still the Wolvertons are too far away from a market to support their winery. They're growing world-class grapes only two hours from Seattle and less than an hour from Portland.

I want them to succeed.

Joan was philosophical: "You know, this has been an incredible struggle, but we managed to raise our children in a healthful environment and they have a great appreciation for farming and family. Those are very important values."

A friend of Joan's and Lincoln's, Liane McIntyre, arrived just as we were finishing dinner. She has a 5-acre vineyard of Pinot Noir just down the road. "I am so glad to finally meet you, Dr. Clore," she tells Walt. "You are the reason that I am in business. Apparently you sat next to my husband at an event of the Enological Society of the Pacific Northwest and convinced him to grow grapes."

Walt chuckled. "Yes, I have gotten a lot of people in trouble," he says.

Separated from her husband, McIntyre now works the vineyard in her spare time. She relies on the Wolvertons for help in managing the vineyard. This evening she brought by a bag full of Pinot Noir grapes for Joan to measure the sugars. McIntyre hoped to sell the grapes to Columbia Winery in Woodinville. The grapes must attain sufficient sugars before the winery will accept them.

This reminded me of a vineyard that had been planted across the street from the Wolvertons. It was owned by an older couple, and the husband had paid Joan to plant Pinot Noir cuttings in his vineyard. It had been painstaking, backbreaking work. But it was well worth the effort—it meant that others were recognizing the Wolvertons' pioneering efforts. Wineries in the Seattle area began to buy grapes from the vineyard. Suddenly Joan had other growers to compare notes with. Then the husband died, and his wife tore out the vineyard, a total of 60 acres planted to Pinot Noir. One reason she pulled it out was that a Seattle-area winery that had shown interest in their grapes refused to buy the fruit during the '90 vintage because the sugar reading wasn't high enough.

"They wanted the sugar reading [measured in Brix] to be up there like the readings in eastern Washington, and you can't do that here," Joan remembers.

Lincoln adds, "It's the flavor. Once you get the flavor, it is ripe." Lincoln pulled out a chart of Bordeaux to highlight his point. "Here is a record of ten vintages of the Merlot grape, and the Brix readings show that often the Brix are less than ideal. Here is the 1963 vintage at 16.5°; here's another at 20°. The grapes can be ripe at 20° Brix." (Brix is a measurement of what percentage of the soluble solids in a grape are sugars; in ripe grapes the available sugars are about 90 percent of the soluble solids. Ideally, winemakers like to see white grapes harvested at 22° Brix and red grapes at 24° Brix.)

Joan says she gleaned her neighbor's vineyard that year and added it to her 1990 wine. But when they pulled out the vineyard, she was crushed. I could almost hear her wail.

As Walt and I had driven up to the Wolvertons', we had noticed a lot of clearing going on along the south side of the road. I remembered from previous visits that the 60-acre vineyard had been on the upside of the hill, across the street from the clearing.

Walt asked Lincoln if someone was planting vineyards.

"No, they are planning on building 400 homes there," he said with a wry smile.

I tried to say something positive even though I cringed, thinking of how good, potential vineyard land was going to more housing. "That should be good for you. Those could be potential customers. And it will make your land more valuable."

"Yeah," says Lincoln. "And we'll be rich when we're dead."

—THE FIRST PROPAGATED VINES—

Except for the planting of grapes at Fort Vancouver, and later at Fort Colvile (later changed to Colville), there are no documented records of grape growing in Washington until about 1854. Yet clearly people were settling in this area, first along the Columbia River, beginning near the Walla Walla area, then in the Willamette Valley, and finally in the river basins south of Puget Sound as well on Puget Sound.

Following the Whitman Massacre in 1847, most of eastern Washington was closed off to settlement during the various wars with Indian tribes. This lasted until 1859, when the area was reopened. During the fighting, many people remained in this area, on friendly terms with the Indians, but little new settlement was allowed to occur. This channeled the settlers further west, then south into the Willamette Valley or north into the Puget Sound region.

The years 1847 and 1848 were pivotal for this region. In 1847 Henderson Luelling arrived in the Willamette Valley with the area's first grafted fruit, brought overland in his wagon from Iowa. Luelling, along with William Meek, established the Luelling and Meek Nurseries in Milwaukie, Oregon, which became the mother nursery of all nurseries in the Northwest. Most of the region's grafted tree fruits originated at this nursery. They also offered early nursery culture and training. The first grape variety to reach the Northwest was the Isabella, a native hybrid. William Meek won an award for his white Isabella wine at the 1859 California State Fair. This is one of the earliest recorded wines produced in the Northwest.

The discovery of gold at Sutter's Creek in California in July 1848 put the Pacific Northwest's development on hold. California became the rallying cry for new settlement. All of America's, and the Northwest's, attention was suddenly focused south. Even Henderson Luelling took the plunge and set out for California, not as a gold digger but as a nurseryman, selling to the newly cash-rich settlers. Luelling and Meek sold their nursery interests to Seth Llewellyn, Henderson's younger brother (who spelled the family name differently).

Because the Mission grape proved that *Vitis vinifera* could be grown successfully, other varieties soon followed. Grape fever in California was second only to gold fever. The growth in vineyards and wineries was spectacular, reflecting a heightened interest in grapes in the United States.

At the beginning of the 1850s, America—which essentially ended in the Mississippi Valley—was entering a new phase of excitement with

grapes. Cincinnati, Ohio, was the wine capital of America, with sprawling vineyards of Catawba along the banks of the Ohio River. German
and French immigrants planted new vineyards in Missouri as well. The
real commotion, however, was taking place back east in New York and
Massachusetts as horticulturists were busy developing new grape varieties through improved methods of hybridization. From this important
work came the Concord grape, developed by Ephraim Ball in Concord,
Massachusetts. Literally hundreds of new grapes were being created by
cross-fertilization and selection. There were even efforts to cross *Vitis
vinifera* and *Vitis labrusca:* The Diana and the Catawba were born of
these crossings.

In addition to the expansion of vineyards in the New York and
Great Lakes regions, spawned primarily by the Concord grape, *vinifera*
was being planted at a feverish pace in California. Most of the original
plantings there had occurred in Los Angeles, but with the discovery of
gold in the Sierras, efforts quickly turned to northern California.
America had found its "new France" capable of growing the classic
European wine grapes, at a time when many of Europe's vineyards were
being devastated by disease.

By about 1850, the Northwest witnessed a new pattern of settlement. Many of the new settlers were arriving after they had been in
California, and they brought with them the enthusiasm for *vinifera*
grapes that was sweeping California. They saw Washington as an
unclaimed area ripe for planting.

It probably took some time to develop nursery stock at the Luelling
and Meek Nursery and to receive new varieties from sources back in
Iowa. David Chambers brought the first nursery stock (obtained from
Luelling and Meek) to Puget Sound when he arrived in the Olympia
area in 1849 or 1850. Luther Collins arrived at the head of the
Duwamish River in 1851 and immediately set up a nursery with stock
from Luelling and Meek as well. Collins's nursery advertised "100,000
TREES FOR SALE." It isn't known if grapes were among the initial offering, although they likely would have been. Grapes were cherished: as a
table fruit they were refreshing and exotic, they allowed settlers to make
their own wine, and the yeast derived from the grapes' skin could be
used for making bread.

By 1853 newspapers in Steilacoom and Olympia were advertising
wine, both California and foreign. Almost all grocery and general
stores, as well as saloons, offered a selection of whiskeys, beers, and
wines supplied by wholesale houses in San Francisco or by the

Hudson's Bay Company, which continued to operate out of Fort Vancouver until 1868. Goods were shipped directly up the Pacific Coast and brought to Steilacoom and Olympia, and possibly the earliest settlements of Seattle and Tacoma, by way of Grays Harbor or Puget Sound.

By 1854, according to advertisements in the *Pioneer and Democrat* from Olympia, at least three nurserymen were operating in the region. To the south at Cowlitz Landing was Eden Farm, owned by E. D. Warbabs. Near Steilacoom, the Washington Nursery was operated by Hugh Pattison, who was the Puget Sound agent for Seth Llewellyn. Two miles south of Olympia, another nursery was operated by B. F. Brown. Well-known American grapes available at that time included Catawba, Isabella, Clinton, Norton, Winchell, Diana, Ives, Concord, Eumelan, Delaware, and Walter. European grapes that were likely available were Black Hamburg, Grey Riesling, Black Prince, Gutedel, Mission, Muscat of Alexandria, Riesling, Sylvaner, Tokay, Traminer, and Zinfandel.

Reading through the diaries of Seth Llewellyn, one senses that he took an interest in wine. There are notes on wine orders that he placed with California companies, including some wine lists from the late 1880s. Llewellyn was also buying nursery stock out of California, possibly from his brother, Henderson, at Fruitvale. This meant he was no longer restrained to offering primarily American varieties from his original sources.

Most of the early grape culture took place in the Willamette Valley in an area called the French Prairie, originally settled by Red River French Canadians and other former employees of the North West Company, the Pacific Fur Company, and the Hudson's Bay Company. Later nurserymen flourished, selling their cuttings and starts to new settlers. Their efforts also blossomed in Washington once eastern Washington was reopened for settlement.

Census reports from 1850 and 1860 shed some light on the early development of Washington state. In 1850 there were only 62 farms north of the Columbia River. Almost all were located in the valleys south of Puget Sound or near Fort Vancouver. By 1860 there were 330 farms, almost all in western Washington, with the slow but steady growth taking place along the shores of Puget Sound. Most of the open land in western Washington consisted of drainage land around the mouths of rivers and creeks. The rest was heavily wooded. Settlers literally clung to the edge of the wilderness. Access to rivers and the

Sound allowed them to move freely between colonies, but it was a number of years before the pioneers were able to clear the land of light-shielding trees of monster proportions.

Grape culture probably occurred initially around the Cowlitz Landing and to the north near Centralia. This area was settled by French Canadians in about 1837, and was also home to the Catholic mission. Grapes and wine were part of their culture and ceremony, and they likely would have satisfied this need, very likely getting their cuttings from the nursery at Fort Vancouver.

Chapter Three

WALLA WALLA

—*LEONETTI CELLARS, OCTOBER 1992*—

Gary Figgins is driven. I watched him at the end of a long day; the October night descended on a hectic day of crushing grapes. Gary is driven by his own personality, being a perfectionist. He wants his wine to be the very best.

He is also driven by his market.

"If I didn't worry about making really good wine, I wouldn't be able to ask the prices that I do. And I couldn't make it on our small quantities."

But he does. He makes one of America's finest red wines. Wine aficionados across the country have discovered his wine, thanks to recent acclaim in the *Wine Spectator.* Leonetti Cellars has been producing about 3,000 cases of wine a year (as of 1993). That's 36,000 bottles. About 50 tons of grapes.

Normally, the crush occurs over a five-week period because Gary buys his grapes from various vineyards, and even grapes of one variety ripen at different rates. This year it all happened in about two weeks, and he was crushing 70 tons. The strain showed on his face and in his back. More wine in less time. Gary's wife, Nancy, and her parents, Bob and Patty Cosgrove, worked to crush 12 tons of Cabernet Sauvignon grapes from the Seven Hills Vineyard just south of the state line, but still part of the Walla Walla Valley appellation. The previous year Gary got 2 tons, not enough to make a designated wine. Now this—12 tons.

Gary drove the forklift, feeding the bins of tiny dark blue grapes to Nancy and her parents. He deftly picked up a wooden bin of grapes, about four feet square and a foot and a half deep, and placed it on a hydraulic lift. As he backed up the forklift, Nancy set the hydraulic lift in motion, which tilted the bin up so that she and her mother could push the grapes down a slanted stainless steel chute, or hopper, into the stemmer-crusher. To accomplish this, they had to climb on top of the stemmer-crusher, about ten feet off the ground, where the grapes entered the hopper.

Bob ran the crusher. As the grape clusters dropped down into the crusher-stemmer, the crusher broke the grapes' skin and separated the grapes from the stems. Steel rods turned the clusters of grapes in a drum with holes that captured any wayward grapes. The stems were spit out the end of the cylinder for Bob to pitchfork into an empty bin.

Gary roared back on the forklift, picking up the bin of stems, a jungle of green skeletons, and dumped them in a new vineyard he was developing.

"We did that last batch in two minutes," announced Nancy.

To do this Gary had to keep moving: loading the new bin, unloading the empty bin, bringing loaded grapes over, dumping the stems, and stacking the empty bins.

Figgins, forty-four years old, is a retired toolroom machinist at Continental Can in Walla Walla. He made tool dies and parts for precision grinding. He also became a major fixer. These skills are an advantage in a small winery where everything—electrical pumps, heaters, hoses, bottling equipment, barrels, labeling machines—has to be kept going. I was impressed by some of Figgins's winery gadgets, such as the 5-gallon recycled soda pop container rigged with a long plastic hose and a dispensing rod, then put under pressure and used to top barrels. It speeds up the job and allows for good sanitation, and the winemaker doesn't have to cart the container around the room with him.

Still, a winemaker is more than just a mechanic who crushes grapes, adds yeast, puts the wine in barrels, and filters and bottles the wine. "Winemaking is intuitive, knowing how to put something together," Gary said in his cocky, self-assured way.

Winemaking starts with the grapes. Figgins likes to get ripe grapes. Usually, because of his reputation, vineyardists will save him some of the best fruit—and he can pick his own sources. He likes to purchase grapes from different vineyards to add depth to the wine. He buys grapes from, among others, the Portteus Vineyards in Zillah in the central Yakima Valley, from Sagemoor Farms on the Columbia River northwest of Pasco, and from Seven Hills Vineyard in Oregon, across the state line but still in the Walla Walla Valley.

Everything Figgins does seems to highlight drawing out the grapes' fruitiness, not in the juicy sense of the word, but rather the flavor. He uses a special yeast to highlight the fruit, adds nutrients to encourage a quick fermentation, and reduces the length of time the grape skins are in contact with the juice. Then he pays close attention to the temperature of the wine while it is fermenting.

"Everything I do is in the books. You just have to look closely," he points out when people wonder why his wines are so good.

He ran to check the freshly crushed grape juice. The juice, skins and all, had been captured at the bottom of the crusher. Bob, using a small plastic bottle, sprayed forty cubic centimeters of dissolved sulfur dioxide to each batch of grapes—about fifty parts per million. This stuns the natural yeasts on the grape skins and kills any unwanted bacteria. The sulfited juice was then pumped through a three-inch-diameter plastic hose to one of Figgins's new 1,500-gallon jacketed stainless steel tanks.

Because of the vintage, the grape clusters were small. The electronic pump was working especially hard because the grape juice was thick.

"It's hard to pump the juice," yelled Bob. Gary came over a minute later and added, "It's hard pumping the juice because there is so much skin in the juice. That's why it will make such a good wine." [This suggests that the skin-to-juice ratio will be high, which concentrates the flavors.]

The tiny Cabernet Sauvignon grapes were about a quarter inch in diameter and deep navy blue in color. It was hard to describe their flavor when eaten directly out of the bin. They were fruity and slightly sharp: a combination of grape acidity and tannins, fruity but also slightly stemmy from the tiny, tannic seeds. It's a long way from the eventual taste of the matured wine, when the flavors will resonate with cedar and oak, raspberry and black currants.

"Right now, everyone is jumping on the bandwagon and fermenting on the wild yeasts," Gary said.

That scares Figgins. He wants something predictable. He asked out loud, "What is cultured yeast, if not natural?" And answered, "It is just cultivated and grown in a known environment."

Figgins uses Pris de Mousse yeast because it encourages a rapid fermentation and tends to highlight the fruitiness of the grape. He mixed up a batch of yeast to put into the juice of the Merlot grapes they crushed the day before. Usually he waits overnight before adding the yeast, to allow the natural yeast to die down.

Gary's brother, Rusty, joined us for a minute. He is eighteen years younger. Rusty is also interested in wine—though more in the management of vineyards—and has trained in Australia. He shares Gary's dark features, slightly softened. He manages a few vineyards in nearby valleys.

Gary offered Rusty and me a taste of the fresh juice. It was sweet and concentrated, almost like pomegranate.

Leonetti is a family operation. The winery is set behind the Figgins's home on School Avenue on the outskirts of town. It feels like it is inside the city until you get out by the winery. To the east were the Blue Mountains and a backdrop of rolling fields of grain. To the west, about sixty feet away, was Gary and Nancy's home, a neatly maintained modern rambler, and the town was just beyond the front lawn.

The sophisticated winery seemed like an odd monument to have in the backyard of someone's home. It was still incomplete, but the basics were there. Underground was a cellar encased in thick concrete with walls about sixteen feet high. The winery foundation was about thirty feet by thirty feet. The outer walls of the winery, nearly a foot thick, were built of nearby river rock from Tiger Gate Creek. Twelve-foot-tall doors handmade of solid wood opened into the winery. It all felt very French, both in style and in purpose.

Once the wine has completed fermentation, it is pressed and then stored in the jacketed tanks. From there the wine is gravity-fed downstairs to the barrel room, where the wine goes directly into American or French oak barrels. Chris Figgins, Gary and Nancy's son, was downstairs, calling up to his dad, giving Gary instructions on when to cut the flow of wine. Gary was very happy that his son had chosen to work at the winery.

Gary and I descended into the cellar, which was moist and heavy with smells of oak and fermenting wine. It was almost overwhelming at first, especially trying to decipher the various aromas. The oak barrels smelled like crushed cedar boughs. The wine was richly vinous, heady stuff. Together the oak and fruit were sharp to the nose. The aisle between the neatly stacked barrels was lighted with European-style lantern lights at the ends of the rows. The barrels were all marked with chalk, showing the grape type and the vineyard source.

Gary grabbed a thief, a clear glass cylindrical tube about eighteen inches long and an inch and a half in diameter that is inserted into the bunghole of the barrel. Wine is drawn up into the thief by vacuum, the end stoppered with the thumb, and the thief removed from the barrel full of dark red wine. Gary put the thief over my glass, lifted his thumb, and the wine slowly drained into my glass. Gary poured some wine into his glass too.

We tasted a variety of wines; each time the thief slowly drew out the red wine and slowly released it into the glass. It is a ritual that winemakers particularly like: tasting the wines from the barrels as the flavors emerge and evolve. As the wine sits in oak, its personality begins to reveal itself. Gary and I tasted the 1991 Merlot, which was being aged in three different types of oak, one American and two different French oaks. The differences were remarkable. The wine in the American oak was more vanillan, and slightly prickly to the tongue. The wine from the French oak barrels was more spicy, cedary, and smoother. The wines were tannic and young, but flavors of plum, raspberry, and ripe cherry were beginning to assert themselves. We tasted some of the '91 Cabernet Sauvignons, then some '90s. One of the '90 Cabernet Sauvignons was made entirely of Walla Walla Valley grapes, a combination of Cabernet Sauvignon, Merlot, and Cabernet Franc.

Gary finished the tasting by opening an '87 Leonetti Cellars Reserve. This wine was made of Seven Hills Vineyard fruit. The wine's aroma was momentarily lost, but then it opened up—a tamed animal no longer bound by the oak. The smells were of young, taut Cabernet Sauvignon; beneath was the telltale concentrated raspberry aroma of grapes from Seven Hills Vineyard. At five years old, the wine seemed still very young. Its youthful tannins were prickly on the tongue. This wine seemed destined to live a long time: easily ten more years, maybe twenty. It will probably be best when Gary and Nancy's son, Chris, or daughter, Amy, is their age.

Gary credits his interest in wine to his grandfather on his mother's side. His mother was a Leonetti, thus the name of the winery. Grandpa and Grandma Leonetti immigrated to Walla Walla from Calabria, Italy. Grandpa always maintained an acre of Black Prince grapes for his homemade wine.

"Those are my winemaking roots. I think they have served me well," Gary stated matter-of-factly.

On the walls of the winery was a stellar collection of medals awarded to Leonetti Cellars. Close by were family pictures taken in about 1978 of Gary and Nancy and their two children—everyone was quite a bit younger when they got started. Then, they made the wine in the basement of their home. Only a few barrels were noticeable in the pictures.

The Figginses have come a long way in a short time. It is Gary's nature to work on all aspects of his winery. This year he was growing Sangiovese grapes in his experimental vineyard out back, constantly striving to make the best wine, and to discover the best wine that expresses his heritage and his location. He continues to seek, whenever possible, local sources for his grapes. In fact, his father has put in a vineyard along the Snake River. And Gary hopes that his brother Rusty will also provide him with sources for Walla Walla grapes.

Knowing Gary, I suspect he would love nothing better than to produce a wine solely from local grapes. He will approach this goal cautiously. He is concerned about the history of grape growing in Walla Walla. He knows well enough that it can get very cold in this valley. He remembers a story his dad told him about the time his dad was attending a local football game. Sitting in the stands, his father noticed how cold it suddenly became. Then, Gary's father told him, he could hear loud popping noises. It was the sound of trees and vines bursting. Walt later told me that would have been in November 1955, between the 11th and the 14th, remembered as the Black Frost, a devastating frost that nearly wiped out all of the ornamental plants in Washington State.

The Walla Walla Valley tends to be colder than the Columbia Valley to the west and north. Often the cold air gets caught in the southerly border of the Blue Mountains as it comes down the Columbia and Snake River valleys. Temperatures can occasionally go down to -20° Fahrenheit. But the greatest danger is a sudden shift in the temperature, like the one his father described.

—L'ECOLE NO. 41, AUGUST 1991—

I sat at the backyard patio with Jean and Baker Ferguson. Their lovely modern ranch house was situated alongside a golf course in Walla Walla. It was late at night, after ten. The air was warm and light, and moonlight gently filtered through the trees of the fairway. We had been out to dinner; afterward Baker suggested we have a glass of port. He carefully decanted a bottle of 1957 Krohn Port with his mechanical wine decanter, a recent gift from Whitman College, given for his service as a regent of the college.

Baker is an imposing person, tall and flamboyant. He is

distinguished by his mop of white hair and great white mustache, set on a tanned face. Baker and Jean are a wonderful couple. Her quiet, yet assertive manner balances Baker's excesses. Both, I guessed, were in their early seventies at the time.

About ten years earlier, they began to get interested in wine. Eventually they opened up a winery in Lowden, just west of Walla Walla. Named L'Ecole No. 41, it was housed in an old schoolhouse, School No. 41. The label featured a child's colorful rendition of the old school. Baker was the marketing director; Jean, the winemaker. They produced richly textured and flavored Merlot and Semillon; their 1983 Merlot helped propel this variety into prominence. The wines, bold and distinctive, matched the people.

At the time of my visit, the winery was operated by their daughter, Megan, and her husband, Marty Clubb. Megan worked at the family bank, while the winery was run by Marty, an excellent winemaker who has toned down the wines slightly and broadened their appeal. He also produced an excellent Cabernet Sauvignon.

As we savored the port, Baker told me of his family's long history in the area, going back several generations, and about early efforts to grow grapes in the Walla Walla Valley. He is convinced that the early French Canadians who settled in the area between 1812 and 1821 would have planted grapes. According to Baker, "There is no way that they wouldn't have. Wine was a part of their life, like fresh water to us. Most of the French Canadians married Indian women who were highly capable of working vineyards."

Baker inferred that there was a demand for wine early on. Wine was a cherished beverage among these early European settlers; even the fresh, pristine water that abounded then would have tasted unfamiliar. Wine was their water.

As Baker spun stories of early Walla Walla and the advanced culture of these early immigrants, he excited my interest. And though Walt and I have not been able to establish that grapevines were planted this early in Walla Walla, the possibility is very real.

—EARLY WALLA WALLA—

In 1859, following fighting between the Indians and the Oregon Volunteers (and the U.S. Army) and the resulting treaty negotiations, the Walla Walla Valley was reopened and resettlement began. Immigrants who in the past had been encouraged to continue south into the Willamette Valley were quick to move into this promising valley. Devoid of substantial trees, its open basins were filled with swaying grasses. It was easy to travel through, and much easier to work than the land in western Washington.

Walla Walla remained a valuable trading center for the Hudson's Bay Company, although its operations were reduced considerably during the skirmishes between the Oregon Volunteers and the Indians. Near Walla Walla, in the tiny hamlet of Lowden, a small French community called Frenchtown arose. Many of these settlers were French Canadians who had banded together and farmed. Because most of these men had married Native women, they were tolerated by the local Indian tribes, who didn't feel as threatened by the Frenchmen as they did by the Americans or the British. Most French Canadians were willing to live peacefully side by side with the Native people, whereas the Indians felt that Americans in particular were interested in driving the Indians off their lands.

The French Canadians suffered the same fate as the Indians. Once the Americans started to settle the valley, the earlier claims of the French Canadians were ignored. It was similar to what had occurred in western Washington in the Cowlitz Valley, where American settlers had usurped the early settlements of the Puget's Sound Agricultural Company's employees.

A letter to the editor on this very subject appeared in the January 29, 1869, edition of the *Walla Walla Statesman*. The writer, signed Cumrux, was interested in setting the record straight and pointed out the mistreatment of the French Canadians. Many had arrived in the Oregon Country as early as 1823, and most had settled in the Walla Walla area between 1852 and 1857. The writer suggested that as a group they probably did not farm more than a thousand acres, although he admits that there may have been other settlers unknown to him.

Following the wars between the Americans and the Indians, a number of American soldiers settled in the valley. These settlers represented the first drops of what became a human flood that dramatically changed the geography of the region.

One of the first settlers in this wave was A. B. Roberts. Roberts remained a resident of Walla Walla for many years and left an amazing assortment of descriptions of early pioneer life in newspapers of the day. (Although, I must tell you, Baker Ferguson has described him as "an airbag.") He is credited with establishing one of the first nurseries in the Walla Walla Valley upon his arrival in 1859. He wrote of purchasing his original grape nursery stock from French Canadians living on the French Prairie at Champoeg in the Willamette Valley, and referred to one of the nurserymen as Mr. A. Mathias, a Frenchman who was said to have settled the French Prairie in 1831. Roberts imported, either directly or through Mathias, 80 different varieties of European grapes from Orleans, France.

In 1861, another important Walla Walla settler, Philip Ritz, also founded a nursery. He had come to Walla Walla by way of California and Oregon, and he brought some of his stock with him from his Oregon nursery. His Columbia Valley Nursery became enormously successful, and he assigned agents throughout the Northwest to sell his stock. Like Roberts, he imported cuttings from Europe and was excited about the possibilities for a grape industry in the Walla Walla Valley. He ultimately owned 10,000 acres of land with an inventory of more than a million trees, and had 21 varieties of grapes in his vineyard.

Ritz and Roberts were important propagandists for the budding grape industry. They knew quite well that vineyards in Ohio and Missouri were in decline because of disease, especially black rot. They also knew that local editions of the Walla Walla newpapers were eagerly read by potential immigrants. The nursery business was probably very profitable, and they understood well their position of prominence. Both men had been in California and Oregon, and when gold was discovered in northern Idaho in 1860 they understood how this discovery would launch an incredible influx of new settlers.

The discovery of gold created a boom economy that lasted well into the 1870s as new mines were opened. Of course, the real boom took place in the businesses that catered to the prospectors and settlers. Walla Walla grew to become Washington Territory's most important town. Detailed sketches by Frank T. Gilbert show the magnificence of some of Walla Walla's early farms and businesses.

Grapes and wine were part of the growing economy. On April 1, 1871, an editorial in the *Walla Walla Statesman* commented, "Grape culture is fast becoming an important feature with our husbandmen. It is now an established fact that grapes, of all kinds, do as well here as in any part of the habitable globe. Some are engaging in the business largely, by planting from one to fifteen acres in grapes exclusively." In June of the same year, A. B. Roberts advertised, "I have on hand 50 tons of grapes."

An article in the October 21, 1876, *Walla Walla Statesman* reported:

The cultivation of the grape in this country is no longer an experiment. Indeed, the success is so great that the more sanguine claim that our climate is as favorable to the growth of the grape as that of California. This being the case, our grape growers are already considering the question—Whence can they find a market for the surplus crop? Mr. [Frank] Orselli, a native of vine-clad Italy, is about to solve this question, and to that end is arranging to convert the grape crop into wine. A day or two since we visited his ranch, a short distance below town, and were shown his vats, barrels and other arrangements for manufacturing wine on an extensive scale. One of the vats he has now in use has a capacity of 1600 gallons, and others are on a smaller scale. Mr. Orselli informs us that this season he expects to make 2500 gallons of wine, mainly from grapes raised on his own place. Should the experiment prove a success, with another year he will buy all the grapes that offer, and engage in the manufacture of wine on an extensive scale. In the room adjoining the vats, we counted 34 casks ready to be filled with wine. These casks are of a capacity ranging from 40 to 80 gallons, and will all be brought into use. With cheap wines there will be less demand for poor whiskey, and thus much of the money that is now sent abroad will be retained at home.

Orselli, an Italian immigrant from Lucca, Italy, had come to the Walla Walla Valley as a soldier in the U. S. Army. He remained in the area in 1859 and set about planting his farm to grapes and other nursery stock. In 1865 he bought the California Bakery in Walla Walla. Among his offerings were wines; however, it isn't known whether he sold his own wine. I assume he did because Orselli was looked to for his experience in winemaking, and newspaper articles mention that he was supplied with grapes by area growers.

Grapes were likely offered to local residents to make homemade wine, as well as to saloon keepers who might produce a local product. Saloons were big business in Walla Walla; by 1882 there were twenty-six saloons for a population of about 4,000 people, or about one saloon for each 150 residents (two-thirds of whom were men).

Another early Walla Walla winemaker was Jean Marie Abadie, one of the first settlers at Frenchtown. Reports indicate that he made 400 gallons of white wine and 150 gallons of red wine in 1876. His efforts were short-lived, however, and he faded from history shortly after.

Although Washington's early wine industry probably got its start in Walla Walla, two important factors played against the area's grape growers. Foremost, they were isolated. By 1883 the Northern Pacific Railway had bypassed Walla Walla and built a spur from Spokane through Clarkston and Lewiston to the north. A private narrow-gauge railroad to Wallula, where the Walla Walla River joins the Columbia, with its access to Portland, offered a primitive outlet for the harvest, but it was never like being on the main road. As the mines diminished in importance, Walla Walla faded, and immigration began to shift to the north. The grape and wine industry was left standing with its grape-stained toe wedged in the door of success. Then, in 1883, temperatures fell to 20° below zero, likely damaging the grapevines and severely affecting production, and nature slammed the door shut.

Despite these setbacks, individuals still grew grapes in Walla Walla. An 1891 agricultural inventory lists scattered growers of grapes. Missing from this list, however, are some of the great names of the past, including Orselli, Ritz, and Roberts. What happened to this burgeoning industry? Did the growers collectively decide that Walla Walla was too cold for grapes?

In the 1870s, Walla Walla had been the star metropolis of the newly formed Washington Territory. But development was also occurring elsewhere in this vast tract that included most of Idaho and western Montana. Pioneer families explored the river valleys throughout the territory. It was clearly a land with vast natural advantages to exploit. Settlers began to settle in the Yakima Valley, the Wenatchee Valley, the Lewiston-Clarkston Valley, and the vast Columbia Basin. Because of the region's dryness, the initial agriculture in these areas was concentrated near the rivers and their tributaries. During these years, immigration into the area hit a critical mass. Portland, The Dalles, and Walla Walla continued to play important roles as jump-off points, but new cities were fast developing this role: Seattle and Tacoma on Puget Sound, Lewiston-Clarkston in the east, and Yakima in the center of this region.

Chapter Four

LEWISTON-CLARKSTON

—WING VINEYARD, IDAHO, MAY 1993—

The Wing Vineyard perches 700 feet above the confluence of the Clearwater and Snake Rivers in Lewiston, Idaho. It is a humble vineyard, less than half an acre, set amid neighboring homes and yards. Bob Wing tends his vineyard with all the care a parent might provide a child. Vines stretch across the trellises in orderly rows separated by neatly cropped lawn.

Wing and his wife, Dorothy, began planting the vineyard twenty-one years ago, in 1972. Contacted by the Idaho Research Foundation of the University of Idaho, they were asked to plant a test plot of wine grapes. The foundation would then collect the grapes and use them to make experimental wines. After the first year the foundation would turn the project over to the College of Agriculture of the University of Idaho. (Three such experimental plots were established in Lewiston, all in what is known as the Lewiston Orchards. They were the northernmost of fourteen test sites established in favorable growing areas of the state.) The Wings agreed to devote a quarter of an acre to the project.

The Wings started with 81 first-year plants of 19 varieties, a mixture of *vinifera* and French-American hybrids. Bob recalls, "The project was off to a great start in 1972. The National Weather Service at Boise cooperated in the study with the agricultural meteorologist, Jim McCoy, who wrote and circulated a regular newsletter to all the sites. Tony Horn, who was a horticultural extension agent for Idaho stationed in Boise, also visited the vineyards, offering advice and collecting samples."

Wing says it was all so promising. Then, in the spring of 1973, when the grant money from the foundation ran out, as expected, the University of Idaho failed to take up the project. "The project was leaderless and essentially ended. A few growers over the years held on to their vineyards, but there was no longer an organized effort on the part of the University of Idaho to further a wine industry in the state," he laments.

That didn't stop Bob Wing, a retired meteorological technician, who began making daily observations and wrote up monthly summaries of the vineyard's progress. When he had accumulated a year's worth of data, he sent it off to Dr. Walter Clore at the Irrigated Agricultural Research Extension Center (IAREC) in Prosser.

"The response was so kind and encouraging. He accepted the information and suggested that the vineyard, being so close to Clarkston, could be included with the sixteen test plots underway in Washington," Wing says. It was an association that Wing credits with nurturing and developing his interest in wine. He became good friends with Dr. Chas Nagel, George Carter, and Dr. Clore. Through correspondence and regular meetings, he was kept abreast of developments in the wine industry.

Bob Wing still makes wine from grapes grown in his vineyard. All of his grapes are crushed and pressed on the cement patio just outside his back door. The juice is then lowered on a hydraulic elevator to the basement for fermentation and racking.

From his upstairs living area, I entered the basement, where stacks of wine boxes filled with empty bottles were neatly stored along the walls. The wine room was spartan, spotless, and functional, with all the necessary winemaking accoutrements: 5-gallon glass carboys, funnels, siphoning tubes, and plastic jugs.

In an adjoining room, Bob Wing maintains an orderly cellar, designed and built for him by his grown children. Two walls are covered with vertical storage space for multiple bottles of wine. In the middle of the room is additional space, including room for large bottles. Each storage space is lettered and numbered, then catalogued on his computer. For Bob, winemaking is more than a hobby; it is a love affair.

Half of the Wings' home and yard has been given over to growing and making wine. Bob's enthusiasm for wine is undaunted by his frustration that no winery has taken note of his work and expanded into this area. He has enjoyed his long association with wine. His greatest joy is to have someone sample his wines, to begin a conversation and friendship with wine as a bond.

He served me a glass of Chardonnay. It was fresh and clean, with delicate Chardonnay fruit; dry with surprisingly soft acids. I read the computer-generated label on the bottle: *Harvest date, October 20, 1990; Brix, 21.5°, T.A. (total acidity), 1.06; pH, 3.20; bottled, April 25, 1991; T.A. at bottling, 0.70; pH at bottling, 3.55.* Wing also showed me precise weather data for the vineyard. Through his detailed notes I was able to trace how the grapes and wine evolved.

Over a bottle of wine we talked about his epiphany with wine. He first got interested in wine after tasting an Almaden Rosé. He and some friends were on a hiking trip to Mount St. Helens, and they were forced to camp when they got stuck in a rainstorm. Everyone was sitting around a campfire under a big tarp, drinking coffee, when one of his friends pulled out the Rosé. Wing says, "I reached over, rinsed my cup with rain cascading off the tarp, poured a bit of wine into the cup, and raised it to my nose. I was suddenly struck with the aroma that filled my nostrils. I had not experienced a more pleasant olfactory event. It marked the beginning of my association with the world of wine. What followed was reading on wine, trips to California, much experimenting, the first tentative steps of making my own wine, and, finally, planting the experimental vineyard of winemaking grapes in 1972."

Bob Wing eventually wrote a regular wine column, entitled "Wing on Wine," for the *Lewiston Morning Tribune.* Through his column he explored and reported on the great wines of the world. Nevertheless, he kept coming back to his own wines and the pleasure of tasting his wines with friends and fellow wine lovers. For many years he conducted regular wine tastings at his home with a devoted group of people. These tastings allowed him to compare his own wines against commercial wines, and convinced him that his wines were as good as any. And if his wines could be that good, he thought, imagine the kind of wines a commercial winery could make from grapes grown in the Clearwater Valley.

For Wing the meteorologist, weather is the key. He explained to me that in the Pacific Northwest we live in a dynamic climate system, with long wave/trough circulation patterns that occur between 40 degrees and 50 degrees in latitude. Long wave patterns are associated with cooler weather. Bob Wing is fascinated by historical temperature averages. He can pinpoint yearly averages in Lewiston back to 1916.

Wing also takes an interest in the early grape and wine industry in this area. That afternoon he and I had visited a farm high above the

Clearwater River, slightly northeast of town, on a site originally planted by Robert Schleicher in 1883. Schleicher's vineyard was possibly the most important vineyard planting in the area, maybe even the entire Pacific Northwest. It covered 130 acres. A 130-acre vineyard can produce nearly 650 tons of grapes, enough to make more than 40,000 cases of wine.

—EARLY LEWISTON-CLARKSTON VALLEY—

Robert Schleicher was born in Lorraine, France, and studied grape culture and viticulture there before moving to the Washington Territory. Schleicher was convinced that the Clearwater Valley was ideally situated to make wines comparable to the great wines of Europe. Like Philip Ritz in Walla Walla, he brought in grapes of many varieties from both Europe and California. For well over twenty years he experimented with different varieties, made wines, and argued that this region was second to none. One of his wines, a 1902 Sauterne type, won critical praise from George C. Hussman, a pomologist in charge of viticulture for the U. S. Department of Agriculture at Napa, California, and one of America's great wine men. Hussman pronounced Schleicher's effort "a very good wine, equal to the best wines made in (Napa) County, which we claim makes the best dry wine in the state."

Everything about Schleicher's wine was first class: the heavy, dark green bottle featured a deep indent, or punt, on the bottom; the white label proudly proclaimed, *Idaho Wine / Sauterne / Type* [indicating that it was made from Bordeaux grapes, most likely Semillon] */ vintage of 1902 / from the vineyards of R. Schleicher, Lewiston, Idaho.* A bird's-eye view sketch of the Schleicher vineyard on the label shows the Clearwater River and the valley in the background; the signature "R. SCHLEICHER" is emblazoned diagonally at the bottom right of the label; on the bottom left is a description of awards the wine received at expositions in Buffalo, St. Louis, and Portland. The entire package (as the bottle and label are called in today's marketing lingo) is remarkable evidence of Schleicher's sophistication.

In 1906 Schleicher wrote a twenty-two-page booklet entitled "Grape Culture in Lewiston-Clarkston Valley," which was published by the Lewiston-Clarkston Irrigation Company. The cover describes Schleicher matter-of-factly: "Grape grower of twenty years' experience in this valley. Winner of gold medals, all first prizes, for grapes at the International Expositions at Omaha, Buffalo, St. Louis and Portland;

Robert Schleicher's vineyard on the Clearwater River outside Lewiston, Idaho. 1909.
—Photo courtesy of the Teats family.

open to world competition. Won honorable mention for exhibit of pure grape wines at the Buffalo Exposition, the twenty-first among six hundred competitors; at St. Louis, a bronze medal in a strictly international competition and with an international jury; at Portland, a silver medal."

In the book he states, "It is always a surprise to people unacquainted with the climate of the valleys of the Snake and Clearwater rivers, in Washington and Idaho, to be told that the tender foreign varieties of grapes *(Vitis vinifera)* grow there in as great perfection as they do either in California, Europe or Asia. This surprise is often so great that it degenerates into doubt, and can be removed only by ocular demonstration. If one will take the trouble, however, to ascertain what is needed for the production of these varieties, he will find that this portion of the Pacific Northwest possesses those requirements to such a degree as to make it an ideal climate for that purpose."

Schleicher's contemporary knowledge of viticulture shows considerable market savvy regarding conditions in California and in his valley. He refers to several different sources in discussions of the importance of temperature during the critical time of harvest, the effect of a dry climate, and the choice of grape variety. Schleicher had a collection of more than 50 different varieties, mostly *vinifera* from northern Europe, and he describes his efforts to make wine from these grapes: "The experiments in wine-making, conducted here for some years, have resulted in notable success; the dry wines of the Sauterne and Rhenish types having been pronounced by connoisseurs as coming nearer to the

European wines than any grown in California. It has been known for hundreds of years that the best wines were produced near the northern limit of possible grape culture and mostly on the slopes overlooking large rivers."

Continuing, he says,

As these wines were made from grapes which have more of a reputation for table use than for wine-making, and as none of the makers had any previous experience in wine-making in other countries, and as the encouraging results so far are due entirely to soil and climate, there is justification for the belief that when wines made here within the last two years, from grapes used in making the celebrated growths of France and Germany, get age enough to develop their highest quality, there is a possibility of results that might realize the most sanguine hopes. At all events, there is a spendid field for intelligent experimentation in this line, and it may not be too visionary to dream of the slopes and hillsides of the Snake and Clearwater rivers being in the near future covered with thrifty vineyards, drawing on the accumulated fertility of the past ages, and transforming it into wealth, as have those on the hills of the Rhine and the Moselle, the Rhone and the Garonne, the quality of whose products have inspired poetry and song for the past thousand years, and made them the wealthiest sections of the world.

These compelling remarks ring true today in Bob Wing's mind. However, one remark by Schleicher must really rile Wing. Schleicher states, "Under the direction of the Experiment Station of the University of Idaho, the writer is at present testing the different kinds of resistant roots, also some grafted vines upon different stocks. These were procured from the University of California, with the kindly assistance of the viticulturists of that institution, selections being made which, from their experience, would be most likely to prove successful in this locality." Nearly a hundred years later, Bob Wing had been abandoned by the University of Idaho.

Bob and I stood at the site of Robert Schleicher's former vineyard, some 300 feet above the Clearwater River. The site faces north and east, and looks up the valley with the Clearwater River at center stage. Schleicher's dream of vineyard-draped hills is yet to be realized, but it may someday come to pass. We visited the cellar where Schleicher made wines. The walls are thick rock. It is all underground and measures about 30 feet by 20 feet. Using our imaginations, Bob and I reasoned out how Schleicher would have brought the grapes into the building, which is situated directly above his vineyards; how he might have crushed the grapes into a cisternlike storage tank, then settled the wine before passing it through iron pipes, still in evidence on the west wall of the cellar, to barrels for fermentation and storage.

It was not difficult to imagine the aroma of fermenting juice, which has not changed. But the sounds of that early winery would have been quite unlike those in today's wineries. Without the benefit of electricity (and the sound of pumps), the wine would have been moved by gravity from one stage of development to the next. Most of the wine was probably sold in barrels, with a small amount sold in bottles. Bottling would have been done by hand. The sound of glass clinking might be one of the only sounds common to both modern and early wineries. But even that sound would have been muffled by the wooden boxes used back then. I smelled the earthy, compostlike fragrance of the cellar: the fruit, the cemented rock walls, and the wood—the wood of the barrels, the wood of the tools, the thick wooden door, the wooden boxes, even the wooden wheelbarrow. For a moment, Wing and I took flight back into time.

Besides Schleicher, at least two other very important winemakers lived in this region. One of the first known plantings was made by Louis Delsol in 1872. A Frenchman, Delsol planted his vineyard on the flatland next to the Clearwater River. Delsol is said to have produced and sold his first wine by 1875, likely made from the Black Hamburg, the dominant grape planted in his vineyard.

Delsol's home still stands. The imposing two-story, thirteen-room French Provincial house once had a walk-around deck at the second level. Wing and I stood by the front porch and looked out across the old vineyard site toward the river. A nearby lumber mill and unsightly mill ponds dominate the area, and Delsol's estate lies forgotten and hidden in thick underbrush.

Also hidden are two old wine cellars set into the hill behind the home. One of the cellars is still accessible, the wood and rock structure completely blended into the hillside. Moss and flowers grow out of the berm over the wooden doorways. Wing told me that farther up the hill, through a violent sea of blackberries, is another cellar that has collapsed.

Wing once attempted to excavate the hidden cellar. Newspaper accounts suggest the cellars go back 100 to 250 feet into the hillside. These accounts report that when one of the cellars collapsed, 400 bottles of wine were trapped. Spurred on by these accounts, Bob dug down to the fallen hewn logs and wisely decided to stop his dig. Another collapse and he risked being stored with those 400 bottles.

Wing would like to see the cellar dug up again and believes that the bottles would reveal the kinds of wines Delsol produced. There is also the twinge of hope that maybe the wine is still living: To study the past is one thing, to taste it is another. Wing also hopes that winemaking equipment or notes are buried in the rubble. If so, they would help shed light on the early winemaking practices of these pioneer winemakers.

Delsol continued to live in the home until 1914, when he moved into the nearby De France Hotel. He had expanded his original vineyard and acquired more land in the vicinity. Eventually he developed Delsol Park, complete with an open-air dance pavilion, a band shell, and five ponds for boating. Delsol supposedly gave the musicians a taste of his wine. The image is appealing: the band members standing on the steps of the pavillon in dark blue uniforms, holding a delicate glass of wine. In the distance, canoes and boats glide across the water. It is all so civilized, so French.

Jacob Schaefer, a native of Germany, arrived in Lewiston in 1896. His skills as a butcher in Lewiston, and as a buyer and seller of cattle, allowed him to purchase 160 acres of farmland at Agatha, on the north side of the Clearwater River, and 20 acres of land at Vineland, today part of Clarkston.

Those Europeans built homes to last. Schaefer's home and winery, a very modern-appearing two-story boxed structure, still stands in the old Orchard Tract area above Clarkston. Today the home is surrounded by neighboring homes, and without knowing the history one would hardly believe that Schaefer operated a profitable winery from this location. Schaefer planted 60 acres of vineyard at his Agatha acreage and built the winery at his home in Vineland. Ten years after his arrival, he was producing wines alongside Delsol and Schleicher. All three men used classic European grapes to make wine, and Bob Wing notes that they had no trouble selling the wine.

Lewiston-Clarkston remained a healthy inland port. Immigrants came to the area on the Northern Pacific. Products from the nearby valleys could be shipped west to Seattle or to eastern markets. This accessibility to markets allowed the Lewiston-Clarkston Valley to eclipse Walla Walla to the southwest and helped it survive the downturns of the economy. Also, the Northern Pacific financed and built major irrigation systems and did much to promote the region.

In 1909 the Idaho Legislature passed a local-option law that allowed counties to vote themselves dry if they chose. Lewiston went dry in 1910. In 1911, J. E. Moore of Portland purchased the Inland Empire Vineyards Company, the formal name of Schaefer's vineyard and winery. Moore was said to be prepared to produce 30,000 gallons of wine the next year using Schaefer's 65 acres of vineyard in Agatha and another 14 acres of grapes at Vineland.

Wing, writing in *The Journal,* published by the Nez Perce County Historical Society in 1990, quotes Moore from 1911: "There is no doubt as to the opportunity afforded here to make the finest kinds of wines, and I have already arranged for a market for our product. The wines will be shipped to Portland for marketing from that point. We can make wine here that cannot be surpassed. With undue restrictions removed, this valley should be the wine supply point for all the Northwest."

In 1911 improvements were made to the winery; its capacity was increased to 48,000 gallons with the installation of eight 6,000-gallon concrete fermenting vats.

Meanwhile, the dark cloud of Prohibition that had started in Lewiston, Idaho, began to spread over Clarkston, in Washington. In 1916 Prohibition was voted in in both areas, ending the growing wine industry. Surely more vineyards would have been planted with the increased availability of irrigated land. Schleicher, Delsol, and Moore all had thriving, grand wineries. The combined vineyard land amounted to over 200 acres. Assuming that they achieved about 5 tons to the acre, this would translate to 1,000 tons of grapes. A ton of grapes produces about 150 gallons of wine. Therefore they were capable of producing 150,000 gallons of wine annually. That is a healthy output—the equivalent of what eight of Washington's current smaller wineries together might produce in a year, with wine left over.

Wing brought up an interesting question, a point also raised by Baker Ferguson of Walla Walla: Why were the wineries and vineyards in the Lewiston-Clarkston Valley able to thrive and continue until Prohibition, while the vineyards in the Walla Walla area struggled after about 1880? One plausible answer, supported by Wing and Ferguson, is that the Lewiston-Clarkston vintners were primarily of Germanic stock and were aware of the need to cover the tender European vines by bending over the vine's shoots and cultivating soil over the shoots and trunk to protect them against the cold northern climate. That was possible, but there were also Germans growing grapes in the Walla Walla area. Perhaps Orselli, an Italian, favored growing practices typical of southern Europe and influenced other Walla Walla Valley growers. Dr. Clore has suggested that "winterizing" the *vinifera* varieties would have been difficult in the Walla Walla Valley because of the highly fertile soils and the higher rainfall.

Another possibility, I believe, is that a number of events conspired against the Walla Walla winemakers. In 1883 and 1884, winter temperatures hit 20° below zero and 17° below zero, respectively. Also in 1883, the more chilling news came that Walla Walla would be bypassed by the Northern Pacific Railway. That really hit hard. Suddenly Walla Walla was removed from the immigration trail and its ability to get grapes to market was severely limited, while Lewiston and Clarkston had new markets opening up to both east and west.

In a series of articles in 1909 and 1910 in the Walla Walla magazine *Up to the Times*, A. B. Roberts recalls early fruit-growing efforts in the Walla Walla Valley:

> But the culture of grapes was our greatest success. We found that we could not only succeed with the *Vitis Tabruska* [sic], the native of the eastern country such as the Concord, the Isabella and the Catawby [sic], but we found we could succeed with the *Vinivera* [sic] or European table or wine grape, and we introduced stock from the French vineyards of the Willamette and the vineyards of California and we sent to Orleans, France, and imported 80 different varieties, among them the Chassalas Rosi [sic], Flanin Tokay [sic], the Muscat and other kinds that were the latest and finest. And we found here the identical climate for all the fine fruits we undertook to handle.
>
> And now we find ourselves in the position of the miner who we often meet, who develops a rich mine and from which he extracts great amounts of the golden treasure, but sinking the vein to considerable depth, he comes to a "horse," or slip,

and he loses the vein and he spends his fortune on an attempt to recover the pay streak but in vain, and he is busted up and leaves. Another, more lucky miner, takes hold of his mine and with a few blasts he opens into the golden ledge again and for all time the vein is continuous.

Now here is where our "horse" came in. We had pushed our fruit business into the fine valleys near the mines which were our best and principal markets, and when fruit was produced in quantities there, we had nothing but our local market for our large product, so we were loaded down and put out of business, for at that time we had no railroads by which to ship to distant markets.

Roberts doesn't mention it, but surely the freeze of 1883 didn't help those poor growers who envisioned a Washington wine industry growing out of the Walla Walla Valley.

Chapter Five

THE YAKIMA TRAIL

—*HERKE VINEYARD, SEPTEMBER 1993*—
I was heading home from Prosser when I stopped by the Herke farm in Tampico, about twelve miles west of Union Gap and Yakima. To get there I hung a left at Ahtanum Road and drove straight west. As I left the malls and roadside businesses, I entered a broad valley set between Ahtanum Ridge to the south and Cowiche Mountain to the north. There is evidence of a good-sized creek lined with cottonwoods and other bushy trees. In a land of sage and grass, trees are a welcome sight.

Steve Herke, a tanned and solid young man in his early twenties, jumped down out of his rig. We were surrounded by large, heavy equipment, primarily road-building rigs and trucks. Steve showed me to a small old house and we went down to the basement, where three other men were just getting ready to eat lunch. The house was in the process of being renovated, so the family was forced to serve its meals in the basement. Steve introduced me to his father, John Herke, and his older brother, Mark.

Between bites of chili and bread, John talked about his family. John Herke was sixty-five years old when I met him, wiry and thin, but strong-looking, with blue eyes and thinning brown hair. He wore a hearing aid. His jeans were dirty and oiled; his shirt pockets were crammed with notes, old receipts, and pens.

John's great-grandfather, Anthony Herke, homesteaded in this house in 1871. On their property is the original vineyard he planted in 1871, one of the earliest known plantings of grapes in the Yakima Valley.

The Herke family emigrated from Germany and made their way up to this area, John Herke explained, "because they knew that the Catholic mission was here." I told John that I had read that his family had originally come through Missouri and spent some time in California before arriving here. They came up through the Willamette Valley, then on to The Dalles. "Um, I haven't heard that," he says. "You know more about it than I do." John says that back then the road from The Dalles went up over Ahtanum Ridge after passing through Fort Simcoe in the Wapato Flats near White Swan.

The Herke family were among the first settlers in this area. Ahtanum Creek provided plenty of water. Most of the land south of the creek is part of the Yakama Indian Reservation. Kamiakin, the great chief of the Yakama Nation, summered in this area and was friendly to the Catholics, including the Herke family. Kamiakin was one of the first in eastern Washington to use irrigation, having learned irrigation from Fort Vancouver, and was known for his well-tended garden.

John Herke recalls that he once heard from a cousin in Germany, Kaspar Herke, who had found a letter dating from 1879 that was addressed to his family in Germany from the Herkes in Tampico. Kaspar wrote the county clerk in Yakima in an attempt to see if any Herkes still lived there. After he made contact with John Herke, he came here from Germany in 1969 to meet the family.

Kaspar Herke owns a winery on the Rheingau, at Oestrich, near the famed Kloster Eberbach, an old monastery that today houses the German Wine Academy, between Hattenheim and Mittelheim on the Rhine River, an area that produces Germany's greatest wines. Kaspar was fascinated with the Yakima Valley. What a sharp contrast to his Germany. There, the land, their business, and the environment are tightly controlled and regulated. Tampico is a little bit like the Wild West: open, unregulated (though don't get John talking about the state), undeveloped, and remote. John says that Kaspar was interested in Washington's grape industry, so John took him to the research center at Prosser, where he met Dr. Clore and tasted some of the wines that the center was producing. Twenty years later, Dr. Clore attended a short seminar on German wines at the famed wine school in Geisenheim, Germany. The instructor took the class to visit a nearby winery. When they walked in, Dr. Clore heard his name called out. It was Kaspar Herke. They were visiting Kaspar Herke's winery!

I asked John Herke to show me the original vineyard that had been planted in 1871. We climbed into his big pickup, drove to a dirt road, and turned. Leaving the road, we bounced over grass and sage to a point overlooking a small gully. John pointed out where the vineyard was; from the ridge it was difficult to distinguish the grapevines from the sagebrush. We walked down into the area, about fifty yards away, through tall bunchgrass and cheatgrass. Soon we discovered grapevines. Some were entwined in the sagebrush, and we could hardly tell their trunks apart from one another. Then a clear pattern emerged. The vines were spaced evenly, about every eight feet, and planted in north-south rows along the small slope of the gully. John pointed out, "It is almost an acre, planted 207 feet by 207 feet." Some of the vines bore sparse bunches of grapes. I was astonished. This was some kind of miracle. These vines were over a hundred years old, they had never been irrigated, yet they continued to produce grapes. John told me they are probably subirrigated by underground springs that run through the gully. Alas, most of the grape clusters were just shells of dried-out grape skins. We were here two weeks too late. The stress caused by lack of water made these grapes mature sooner. The grapes in the irrigated vineyards in the valley were just then maturing.

The grapes in the Herke Vineyard were both red (actually dark blue) and white. Some of the white grapes had a purplish blush to them and looked more like Gewurztraminer. (Apparently Dr. Sarah Spayd and Dr. Robert Wample of the research center in Prosser visited the vineyard a few years back and decided it was planted with 4 grape varieties. They felt confident that 2 of them were Lemberger and Riesling. I revisited the vineyard in 1995, when more grapes were accessible, and believe that besides the varieties mentioned above, there may also be Chasselas and a Muscat-like variety, as well as a *labrusca*-appearing variety. The vines are so stingy it is difficult to get good specimen grapes.)

John believed the vines came from Germany when the family came here. I told him that more likely they got the grapes from Missouri, California, or the Willamette Valley. Or they may have come from another nearby vineyard said to have been planted only a few years earlier by the Schanno family.

John told me that Anthony Herke was not a vintner by trade. In Germany he had been a baker and a butcher. Here in Washington, the family grew and marketed hops on their farm until they were driven out of business by a flooded marketplace. I wonder what they did with the vineyard. An acre might not seem like much, but it is capable of producing enough grapes to make 400 to 500 gallons of wine. They probably made wine from some of the grapes to drink at home and for the church, and the rest of the grapes probably went to neighbors so that they could make their own wine.

Back at the the Herkes' home, Steve drove me out to another portion of the ranch where he has planted a small experimental vineyard. It contained many of the grapes currently popular in the valley: Cabernet Sauvignon, Merlot, Lemberger, Chardonnay, Semillon, and Riesling. Steve had abandoned this project for the time being. He said he felt the pull of his ancestors and would like to one day have a winery and vineyard at this site, but he doubted there was enough money in it. Right now, apples look more promising. The apple market pays immediate cash. Besides, he could make more money running the road rigs. Winemaking and vineyard work were too involved and he believed the market for wine was limited and very fickle.

I think back to 1871. Besides the Herke family, other immigrant families were settling in this part of the Yakima Valley. The Schanno family is said to have maintained a vineyard near Union Gap. The Schannos were a mercantile family. The father, Charles Schanno, was from Alsace-Lorraine, France. After immigrating to America, they had come up from The Dalles, where they owned a supply and general merchandise store. They founded Oregon's first brewery there. In Yakima they set up a similar arrangement, operating a brewery and a store. They arrived about 1869 and likely planted grapevines. Perhaps they supplied the Herke family with grape cuttings supplied from the Willamette Valley.

Little is known of the Schanno family. Apparently Charles Schanno killed one of his employees in his brewery. He was tried and convicted of murder. The Schanno family scattered after the trial, but descendants still live in the Yakima area.

A few years ago, when I attended the Northwest Wine Festival sponsored by the Enological Society of the Pacific Northwest, I talked to Mary Benoit of Benoit Winery in Oregon. When she learned that I was writing a book about the history of wine in Washington state, she mentioned that her family was related to the Schannos. She later sent me a photocopy of an October 1933 newspaper clipping from the *Yakima Herald.* In the article, Marie Catron, Charles Schanno's daughter, claims that her father planted the first grapevines in the Yakima Valley. She describes in quite substantial detail how her father brought cuttings from The Dalles, "wrapped in wet straw on horseback." She also says that he obtained the cuttings from the Hudson's Bay Company at Fort Vancouver. (Although the fort had been turned over to the Americans by 1848, the Hudson's Bay Company continued to do business out of the fort at least until 1868.) According to Catron, the vines "were placed in the spring on the place as the water was warm. [T]he cuttings [were examined] at times to see whether they were striking root. All the cuttings put out roots and were planted on the home place where they grew and bore fruit that was the wonder of visitors in the early days."

If the cuttings were in fact bought from the Hudson's Bay Company, they likely would have included *vinifera* stock. Cuttings from the Willamette might have included either *labrusca* or *vinifera,* as both were favored by that time by Seth Llewellyn, one of the major grape suppliers.

Catron also states that her father provided grape cuttings to Philip Miller, who settled in the "north central district" near Wenatchee.

—EAST WENATCHEE, AUGUST 1993—

I drove north to Winthrop on State Highway 241. The road goes directly north out of Sunnyside, pretty much mid-Yakima Valley. It wanders past vineyards, orchards, and hop fields until it reaches the gently rolling foothills of the Rattlesnake Hills. There it cuts through a small pass that runs down through the western edge of the Cold Creek Valley. Although it was August, I was thinking about winter.

I have never driven over the Cascade Mountains in the winter. When I was younger I skied at Snoqualmie Pass and was always impressed by the amount of snow that accumulated on the slopes of the mountains. Because Seattle television weather reports always indicated that eastern Washington was considerably colder than western Washington, I assumed that in winter everything east of the pass was covered with snow or ice.

I still have this ice-sheet mentality, although it is slowly melting as I begin to understand weather. For one thing, I now know that the Cascade Mountains act as a barrier to the ocean air mass; one result is that the annual rainfall in the Columbia Valley ranges from three to twelve inches. Even if it all fell as snow, it wouldn't amount to very much. Nevertheless, it is easy to understand how Californians must shiver at the thought of grape growing in Washington state. We are so far north, it's cold, and it rains all the time, doesn't it?

Dr. Clore once told me of a *Wall Street Journal* article that quoted Dr. Maynard Amerine, distinguished professor of enology at the University of California Davis, as saying that the "Pacific Northwest is a climatic nightmare." To Dr. Amerine, Washington state must have seemed like the end of the viticultural universe.

Believing that wine grapes can be grown in Washington does take a monumental leap of faith, from a Californian's point of view. A wine-maker in Napa, or even Sonoma, has a difficult time imagining grapes being grown north of Ukiah, in Mendocino County, because of frost dangers. Anything farther north can only be more dangerous and uncertain. And then there's the erroneous perception that everything north of the California border is like a huge wet sponge.

Unfortunately, this perception of excessive rainfall has even been propagated by the Washington wine industry. Too many wineries praise the dry conditions of eastern Washington by slandering the climate west of the Cascades. In order to overcome the perception of rain-drenched Northwest vineyards and wineries, propagandists have inadvertently dumped all the water on the west.

Descending into the Cold Creek Valley, I drove past the Cold Creek Vineyard and I remembered Walt telling me it is one of the very best sites in the state because of its excellent air drainage and southeast exposure. Walt helped Chateau Ste. Michelle select the site nearly twenty years ago. At this point, beyond the vineyard the road turns slightly east and abuts the Hanford Nuclear Reservation. Beyond the fence and a guard station is a fine view of the Columbia River and rolling grasslands.

Crossing the river, I shook my head at the beauty of the land. To the north is the Wahluke Slope, with the abrupt uplift of the Saddle Mountains farther north. The Wahluke Slope descends to the Columbia River before turning to the southeast. From east to west the slope is nearly thirty-seven miles long. It is like seeing a topographical slice of a mountain with two-thirds of its top sheared off.

I recalled the Langguth Winery of Germany, which started vine-yards and a winery twelve miles from Mattawa, which is still eight miles northeast of where I crossed the river. Langguth, one of the larger German wineries, also owns vineyards and wineries in South America and Australia. Much of Germany's prized vineyard land is located on the 50th parallel, especially in the area near the great Rhine River. Wolfgang Langguth, owner and director of the family winery, must have looked at a map of Washington state, where he would have seen that the Wahluke Slope is located between the 46th and 47th parallels, and the mighty Columbia River is very similar in size to the Rhine. This insight resulted in a mammoth undertaking.

Langguth brought in the very best winemaking equipment and planted vineyards. The Mattawa winery was ultra-modern, and its size made it one of the larger wineries in Washington in the early 1980s. It created quite a sensation: a top-quality German wine company was going to show Washington how to grow Riesling grapes and produce Riesling-based wines. (At that time, Riesling was the most planted wine grape in Washington.)

The first Langguth wines were very disappointing. The wines were trying to be Germanic, even though they were produced in Washington. They were dry and refreshing, but they lacked character. They were also criticized for being overprocessed. The winery had all that fancy equipment, massive stainless steel tanks, the latest filtration systems, and everything was tied in to a computer. The juice was ana-lyzed in Washington, and the information was sent to Germany. Then Max Zellweger, the Swiss-born winemaker hired from Chateau Benoit in Oregon, was told how to process the wine. The results were dead wines, wines without soul.

Zellweger did eventually make some wonderful wines, both sweet and dry, but it was too late. The wines never recovered from their ini-tial bad impression. The marketplace was, and is, unforgiving.

—WHITE HERON WINERY, AUGUST 1993—

Past Mattawa, the road followed the Columbia River north. At George, Washington, I decided to stop to eat lunch. I drove into the small town, but the restaurant I planned to eat in was closed. As I pulled into a dri-veway to turn around, I noticed a small hand-painted sign; it read WHITE HERON WINERY.

Should I stop? My family was waiting for me, but I decided to visit and try a few wines. How long can that take?

The winery was actually an old garage: small, slightly unkempt, and surely not a beautiful monument. As I entered, I was greeted by Joseph and Dylan, the owners' young children. They sat on a couch behind the counter, reading books. Behind them was a bookshelf, crammed with books—evidence that they spent a lot of time there. Then Rory, a big, handsome young man whose last name I didn't catch, came out. Rory helped at the winery, both in winemaking and sales. He poured me a taste of white and suggested that I go in the back and talk to the owners.

In the back room there were about 30 oak barrels. And behind the barrels were the winery's owners, Cameron and Phyllis Fries. Cameron is a big man, with a toothy, broad smile and a deep baritone voice. He sat at an old picnic table crowded with bottles of Riesling that he was labeling. His wife, Phyllis, an attractive, dark-haired, serious-looking woman, sat at her own table next to him, also labeling bottles. Both were in their mid-thirties.

The wine tasted good, and everyone appeared in good spirits. Rory acted as master of ceremonies, cracking jokes and being goofy. As Cameron and Phyllis worked, he brought them more of the various wines. I had started with the Riesling. It was dry, more like a young unoaked Chardonnay, slightly tart from crisp acids, and displayed the refreshing apple/butter flavor of Riesling. Cameron explained that he prefers to have the wine undergo malolactic fermentation, which reduces the acidity and allows him to make a totally dry wine. He claims that most Riesling wines, even though they are called "dry" on their label, are in fact slightly sweet, with about 1 percent residual sugar and rarely are they allowed to undergo malolactic fermentation.

Cameron and Phyllis graduated from Pacific Lutheran College in Tacoma. After they married, they went to Europe together. They lived for a while in France and later in Switzerland. Cam apprenticed at a winery during their stay. Charged up with all they had learned, they decided to come back to the States. Cam eventually ended up at the Champs de Brionne Winery in George. (Champs de Brionne is now more famous for concerts overlooking the Columbia Gorge. In fact, the winery has ceased operations.) White Heron's first crush was in 1986. The family now lives in Trinidad, a half-hour drive from the winery. There they have planted a small vineyard using some of the viticultural methods they learned in Europe, with closer plantings of the vines.

I asked them how they ended up here. Why didn't they grow grapes and make their wines on the west side of the mountains in growing conditions more like those in Switzerland?

Cameron laughed a booming laugh. Both of them fell in love with this country, he says. Besides, he argues, the west side is too cool to grow grapes with any success. At one point, he looked at the Puyallup

Valley, but after working in eastern Washington, he decided that it was easier and cheaper to grow grapes on this side. He says in eastern Washington he could buy unimproved "ground" for $250 an acre. Comparable land in western Washington would cost about $6,000 an acre. In his opinion, both eastern and western Washington are "on the edge," which means they each present plenty of risks to growing grapes. The grapes' struggle, with the environment and the northern climate, contributes to powerful flavors expressed in the wines. Cameron is convinced that eastern Washington, with its dry, cool conditions during harvest, can produce wines that are unique in the world. The weather in the Puget Sound area is less conducive to such wines, in his view.

After the Riesling, we tasted a 1992 Pinot Noir. It was good but slightly sharp at the edge of the tongue. The nose smelled faintly of fresh raspberries. Drawn directly from barrel, it was a youthful wine. The '90 was dry and fruity with just a little sharpness. A 1989 blend of Cabernet Sauvignon and Merlot, called Chantepiere, was delightfully balanced. Barrel samples of the same blend, from '90 and'92, were also very good.

As I sampled the wines, I viewed the interior of the winery. It was funky, basic, and raw. Wood pallets were stored against the roll-up door of an old garage. Music played on a radio tuned to a station in Wenatchee. Unlabeled bottles of wine lined the walls in the style of European cellars: the bottles lie side by side alternately, neck to bottom and bottom to neck, in long stacks.

The Frieses appeared financially strapped. I knew they had struggled to keep the winery going. The wines were very reasonably priced, but I couldn't see how Cameron and Phyllis could afford to sell their wines in Seattle at a price discounted to allow both the wholesaler and the retailer to add their markups.

The kids were part of the winery, by necessity, as both parents worked here. Out back they had a yard to play in, and they were building a make-believe city. Cam says, "We are in this for the long haul. We are building something for our children."

When I left the winery I felt richer, having experienced a real winery with real people. These folks had a dream, and the determination to follow their dream.

I hope it comes true.

As I left the winery, Cameron handed me a newspaper article from a recent edition of the *Wenatchee World*. Written by Steven Smith, it chronicled the life of Wenatchee's first European-American settler, "Dutch John" Galler.

John Galler, born about 1813 in Baden, then an independent German state, fought on the side of rebels during an unsuccessful revolution to establish a representative government.

He came to America in 1849 and lived for a time in Philadelphia. After his wife died, he left his two children in the care of his sister and struck out west, living among Nebraska Indians for a couple of years before heading further west. After living in Montana, he arrived in Ellensburg in 1867, one of the first settlers in that area. In 1868 he made his way over Colockum Pass, then an Indian trail.

He settled below Wenatchee along the south side of the Columbia River in an area known as Malaga. After initially roaming the area hunting furs, he established a homesite when he married a young Indian girl who had saved his life. He had fallen into a river while traveling with a group of Indians. He had been abandoned by all except the young girl, Mary, who lay with him and kept him warm, and later married him.

At his homesite he was the first settler to irrigate his orchards. He added a vineyard in about 1873, planting 300 grapevines. Galler's neighbor, G. Earl Young, recalled in the *Wenatchee Daily* in 1921 that Galler had 20 acres of grapes and that he made 15 to 20 barrels of "sour German wine" a year. Galler told of making $2,000 a year from the sale of his wine. By 1890 Galler's ranch was located close by the new wagon road that came from the Kittitas Valley. Many accounts are given by travelers of the beauty of Galler's home.

The name Malaga was given to his ranch by railroad men who would stop to buy some of Galler's wine, believed to be made from the Malaga grape. Additionally he was said to have sold a large portion of his wine to Chinese miners who worked the area.

Galler moved from his homestead sometime after the turn of the century to the Colville Indian Reservation. He died in 1921, supposedly at the age of 108.

—THE TRAIL NORTH—

Other Wenatchee residents also had vineyards about this time. One of the more prominent was Philip Miller, who had arrived in 1872. His history follows closely on the heels of Galler. Miller, also German, came west from Pennsylvania, then Montana, and came up through the Yakima Valley by way of The Dalles.

Miller planted his vineyard about 1874. His nephew, Jacob Miller, in an interview in *The Wenatchee Daily World*, on June 30, 1927, described the Miller ranch as quite spectacular. It encompassed 640 acres, as part of a desert claim, and was planted to 40 acres of fruit, including 5 to 8 acres of grapes.

In a letter to the *Wenatchee Advance* in 1894, Miller writes that he made about 1,400 to 1,500 gallons of wine a year. Any excess grapes or wine he turned into brandy, using a four-year-old copper still that allowed him to make 500 gallons a year, which he sold for $5 a gallon.

There were other vineyardists and winemakers as well. H. S. Simmons, writing in 1894, provides a rare insight into the variety of grapes grown at that time. He writes, "I have 100 Zinfandels, four years old, from which I made last fall six barrels of wine. You can grow 700 vines on an acre and at this calculation you would get 42 barrels of wine a year, worth at least 50 cts. a gallon, or $1,050."

Add to this Conrad Rose, who claimed to grow "most of the European varieties of grapes grown in California with great success, also some American varieties, we produce and make wines that are pronounced good by all."

One of those proclaiming the wines good was a Frenchman, John Durieux. In 1894 he prophesied "that in a few years wines will be produced in Wenatchee valley equal to the famous red wines that have made the district of Macon popular throughout the civilized world."

In 1901 he served Wenatchee White Claret at dinner. Is it possible that the wine could have been a forerunner to today's White Zinfandel?

Chapter Six

CALIFORNIA
WINE GOES WEST

Shortly after 1850, the wine capital of America shifted from Ohio to California. California's wine industry grew out of the Los Angeles desert and drifted northward to the Napa and Sonoma areas of California. Grape growing and winemaking were pursued with the same frenzy as gold digging in the Sierras. The ease of growing grapes in California, without the fear of winter damage, combined with the rapidly growing population, caused an outright stampede to plant vineyards and put up wineries. Merchants in Los Angeles and San Francisco sold the wine to a curious world.

By 1860 California was on its way to becoming the wine world's "new vineyard." With disease attacking the vineyards of the Old World and the eastern United States, California was truly a promised land. It was still far away, however, from the markets of the east. Without a transcontinental railroad, the California industry was awash in wine.

Thomas Pinney's *A History of Wine in America,* published in 1989, carefully documents that *vinifera* grapes were widely planted throughout California by the mid-1860s. Many of the earlier pioneer grape growers had been skeptical of *vinifera's* ability to flourish in California and often hedged their bets with hybrid or *labrusca* grapes. Early vineyardists intermixed Mission and Riesling, *vinifera* grapes, with Catawba and Isabella, hybrid grapes.

By the 1870s, California was truly on course: *viniferas* were the grapes of choice, and notable dry table wines were made from Riesling and Zinfandel. With the completion of the transcontinental railroad in 1869, California wines began to expand their sales into the eastern and

Midwest markets, competing directly with the established grape-growing regions of the east.

California was also the source of most of the wine that came to the Pacific Northwest. It was brought up the coast by ship through wholesale wine merchants in San Francisco. Early newspaper ads in all the major towns of the Northwest indicated the availability of wine. A standard advertisement might list LIQUORS, WINES, AND CIGARS. Occasionally ads would specify California Wines, Port, Sherry, Madeira, and California Champagne. Ads sometimes mentioned a particular grape variety such as Riesling or Muscat, but usually the wines were sold generically, based on a place name.

This is how the California wine industry developed its mistaken practice of using Old World wine names to help sell its products. Because California wines were initially based on the Mission grape, producers sold their wines under generic names then popular in America such as Port, Sherry, or Burgundy.

George Hussman, writing in the *Yearbook of the United States: Department of Agriculture* in 1898, details the early history of wine in America and California. He writes, in describing the early California industry:

> This may be called the first or trial era of the young industry, extending from 1855 to 1875, at which time wines and grapes fell to a price so low that they would not pay for the picking, and in many cases hogs were turned into the vineyards to utilize the crop.
>
> But still some of the wines, especially the finer grades, found favor and created a demand which exceeded the supply. Then, however, began the sale by the producers of their entire products, as already stated, and the injurious practices growing out of such a system. The dealers who bought the wines disposed of the low-grade goods as California wines, while the better qualities, sufficiently aged, to be found in nearly every cellar, were generally sold at high prices as French and German wines. The State thus suffered all the discredit for the poor wines, but obtained no credit for the really fine wines which were produced. This practice prevails to a certain extent to-day, fostered by a false idea which leads many people to pay high prices for foreign goods, while scorning the home product, even though this may be better in quality.

Clearly, California's future lay with *Vitis vinifera,* but winemakers were unable, or unwilling, to market their wines as varietal wines. This led to outright fraud by many producers and merchants and, coupled with overproduction and limited market demand, the California wine industry was cast into a depression that lasted until the late 1890s.

Hussman also mentions the devastation to California's vineyards from phylloxera and the growers' failure to use resistant rootstock. Meanwhile, the vineyards of Southern California were being wiped out by what was referred to as the Anaheim disease, today known as Pierce's disease. The California wine industry was reeling.

By 1898, the year of Hussman's report, the marketplace had begun to catch up to the supply and the California wine industry was starting to realize its potential. Hussman notes that in 1897 the wine industry produced 34 million gallons of wine. Of that, 27 million gallons were dry wines, and the remaining 7 million gallons were sweet wines. He also states that in Napa County alone, in 1898, there were "over two hundred cellars and wineries, ranging in capacity from 10,000 gallons up to 3.5 million gallons, that of the largest cellar, the Greystone, above St. Helena."

Hussman was describing a mature industry that had learned to diversify its product, and to rely on the resources of the state of California to promote and market its product.

Chapter Seven

BINGEN
WHERE RAIN AND SUNSHINE MEET

—*MONT ELISE VINEYARDS, JANUARY 1994*—

Bingen, Washington, is located along the Columbia River, just below White Salmon, across from the Oregon town of Hood River and about an hour's drive from Vancouver, Washington, on Highway 14, a winding, difficult highway that hugs the mountainside above the river. It was wet and misty. I kept my hands on the wheel and my eyes straight ahead, ready for the next sharp bend in the road. Forget about the beauty of the Columbia Gorge; right then, there wasn't much to see other than a river of thick, soupy fog.

I did notice a dramatic shift in the vegetation as I got closer to Bingen. Ponderosa pine and oak became more prevalent, and there was generally less underbrush. Officially, I was in eastern Washington.

Bingen, during this winter visit, was a quiet town. The roads were covered with sand, strewn on the roads to give drivers better traction, and the main route through town was cluttered with small cafes and mini-marts. One building stood out: the Mont Elise Winery, a somewhat Bavarian-style building on the river side of the road.

German immigrants named the town after the German wine-town of Bingen am Rhein, as the site reminded them of their village on the Rhine River. The German pronunciation, *BING-in*, was corrupted over the years to *BIN-jen*, as it is pronounced today.

Chuck Henderson greeted me warmly. It has been at least twelve years since I last visited him at the winery. He looked good, with good color in his face. In May, Chuck underwent quadruple bypass heart surgery. Chuck's broad, strong hands belied his crippled heart. A hardworking man, his deepset blue eyes were shiny and bright. At seventy-three, he was slightly balding, with silver and brown hair brushed back on the sides. His mouth bent down at the corners, giving him a sad look. His voice was soft, like the fog that muffles the valley.

Henderson came to Bingen from Fargo, North Dakota. He had bought a farm there and planned to go into general farming. The man he bought the farm from went west and bought a farm at Bingen, but after he and his wife had been here a while, they decided they hated it out here and in 1961 they arranged to swap farms with Chuck and his wife, Bella.

Although the Hendersons' land was mostly planted to cherries, Chuck began to wonder if German grapes wouldn't do well here on the Columbia River. He remembered learning to drink good German wines back in Wisconsin, where he had once lived. At first he thought the wines tasted like vinegar, but slowly he began to appreciate their complex, fruity flavors. "This was back in '54, when Germany was desperate for money; you could buy really good German wines for $1.35 a bottle." So when Dick Adler, the local extension agent, approached him about growing grapes, there was little hesitation. Chuck was looking for another crop to plant. He was tired of working with the big company that bought the cherries, and when one crop was completely lost due to the company's spoilage problems, he had finally had enough.

Chuck Henderson was one of the first test-site cooperators with the Wine Project. In 1968, Walt Clore brought him 20 grapevines to plant, including White Riesling, Chenin Blanc, Gewurztraminer, Gamay Beaujolais, and Pinot Noir. The Wine Project was interested in finding different test sites to grow wine grapes, especially in different areas of Washington. The Bingen/White Salmon area is what Walt calls a "transitional zone," where the Pacific Ocean breeze coming up the gorge meets the continental winds from eastern Washington, moderating the weather. Because of this unique combination of climatic conditions, the area always receives a protective blanket of snow when extreme cold occurs. Rainfall here is three times greater than in the Yakima Valley, averaging close to thirty-five inches a year. Additionally, Henderson's test site is magnificent, perched high above the river at 1,750 feet elevation. The topsoils are ten feet thick, with ancient soils unmolested by the Bretz Floods 10,000 years ago that stripped much of the soil away from the banks of the Columbia River.

Initially, Henderson wanted to irrigate his vineyard, but Dr. Clore said that the combination of adequate rainfall, deep topsoils, and the

Chuck Henderson in his vineyard
at Bingen, Washington. 1977.
—*Photo by Lawrence J. Allen.
Courtesy of Elizabeth
Purser-Hendricks.*

protection of snow in cold weather would make irrigation unnecessary. He was right. Chuck told me, "I got some gypsum block that they use to test moisture content in the soil. In August, the top two or three feet would be bone dry. When you get down to about four feet it is about 25 percent to 35 percent field capacity (wetness); at six feet it is about 70 percent capacity; when you get down to about ten feet it is still pretty wet. I have never, even in the driest of years, ever seen any evidence of moisture deprivation to the plants. My biggest problem is that I can't stop the darn plants from growing."

Based on the initial trials in his test plot, Henderson planted his first vineyard, of 3 acres, in 1971, mostly to Pinot Noir. He planted an additional 3-acre vineyard in 1972, and in 1979 he planted 7 more acres. He planted Pinot Noir, Gewurztraminer, Chenin Blanc, and Gamay Beaujolais.

I asked why he had chosen these varieties. Was it because these were the varieties that grew best in his vineyard or was it because that is what the marketplace demanded? "Both!" he says emphatically.

Henderson opened his winery in 1975. He had traveled to Prosser to taste the wines at the research station: "I liked the Cabernets; the

Pinots were not very exciting. I had already made from my own grapes some Gewurztraminer that I liked. I was interested in the Gewurztraminer because it is a hardy grape and I didn't know what the winters were going to do to the grapevines. Since I started, I have had little winter damage to the grapevines.

"When we first started, it was real fun. There was such camaraderie among the group of people. We hadn't gotten so commercial as we are now. Everyone was trading information and helping each other out. A lot of friendships were made."

At first the winery was called Bingen Wine Cellars, but it was later renamed Mont Elise Vineyards. Elise is Chuck and Bella's daughter. They also have a son, Charles, who showed an early interest in the winery by attending UC Davis. Chuck and Bella always hoped that Charles would take over the day-to-day operation of the winery. Running both a vineyard and winery is very difficult; there aren't enough hours in the day. For Chuck, with his weakened heart, it was taxing to the point that he felt he literally lost a year prior to his bypass surgery. He remembers very little from the '92 vintage.

Sitting across from Chuck Henderson, I felt great sorrow for him. His early vision of the winery and vineyard has eluded him. He has done so many things right: he has a wonderful building, with an underground cellar and thick rock walls, and he has a manageable vineyard of about 15 acres in a spectacular setting with a perfect microclimate.

But so many other things haven't gone the way he had hoped. For one thing, his location is isolated. Though it is only an hour's drive from Vancouver and Portland, it seems much farther away, especially in the wet and cold months of winter.

The tasting room sits up above the cellar; large windows in the west wall allow visitors to oversee the operations in the cellar. Most of the equipment was put together by Henderson. Besides the stainless steel tanks, Henderson also was an early experimenter with white oak from the Northwest. He even constructed his own barrels, shaped square, because of the difficulty of curving the oak.

Chuck poured me a glass of sparkling wine, made in the method of Champagne. It was crystal clear with tiny bubbles. From the 1984 vintage, the wine had been recently disgorged after having sat on the spent yeast in the bottle for nearly nine years, an enormous amount of time even by French Champagne standards. This sparkling wine was made out of 100 percent Pinot Noir, grown in the Hendersons' vineyard.

The aromas were fresh and delicate, suggesting apple with clean hints of yeast, not doughy or breadlike. On the palate the wine was intensely fruity—not sweet—although there was an accompanying sweet taste. But the finish was bone dry, chalky, almost tannic, a refreshing balance to the intense fruit in the middle palate. The residual sweetness was only 0.65 percent, well below the residual sugars found in most dry sparkling wines.

This was very good, world-class sparkling wine. Alas, only about 7,500 bottles of it were made.

The Hendersons have proven, beyond a doubt, that grapes can be successfully cultivated in this area, and that the microclimate produces grapes and wines of unique flavors.

—CHAMPAGNE FOR KINGS—

Making world-class champagne (best called sparkling wine) was a dream of Sam Hill's. Sam Hill arrived in Washington at the turn of the century. He had come west with the railroad; his father-in-law was James J. Hill, builder of the Great Northern Railway. Sam Hill, an attorney and road builder, was an eccentric man of great vision. Early on he argued for development of the Pacific Northwest to supply the needs of the developing Asian continent. He hobnobbed with the Queen of Romania, knew the Russian aristocracy, and was a close friend of the Prince of Belgium, who later became king. Hill envisioned building a large summer house overlooking the Columbia River, surrounded by vineyards worked by Belgian vineyardists, which would become a second home for the prince.

Originally Hill sought to buy vineyards owned by the Jewett family, located near White Salmon, not far from where Bella and Chuck Henderson now live. The Jewetts had a beautiful vineyard that Hill wanted badly. Planted in the late 1880s, the vineyard was at its peak around 1905 when Hill made his move to buy it. Hill coined the phrase "where the rain and sunshine meet" to describe the site. The Jewett family was reluctant to give up the vineyard, but Hill pressed them into submission. Finally they relented, but only verbally.

Sam Hill, excited with his catch, brought out a bottle of spirits and proposed a toast. Big mistake. The Jewetts were teetotalers, and they told Sam Hill the sale was off and hurried him away.

Disappointed but undaunted, Hill took his idea farther east to the small, thriving farming community surrounding Columbus, situated on a benchland that rises up from the Columbia River eleven miles south of (and below) the town of Goldendale. Columbus was founded in about 1852 by Amos Stark, who placed an early claim but then went south to California to mine gold. Some think Stark may have brought grapes back with him from California upon his return. Other growers followed, including the Gillenwater family; prior to 1905, they raised 21 different varieties of grapes on their 240-acre farm.

The Reverend W. T. Jordan, a Baptist minister from Portland, also had a beautiful vineyard, down along the river. Jordan's vineyard had originally been planted by Winthrop Presby, a prominent attorney in Goldendale. Presby planted the vineyards in about 1900 after securing a loan of $10,000 from Jordan's mother-in-law, Lucy Palmer Maddock. Presby used the money to go to Europe to find the best grapes for his vineyard. Unfortunately, he was not able to make his payments and the property was foreclosed. Mrs. Maddock continued to rent the vineyards until her death. Jordan and his wife, Birdie, then took over the operations of the vineyards, naming it the Tokay Ranch. Jordan loved his vineyard of Muscats; eventually he was selling, and shipping, 80 to 100 crates of grapes a day to the ethnic communities up north in Roslyn and Cle Elum.

When Sam Hill arrived in 1907, Columbus boasted acres of peaches and grains, as well as grapes, growing along the hillsides. The Gillenwater farm was Hill's first major purchase; it became the location of what is now the Maryhill Museum. (Hill was also interested in the Reverend Jordan's vineyard, but Jordan refused to sell.)

In the fall of 1984, Walt and I drove over to Goldendale from Prosser and continued on down and visited the Maryhill Museum. Walt told me that in 1938, at the urging of O. Z. Brooks, the Maryhill estate attorney, and William Bridgman, a Sunnyside vineyard and winery owner, plans were made to plant the vineyard that Hill had originally envisioned. Bridgman recommended a number of varieties, *vinifera* as well as American hybrids, relying on T. V. Munson of Texas and his experimental work with American hybrid grapes. There are no records of any harvests or wine being made before a series of grass fires destroyed most of the grapes, and the vineyards were abandoned shortly after. Remnants of a few vines can still be spotted on the hillside along the driveway entering the museum from Highway 14.

In the spring of 1975, Dr. Clore and Mel Hagood, a Washington State University irrigation specialist, consulted with the museum director about growing wine grapes and developing an irrigation system on the museum grounds. For lack of funds, development never took place.

Maryhill Museum vineyard about 1940. —*Photo courtesy of the Maryhill Museum of Art.*

Chuck Henderson also told me about efforts by the museum's director back in the mid-'70s to resurrect the property's vineyards. There was even talk of Henderson's winery making wine for the museum. Something happened to infuriate Henderson, and in his wrath he threw all of the records of the area's early grape history into the museum's boiler. (Walt thinks that Henderson's fury came when the director allegedly took off with the funds.)

Walt and I also drove down to the river and tried to visit, unannounced, the Takahashi family at their fruit stand. Unfortunately, none of the family was in. Tsugio "Doc" Takahashi owned the old Jordan vineyards. Today his son farms that land. Takahashi had told Walt back in 1965 that he believed some of the Muscat vines were a hundred years old, claiming they were among the oldest in the state. (We have not been able to confirm that.)

We were then directed to a nearby fruit stand, run by Gunkel Farms. Here we were told we could visit with George Gunkel at his home next door. George Gunkel answered his door and led us down his porch stairs to his front lawn, where we sat on well-used garden chairs. The September sun was warm and comfortable under the shade of the trees. Gunkel, now in his seventies, grew up on this farm. As a child he occasionally accompanied Jordan up to Roslyn to deliver grapes.

George gave us a tour of the area. His land is on the river below and to the east of the Maryhill Museum and the Highway 97 bridge. We piled into his enormous pink Cadillac, about ten years old with tools scattered on the seats, and drove through his peach orchards. The red- and yellow-streaked peaches were absolutely beautiful in the slanting autumn sun. We also visited his vineyard of Muscat of Alexandria, which was just ripening. The grapes were bursting with flavors of peach and apple.

Alongside Gunkel's vineyard is the old site of the town of Columbus and the home of W. T. Jordan. Gunkel showed us Jordan's stately white home, surrounded by its picket fence, and the church next door. Next to them are vineyards and farmland owned by the Takahashis. Then we drove up the hill to the abandoned townsite of Maryhill. Not far away is a replica of Stonehenge, an eerie memorial built by Sam Hill as a tribute to county residents who died in World War I.

Gunkel showed us grapes planted by Hill that were growing along a dirt wall. The grapes were definitely *vinifera*, but difficult to identify. At the Maryhill townsite there was an abandoned little store that was to have been part of the larger town. We munched on fresh Muscat grapes as Gunkel told us some of the area's history.

Sam Hill bought his first property around 1907 and expanded his holdings to over 7,000 acres. Hill said he wanted to build a Quaker community of independent farmers, "to organize a company of $100,000 capital and buy the fruitland and vineyards. . . . [T]he plan is to sell a man a piece of fruitland and a piece of timberland so he can have material for fuel and boxes for his fruit." He knew that with the coming of the Spokane, Portland, and Seattle Railway, markets would open up.

Regrettably, Sam Hill destroyed an established farming community while trying to build a new one. The new one, called Maryhill after his wife, never attracted the farmers he had hoped for. Problems developed that he didn't anticipate. For one thing, much of the land needed irri- gation. Unlike the thirty inches of annual rain at Bingen, Maryhill receives only eleven inches of rain. The Gillenwaters' farm that had so attracted him was subirrigated, but much of the remaining farmland required a source of water.

Then there were the problems with the site. When I asked Gunkel how he viewed this spectacular area, he said, "You see it as beautiful. I see it for what it is. It is a desert; it is dry, windy, sandy, and hot."

Eventually, Sam Hill lost interest in his planned community and instead tried to build a home as a retreat for his fractured family. But

Maryhill vicinity about 1910. Tokay Ranch in lower left.
—*Photo courtesy of the Marhill Museum of Art*

his wife refused to live with him there, and his son and daughter were often elsewhere. The house that Sam designed and constructed was finally finished after his death in 1931. It became the Maryhill Museum, dedicated by the Queen of Romania during its opening celebration in 1926.

Grape growing in this area continues to this day. Given the right strategy (and financing), the Maryhill Museum would gladly entertain the idea of replanting the museum vineyard, with wines made for the museum or possibly by them.

Chapter Eight

STRETCH ISLAND
ISLAND BELLE

"I know what I will call it! It will be the Island Belle," exclaimed Adam Eckert. The story, as related by Mary Sagerson and Duane Robinson in their book *Grapeview, the Detroit of the West*, goes that Adam Eckert's daughter, Lottie, had attended a dance on Stretch Island where she was clearly the belle of the ball. Eckert, while attending a growers' convention in San Francisco sometime after 1905, wanted to talk to the conventioneers about his discovery of a new grape and needed a name for it. A different version of how Island Belle was named credits Augusta Eckert, Adam's daughter-in-law, married to Walter Eckert.

Modern horticulturists, including Walt Clore, remain unconvinced that Adam Eckert developed a new variety of grape, stating that the Island Belle grape is identical to the Campbell Early. Both are slip-skin grapes, meaning the skins easily slip or slide off the pulp when the grape is pinched; both are dark blue-black in color and adapt well to the climate in western Washington; both are hybrid grapes; and both are part *labrusca* and part *vinifera*.

The Campbell Early and the Island Belle emerged at about the same time. The Campbell Early was developed in Ohio in 1892. It was a cross between a seedling of Moore Early pollinated by a *labrusca-vinifera* hybrid (a seedling of Belvidere pollinated by a Muscat Hamburg). Campbell Early was readily available through Puget Sound nurseries, along with numerous other hybrid grapes of the time.

No credible records have been found to authenticate Eckert's work with the grape. Clearly, though, he was an enthusiastic nurseryman who was constantly working in the vineyard and sought the perfect grape for his region. But as Dr. Clore would say, "Nurserymen aren't necessarily plant breeders; they are propagators." Walt doubts very much that Eckert ever did any breeding. He has pointed out to me the great technical difficulties, and time-consuming efforts, of plant breeding. Eckert probably selected a vine, or sport, of Campbell Early that he thought was superior to the other Campbell Early vines in his nursery. As a businessman, he understood the marketing advantages of calling the grape Island Belle. But according to Walt, and most horticulturists, the Island Belle is the same as the Campbell Early.

Adam Eckert was more a businessman than a farmer. He was originally from Auburn, New York, in the Chautauqua District, an area noted for grape growing. Eckert had owned his own liquor business and was also a butcher. Eckert himself writes in the 1905 *Mason County Journal,* "In 1889 Mr. Adam Eckert, on his way to California in search of a new home where he could engage in grape culture, stopped at Seattle to visit his friend, Mr. Charles Gould. At Mr. Gould's request, he went with him to a place he had pre-empted, adjoining Mr. Evans. The fact that Mr. Evans was growing grapes successfully interested Mr. Eckert at once, as many had told him grapes could not be grown in the Sound country." It isn't clear whether he ever made it to California; rather, he may have gone straight to Mr. Evans.

According to most sources, Lambert Evans, twenty-nine years old, arrived by skiff from the Olympia area in 1872 (although Eckert noted that he arrived in 1878.) He was a very long way from his native Florida, where it is believed his family had engaged in grape growing. Evans, a Confederate soldier, had been imprisoned in St. Louis during the Civil War. Upon his release, he walked the entire way to Los Angeles. Unhappy with the heat of Southern California, he turned his sights northward and came to the Olympia area to look for a new home. Rowing his skiff along the waters of the South Sound, he happened on Stretch Island. He chose as his site a gently sloping hillside close to the water, with a southeasterly exposure ideal for fruit cultivation. He planted apples and grapes.

Grapes were certainly a source of needed cash for Lambert Evans. He was known to take his skiff into Olympia to sell his produce. It is even thought that he made and sold a little wine. With his long, wavy white hair and beard, he was considered a local character, a survivalist who had carved a home out of the forested land with Natives as his primary companions.

Eckert's business in Auburn, New York, had been declining. He

Lambert Evans in Evans's vineyard on Stretch Island. —*Photo courtesy of the Somers' family.*

came out west to explore new opportunities, arriving on Evans's Island (then the name for Stretch Island) in 1889. What he saw was an island with a nearly pristine landscape, set in the middle of a water highway that connected two growing metropolises—Olympia and Tacoma—twenty and twenty-five miles south by water, respectively, with Seattle to the north, nearly fifty miles by boat. Within a year Eckert brought his wife and children west. The family immediately set out to clear the heavy timber on 40 acres purchased from Lambert Evans. They built their home on the north end of the property, right at the edge of the cliff looking north to North Bay in Case Inlet.

To Eckert, the future was bright and the area ripe for development. In 1883, the Northern Pacific had completed its transcontinental route, with Tacoma as its western terminus. Additionally, the Great Northern was headed toward completion in Seattle, in 1893.

Eckert's farm prospered. He raised primarily apples and grapes, but he was most excited about the grapes: "I'd rather take care of five acres of grapes than one acre of apples." Raising nursery stock and selling vines for a premium price was a very profitable sideline. Eckert became more and more enthused about grape growing, and a larger and larger portion of his land was given over to grape production and nursery work.

Eckert became a leading spokesman for grape growing in the Puget Sound region. His eloquence was rewarded when he was elected

Adam Eckert standing next to
Island Belle grapevine in the
Eckert vineyard. —*Photo courtesy
of Robert and Shirley Eacrett.*

president of the West Coast Growers. It was at their meeting in San Francisco that he may have planned to unveil the Island Belle.

Eckert wrote a small booklet, "Grape Growing in the Pacific Northwest: From Practical Experience of Twenty Years in the State of Washington," in 1910. It is a complete treatise on everything needed to grow and market grapes. In the opening remarks, he writes, "That the grape can be successfully grown, not only in the home garden, but for commercial purposes in the Sound country and Pacific Northwest, that many portions of this country are well adapted to grape culture, and that it is a profitable branch of horticulture, is now settled beyond any controversy."

Having lived in the middle of the New York grape-growing district, Eckert would have known the value of promoting a grape variety especially adapted to the Puget Sound country. We will never know whether he arrived at the Island Belle grape on his own or whether he happened to select a particularly likely-looking cutting of the Campbell

Early. Is it possible that he crossed the Hartford Prolific and the Concord? Walt says it is very unlikely. It would have been difficult to cross-pollinate them because they do not bloom at the same time; Concord is a late bloomer and Hartford Prolific is an early bloomer.

In his book, Eckert mentions both Campbell Early and Island Belle. In the document Eckert clearly distinguishes the grapes as different varieties, but in a confusing way. Surprisingly, he mentions Island Belle only once, saying that the Island Belle is grown on the same system as the Campbell Early. Eckert does describe the Campbell Early:

> Campbell—Black. Of recent origin, has been extensively advertised as the one grape to grow. In the hands of those who have a good knowledge of grape culture or those who will give it close attention it will prove a success. With the average grower, a failure and disappointment. The vine is fairly vigorous, weak in foliage, often shedding most of its leaves before the fruit is fully matured. Bunch large, shouldered if properly pruned, compact; quality good; better than Concord. Colors as early as Moore's Early, but is not sweet or marketable, but a few days before Concord. It does not crack or shell; will hang on the vine retaining all its good qualities till very late. The vine is very difficult to handle or renew. After a few years in the vineyard making all its growth from the last few buds. Owing to its weak foliage the new growth near the stock will not mature. From the fact of its early coloring and lateness in becoming sweet and the difficulty of handling the vine, we do not recommend it to the vineyardist unless he will give it the necessary attention.

Why doesn't he mention Island Belle as a variety of grape to grow? Walt has pointed out that in order for Eckert to have used the Island Belle name, even in passing, he would have had to have seen and evaluated the fruit, which indicates that it would have been planted earlier than 1910, at least six to eight years earlier. On the other hand, he seems to give it such little attention in his book. He says that Campbell Early is of recent origin; what might that mean in regard to Island Belle? It does suggest that Campbell Early was already established in his vineyard and, even though he found it finicky, it is still one of his preferred grapes; its major drawback is that it is difficult to manage.

Adam Eckert also wrote an article in *The Mason County Journal* in August 1905 detailing his experiments with numerous varieties of grapes, but fails to mention Island Belle. He writes: "Under the name of the Eckert Fruit Co., Mr Eckert and his two sons have increased their plantings each year; they now have about six acres or more of grapes, but not all in bearing. They also have the largest Grape Nursery in the Pacific Northwest, and each year every new and many of the older varieties are planted for trial purposes, as they are constantly seeking after the very best varieties."

In 1918 Adam Eckert founded the Island Belle Grape Growers' Union, noting that 25,000 baskets (about 62 tons) of grapes sold in nearby markets and an equal amount was used for juice "into what is fast becoming our national beverage."

Eckert did manage to convince grape growers that he had developed something special; Island Belle became the most planted grape in the state. Most of the plantings were in Mason County, although the grape was planted throughout the Puget Sound country. Originally it was used primarily as a table grape and later as a juice grape. With the dawning of national prohibition (in 1919), and beginning with severe state restrictions in 1914, it became widely used as a wine grape by home winemakers.

—ST. CHARLES WINERY, APRIL 1991—

I have driven to Stretch Island numerous times in the last few years. Although it is an easy drive from Tacoma, Olympia, Shelton, and Bremerton, it somehow remains isolated. On one of my visits, I arranged to meet with Bill Somers. He agreed to show me the old St. Charles Winery, which his family operated up until about 1965. The state's first bonded winery, it emerged at the end of Prohibition, in 1933, and Bill's father, Charles Somers, was able to begin production and sell wine prior to the official national Repeal, by taking advantage of a very confusing time between state's rights and the changing national laws.

The winery and property were basically intact. Bill Somers and his family operate the winery as a museum open to the public. The square, plain white winery building had a stunning setting, with a view south to a picturesque cove about midway on the western edge of the island. A pretty little blue house, with curtains billowing in the open wood-framed windows, sat just below the winery near the water's edge.

Between the home and the winery was a vineyard that sloped down from the north and west. Sheep grazed in a nearby pasture.

Bill Somers spoke quietly. His jovial face, round and bright, was accented by penetrating blue eyes. He walked me over to the vineyard, where a series of old grapevines lay on or near the ground, with shoots reaching horizontally between the trunks. Each trunk was about ten inches thick. They looked like old men sunning themselves in the morning sun, stooped low to the ground for additional warmth.

Bill told me that these were the original grapes planted by Lambert Evans when he arrived in 1872. They have since been top-grafted with the Island Belle grape. Their production is limited because of the age of the vines, but also because the deer like to eat the new shoots that appear in the spring.

Bill was proud of the history behind his family's farm and winery, and had his own theory about how the Island Belle grew out of this bucolic island garden. He thought that Lambert Evans might have sent for cuttings from his family in Florida. A favorite variety of that time in the South was the Scuppernong grape, a *Vitis rotundifolia*. Bill suggested that this grape might have been crossed with the Concord. Later, it may have been crossed with the Hartford Prolific. Evans was enthralled by grapes, and Bill Somers believed that he was an accomplished nurseryman.

I later related this to Walt; Dr. Clore is critical of Somers's story. He says that the Scuppernong is a pistillate variety that produces no viable pollen. The Concord is a bunch grape and has thirty-eight chromosomes, and the Scuppernong is a cluster grape that has forty chromosomes, making a cross impossible at that time. Additionally, Walt believes the Hartford Prolific would have been a very poor choice for a cross.

It is also doubtful Evans would have been able to receive cuttings from Florida, especially immediately following the Civil War. More likely he brought cuttings with him from California. Also, by 1872 numerous nurseries were already established west of the Cascades, from Luelling and Sons in Milwaukie, Oregon, to the Washington Nursery in Steilacoom. There was even a nursery at Arcadia, on Pickering Passage, along the route that Evans would have rowed on the inside passage of Harstene Island to the south.

Archival nursery catalogues show that locally the grapes of choice were Worden, Concord, Hartford Prolific, Catawba, Isabella, Diana, Clinton, Allen's Hybrid, and Mission. The list is strong on *labrusca* parentage and newly developed hybrid grapes. Concord, developed twenty years earlier in Massachusetts and widely planted in the Great Lakes area and in New York state, was probably the most planted variety in the nation at the time. The Catawba was particularly popular in Ohio and Missouri. Locally, Seth Llewellyn of Luelling and Sons preferred Worden, Catawba, Hartford Prolific, and Isabella. By the 1880s the northeastern states were experiencing a genuine grape mania. Out of this unbridled activity, "new" varieties emerged whose promoters unself-consciously proclaimed them the "latest and best," only to be replaced by other, better varieties. Any of these might have appealed to Evans and, later, Eckert.

What is the big deal? Does anyone care if the Campbell Early and the Island Belle are the same? The Bureau of Alcohol, Tobacco and Firearms (BATF) seems to. In 1994 it sent out a memo to the wine industry with a list of grape variety names it would no longer recognize, starting in 1995. One of them was the Island Belle. Wines made from those grapes would have had to use the Campbell Early name.

—HOODSPORT WINERY, OCTOBER 1992—

Since 1981, Hoodsport Winery, a small family winery located in Hoodsport, has produced an Island Belle wine from grapes harvested on Stretch Island. Disgruntled Island Belle growers suggest that the BATF edict was probably initiated by other wineries in the industry, wineries that felt Island Belle was being passed off as a *vinifera* variety rather than an American hybrid. Walt assures me, however, that the BATF began this kind of review when he retired in 1976: "(The BATF) would have relied on dependable published data, not hearsay." If Hoodsport wished to continue using the name, it would have had to classify its Island Belle wine as a proprietary wine instead of a varietal wine.

That has changed. In a ruling that went into effect in October 1995, the BATF allowed the use of the Island Belle name, and recognized it as a synonym for Campbell Early.

Recently I tasted a '92 vintage of the Hoodsport Island Belle. It was remarkably fruity and intense; in style and taste it was somewhere between the Gamay of Beaujolais, France, the Barbera of Piedmont, Italy, and the Zinfandel of California. The color was Beaujolais-like, a bright red-blue. It had a grapy, ripe-fruity nose with little of the foxiness often associated with American grapes, and Campbell Early. I felt a personal interest in this particular wine because I had taken my son, Andrew, and his friend, Jonathan, to Stretch Island in 1992 to help with the grape harvest.

We got a late start on the morning we went to Stretch Island to help pick grapes. Perhaps it was the nasty grayness of the day, with the accompanying heavy mist and blustery wind, that slowed us down. At the vineyard, the dismal weather gave way to a beautiful autumn day. The grapevines were spectacular; their fall foliage of yellow and orange exposed large clusters of blue-black grapes. Over the tops of the vines we could see people in the vineyards picking grapes. Beyond them several historic-looking homes sat on a bluff overlooking the dark blue waters of Puget Sound to the north. (I learned later that one was the original home built by Adam Eckert.) The air was unbelievably fresh, and accented by the smell of grapes. The weight of the fall day and the warmth of the October sun, the setting and the pace, reminded me of a tiny wine village in France.

We had been invited to Stretch Island by Mary and Harry Branch, who owned and managed this vineyard and were stockholders in the Hoodsport Winery. Mr. Branch—tall, slender, wiry, and probably in his seventies—got us our shears and showed the boys and me how to cut off the clusters. The clusters were about six to eight inches long, and very tight. The dark blue grapes were about an inch in diameter, larger than most *vinifera* grapes. Cordon-trained, they hung from chest-high wires and were easy to snip with the shears because much of the foliage had dropped off, exposing the thick clusters.

The low sun was hot on our faces as we plunked the grapes into plastic buckets. It seemed so simple—and the buckets filled so quickly. I tasted the grapes quite often. They were delicious, grapy like Concord grapes but with a spiciness a bit like cardamom. I noticed that when I pinched an individual grape between my thumb and forefinger, the skin slipped off easily from the pulp. This is a *labrusca* characteristic.

While picking, I talked briefly with Peggy and Dick Patterson, majority owners of and managers of the Hoodsport Winery. The winery's location caters to tourists, but the winery long ago reached out to markets in the nearby cities of the Northwest. A watercolor rendition of Puget Sound and its landscape—a mixture of hills, islands, sky, and water, not unlike the scene on the horizon above the vines where I was standing—adorns their label.

Peggy talked about how they got started in the wine business. They began the winery with a friend, Wayne Hazel, who was about to get laid off at Boeing in the recession of the 1970s. Both Dick and Peggy were teachers in Tacoma, having moved to Washington from Montana. The wine industry sounded romantic to them, and it was something they could do with their family. Hoodsport began as a gift shop and slowly progressed into a full-time winery. The new label, and two energetic daughters who marketed their wines, helped establish the winery.

Originally Hoodsport was known for its distinctive fruit wines, especially a delicious raspberry wine that was bursting with flavor. Slowly the table wines came along, first a Johannisberg Riesling and a spicy Gewurztraminer, followed by a Chardonnay and a Merlot. Along the way they also added a rhubarb wine that is today one of the line's top sellers. One of their specialties is the Island Belle wine, first made by them in 1981, from grapes harvested on Stretch Island. No other commercial winery uses this grape. The Pattersons rely on a couple of sources for the grape. Besides the Branch Vineyard, they get grapes from Misty Isle Vineyards, also on Stretch Island, and others.

Peggy finished her story just as we were picking the last rows of grapes. It was almost two o'clock in the afternoon. We had picked through lunch, and now we were hungry.

Harry Branch called out that lunch was ready.

We walked through the 4-acre vineyard to the house, where we found potato salad, cabbage salad, green beans, bread, and a roast turkey that had been barbecued.

I was more interested in tasting the Island Belle wine. I had read about the grape, about its importance to the local economy during the early 1900s. At least four wineries had once based their production on this hearty grape. Even as late as the 1950s, nearly 250 acres of the 300 acres of land on Stretch Island were planted primarily to this grape.

Harry Branch came around with two bottles of Hoodsport wine, one a Johannisberg Riesling, the other the Island Belle. The Island Belle was not vintage dated. Dick Patterson explained that it was a blend of years. Sometimes they don't get enough grapes to make enough wine to vintage date it, or the weather makes a less than desirable vintage wine, so they blend it. Branch poured me a glass. It was round and smooth; the nose was fruity and musky. It reminded me of an older Beaujolais. It was a perfect accompaniment to the roast turkey. As we sat on the lawn overlooking the north bay, talking about wine and grapes, I reflected on the perfect afternoon. There I was, sitting in the sunny present, with shadows of the past in my glass, in the vineyard, in the conversation, and in the sweeping view of the Sound.

Chapter Nine

THE GOOD LIFE AND WINE

In 1889 Seattle began the slow process of rebuilding after the great fire that left much of the modern Pioneer Square district in shambles. One of the businesses that located there was a winery owned by Louis Jaffe and his family. Jaffe also owned vineyards and a winery in the Dry Creek region of Sonoma County in northern coastal California. Jaffe founded the winery there in 1888 and was the first kosher winemaker in the Dry Creek area. Records, in *The Vineyards in Sonoma County,* published in 1893, and in the *Directory of the Grape Growers, Wine Makers and Distillers of California,* published in 1891, indicate that he owned 15 acres of vineyards and was growing Zinfandel and Mission grapes. Records are conflicting; although the winery's capacity in 1893 was 20,000 gallons, other records from the same year, relayed to me by a researcher in Sonoma, show that the winery shipped 30,000 gallons of Johannisberg Riesling to New York City. The winery was called the Wine Creek Winery, named after a tributary stream of Dry Creek. At some point, likely in 1889, Jaffe and his family moved to Seattle, and they operated a winery, using the Wine Creek Winery name, in Pioneer Square for nearly twenty-five years, from 1889 until 1914, in conjunction with their wholesale liquor and wine business. It is not clear if the winery in Seattle was producing wine or only wholesaling the wine produced in Sonoma.

Louis Jaffe died in 1904 or 1905, but the winery continued in operation until at least 1910, with Mrs. Johanna Jaffe, his wife, as president. The Jaffes' sons remained active in the wine business in Seattle, and I suspect in California too, until Prohibition forced them out.

Listings of saloons and liquor wholesalers in early Seattle directories provide an insight into the culture of alcoholic beverages. Wine gained momentum in the Seattle area during the mid-1890s and kicked into high gear around 1905. Some wholesalers featured specific wineries; others carried a broader selection. A few examples: in 1893 and 1894, Louis Chopard listed Almaden Vineyard and California table wines as a specialty; in 1903, The California Wine Company (formerly the Ballard Wine House) purveyed wines from the Golden State; in 1910, Louis Roederer Champagne maintained an office in Seattle; and in 1914, the Santa Rosa Wine Company showed up.

By the turn of the century, Seattle consumers had access to a number of high-quality California wines. And Seattle was a very important market for wine, especially after 1893, the year James J. Hill's Great Northern Railway finally reached Seattle. That meant two great transcontinental railways connected the Seattle area with the Midwest and the East Coast.

With the discovery of gold in the Canadian Klondike in 1897, Seattle became the new gold crossroads, causing a flurry of economic activity unmatched in the city's history. It launched the city on a path of great wealth that was sustained throughout most of the early 1900s.

Wine was part of this new wealth, in part because this was a new generation but also because the first rumblings of Prohibition had been heard. Wine was considered a temperate alternative to whiskey; it could be drunk at home with a meal, to toast the good life. There is very little to suggest that Washington grapes were used, except in isolated circumstances, to satisfy this demand that was easily met by the overproduction of California wine.

It is likely, however, that Robert Schleicher of Schleicher Vineyards in Lewiston, Idaho, was shipping some of his wine to Seattle or Portland. It is also very likely that passengers on the Great Northern and the Northern Pacific were offered wine from one of the wineries of Clarkston or Lewiston as a way of promoting the area's offerings.

It was an extraordinary time for the Pacific Northwest. Waiting around the corner were the discovery of the automobile and the airplane. Humankind, and American ingenuity, could do almost anything. This spirit was most evident in eastern Washington. The great Columbia Basin awaited large-scale irrigation to transform the dry desert that claimed most of the state from Yakima east to Clarkston, and from Spokane south to Maryhill. It was a vast area of boundless potential.

Irrigation had been practiced extensively along streams and rivers throughout eastern Washington prior to 1900. Kamiakin, the great leader of the Yakama Nation, was an early irrigator at his summer retreat near Tampico. The Schanno family followed his example, as did others in the vicinity of the Yakima River. Near East Wenatchee, John Galler relied extensively on irrigation to water his vineyards.

One large-scale irrigation project took place between 1892 and 1893 in the Kennewick area, where farmers planted *vinifera* grapes, primarily as table varieties. Due to a break in the irrigation ditch and the economic panic of 1893, the project was abandoned and most of the farms were deserted.

Another major irrigation development was started at Moxee City by the Moxee Company. The Moxee Company encompassed 6,400 acres in the area just east of Yakima. It was owned by Gardiner Hubbard, founder of the National Geographic Society, and his son-in-law, Alexander Graham Bell. Nancy Davidson-Short, one of the founders of the Enological Society of the Pacific Northwest, told me that her grandfather, Harry Scudder, was brought out from Boston to manage the Moxee Company. Throughout the 1880s, besides tobacco, cotton, and peanuts, the company also planted Johannisberg Riesling and Mission grapes with cuttings brought from California. The financial panic of 1893 put an end to the Moxee Company. However, much of the acreage was sold to French Canadians from the Great Lakes region who eventually turned Moxee into the hop capital of the world, relying on more and more sophisticated irrigation, and a hybrid Moxee Company continued in business until at least 1925.

It took the capital and the organization of the great Northern Pacific Railroad to foster larger irrigation projects. The Northern Pacific, headed by financier Henry Villard, took the lead in opening up new irrigation systems throughout the Pacific Northwest. The railroad owned the odd-numbered sections for twenty miles on both sides of the railroad track right-of-way, granted to it by the U. S. government in exchange for building the railroad across the United States. The company had a rare opportunity: it could sell the land and then control access to markets. Controlling irrigation was the key to making the land productive. Villard and the Northern Pacific were instrumental in selling these projects to people through colorful and extravagant promotions. Villard, a German immigrant, heavily advertised these projects in Europe, and especially in Germany.

In 1903, the Northwest Improvement Company, a subsidiary of the

Vineyard workers in the Dam vineyard at Nob Hill, Yakima.
—Photo by Asahel Curtis, courtesy of Washington State Historical Society.

Northern Pacific Railroad, developed one of the first successful projects, in Kennewick. Included in the plantings were a number of grape varieties, both *labrusca* and *vinifera,* aimed at the table market. By 1909, Frank Cole had planted 2 Italian wine varieties and 1 German wine variety at Finley, southwest of Kennewick. So extensive were the planting of grapes in the Tri-Cities region that Kennewick, in September 1910, held its first annual Grape Festival. One of the esteemed lecturers was Robert Schleicher of Lewiston, Idaho. Grape varieties judged in the European category included Tokay, Muscat, Malaga, Thompson Seedless, Black Hamburg, Rose of Peru, Black Prince, Emperor, Muscat of Alexandria, Muscatel, Sweetwater, Romania, Chasselas-Victoria, Fararar, and Cornichon. American varieties included Concord, Niagara, Moore's Early, Campbell Early, Delaware, and Catawba.

Out of this captivation with grapes grew one of the most successful early juice companies: the Church Grape Juice Company of Kennewick, first known as the Twin City Ice and Cold Storage Company, pressed its first grapes in 1913. In 1918, it processed nearly 40,000 gallons of grape juice (Concord and Worden only) and 135,000 gallons of cider that the company intended to market up and down the Pacific Coast. It was the beginning of the large commercial processing plants in eastern Washington, which set in motion larger grape plantings.

Concord was first planted in 1904 near Outlook by Ellsworth Dopps, and it quickly became the most popular grape in the semi-arid areas of eastern Washington, especially for many of the new arrivals, who brought with them the East Coast prejudice against *vinifera.*

There was no denying that Concord adapted beautifully to the conditions in eastern Washington. The same conditions that favor *vinifera* also concentrate Concord's flavors and produce good sugars and acids in the grapes. But it was the ability to continually boost the production levels, through better farming practices, that excited the early growers. And with infrequent winter damage, Washingon state was on its way to becoming the Concord capital of the nation, despite ongoing efforts by others in the state to establish *vinifera* grapes.

The reorganization of the Yakima Land and Canal Company into the Northern Pacific Yakima and Kittitas Irrigation Company became a major step in the development of the Yakima and Columbia Valleys. The combination of irrigation and railroads sparked one of the great migrations into Washington state. Between 1880 and 1890, the population of the state grew by 380 percent. The migration was further fueled by the Klondike phenomenon in 1897. Washington state was the place to be. If you couldn't find gold in the hills of the north country, you could make gold selling hope to fools. Likewise, if you couldn't realize money as a farmer, you could sell the promise of wealth. It was an era rich in schemes.

It represented the best and the worst of America's entrepreneurial spirit, but it was different from past efforts at development in Washington state. For the first time, many of these developers were American-born, not immigrants. These new settlers were bringing their farming knowledge from the Midwest and the East Coast. More important, many of the organizers of these land and irrigation projects were from privileged families or centers of culture, such as Minneapolis and St. Paul or Chicago. They brought with them a whole new set of values, rooted in America's emerging middle class.

One of these values was a preference for wine as a temperate beverage. America was becoming less tolerant of alcohol and its abuse. The railroad companies helped establish many of the towns along their rights-of-way and and then shipped in beer, wine, and spiritous liquors from all over the world. Saloons sprang up overnight. Often, families were torn apart by the free-wheeling gambling and drinking that took place in saloons.

Norman Clark makes a strong case in his book *The Dry Years* that Prohibition set out to destroy the saloon, not the drink. Saloons were seen as the source of all kinds of problems. Originally they served as a meeting house, a place to share information, find a job, reinforce an ethnic community, or seek fellowship. By the turn of the century, their role in society had degenerated. The wrath of prohibitionists was aimed primarily at the liquor and beer companies and their practice of owning drinking establishments as well as producing, distributing, and selling their brand.

—E. F. BLAINE'S STONE HOUSE WINERY—

At Walnut Street and Apple Way in the Orchard Tract district of Grandview is an old brick water tower, about twelve feet tall. It stands across from E. F. Blaine's old farm on Apple Way. From atop this tower Asahel Curtis, Blaine's neighbor, took a number of photographs of the surrounding farms being developed between 1905 and 1910.

Curtis was one of the most prolific photographers of his day. His work, commissioned by railroad and irrigation companies, concentrated on agricultural and industrial development throughout the Pacific Northwest, and one of his favorite subjects was the agricultural bounty of the Yakima Valley. Curtis's photographs played a major role in selling the companies' developments; many of the brochures of the day carry his stunning pictures. His photographic trail recorded numerous efforts to grow grapes in the Yakima Valley.

One of his favorite farms to photograph was owned by his colleague, Elbert F. Blaine, a prominent and successful attorney from Seattle. Blaine arrived in Grandview in 1902 as the manager for the Washington Irrigation Company. He had organized the company on behalf of the Denny estate. When the Washington Irrigation Company acquired the Sunnyside Irrigation Canal at a receiver's sale, it suddenly owned in excess of 60,000 acres. In 1905 Blaine successfully sold the company's holdings to the federal government, under the Reclamation Act, netting the Washington Irrigation Company about $250,000.

Blaine used some of this money to develop the Orchard Tract area. He personally bought a section of 160 acres. Beginning in 1905, he began to advertise and promote the sale of parcels of land in this area. He also began to cultivate the area. Before-and-after pictures of its development are astonishing.

I remember a day when Walt and I visited the Blaine farm. We stopped earlier at the Grandview Museum to see if there might be some pictures of the Orchard Tract. We went through various scrapbooks and were about to leave when Walt found a picture of a booth at a fair in Seattle. The booth displayed promotional information about the Orchard Tract area, including a large topographical map on a table and a couple of pictures on the wall behind some salesmen.

As I looked up from the picture in the scrapbook, I noticed for the first time two enormous pictures on the wall, each about five feet long by three feet high. They were the same pictures that were behind the table in the picture we were looking at, so large we had almost missed them. They were sequential pictures of Blaine's farm, one taken in 1905 and the other taken about three years later. The former showed a barren landscape; the latter depicted a sprouting farm of orchards and vineyards. No doubt the picture had been taken from the water tower across the street, probably by Asahel Curtis.

Walt and I went on to visit Blaine's farm, where we toured an underground winery Blaine had built between 1907 and 1910. The winery was quite substantial, and of solid concrete. Submerged, it was divided into three areas accessible by a steep concrete ramp: one twelve-by-fifteen-foot area was for receiving grapes and crushing; another, thirty feet by thirty feet, was used for fermentation; and a larger room, thirty feet by fifty feet, was used for wine storage. The dimensions suggested a winery capable of producing about 2,500 gallons of wine.

Blaine's winemaker was Paul Charvet, a Canadian who had moved to the Yakima Valley from Montreal. Charvet also maintained a winery at his home nearby, on what is now called Charvet Road. Both wineries shipped wine in barrels up to Roslyn, a tiny mining town on the east side of Snoqualmie Pass.

Blaine produced a table wine made from Concord, Zinfandel, and White Diamond grapes, and a sparkling wine made from White Diamond grapes. (There are no records of how much wine was actually sold.) He also grew Campbell Early, primarily for the table, and Black Prince, which would have gone into table wine. Charvet's stepson, Leo Dion, who lives nearby, has in his possession a sparkling wine bottle from the Blaine winery. He can still recall his stepfather's wine. It was made in a light, effervescent style. Usually the alcohol content was low because the wine was bottled prior to the fermentation finishing. According to Dion, a lot of Italians living in the area also made wine, particularly the Brignolio family on Walnut Lane, just east of Blaine's estate.

Blaine's winery was named the Stone House Winery, after the distinctive house he built beside the winery. The house, which still stands, was patterned after houses Blaine had seen in Normandy, France.

Yakima Chamber of Commerce visiting E. F. Blaine's vineyard in Grandview's Orchard Tract area about 1912. —*Photo by Asahel Curtis, courtesy of Washington State Historical Society.*

Beside the house were smaller, matching buildings that were the servant quarters and the barn. He abandoned the winery shortly after 1910, possibly because of the threat of Prohibition.

Blaine then built a large home north of Grandview, on Hahn Hill, and named it LaPanorama for the exceptional view it commanded of the Yakima Valley. Dr. Clore recalls attending a party at LaPanorama thrown by Blaine in 1942. He was invited as a guest of the superintendent of the research station. Blaine was celebrating his eighty-fifth birthday; Dr. Clore was about thirty-one years old. By that time, Blaine had become quite an important person of substantial wealth, and was known as the "father of irrigation" for the lower valley.

E. F. Blaine's eighty-fifth birthday party, in 1942, in some ways symbolizes the passing of the torch in Washington's wine industry. The year before, Dr. Clore began experimenting with wine grapes at the insistence of William B. Bridgman, an attorney and farmer in Sunnyside. Bridgman, like Blaine, was a local celebrity and early pioneer. Both had played important roles in the development of irrigation in the valley. Bridgman, as manager of the Sunnyside Irrigation Canal, would have negotiated the receiver's sale to Blaine's Washington Irrigation Company. I am sure he would have been at Blaine's party.

I can envision the elaborate gathering on the lawns of Blaine's

LaPanorama, when the hands of history brushed one another, unbeknownst to the participants. I see a young scientist, Walt Clore, his head protected from the sun with a Stetson. Across the way is the elderly E. F. Blaine, perhaps talking to his old acquaintance William Bridgman, a man in his prime at sixty-four.

Bridgman and Blaine, both grape growers and promoters, could look back on lives of accomplishment with satisfaction. Perhaps they expressed amazement as they viewed the Yakima Valley, astonished at the progress they helped initiate forty years earlier. For when they first arrived, the Yakima Valley had appeared to be a sand bowl, a vast open canvas of sage and barren hills. Both Blaine and Bridgman had recognized the potential for agriculture, both had recognized the potential for gain, and both had brought a vision of grape growing to the Yakima Valley. But it was William Bridgman who had the greatest impact on Washington's wine industry.

At seventeen, in 1895, Bridgman left his home in the Niagara Peninsula area of Ontario, Canada, to enter Hamline University, in St. Paul, Minnesota, where his uncle was president. He graduated with degrees in the arts and sciences and in law. To pay for his education, in addition to teaching science courses he personally tutored Walter Hill, son of James J. Hill.

As part of his son's education, James J. Hill sent Walter and Bridgman on a trip to the Pacific Northwest in 1899 on his railway, the Great Northern. Bridgman was twenty years old. Hill arranged for visits in Portland, Seattle, and Victoria. Bridgman was very impressed when the train entered the Wenatchee Valley. He saw magnificent fruit, especially peaches, nearing ripeness in late July. His family grew grapes in the Niagara Peninsula, mostly Concord, and he would have quickly grasped the potential for grape growing in the valleys of eastern Washington. If grapes could be successfully grown in Canada, surely they could prosper in a more southerly locale. He saw firsthand the wonders of irrigation when passing through Wenatchee. Perhaps he saw Philip Miller's farm and vineyard in Wenatchee or that of Dutch John Galler in East Wenatchee. He might even have tasted their wine, for both Galler and Miller made considerable quantities of wine by the turn of the century. On his way west, he might have also seen Robert Schleicher's vineyards gracing the hills of the Clearwater River at Lewiston, Idaho.

Bridgman arrived in Sunnyside in 1902 carrying with him a vision articulated by James J. Hill: that the world of trade and commerce was

William B. Bridgman
—Photo courtesy of Robert Sincock family.

at the doorstep of the great valleys of Washington. Bridgman came to the Yakima Valley to nurture his farming instincts.

Sunnyside was a struggling community caught in the grip of its roots. It had been founded in the late 1890s by a group of Midwest religious zealots, members of the Progressive Brethren Church, who were determined to keep the sins of the world at a distance. Organized as The Christian Cooperative Colony, the town had no economic base other than selling land to newcomers. It had not yet been successful at getting products to market. The Sunnyside Irrigation Canal had been in operation nearly ten years but was badly organized and run.

Bridgman's arrival in the "holy city" was a blessing. As a young attorney, he specialized in irrigation law and helped draw up the state's first irrigation laws. Through Bridgman's efforts, orderly guidelines were devised to share and develop water resources. His law practice thrived, allowing him to invest in farmland. He wisely selected choice parcels of land on two nearby uplifts, Harrison Hill and the southeast slopes of Snipes Mountain. He was well aware of the advantage of site selection for air drainage. Farming was in his blood; he had taken a circuitous route to come back to it.

Twice elected mayor of Sunnyside, he set about promoting his young community. He joined forces with the business and farming interests throughout the valley to make improvements and promote the agricultural bounty of the irrigated farmlands.

Sunnyside historian Roscoe Sheller, in *Courage and Water,* relates a story about a huge party thrown atop Harrison Hill, on February 2, 1906, to celebrate the arrival of the railroad in Sunnyside. Over 3,000 people attended, many from other parts of the state. Harrison Hill provided the guests with a sweeping view of the valley's rich promise.

Sheller writes, "The steer had been roasting all of the previous night, under the supervision of Chef Hawn, and dishes of delicious food of all kinds prepared by local housewives appeared in unbelievable quantities to supplement the beef. It was truly a feast."

Mayor Bridgman introduced numerous speakers to extol the virtues of country living at its best and to describe the coming riches with the advent of the train, their tie to the outside world and to markets unimaginable. Sheller continues:

No wonder the attendance at the barbecue was hundreds greater than the population of the entire area at the time.

A special train started from North Yakima was bringing a big delegation, and a welcoming delegation, including a band, was in waiting for the train's arrival, at the depot. As it crossed the Swan Road a mile west of town, its screeching whistle announced its eagerly anticipated arrival. The plainly nervous welcoming committee pulled down its vest and straightened its tie, but something was happening; the train was slowing down. Its whistle changed from a scream to a wail as both stopped half a mile from the station.

The train, larger than any that had yet tested the new roadbed, had pressed the ballast, ties, and rails into the mud so deep that it could no longer move. The passengers were taken from the train, and driven in buggies to Harrison Hill, where the barbecue proceeded.

Progress mired in mud. The train incident quickly pointed out one of the dangers of irrigation: drainage. Bridgman went to work to solve drainage problems and wrote the first drainage laws on record in the Yakima Valley. He even advocated stocking the canals with fish, introducing an ecological awareness to the use of irrigation.

In 1914, when Bridgman planted his first grapes at Harrison Hill, the first rumblings of Prohibition could be heard in Washington state. Bridgman's first grapes were mostly meant for the table market. They included Ribier, Flame Tokay, and Black Prince.

In 1917 Bridgman made another planting at Snipes Mountain, across from Harrison Hill. This time he planted wine grapes; he had noted a developing demand for wine grapes, which were more profitable than the table market. That first planting was supposed to be of 1 variety, but it turned out to have about 8 different varieties. Bridgman, in *Notes on Life of W. B. Bridgman, and on the Upland Winery*, describes the mix as "Zinfandel, Mataro, Carignane, and Muscat grapes." Dr. Clore thinks that Semillon, Sultanina Rosea, Sauvignon Blanc, and Black Malvoisie were planted as well. Also included might have been the Thompson Seedless, the Csaba, and the Muscat of Alexandria.

It was a curious time to be planting wine grapes, especially in the "holy city" of Sunnyside. By 1916 Washington state had adopted "totally dry" prohibition laws, more severe than the proposed national laws then gathering steam in Washington, D.C. The result, which Bridgman benefited from, was a boomlet demand for wine grapes. His foresight was rewarded by an increased sale of wine grapes, at prices far greater than his neighbors received for table varieties. (Like the Reverend W. T. Jordan at Maryhill and E. F. Blaine in Grandview, Bridgman sold wine grapes to the various ethnic groups such as the Italians and the Croatians in Cle Elum and Roslyn.)

As Bridgman continued to expand his plantings, he furthered his own education in the varieties of grapes needed to produce quality wine. For information he turned to the vineyards in California and New York as well as the United States Department of Agriculture. Besides propagating his own nursery stock, Bridgman also imported cuttings from vineyards in California, New York, and Europe. Eventually he began to sell cuttings to friends and neighbors, and created a network of vineyards throughout the Yakima Valley and into the Columbia Basin. By 1934 Bridgman had more than 165 acres of wine grapes under contract with over seventy growers.

—SUNNYSIDE, OCTOBER 1991—

Sunnyside is the heart of the Yakima Valley, practically mid-valley between Yakima to the northwest and Richland to the east. Sunnyside sits on a slight plateau north of the valley floor as the valley begins to rise gently on the south slope of the Rattlesnake Hills.

Interstate 82 borders the town in its general east-west direction. As I approached Sunnyside from the east, traveling west and slightly north, I recognized the uplifts where Bridgman first planted his grapes. Harrison Hill, a small round hill to the north of the interstate, with perfect exposure to the south, was dotted with comfortable homes and small farms.

Directly across the interstate, on the south side of the highway, is a more pronounced uplift. It is Snipes Mountain. From the highway it looked like a round, tubular formation, rising about 400 feet above the valley floor, covered with uniform orchards and rows of vineyards. This was the home of Bridgman's first wine grapes. Continuing west, Snipes Mountain gradually tapers off, although it continues about eight miles to Granger on its western flank. In the summer the mountain is a combination of brown and deep green. It looks like a scantily clad goddess, lying on her side with her head cradled in her palm, her elbow resting on the valley floor, the green of the valley floor creeping up to cover her.

Walt and I drove to the top of Snipes Mountain, to a water tower that looks like a castle turret from below. The view was spectacular, as the grand expanse of the Sunnyside Valley leads up to the Horse Heaven Hills. At the top of Snipes Mountain, vineyards sloped to the south. The soil here is rocky, unlike the soil on the valley floor, which is much lighter and fluffier; one can sink two or three inches in the sand there. But here the soil is denser, with rocks on the surface. It reminded me of the soils in Burgundy, France.

We arranged to meet Al Newhouse in the vineyard. His family then owned the old Bridgman property. Al appeared to be about sixty years old. His tanned face was drawn with great creases; he wore his baseball cap slightly askew. As he showed us the vineyard, he picked clusters of grapes for us to taste. One cluster came from an unbelievably old gnarled grapevine. The grapes were Black Muscat, or Muscat Hamburg, grown chiefly as a table grape but also used to make wine, both sweet and dry.

The grapes tasted exotic, with lush fruity and floral overtones. Newhouse believed these grapevines were about eighty years old. That means they were among the first grapes Bridgman planted.

Then I remembered that Dr. Wade Wolfe, of Thurston-Wolfe Winery, produced a wine called Black Muscat. It was especially fruity, with rich but delicate flavors on the palate. The smells were reminiscent of roses and fresh grapes. I chuckled to myself: Dr. Wade Wolfe, a most modern man, well educated in viticulture and enology and with a good sense of the modern marketplace, was making a wine not unlike some of the earlier wines made in the state. It was a wonderful contrast of old and new.

Newhouse was proud of the grapes that came off of his Snipes Mountain site. Nearly all of his grapes go to Stimson Lane. He was particularly proud of the Chardonnay, and boasted, "This is the best site for Chardonnay in the state." Walt responded, "It is unquestionably an excellent site."

Someday, maybe the wine will be vineyard-designated: Upland Vineyards, or Snipes Mountain Vineyards, or even Newhouse Vineyards.

Chapter Ten

WINE AND VINE SURVIVE PROHIBITION

Prohibition began in Washington state in 1917 with the enactment of House Bill 4, a set of absolutely unequivocal dry laws, that eclipsed already severe laws drawn up the year before, by forbidding the manufacture, distribution, sale, and consumption of alcoholic beverages. It was the most severe anti-alcohol legislation passed by the state legislature. Prior to this time, communities were deeply divided over the issue of alcohol. Through the strength of the Anti-Saloon League, pressure was brought to bear to enact this tough legislation. One reason House Bill 4 passed was that many young men, the frequenters of the saloons, were away fighting in World War I. Meanwhile, they were losing a battle at home.

In 1919 the Washington State Legislature ratified the Eighteenth Amendment to the United States Constitution. Prohibition began nationwide when the amendment went into effect on January 16, 1920. National Prohibition superseded the state's own tough anti-alcohol laws. National Prohibition aimed its sights at the sale and distribution of alcohol. It didn't outlaw drinking. In fact, it accommodated the moderate use of beer and wine made at home. To this day, as a head of household, citizens are allowed to produce up to 200 gallons of wine annually without a permit.

The effect of this was to create an immediate nation of home winemakers and a boom in the demand for wine grapes. Many ethnic communities already made wine at home. In Washington state, these communities often relied on grapes from places like Jordan's 40-acre vineyard in Maryhill, Eckert's vineyard on Stretch Island, or

Bridgman's vineyard in Sunnyside. The home winemaker could get Zinfandel, Island Belle, Concord, Muscat of Alexandria, Black Monukka, Black Prince, Riesling, Sweetwater, Sultana, and Flame Tokay grapes grown in Washington. Local winemakers also bought California grapes by the trainload. Bridgman estimated that, during Prohibition, California was shipping annually between 5,000 to 10,000 tons of wine grapes, mostly Zinfandel, into the state. That represents nearly a sixth of Washington state's production of wine grapes today.

Bridgman responded to the demand by planting more wine grapes. In western Washington, more grapes from Stretch Island also were going to home winemakers. There was even a demand for Island Belle in California, because it delivered a rich flavor that could be blended with ordinary California table grapes to make a palatable table wine. However, California growers derailed these shipments by persuading the California legislature to pass a law requiring grapes to have a minimum Brix (a meaurement of sugar) above the capabilities of the Island Belle.

The wine industry was profoundly affected by Prohibition. First, it created a new market of wine drinkers, primarily middle-class Americans who began to use wine as an alternative to spirits and whiskey. Making wine at home was relatively easy. Basically, it required finding mature grapes with natural sugars of between 21° and 24° Brix. This allowed the home winemaker to make a good table wine without the addition of sugar. By avoiding large sugar purchases that might bring unwanted attention from authorities, home winemakers could even indulge in making extra wine to sell on the side.

Although grape growers prospered, the wine industry suffered. The earlier promise of a wine industry developing out of the irrigation projects of eastern Washington vanished overnight. Gone were the Stone House Winery in Grandview, Galler's winery in Wenatchee, the Wine Creek Winery in Seattle's Pioneer Square, and Shaefer's winery in Clarkston and other efforts along the Idaho border. The opportunity to build upon the continuous efforts of the past appeared lost.

Fortunately William Bridgman, in particular, kept the wine torch burning. He continued to plant new varieties each year. In 1920 he planted Alicante Bouschet, Black Malvoisie, Carignane, Csaba, Muscat of Alexandria, Sauvignon Blanc, Semillon, Sultanina Rosea, Thompson Seedless, Tokay, and Ribier. He found ready markets for his grapes.

Another grower, Frank Subucco of Walla Walla, planted wine grapes at about this time in a 36-acre vineyard in the Attalia area northwest of Walla Walla, along the Columbia River. Included in his vineyard were Black Prince, Muscat of Alexandria, Sweetwater, and Concord. (Nearly all of his grapes were used by a Seattle winery following Repeal.) The Italians of Walla Walla continued to grow wine grapes for their own home use.

Bert Pesciallo of Milton-Freewater, Oregon, a small town at the southern edges of Walla Walla, shared with me some of his memories of that time. I had been told to visit him by both Rick Small of Woodward Canyon Winery and Gary Figgins of Leonetti Cellars. They both said that Bert Pesciallo's winery was the first winery in the Walla Walla area after Prohibition was repealed.

When I met him, Pesciallo was a small, gentle man, quite elderly. As we sat outside in the shade, sipping iced tea, he told me about his family. Both his parents and his wife's parents came directly from Italy between 1900 and 1910. Joe Locati, in his book *The Horticulture Heritage of Walla Walla County, 1818-1977*, chronicled the development of the Italian community in this area. Frank Orselli, the vineyardist, winemaker, and baker, arrived in 1857, and was followed by a few more Italians in the 1870s to 1890s. By 1900 nearly twenty Italian families were living in the area and growing fruits and vegetables. Quite a community evolved (Locati estimates that about 200 Italian gardeners called Walla Walla home by 1940), and you can bet this group made wine, a lot of wine.

Not many had grapes, however. Bert recalled, "Most of the gardeners would come over to my dad's farm on Sunday and get their grapes. It was their only day free from work. They would bring their wagons over about October 1 or a little later. They liked my dad and he was able to bring people together, those that were from northern Italy with those from the south."

Bert said his father didn't make wine during Prohibition: "He sold all of his grapes to some big businesspeople in Walla Walla, people he had never sold to before. They asked him to make wine for them but he refused because he was afraid of getting caught."

Bert Pesciallo inherited his father's farm. It came with the 2 acres of grapes, including Black Prince, Chasselas-Rose, Tokay, Malaga, and Concord. From our chairs we looked out on the apple orchard. There were no longer any grapes on his property.

Later in my visit, we went into the house. Downstairs, Bert dug out a couple of bottles of his Blue Mountain Vineyards wine to show me. These wines came from his winery that he began in 1950. Both bottles were gallons; one was Black Prince, the other was Rose of Peru (another name for Black Prince). He said that every once in a while the family opened a bottle and the wine tasted wonderful, with a smooth, velvety texture.

Pesciallo's winery didn't last very long—a killer freeze in November 1955, called Black Frost, devastated the vineyards. Nearly all of his vines were killed back to their roots. Pesciallo said this happened about every three years; he never lost the vines, but it took them a year to grow back. The winery never recovered. He closed it down and found outside work.

Another winemaker who emerged at Repeal was Rudolf Werberger. Werberger emigrated to America from Germany and worked as a miner in Roslyn, where he married Marie, also from Germany, in 1904.

Shortly after their marriage, they left Washington state to go to St. Louis to work with Rudy's brother, who had a liquor and wine wholesale business. In 1918 Rudy and Marie returned to Washington. This time they bought property in the Puget Sound area, along Pickering Pass across from Harstene Island (located just south of Stretch Island), on land that sloped gently toward the water in a southeasterly direction. On their land they planted a thousand cuttings, mostly Island Belle and White Diamond (more likely, Chasselas), that they got from Adam Eckert on Stretch Island. Like Bridgman, the Werbergers recognized that the grape business was going to expand with the coming of Prohibition.

While Prohibition might have destroyed legitimate winemaking, it definitely accelerated the planting of wine grapes, as well as juice grapes, in Washington state, and increased the production of grape juice. As early as 1890, Charles E. Welch in New York state claimed to have created "a non-alcoholic Port wine" from Concord juice. It proved to be very popular and ushered in a major grape-growing effort in the Chautauqua district of New York. (It is not known how much grape juice went into the production of wine, but it is likely that it was a considerable amount.) Concord became the grape of the north because of its winter hardiness, its ability to adapt to a wide range of soils, its prolific growth, its volatile aromatics, and its consistent production. It soon became widely planted in Washinton state.

In California, as in Washington, wine grape plantings increased significantly during the first years of Prohibition. The Californians

Werberger Winery at Pickering Pass. —*Photo courtesy of Don Wilson.*

found that the Alicante Bouschet was their workhorse. Thick-skinned and sturdy, it was an excellent shipping grape and became the grape of California, which began to ship carloads of the grape to all the major cities of the country, including Seattle. From Seattle the grapes were routed to Roslyn, Spokane, Tacoma, Walla Walla, and other small towns on the railroad network. Home winemakers could get fresh Alicante Bouschet, Zinfandel, and Muscats shipped almost directly to their door.

Prohibition created a vast national market for California grapes, and set into place a distribution network that was easily transferable to wine once Prohibition ended in 1933.

Ironically, Prohibition created a thirst for wine and alcohol. Because alcoholic beverages were forbidden fruit, people who otherwise might not have been interested in wine were more inclined to taste it. Imagine some of the horrible homemade wines that people were making and drinking. Most of the wines were very dry because home winemakers didn't know how to leave residual sugar in the wines without the wines refermenting. Often they were also quite tannic, with a mouth-puckering quality expressed from the grape's skin as grape tannins. No doubt these wines were drunk before their time. These faults would contribute later to a taste for sweet wines. Besides, consumers of these wines were not using them for the table. Wine, like whiskey, was served as a social beverage. Few people argued the merits of a wine's flavor; it was more important that it loosened up the drinker, that the person could get inebriated.

The Eighteenth Amendment to the United States Constitution was annulled by the adoption of the Twenty-first Amendment to the constitution on December 5, 1933. Locally, the citizens of Washington state had already begun to loosen the laws restricting the use and sale of alcoholic beverages. Initially anarchy prevailed, as there were no laws governing how wines or any alcoholic beverages could be sold or used while the state and federal governments grappled with this issue. The people knew that they were fed up with Prohibition; they just did not yet know what they wanted to replace it with.

Part II

WILD, WOOLLY, AND WONDROUS WINES AFTER PROHIBITION

"The entire industry, however, is still in a sort of embryonic state and the most significant thing that one can say about it is that Washington, sooner or later, will produce fine wines and will rank among the best viticultural regions of the United States."

Frank Schoonmacker, *American Wines,* 1941

Chapter Eleven

ST. CHARLES WINERY

In December 1933, Charles Somers of Seattle was given the first bonded license in the Pacific Northwest to operate a winery, on Stretch Island. Naming it St. Charles Winery, he had to petition the Treasury Department in Washington, D.C., as there was no state agency in charge of wine or liquor permits. The license allowed him to produce wine for medicinal purposes, and his first wines were sold in drugstores.

Charles Somers wasn't a home winemaker, nor did he drink wine, but he saw a potentially lucrative business opportunity; there was a market for his grapes. The timing couldn't have been more perfect: the grapy smell of harvest dominated tiny Stretch Island. News that the nation was going to repeal the Eighteenth Amendment encouraged him to store his grape juice with the idea that maybe he could turn it into wine. It was a very depressed market for fruit of any kind; it was even worse for Island Belle grapes.

When Somers bought Lambert Evans's farm from Evans's widow in 1918, he was a real estate agent living in Seattle. He sold property on Stretch Island to Seattle people, many of them retirees or soon to be. Each time he sold a piece of property, he recommended that the buyers plant grapes as a cash cow, something to milk for future retirement funds.

He would point to the Grapeview Juice Company, begun by Adam Eckert and managed by Walter Eckert, and the Belle Island Grapejuice Company (which, coincidentally, purposely put Campbell Early on its label to irk the Eckerts). These companies were a ready market for the fresh grapes. He could even show prospective buyers that there was a

Bill and Howard Somers in their family vineyard on Stretch Island.
—*Photo by Heckman. Courtesy of Mason County Historical Society.*

market for their grapes in California. Charles Somers was a very good real estate agent, persuasive and tasteful. He helped transform this isolated island into a verdant vineyard. Of the 350 acres on the island, nearly 200 acres were planted in grapes, primarily Island Belle.

Then the Depression hit, after the stock market crash of October 1929. The price of grapes plummeted. Worse yet, there was no market for them. Charles Somers was crushed. He felt responsible to all of his former clients, most of whom had retired to the island and expected to make a little extra cash from their grapes.

With the hope of Repeal, Somers and his friends saw the opportunity they needed. They reasoned that a winery could use all of their excess grapes. They were hopeful enough that they were willing to wade through the bureaucratic minefield to get the first license.

It was a remarkable time for the wine industry: the nation's and the state's alcoholic beverage laws were turned upside down, and suddenly there was a monstrous market of potential wine drinkers. The idea of wine was rudimentary at best. Very few, if any, thought about wine with food. Wine was meant for Friday night, for easing the economic pain of the Depression.

Not only were consumers uneducated about the uses of wine, but the producers too were starting out from scratch. No one knew anything about the rigors of commercial wine production or had any idea of the kinds of wines consumers might want. Their primary models were the wines made during Prohibition, which included just about anything that fermented, with or without the addition of sugar.

Prohibition had successfully destroyed a blossoming culture that had begun to discover what kind of beverage wine was. Repeal provided a new beginning.

The Depression furnished reason enough for men like Charles Somers to try making wine. With grapes on hand, they had nothing to lose. Somers had two strong sons to help with the harvest and the winemaking: eighteen-year-old Charles Jr., known as Bill, and fifteen-year-old Howard. Neither of them could foresee that they would be intricately involved with the wine business for most of their adult lives.

Today, Howard Somers lives in a new home on Bainbridge Island. He remains active as a real estate agent, a second career that he began when he retired from the wine industry back in 1987, just before his seventieth birthday. Howard can look back on a career that began when his father first purchased Lambert Evans's farm; in a very real sense, his roots are tied to the vines planted by Evans in 1872.

Howard Somers, a tall, slightly balding man, was healthy and active when I met him. He had a thin nose and a bulldog jowl, and his voice was soft and direct. He spoke reflectively on the past, aware of his preeminent place in Washington wine history.

Howard Somers, barely fifteen years old at the end of Prohibition, lifted his eyes toward the ceiling and looked across the room, picturing the winery as it looked in 1933, when his family first made wine. "We had about fifty 50-gallon wood barrels, open at the top, with about 30 gallons of juice in each, that we fermented all of the grapes in. I think there were about 1,500 gallons of wine made that first year." The first wines were made by a Frenchman—Somers can't recall his name—who claimed he knew how to make wines. Somers remarks, "Of course, at the end of Prohibition, during the Depression, there were quite a few people, mainly recent immigrants, who said they were winemakers. They recognized that there was an opportunity there." Bill Somers and Wilbur Reeves also helped make the first wines. Reeves later was involved with another winery, the Stretch Island Winery.

Somers continued, "In 1934 we got a row of 600-gallon redwood tanks, broken down, that came by steamboat. Then in '36 we built a second building and put in a row of 2,500-gallon redwood tanks. It seems like we were doubling production every year. In '39 we added a third cellar with 5,000-gallon redwood tanks." Nearly all of the wines were made from the local Island Belle grape. It wasn't until later that they began to buy Campbell Early grapes from eastern Washington to supplement their supply of locally grown grapes.

The following vintage, in 1935, the wines were made by Erich Steenborg, a young German immigrant who was then living in Tacoma. Although Steenborg was working for Puget Power and Light as a draftsman, he had been trained as an enologist at Germany's finest wine school, at Geisenheim. Of course, he had been taught to make wines using *vinifera* grapes, most likely mainly German wine grapes such as Riesling, Sylvaner, Pinot Noir, and possibly Lemberger. But Island Belle?

Steenborg came from a family interested in wine. His father operated a hotel on the Baltic Sea and was also in the restaurant and wholesale wine business. He sent his son to the Geisenheim wine school to learn to make wine as well as manage the hotel's wine cellar. For a time Steenborg made wine at Bernkastel, a famous wine town on the Mosel River.

The ravages of the first world war and inflation crushed the family business, and young Steenborg sought a new start in life. Through family friends he relocated in the Pacific Northwest. Steenborg arrived in Tacoma in 1926, at the age of twenty-three.

Steenborg's daughter, Erica Swanson, told me her father made wine during Prohibition because it was an easy way to make some extra cash. She said he didn't make much wine, and she couldn't recall where he got his grapes. She also remembered that when her family lived in Seattle, a friend of her dad's, Joe Molz (who later founded Pommerelle Company), would come by and look at some wine they were making in the basement of their home. She remembered this as a sweet dessert-type wine, somewhat like Irish Cream.

At Repeal in 1933, Steenborg was the only trained winemaker in the Pacific Northwest, and his services were coveted by a number of people. Erica said her dad knew the difference between wine grapes and table grapes, but he also understood that the consumers knew very little about wine; he wasn't about to let his noble sense of wine impede the commercial reality. He decided to go with the market, and got caught up in the excitement of the burgeoning wine industry. He tried to make the best wines that he could with what was handed him.

The idea that you should make what the market wants was central to the wine industry in those days. Bill Somers recalled that his dad always said it was too hard to educate the consumer about wine, that it was more important to make a wine that consumers wanted. Wineries that tried to produce wine according to their ideal concept of what wine was found that there was little demand for their wines.

Wine drinkers of that time wanted something sweet to sip. Hoping to capture the market, the St. Charles Winery produced a richly flavored sweet red wine. The winery used fermentation techniques developed by Dr. Bernard Henry, head of the bacteriology department at the University of Washington, to produce "high-fermentation wines." Dr. Henry, in conjunction with Dr. Henry Benson of the chemistry department, had written a pamphlet on the fermentation of fruit and berry wines as part of a Works Project Administration (WPA) project during the Depression.

Steenborg worked closely with Dr. Benson, who was so fond of Steenborg that he kept an extra desk for him in his department. Steenborg helped St. Charles Winery perfect the high-fermentation technique. High fermentation involves using a cultured yeast that will ferment in a solution high in alcohol. The winemaker needs to know when to add more sugar to the solution to keep feeding the yeast. At about 17 percent alcohol, the yeast can no longer live. Using this technique allowed the winery to make wines that were about 17 percent alcohol from grapes whose sugars would normally produce wines of only 9 percent to 11 percent alcohol. It meant that the winery could produce a full-flavored, high-alcohol wine without fortifying the wine with brandy. This was especially important at first, because initially state or federal law prohibited wineries from fortifying their wines.

Steenborg also worked at, and later became a partner of, Stretch Island Winery, a small winery begun in 1936 by Dr. Benson, Herb Drew, Ed Wright, and Wilbur Reeves. There Steenborg made a table wine called Belle Isle, from the Island Belle grape.

Chapter Twelve

UPLAND WINERY

In November 1934, William B. Bridgman started Upland Winery, producing 7,000 gallons of wine made from his own wine grapes. However, recognizing that there was an art to winemaking, he put out word through the Washington State Liquor Control Board that he wanted an experienced winemaker. Today it seems unbelievable that the liquor board would be helpful to a winery, but in those days it was quite common. In fact, the wine industry relied heavily on Fred Gibson, the liquor board's supervisor of winery operations. Gibson worked closely with wineries that were trying to adopt good winemaking techniques. It is very likely that Gibson was the person who recommended that Bridgman contact Erich Steenborg.

For Steenborg, it was a dream come true. Here, in Washington state, were European wine grapes! In Bridgman's vineyard he found a grape smorgasbord: Semillon, Pinot Noir, Cabernet Sauvignon, Palomino, Thompson Seedless, Sauvignon Blanc, Sultana, Tokay, Zinfandel, Black Muscat, Black Monukka, Alicante Bouschet, Csaba, Muscat of Alexandria, Carignane, Black Malvoisie, and Ribier.

Bridgman, committed to making table wines had long thought that Washington wines would someday rival the wines of Europe and California. He was also active with the Washington Wine Producers Association, founded in 1935, although its charter members were then all western Washington producers: St. Charles Winery, Davis Winery, Pommerelle Winery, Wright Winery, and Werberger Winery. Through the association, Bridgman continually argued for the production of traditional table wines made from European grapes.

Early picture of winery workers at Upland Winery.
—*Photo courtesy of Erica Swanson Steenborg.*

Steenborg was his key to these kinds of wines. One of the first things Steenborg did was to help Bridgman procure his first shipment of grape cuttings from Europe. Included was the Scheurebe grape, then mistakenly thought by Bridgman and Steenborg to be Riesling. It wasn't until years later that one of Walt Clore's field aides, Vere Brummund, had the vine identified as Scheurebe by Dr. Helmut Becker, of the Wine Institute at Geisenheim. The Scheurebe, a cross between Sylvaner and Riesling, is very much like Riesling, enough so that Upland Winery was producing a wine labeled Riesling, from the Scheurebe grape.

Steenborg went on to make a dry Semillon, a slightly sweet Bordeaux-type blend called Chateau Rouge that included Cabernet Sauvignon, and a Burgundy blend made primarily with Pinot Noir. He sold these wines primarily to restaurants and hotels, but it was always an uphill battle. The market for these wines was small.

Bridgman often lamented to Dr. Clore that the premium wines he was producing were only about 10 percent of his business—a tough 10 percent. Louise Durfy, who I met at a reunion of former Upland Winery workers, was one of the winery's bookkeepers; she recalled that Steenborg would get on the telephone and call some accounts, and they would place an order. But it always required his personal attention, convincing clients that they could sell table wines.

Erich Steenborg passed away in 1991, forgotten by an industry that today is producing the kinds of wines he was trying to make and sell sixty years earlier. He even wrote articles in newspapers and magazines to educate the public about the virtues of table wine. In one article dated May 19, 1947, from an unidentified source, he states:

> Education and still more education all along the line, from producer to consumer, is needed to meet the problems that face the wine industry in this period of reconversion and adjustment. . . .
>
> Wines must be properly aged, and it takes time to make quality wines. People who really know wine want certain standard types and we must supply them. They are not going to change their likes and tastes to suit us. We must give them what they desire, a true riesling, a sauterne, a burgundy, a sherry, a port or a muscatel. It's just like music. Hundred-year-old compositions that have charm and merit are always in demand. You hear them each day on the radio, you play them on the piano, you listen to them at concerts, the lovely music lingers on and on. Not so with most of the modern music that is popular one day and forgotten the next. People know the music they want. That also goes for wine; the consumers know the types and I have insisted that if we expect our industry to grow in Washington, we must give the consumer the very best traditional wines.
>
> I am glad to report that some of the Washington wineries are working to this end. Our own winery is specializing in table wine, making the proper blends from the proper types of grapes and getting excellent results. We have had great success in growing the European grape varieties in eastern Washington.

He might have concluded the article by admitting that selling table wines was extremely difficult because the public wasn't ready.

This was also true in California. Table wines represented less than 10 percent of the total production of California wines. Leading educators and researchers of the California wine industry strongly favored table wines, and were chagrined at the industry's production of sweet dessert wines.

View of Upland Winery and Upland Farms looking southwest.
—Photo courtesy of Erica Swanson Steenborg.

In one of the cellar books uncovered from Upland Winery are clippings of magazine articles from the first issues of the *Wine Review* and *Wine and Vines*. One article, "Tests on Unsweetened Sweet Wines," by W. V. Cruess, is interesting for its candor:

> Since repeal there has been a marked trend in consumer preference toward sweet wines, including both the fortified and those of less than 14 per cent alcohol, such as sweet Sauterne and the "Chateau"-type white wines. There has also developed a considerable demand for what might be termed "natural sweet Claret and Burgundy," strange as that statement may seem.
>
> The writer is frank to admit that he does not like these unfortified sweet wines nearly so well for table use as he does dry white and red wines. Yet, two years ago, from observations made with students and others unfamiliar with the proper use of dry wines, it appeared that there was a potential demand for unfortified sweet wines in bottled form and we so reported at the first Wine Conference.
>
> Perhaps, if consumers could be given the unfortified, natural, sweet wines they might in time take the next step and learn to appreciate dry wines; because except for their mild

sweetness, the wines which I am discussing have the flavor of
dry wines rather than the flavor and bouquet of fortified wines
such as Sherry, Port and Muscatel.

Cruess was then a professor at the University of California
Berkeley. He was part of the noted microbiology department that
housed the California wine industry's first wine courses. Jules Fessler
graduated from this department in about 1933 and went on to found
the Berkeley Yeast Laboratory, the source for most of the yeast in the
American wine industry. Through the laboratory, Fessler's influence
spread throughout the country. The lab became a clearinghouse for
information. Wineries and winemakers could get up-to-date information about winemaking and wine marketing. Washington winemakers
didn't have this centralized source for information, and although they
relied on people like Fessler and Cruess in California, locally they got
their information from Fred Gibson or Dr. Henry Benson.

The distinguished Berkeley class of 1941 included Carl Wente,
Louis Martini, Myron Nightingale, and other famous California winemakers who promoted the use of table wines. For many of these pioneers, who were German or Italian, it was a return to their winemaking
heritage. In contrast, Howard Somers, who graduated from the
University of Washington in 1941, was the lone Washington winemaker in his class.

Chapter Thirteen

THE WASHINGTON STATE LIQUOR ACT

Upland Winery, St. Charles Winery, and Stretch Island Winery were not the only wineries that started immediately after Prohibition. By 1938 there were 42 wineries in the state of Washington. These post-Prohibition wineries tended to spring up in small communities and were mostly small owner-operated ventures that relied on local fruit or grapes. Washington state wineries included the Morton Winery in Montesano; the L. R. Autry Winery and Columbia Winery (not related to today's winery of the same name) in Vancouver; Young's Winery in Olympia; Bert Kellett Winery in Yakima; and Bert Dana's Winery in Hanford. Clarkston, Burlington, Sultan, Dockton, Lake Stevens, Vaughn, Edmonds, and Cape Horn also had wineries.

Tacoma was home to the Interstate Winery, Berryland Wineries, and Washington Wineries; the Wright Winery was located in Everett. Grapeview, at Stretch Island, boasted three wineries: Stretch Island Winery, St. Charles Winery, and Davis Winery. Just south across from Harstene Island was the Werberger Winery, and nearby Gig Harbor had the Gottlieb Stock Winery.

Most important were the wineries located in Seattle, only because a few would grow to dominate the marketplace. These included Pommerelle Company, National Wine Company, Washington Distilleries, Connoisseur Winery, Mount Rainier Winery, Union Wines, and Sunset Fruit Products Company. Together, they commanded slightly over 45 percent of the very lucrative Seattle market in the late '30s.

It was a wild time for wine: anything went, as long as it fermented.

Wines were made from all kinds of fruits and berries: loganberry, blackberry, gooseberry, currant, apple, cherry, raspberry, pear, and even melon. Grape wines initially used mostly Island Belle grapes; later wines also used Campbell Early, Concord, and *vinifera* grapes such as Muscat, Zinfandel, Alicante Bouschet, Tokay, and a smattering of others.

One of the unifying influences of this emerging wine industry was the Washington Liquor Act, also known as the Steele Act, named for Earl N. Steele of Thurston County. In an extraordinary session in December 1933, Steele introduced Senate Bill 7, a wide-ranging law that pushed the state in the direction of "modern temperance." It became law in 1934. Steele's bill was based on the results of a study conducted by a liquor commission directed by Governor Martin and headed by Alfred J. Schweppe, former dean of the University of Washington Law School. In the study's summary, Schweppe noted that "true temperance is best promoted by making widely available intoxicating beverages of low alcoholic content such as beer and light wines, but limiting so far as humanly possible the promotion of the sale of intoxicants of heavy alcoholic content through making them available in Government dispensaries. The sale and drinking of hard liquor in public places should be prohibited."

Norman Clark, in his outstanding book *The Dry Years,* points out that behind this directive was the simple and clear desire to avoid the re-institution of the saloon. In its place, the Steele Act created the tavern, envisioned as a place where light alcoholic beverages could be enjoyed without the pitfalls of hard liquor and the lawlessness of the saloons. At first only beer was allowed to be sold by the glass. By 1935, wine was added. Hard liquor could be purchased only through Washington State Liquor Control Board stores. If a person wanted to drink whiskey, he or she was required to drink in the privacy of his or her own home, and later in private clubs. Liquor by the glass was not allowed until 1948, when an initiative passed that permitted restaurants to serve hard liquor.

The Steele Act defined and classified wine as ". . . any alcoholic beverage obtained by fermentation of fruits (grapes, berries, apples, etc.) or other agricultural product containing sugar, to which any saccharine substances may have been added before, during or after fermentation. . . ." The bill, as amended, allowed sugaring (adding sugar to the grape juice prior to fermentation); raised the maximum alcohol from 14 percent to 17 percent; created a category called "Farmer's Winery" (wineries that used their own farm-grown fruit to produce their wines—what today we might call "estate-bottled" wines); allowed wineries in that category to pay lower licensing fees and lower taxes; allowed private wine wholesalers to sell only Washington wines directly to the retail trade; and allowed retailers to sell wine in unopened bottles for off-premise consumption. Other amendments were added over the years.

The Steele Bill was battered by special interests in the wine industry that wanted to change the definition of wine to make it a higher-proof replacement for liquor. This was an issue that tore at the industry for many years. Initially the Steele Bill eliminated the references to "fortified" and "unfortified" in its definition of wine. The wine industry continually increased the amount of alcohol in its wines. The *Seattle Daily Times,* on April 8, 1938, editorialized that "many purchasers ask the alcoholic content of the wine, and choose the stronger beverage," which helped fuel a proof war amongst competing wineries.

In general, the Washington State Liquor Act provided for the "control and regulation" of intoxicating liquors. As stated in the act, it was deemed "an exercise of the police power of the state, for the protection of the welfare, health, peace, morals, and safety of the people of the state, and all its provisions shall be liberally construed for the accomplishment of that purpose." Jean Jules Boddewyn, in his doctoral thesis for the University of Washington school of business administration (published in 1964), *The Protection of Washington Wines: A Case Study in the State Regulation of Business,* stated, "Like many government regulatory acts, its purpose was vague and its powers were broad."

Boddewyn's work, an incisive, comprehensive historical piece (in retrospect), included interviews with some of the key people in the Washington wine industry. The conclusion of Boddewyn's thesis was that Washington state consistently and purposely erected trade barriers and measures whose effects were to protect the Washington state wine industry.

Boddewyn noted that besides attempting to define public drinking patterns, the Washington State Liquor Act created the Washington State Liquor Control Board. Boddewyn's thesis showed how the protection of Washington wines became a complicated patchwork quilt of competing interests. The Washington State Liquor Control Board, by its own bylaws, was charged with helping and nurturing the local wine and spirits business, and yet it became increasingly important to state administrators to increase the revenue from liquor board sales. To Boddewyn it was like tap dancing in a minefield.

The Washington State Liquor Control Board was created using a national model proposed by John D. Rockefeller Jr., a "dry" turned "moderately wet." In his report (known as the Rockefeller Report) during the waning years of Prohibition, he set forth the principles and elements that became the foundation of most of the states' liquor control systems: state control of alcoholic beverages was preferred because national prohibition hadn't worked, and he noted regional differences that were best dealt with at the state level, the success of the Canadian system as a model, and, lastly, the distrust of county and municipal systems. According to the Rockefeller Report, "The experience of every country supports the idea that light wines and beers do not constitute a serious problem." And, further, Rockefeller anticipated that if unlimited quantities of beer and light wines were made available, the American people would forget their thirst for hard liquor.

Initially, the Washington State Liquor Control Board was empowered to sell hard liquor at a low markup to discourage bootlegging and control sales through state-operated "dispensaries." Customers were given a permit number and had to go to a state liquor store to purchase the liquor from a sales agent who stood behind a wired teller box, much like the old postal operations. The customer ordered the liquor by brand and signed a document that the agent kept at the counter.

In the first state liquor stores, wines were included in the liquor inventories. The board stated a preferential status for Washington wines. The idea was that the young Washington wine industry was starting out from scratch and needed help and guidance from the Washington State Liquor Control Board. If Washington vintners made wine from their own fruit, the wineries—designated "farmer's wineries"—were allowed to pay a low licensing fee; this also cast the wine industry in the light of being part of the agriculture industry. As such, it was able to solicit help from the liquor board and the legislature to "help the state's agriculture."

Initially the liquor board purchased wines from both Washington wineries and out-of-state wineries. In the first price list published by the Washington State Liquor Control Board, in October 1934, only one Washington wine is included; listed as "Yakima Wines," it lists an Ambrosia brand (of unknown origin) which included a Red Table

Wine and White Table Wine, a Red Carbonated and White Carbonated, and a Yakima Muscatel.

The first liquor store lists provide a fascinating view of the kinds of wines initially purchased by the board. Remember, the purchasing agent probably knew nothing about wine. And recall that at the end of Prohibition, there was essentially no American wine available. With that in mind, the purchasing agent sought the best wines from around the world. Offerings included 1923 Charles Heidsick Champagne, 1926 Clos du Vougeot, 1926 Lanson Champagne, 1929 Langenbach Hochheimer, 1929 Langenbach Bernkasteler, a complete line of Barton and Geister (B&G) French wines (including estate bottlings and generic wines), Hungarian Tokay, Brolio Chianti, Duff Gordon Sherry, and Cockburn Port.

When American wines came onto the market, the stores sold bottles from California and Washington. Italian Swiss Colony and Belvista Winery wines, from California, included Port, Sherry, Muscatel, Tipo Red, Burgundy, Zinfandel, Claret, Tipo White, Sauterne, Riesling, and Chablis.

In those first lists, Washington wines were available from J. F. Morton of Montesano, the Wright Winery of Everett, and the Davis Winery on Stretch Island. Davis offered a wine called Chambelle, while Wright sold mainly fruit wines such as blackberry and cherry.

The selection of Washington wines included Sauterne and Chateau from St. Charles Winery. When I visited St. Charles Winery with Bill Somers, he showed me a bottle of St. Charles Winery Sauterne. It was one of the first wines made by Erich Steenborg while he was the wine-maker at St. Charles Winery. The heavy glass bottle was shaped like an expensive Bordeaux bottle, including a deep punt (indentation) in the bottom of the bottle. The label and capsule were gold foil; in every respect it looked like a modern reserve-bottling wine. The wine was crystal clear, with two inches of sediment at the bottom of the upright bottle. Bill told me that the wine was made of 100 percent Island Belle and that it was dry. I really wanted to pull the cork on that bottle: Even though I knew that it was probably long gone, I held out a ridiculous hope that there was something left of the wine.

—WASHINGTON WINES SEEK PROTECTION—

In 1935 the Washington wine industry organized as the Washington Wine Producers Association. Some of the immediate issues it dealt

Washington Wine Council, about 1938. Seated front left is W.B. Bridgman. Directly behind him on his right is John Molz of Pommerelle. At Molz's left is Edgar Wright of Stretch Island Winery. Warren Dewar, the Executive Secretary, sits to his left. Next to Dewar is Dominic Depoulis of Nawico. To the far right is Rudolph Werberger of Werberger Winery. Seated to his left is Ken Tuttle of Connoisseur Winery. Jim Maloney, a salesman, sits in front with Bridgman. Others remain unidentified. —*Photo courtesy of Erica Swanson Steenborg.*

with included labeling requirements, fortified-versus-nonfortified labeling, and direct sales to retail accounts such as taverns, grocery stores, and restaurants. Through the cogent arguments of one of the association's first executive secretaries, Warren Dewar (formerly the supervisor of wineries for the liquor board), Washington wineries in 1935 acquired the right to sell wine directly to retail accounts, either directly from the winery or through wine wholesalers. Other wines, chiefly California and European, had to be purchased from the state liquor stores at the liquor board's marked-up retail price and then sold at the retailer's price.

For the first year after Repeal, Washington wines dominated the local market because of their new-won status as the only wines that could be sold directly to the retail trade, and, additionally, because California wines were taxed at a higher rate. However, there were some problems. Because many of the Washington wineries were exceedingly small, the liquor board had difficulty distributing the wines statewide through its stores. Also, the wines were very young. They had barely finished fermenting before they were pushed onto the market, causing some wines to explode on the shelves of the liquor stores.

Nonetheless, Washington's wine sales expanded rapidly under this system. Howard Somers said the St. Charles Winery doubled production each year for the first few years after Repeal. This double-digit growth was happening everywhere in Washington. Following Repeal, it seemed like consumers couldn't get enough wine. By 1938 there were 42 wineries bonded in the state of Washington, producing 2 million gallons of wine. The state's population in 1938 was 1.5 million people. That works out to a per capita production level of nearly 1.33 gallons. Compared to 1992 numbers, this is phenomenal. In 1992, 87 wineries produced slightly more than 4.5 million gallons. The state population was close to 6 million. That works out to 0.75 gallon per capita. Considering that nearly half of the wine produced in Washington in 1992 was exported, the per capita consumption of Washington-made wine was less than 0.4 gallon.

By modern standards the wine industry in 1938 was dynamic and remarkable. The state was awash in Washington wine. A comparative sales report of wine sold in Washington in March 1938 showed that the leading winery was St. Charles Winery (with 15.9 percent of the total sales), followed by Pommerelle Winery (12.6 percent), National Wine Company (12.1 percent), Wright Winery (11.2 percent), Washington Distilleries (8.6 percent), Connoisseur Winery (8.6 percent), Upland Winery (8.1 percent), Stretch Island Winery (4.1 percent), Rudolf Werberger Winery (3.9 percent), and then others with less than 3 percent of sales. These wineries were producing a lot of wine, in every conceivable color and style.

By 1938 the Washington Wine Producers Association had reorganized as the Washington Wine Council. The new council was made up of a broader base of support reflecting the growth of wineries east of the Cascades. Warren Dewar, secretary of the council, sought and received continued protection from the liquor board, primarily by seeking tax relief. California wines were continually assessed a higher tax rate. The liquor board constantly pushed up its markup on California wines, especially dessert wines, arguing that it would increase its revenues while at the same time protecting the Washington wineries, because Washington wineries could sell directly to taverns.

Without Washington wines in the liquor stores, California wines represented the great bulk of the liquor board's offerings (thus the liquor board became a booster of California wines). Washington wineries went after the very lucrative tavern business, placing themselves in a race to produce increasingly sweeter and more alcoholic wines. Because they could sell directly to the taverns (and thus with lower prices), theirs were usually the first wines of choice. Because sale of liquor by the drink was not authorized until late in the forties, the taverns were the center of the alcoholic-drinks industry. Meanwhile, California wines were the wines selected by restaurants and grocery stores—not until later did California recover a share of the tavern market.

Bill Somers said that Washington wineries were very cognizant of what other wineries were doing, both locally and nationally. If one winery had a product that was selling well in the taverns, other wineries would copy that style. Sometimes the names were amazingly similar. When Tokay, a Muscat-based dessert wine, became popular, it wasn't long before Bokay, made from apples, became an attractive alternative. St. Charles Winery made a local knockoff of Alicante Bouschet called Caliante. Wineries came up with imaginative labels as well. One popular brand, White Mule, pictured a mule with an apple on its back. According to Bill Somers, "If the apple fell off the donkey's back, it was time to quit drinking."

During the first couple of years following Repeal, fortified wines were disdained by many winemakers. It was thought that wine should remain as close to the natural product as possible. Bill Somers said his dad never liked to add spirits to their products, thus they never built a distillery at the winery, and only later, when they had to produce fortified wines to remain competitive, did they begin buying brandy to add to their wines. Instead they preferred to make wine using the "high-fermentation" technique perfected by Dr. Benson and Erich Steenborg.

Chapter Fourteen

FORTIFIED WINE
A RESPONSE TO PROHIBITION

Washington State Liquor Control Board annual reports show that in 1938, nearly 38 percent of all wines sold in the state were from Washington. By the end of 1942, Washington wineries controlled a record 65 percent of the market. This was accomplished by only 24 wineries, down from 42 wineries in 1938. Records also show that the wineries were producing more wine, and the wine was becoming more and more potent. In 1939 less than 31 percent of Washington wines were fortified. By 1943 that number had risen to 50 percent. By 1948, 85 percent of all wines produced in Washington state were fortified.

Part of that increase of fortified wines is attributable to sugar rationing during World War II. Wines formerly made using the high-fermentation technique, which depended on copious quantities of sugar, began to be fortifed with brandy, which could be made from fruit or grapes. Also, consumers became less and less discriminating. During the war years, the Washington economy, especially in the Seattle-Tacoma area, was booming. Youthful workers, with their taste for sweeter beverages and penchant for high-proof wines, earned good money in the war industries and helped fuel this demand.

—POMMERELLE COMPANY—
Pommerelle Company, initially an apple juice company, branched off into apple wine at Repeal, in December 1933, and became one of the first bonded wineries in the Seattle area. Pommerelle was founded by partners Joe Molz, William Braicks, Dr. William Leede, and

Fred Wonn. Both Molz and Braicks were Germans who had immigrated after World War I, settling in Seattle through the help of Leede, a local sponsor. During the Depression, Wonn and Braicks worked for the Dutch Consulate, Mr. Vanderspek, at Holland American.

The guiding principal of Pommerelle was Joe Molz, a German born on the Mosel River whose father had been in the wine business in Germany. Joe Molz had become a successful businessman in the Seattle area, prospering during the Depression by selling distressed mortgages to wealthy Europeans through Vanderspek. It was in this business that Molz met his partners for Pommerelle.

At the end of 1933, these men began to experiment with producing sterilized and filtered apple juice, using German technology that would someday transform the wine industry through controlled fermentations and cleaner finished wines. Starting operation just prior to Repeal, they set out to produce an unpasteurized fresh-bottled apple juice that wouldn't ferment once bottled. They formed Pommerelle Company (named after the French word for apple, *pomme)*, and began to sell their product.

Only a few months later, Prohibition was lifted and they recognized a business opportunity; it was just a simple matter of fermenting their apple juice into hard cider or, more correctly, apple wine. They were in the wine business.

Their first bonded wine facility was in a warehouse on Dearborn Street near where the Kingdome is now located. Some of the first apple wines were weird imitations of German wines but, rather than using grapes, they were using apples. This willingness to copy the only wine they probably knew showed the naiveté (or perhaps the sophistication?) of these budding winemakers. They were working with what was available—apples. Gradually, Pommerelle produced other fruit wines, relying on local fruits to build its brand.

Pommerelle prospered. One of the big sellers was Pommerelle's loganberry wine, which used berries purchased from a farm on Whidbey Island. The winery quickly outgrew the original space and they had to expand to another location on Dearborn, near the old Norway Building. Soon after, they added sparkling apple wine (bottled with an attractive champagne package) and grape wines.

Beginning in 1937, Pommerelle began to fortify its apple wine. The laws then required that whatever fruit a winery was using to make its fortified wine, the same kind of fruit had to be used to make the brandy used to fortify the wine. Here they were, making some of the state's first apple brandy, much like the Calvados of Normandy, France, and they probably didn't even think about it because they couldn't sell it as brandy. (There have been recent proposals by entrepreneurs to make a Calvados-type spirit, often chastising the industry for not having done this already.) For Pommerelle it was merely a means of fortifying its apple wine, which required them to re-open their original site for much-needed space to produce the brandy.

They soon outgrew their two Dearborn locations and bought property on East Marginal Way in south Seattle in 1940. At one point the company even began to ship wine out of state, with sales in Oregon and as far away as New York. It operated bottling plants in Portland and Chicago; the Chicago plant was forced to shut down after a very short time because of World War II.

During the war, Pommerelle had a difficult time. It was having trouble selling its berry wines, and Fred Wonn, Pommerelle's manager, had other interests that kept him from properly managing the company.

In 1949 Ivan Kearns was hired by Pommerelle to replace Wonn. Kearns, a manager popular with employees, brought the company back to its previous stature. He introduced new wines and directed sales to the chain stores that emerged after the war.

—NATIONAL WINE COMPANY—

National Wine Company (Nawico) also began in Seattle in 1935. Nawico was located near today's Fremont District and was originated by Frank Alvau, Dominic Depoulis, and Virgil Layton. Also involved were Joe Carbonatto, Philip Sugia, Dominic Cappellero, James (J. C.) Sams, and Roger McCoubree. Whereas Pommerelle was dominated by Germans, Nawico was dominated by Italians, some with nefarious occupations during Prohibition.

Depoulis's bootlegging and, later, his legitimate beer and beverage distributorship, paved the way for the winery. Additionally, his wife, Mariah, had successfully operated a brothel up on Vancouver Island. Alvau brought to the winery his substantial earnings from years of building illicit stills throughout Washington state during Prohibition. Joe Carbonnato, who saw that the winery was doing well in about 1938, approached the partners and asked if he could put some money in. The partnership voted against him entering, although Alvau voted for him.

Carbonatto then went to the federal authorities and told them of

Layton's, Alvau's, and Cappellero's activities during Prohibition. The federal government took Layton, Alvau, and Cappellero to court for bootlegging, and the Washington State Liquor Control Board removed Layton and Alvau from Nawico. Cappellero turned state's evidence and was able to remain with Nawico. Layton bought vineyards near Wallula that were later flooded by construction of the McNary Dam. Alvau bought the Tokay Ranch at Maryhill, then went to Pommerelle and offered his share of Nawico. In lieu of money, he received a five-year contract in which Pommerelle agreed to purchase grapes from his vineyard, Tokay Ranch, at $50 a ton, considerably higher than the going rate.

Nawico tended to make primarily grape wine, relying principally on grapes purchased from eastern Washington vineyards. In 1937 the winery built a facility in Grandview to handle the grapes closer to the vineyards. Nawico became a strong winery, combining the advantages of grapes grown in eastern Washington with a trained sales staff located in western Washington, where the consumers resided. It was a combination that set it apart from other wineries.

Lester Fleming, a native of Grandview, began working for Nawico in 1937. Fleming's father was one of the very first to settle in the sagebrush town at the turn of the century, opening the town's first general store. Les had been asked by his cousin, Walt Fleming, to help install some wooden tanks at Nawico. It was the beginning of a wine career that lasted over forty years.

It took Fleming a year to help get the winery up and running. By the fall of 1938, everything was set for that year's harvest. Initially Fleming managed the winery and its vineyards in eastern Washington, occasionally dealing with the company managers in Seattle. Generally he was left alone, but once in a while he had to deal with the westsiders.

In 1938, Fleming hired a close friend of his, Victor Allison. Even though Fleming hired Vic, Vic emerged as the manager of the winery. But Fleming recalled, "Titles weren't so important in those days. Everybody had a lot of work to do and we just all did it. I needed some help; he came in to help me. So this title business didn't come along until later." Fleming increasingly took over the management of the vineyard and relationships with the growers. Vic worked directly in the winery and communicated with the Seattle wineries, first Nawico's westside office and later Pommerelle's as well.

Vic and Les worked well together. Allison had also grown up in the Yakima Valley, going to school in Prosser and Sunnyside. As young men, Fleming and Allison had managed competing service stations kitty-corner from one another. Allison started in the wine business in '36 when he took a job at the Wright Winery, located right next door to the Nawico winery in Grandview. He then took a year off before going to work for Les in '38.

Prior to World War II, Pommerelle bought out Nawico. However, separate management was kept for both companies. It was a strange arrangement, pitting one company against the other. They acted as separate companies. One likely reason for this bizarre arrangement was that Nawico had a grandfathered liquor license that allowed it to manufacture everything from covered wagons to airplanes and receive supplies needed for these sorts of operations. This became very critical during the war when supplies were restricted.

During the war, grapes were in short supply. Alcohol produced from grapes, and other fruits, was needed as an alternative fuel supply. With beer and liquor in short supply, further demand was placed on wine. Nawico's manager, J. C. Sams, would not give up Pommerelle's share of the grapes. He did this to strengthen his own part of the business, because he had recently bought into the business. This relationship went on throughout the war years.

After World War II, Molz used Nawico's grandfathered liquor license to resell acquired military vehicles left over from the war. But this arrangement put a considerable strain on the company. It was like a bad marriage; each company refused to recognize shared goals. Although they were essentially one company, salespeople from each company had to compete for shelf space for their own brands.

Times were good in Seattle during the war. The economy was bursting with war industries and with an influx of mostly young people, many of them women. Their nighttime entertainment was mostly in the taverns because they still couldn't get liquor by the drink. Nawico was wed to the tavern business. Wines were at the height of their popularity during the war because wartime restrictions on alcohol made it difficult to get whiskey. Most popular were the ports, sherries, and muscatel wines, along with the fortified grape and apple wines. A wine race developed in the industry as wineries tried to outdo each other with higher alcohol proof or new ways of packaging their products. If one winery's product caught the customers' fancy, other wineries would soon copy it.

In 1943 Fleming's father became ill, and Fleming left the winery to devote himself to his father's farm and his own, which he had purchased in the Orchard Tract, in south Grandview. Fleming continued to help out each fall until 1953, when Allison moved to Seattle to run the winery in Seattle and asked Fleming to come back and manage the Grandview winery. A year later, in 1954, J. C. Sams convinced the owners of Pommerelle that they should at last streamline the two companies, and they became the American Wine Growers. But more on that later.

—UPLAND WINERY—

In the meantime, what had become of Upland Winery? Remember that it had begun in 1934 with a vision of making table wine from *vinifera* grapes, rather than fortified wines made from fruit and *labrusca* grapes.

Under Steenborg's direction and Bridgman's guidance, the winery had progressed steadily to become a prominent winery. Many wineries closed during World War II, but Upland Winery actually prospered. William Bridgman was fortunate. His talented winemaker, Erich Steenborg, had invented a method to extract dry cream of tartar, a natural by-product of wine, which was used in the manufacture of explosives. Bridgman's winery was able to skirt many of the restrictions placed on other wineries due to its special wartime status. While other owners were struggling to staff their wineries, Bridgman was able to maintain his workers and he had less difficulty getting supplies of sugar and bottles.

Wineries that were able to stay in business during the war years were very profitable. Without liquor by the drink, taverns outdid themselves to find wines that delivered the most punch for the buck. Upland Winery too began to find its fortified wines more and more profitable. But eventually this route was to become a dead end.

A handwritten note in faded blue fountain-pen ink, scribbled on a carbon copy of the minutes from a staff meeting, offers a clue to the downfall of Upland Winery. It is dated November 21, 1946. In attendance were W. B. Bridgman, the winery's owner; Bill Barnard, Bridgman's nephew and the vineyard manager; R. C. Hermon, the engineer; Julian Steenbergen, the chemist and cellarmaster; and Erich Steenborg, the winemaker. Each staff member made a presentation about the harvest season just ended. Steenborg reported that sales had slowed a little but Upland was holding up better than average. Steenbergen stated that the winery would produce 280,000 gallons of fortified wine and 100,000 gallons of table wines that year, having

Upland Winery display float used in Sunnyside parade about 1938.
—*Photo courtesy of Erica Swanson Steenborg.*

crushed 2,158 tons of grapes. Barnard discussed vineyard operations and requested a larger machine shop, but was willing to forego this for new fermenters and fortifying tanks.

But it was Hermon's presentation that startled both Steenbergen and Steenborg. Hermon displayed drawn plans for revising winery buildings and future buildings for an "ultimate storage capacity of 2 million gallons." Steenbergen underlined these words on his copy of the minutes and drew a line to the bottom of the page, where he wrote, "Where are we going to sell this?"

For Steenbergen and Steenborg—especially Steenborg—this increase seemed beyond reason. But Steenborg had seen his influence on Bridgman wane after Bridgman hired Barnard to manage the vineyard, and Upland Winery was increasingly directing itself toward fortified wines. Steenborg was growing increasingly frustrated in his efforts to steer the winery toward table wines. He believed that consumers' tastes would change eventually, if he could somehow educate them.

Bridgman was too practical for that kind of thinking: the winery's success with fortified wines was overwhelming. His earlier vision of European table wines had begun to blur. And Barnard, probably without a vision one way or another, fit into Bridgman's revised strategy. The new building was constructed, although it is unclear how long it took to complete the job. Bridgman financed the construction through the bank, using cash flow from the wine sales to buy up new vineyards and orchards, continuing to expand his farm and winery.

Julian Steenbergen and
Erich Steenborg in
Upland Farms' vineyard.
—*Photo courtesy of
Erica Swanson Steenborg.*

At this critical time of expansion, a series of crushing blows hit Upland Winery. Chilling back-to-back winters of 1948–1949 and 1949–1950 devastated Bridgman's vineyards, especially the *vinifera* grapes. Winter damage was nearly complete, although a number of vines survived. Far worse than nature's cruel blow, however, was the state legislature's action: in 1948 it allowed liquor to be sold by the drink in restaurants, either at the table or in the bar. Upland's fortified-wine sales began to decrease significantly, and the winery was left with little cash to pay off the financing on an overbuilt winery.

Steenbergen, Steenborg's confidante, chemist, and cellarmaster, left in 1948 to take over the family orchard, and Barnard took over more and more of the day-to-day management. Another winemaker was imported from California, but he and Steenborg fought. Steenborg decided to concentrate on sales—away from the winery. Barnard's daughter, Marie Christensen, who had worked as Steenbergen's lab assistant, began to take over the winemaking responsibilities. Steenborg eventually left the winery in 1951, bitter and disappointed—both at Bridgman and at the wine industry. He had watched his dream unravel. When Steenborg finally left, Christensen became the full-time wine-maker. The turning point for Upland Winery was 1952. Over the next

Winemaker Marie Christensen in Upland Winery's lab.
—*Photo courtesy of Erica Swanson Steenborg.*

twenty years, the winery died a slow and agonizing death. It went out of business in 1972.

How could a major winery unravel so completely? The answer probably lies in a combination of market forces: changing demographics, changes in the wine laws, increased competition, and Bridgman's decision to focus on fortified wines.

Bridgman found himself defending an industry far removed from his original vision. If he had only said to himself, "This is just a phase; eventually the market will want table wines, and I will be ready to meet that need." Instead he gave in to the market. By 1947, thirty years after he had planted his first wine grapes, he was far from his early goal of making table wines. Whatever hope he had of someday realizing his original vision was shattered by the winters of '48–'49 and '49–'50. He even remarked to Walt Clore, in a moment of despair, that maybe he should have planted only Concords.

In 1960, Bridgman sold the winery to George Thomas, who changed the name to Santa Rosa Winery in a cynical effort to win back its old prominence. The winery revealed the depths of despair to which it had fallen: it tried to appear as a California winery to overcome its unfavorable image. Bridgman died in 1968 at ninety years of age. Though Bridgman proved mortal, his ideas and his vineyards live on, and continue to affect Washington's wine industry today.

Fortunately, Bridgman had encouraged Walt Clore to plant *vinifera* wine grapes at the Irrigation Experiment Station in Prosser in 1940. By providing Clore with cuttings from his own vineyard, Bridgman propagated his vision.

Bridgman's early efforts at wine grape growing and his vision of European-style wines can be viewed as a family tree—or family vine—of Washington's wine industry. The family vine would show Bridgman as the trunk, with branches (canes) to new developments emanating from his efforts. One cane would lead to Dr. Clore, another would lead to Dr. Woodburne and the Associated Vintners, home winemakers who bought their first grapes from Bridgman. Shoots would lead to Dr. George Stewart, who built his home on property with grapes planted by Bridgman and later founded a winery at Granger; American Wine Growers (the forerunner of Stimson Lane Vineyards & Estates); Tucker Wine Cellars in Sunnyside; Maryhill; and the new DeLille Winery in Woodinville. A shoot leading to Sagemoor, Bacchus, and Dionysus Vineyards was nurtured by Bridgman's early acquaintance with Albert Ravenholt, one of Sagemoor's founding partners. And today Bridgman's seminal vision is acknowleged in a brand named for him: W. B. Bridgman, produced by Washington Hills Cellars winery in Sunnyside.

Melvin and Vera Tucker owned one of Bridgman's first contract vineyards; they maintained the relationship from about 1930 to at least 1942. Their son, Clifford, worked for Bridgman, initially in the vineyards, starting in 1935; later, he worked in the winery and, finally, in outside sales. Clifford Tucker enjoyed working for Bridgman. He related a funny story about Bridgman:

Bridgman sent Clifford out to the currant farm. Later, Bridgman showed up in his big black sedan, which he always forgot where he had parked in the vineyard. He asked Clifford how things were going.

Clifford replied, "Oh, pretty good." And then added, "Mr. Bridgman, did you know that the war effort is after you?"

Bridgman responded, "Is that right?"

Clifford told him, "Do you know what they are going to do? They're going to take the silver out of your hair, the gold out of your teeth, and the lead out of your butt." Tucker roared in laughter, but then cut his laughter short.

Tucker said that Bridgman looked at him directly and he thought for sure he was going to get fired. Suddenly Bridgman started laughing and he said, "Tucker, I'm going to give you a raise." At this, Tucker almost fell over; Bridgman hardly ever smiled—and to hear him laugh surprised him.

Tucker enjoyed the work in the vineyard and winery among friends. Much of the work was hand labor. Grapes were picked and put into small wooden boxes that held about thirty-five pounds. The boxes had to be lifted into the crusher-stemmer one at a time. Based on figures recorded by Julien Steenbergen, during the '40s the winery crushed about 2,000 tons of grapes annually, or more than 100,000 boxes of grapes.

Once the grapes were crushed, the juice went into huge cement fermenters, some capable of holding up to 25,000 gallons. Once the wine started fermenting, that was usually the last Tucker saw of it until bottling time. Tucker recalled getting a phone call late one night, asking him to come down to the winery. One of the big tanks had broken: the cement had given way because there wasn't enough rebar in the walls, due to the wartime metal shortage. Tucker said the wine had run down the hill and spilled into an irrigation lateral. He and the other workers quickly stopped up the lateral, which was empty at that time of year, and pumped the wine back up to the winery. The wine was then distilled into alcohol in their still. Tucker let out a huge guffaw as he reminisced.

Chapter Fifteen

VARIETALS
A ROSÉ FUTURE

In 1947 fewer wineries were producing a record amount of wine. But this began to change with the change in liquor-by-the-drink laws, which were liberalized in 1948. From 1947 to 1953, with the consolidation of the industry, fewer wineries were producing less wine. The industry that produced nearly 2.8 million gallons in 1947 produced less than half of that amount in 1953, 1.23 million gallons. In 1948 the Washington wine industry was near bottom.

Twenty years after the repeal of Prohibition, the glamour of the wine industry had worn off. Wineries continued to go out of business or merge with other larger wineries. The early 1950s were a dark era for the Washington wine industry, with 15 wineries, down from the high of 42 wineries in 1938 and 21 wineries in 1947.

The industry was able to pull itself through with effective legislation. The Washington Wine Council in 1949 had effectively sought "minimum prices" on wines sold by the state to curb any dumping of cheap California wine following the prosperous war years.

Another change took place: the marketplace had matured; the tavern crowd of the late 1930s and early '40s was settling down after the war. Chain stores, not taverns, were beginning to dominate wine sales, but the industry and consumers were trying to match their taste to a dramatic shift that was occurring: dessert wine sales were beginning to decrease. In 1952, 84 percent of Washington wines were fortified; in 1953 that had dropped to 70 percent.

In 1953 one of the hot new wines out of California was Almaden's Grenache Rosé. California wineries were leading the way:

with improved technology they were beginning to produce just slightly sweet wines. Improved filtration techniques and jacketed stainless steel tanks allowed the wineries to produce lighter wines. The Grenache Rosé had just a hint of sweetness.

They were perfect wines for the emerging and expanding middle class of the '50s. World War II veterans wanted wines that they had grown fond of in Europe. Housewives in particular were learning the demands and pleasures of the dining experience. The population was aging and had increasingly more time on its hands, a bit more money, and an ever-expanding intellectual interest in the world around it.

—AMERICAN WINE GROWERS—

After World War II, Pommerelle's Ivan Kearns introduced new wines to the new chain stores, while Nawico's J. C. Sams saw his company's sales fall dramatically. In a countermove, he convinced the partners to put the two companies under one roof and one management: the management of Nawico. In 1954 the two wineries formally merged to become the American Wine Growers (AWG). Kearns was out; Sams was in.

This move took two of the strongest and largest companies in the wine industry and made them into a huge company with devastatingly competitive advantages. Even though Pommerelle had first bought Nawico in the late '30s, it wasn't until the merger in '54 that they acted like one company.

American Wine Growers was a good blend of talents and products. Vic Allison was made the general manager. Lester Fleming recalled that he and Vic understood the changing wine market, but that they had no reason to change how they were making wine. The Washington wine industry was still servicing at least half the market. California was progressing with table wines, but there was still enough demand for the kind of dessert wine the Washington wine industry was known for.

Fleming also said that he and Allison talked about *vinifera* wines. They were pretty convinced that they could grow *vinifera* in eastern Washington. They had been buying *vinifera* from numerous sources up and down the valley. Les had been buying *vinifera* grapes for Nawico from a number of growers, especially a few down by the Tri-Cities and toward Finley: Pardini, Subucco, Layton, and others whose names he could no longer recall. Later, as Bridgman's Upland Winery began to fall on hard times, considerable vineyards—which Bridgman had

American Wine Growers at National Wine Company in Grandview. On the left is
Lester Fleming, vineyard manager. Next to him is Vic Allison, manager. On the far right is
John Molz, partner in American Wine Growers. —*Photo courtesy of Lester Fleming.*

developed—in nearby Grandview became available to Fleming for
American Wine Growers.

AWG bought one of Bridgman's most important vineyards in
1956. It is known today as Ranch #6. Fleming recalled that when they
acquired it, it had become quite rundown. Besides *vinifera* grapes, the
ranch also had alfalfa and currants. The vineyard plantings were a wild
hodgepodge of varieties. Les Fleming related, "I couldn't understand
how anyone would plant that way, so I talked to one of the guys working for us who had also worked for Bridgman. I asked, 'Charlie, why in
the world are these grapes so mixed up? It's terrible. We've got to get
this stuff straightened out. Can't make a wine out of four different
kinds of grapes and call it something unless it's red port or white port.'
'Well, the only thing I can think,' he said, 'is ol' Bill (Bridgman) would
come out here if we weren't too busy and he'd grab a bucket of plants
and tell us to go plant the sticks. He'd tell us to plant sticks, but he
wouldn't tell us what kind of grapes they were. We planted sticks.'"

In that vineyard, Bridgman had Chardonnay, Pinot Noir,
Zinfandel, Muscat of Alexandria, and Grenache as well as numerous
other *vinifera* and American and French hybrid varieties. For American
Wine Growers, it became an important source of experimentation with
vinifera grapes.

Later, Allison would have Fleming go out to that vineyard and pick separately some of the Semillon and Pinot Noir for Dr. Lloyd Woodburne and his fellow winemakers of Associated Vintners. Les thought it was pretty funny: "I just thought they were kind of fussy. We picked fancy grapes for them and put them in apple boxes and then they would come over and get them in their truck. Vic used to have me pick so many boxes of this type and so many boxes of that type, and he wanted all good bunches for this guy at the university for this experimental wine."

Fleming continued, "Vic was playing ball because they were experimenting with varietal wines. They weren't fortified wines. Vic was kind of playing along with them to see how that stuff would turn out." Fleming said that he and Vic knew that they would eventually have to go toward varietal wines. That's why they had planted Grenache in 1950. By 1954 American Wine Growers offered Grenache Rosé under their Granada brand and their 100 percent Concord under the Haddasim label.

Under Allison's leadership, American Wine Growers began to buy up vineyards in eastern Washington. In 1955 AWG bought Ranch #4 from the original Pommerelle owners. This vineyard included Grenache, Muscat of Alexandria, Semillon, Sauvignon Blanc, Thompson Seedless, Carignane, Zinfandel, and White Diamond. In 1963 AWG bought from National Grape Growers Cooperative Association its Vineyard #7, a 125-acre Concord vineyard in Benton City, in which AWG planted 15 acres in Cabernet Sauvignon.

American Wine Growers pointed itself toward the future, but it wasn't until 1965 that AWG finally made the plunge into serious production of varietal table wines. Up until that time, AWG, like others in the industry, was mainly putting premium varietals into nondescript generic wines, labeled as burgundy and sauterne. In the early '60s, a consumer could pick up a bottle of burgundy for ninety cents and it might have been made of primarily Cabernet Sauvignon, but the next batch might be Concord. There was no consistency.

Allison and Fleming were practical men and, like others in the wine industry, they understood that it was cheaper and easier to make formula wines, whether it was a fortified port or a burgundy blend. The greatest profit was in using as much Concord as possible, boosting the alcohol with brandy, and getting the wine fermented and out of the winery as quickly as possible.

Table wines of varietal character were a different kind of challenge.

It didn't make sense to pay more for better grapes, then need special equipment such as expensive stainless steel tanks or small oak barrels to make the wines, then hold on to them for a couple of years to mellow them. Sure, you could sell the wines for a bit more money, but there simply wasn't the same amount of profit built into each wine.

In 1961 Vere Brummund, who had been working with the WSU Irrigated Agricultural Research and Extension Center at Prosser, gave a speech in Yakima to the winemakers and grape growers. He urged them to abandon the dessert wines of the past and grasp the future: varietal table wines. Afterward, Vic Allison approached Brummund and told him that table wines would never work for Washington: there just wasn't enough of a market. But Brummund countered by saying "the market was there, it was being developed for the Washington wine industry by California."

Brummund told me he remembered tasting a Semillon wine out of tank at American Wine Growers. He recalled that it was a marvelous wine, better than anything he had tasted out of California, yet when he later asked what had become of the wine, he was shocked to learn that it had become a sauterne and sold for $1.49. Brummund was outraged: that wine could have sold for much more and, with a better presentation—a cork rather than a screw-top—the wine could have attracted more attention.

Vic Allison saw a dramatic change in the consumption habits of consumers in the early '60s. Table wines had been steadily increasing as a percentage of all wines sold in Washington. Prior to 1961, in the late '50s, consumers had a brief affair with fruit-flavored aperitif wines that then declined and gave way to increased table wines. By the end of 1965, for the first time, table wines outsold dessert wines in the state of Washington.

For Allison, that was a compelling argument. He may not have cared too much for what Brummund had declared in 1961, but Allison was a practical man and his winery was market-driven. He moved with the market. He knew that Washington state could grow *vinifera* grapes; his own company had been using *vinifera* grapes for more than thirty years. He understood the risks, as well, of growing *vinifera:* an occasional bone-chiller like the winters of '48–'49 and '49–'50, or the November freeze of 1955.

Lester Fleming, in typical fashion, explained how eastern Washington growers like themselves could look past the risk of growing *vinifera:* "You'd have a bad winter and you'd freeze stuff. You didn't plan your planting by the weather." He implied that a farmer planted according to what the market wanted, and what would yield the highest price—the weather be damned.

Les Fleming has seen—no, he has helped grow—the wine industry in Washington state. When Fleming retired in 1977, he had ridden the industry's roller coaster through two generations and could say in his direct Yogi Berra way, "We've seen it go up and down. It went up and then it went down." And now, looking back, Les can say it went up again, beginning with the interest in varietal table wines.

—OLD WEST WINES—

Old West Wines in Renton, just south of Seattle, was owned by Harry and Meta Buttnick. The Buttnick family was known as an outerwear manufacturer. They entered the wine business when they bought Union Wines, a winery located in Ballard best known for berry wines. In the mid-1950s, Old West Wines produced a wide range of wine styles under numerous brand names, from Victory Apple Wine to Zion Port Wine.

Old West winery had already begun to branch out into table wines, but it took Martha Niblack's vision to focus them on producing a quality table wine.

Martha Niblack was born in Mississippi; she moved to the Pacific Northwest in 1942, when she was an incredibly young sixteen, to work at Hanford, which was then secretly working on the hydrogen bomb. Two years later she moved to Seattle where, she told me in her wonderfully soft southern manner of speaking, "I worked two jobs . . . I worked 8 to 5 and then 11 to 7. I was making money. I had never seen that kind of money, being raised on a farm. I was making $49 a week." In 1957 Niblack, an attractive thirty-one-year-old woman, began working for Old West Wines, first as a secretary and bookkeeper, then taking over more and more management.

Martha Niblack was always a contradiction: being Southern Baptist she refused to drink wine, but she had no qualms selling it or helping make it. She recalled her original vision of wine: "I felt early on that wine was part of gracious living, that it could add to life—even though I didn't drink. I felt that if you were going to be a winery, you should be a Charles Krug. I had visited the Krug winery in California, and that is what I thought a winery should be."

She used the Charles Krug Winery as a model to help Old West

Wines develop its Chateau Merryl wines. She got help from Bud Jones, of California's Gibson Winery, who was then buying Concord wine from Old West. [An interesting aside is that recently I found bottles of Pommerelle Blackberry and Nawico Loganberry in my local grocery store. The fine print indicated that the wines were made by Gibson Vineyards in California.] Jones was particularly excited about the possibility of Old West making a Muscat wine. Old West was buying the Muscat from the Takahashi Vineyard at Maryhill. Ultimately Old West leased the vineyard so that it could get better control over the quality of the grapes.

The Takahashi vineyard provided Old West with Zinfandel, Golden Chasselas, Pinot Noir, Chardonnay, Gewurztraminer, and Thompson Seedless. Niblack wanted to call the winery brand Chateau Maryhill but changed it to Merryl when she realized that some of the wines might not always use grapes or berries from the Maryhill area.

Niblack started working on the Chateau Merryl concept from the day she began at Old West. She helped design an attractive Lancers-type label, a small label in muted beige and red, and originated a unique bottle shape used only for the Chateau Merryl brand. She chose the Chateau moniker to highlight the gracious side to wine, and noted wryly that it was soon after that American Wine Growers developed its Chateau Ste. Michelle Vineyards brand. Chateau Merryl wines began to appear in about 1963, three years after Old West founder Harry Buttnick passed away.

Now Martha Niblack was clearly in control of the winery's direction. Buttnick's son, Jack, started to work at the winery during this time but tended to defer to Niblack's experience and vision. He described her as a "racehorse being held back."

Niblack had plans. She wanted stainless steel tanks, small oak barrels, a proper filtration system, and even a winery in eastern Washington that would be closer to the grapes. She wanted to educate the consumer. She wanted her wines in Safeway. In the hotels. On the family table.

She said, "I had invitation after invitation from people in Bellevue. . . . They had a home economics convention of some sort at Ocean Shores, so I made reservations there. I had recipes and I wanted to show off our product. I called [Ivan] Kearns and told him that I was going to do this and I would be delighted if any other Washington winery wanted to join me. I just wanted to see. . . . Two hundred people showed up! I ran out of everything. Many of those people contacted me; they wanted recipes.

"They wanted that touch of class, that touch of glamour that they associated with wine...and they were hungry for it....We had that window of opportunity to develop and create a taste."

Thoughtfully, she continued, "I don't think California's wines were any better than [Washington's]. The issue that we were addressing was a marketing issue. Ninety-eight percent of the people knew about wine, and 50 percent of the market was women who wanted to learn. We had that market and they were begging. And in California they cultivated it."

Chateau Merryl floundered. American Wine Growers' Vic Allison, always the competitor, kept Niblack's wines off the shelf at Safeway with his influence over the buyers. And the bank that controlled Harry Buttnick's trust tethered her expansion plans.

It was a tough, competitive marketplace. She was one of the only women directly involved in wine marketing in a landscape of men—men who didn't want to upset the status quo, and men who for so long had practiced the rules of competitive restraint.

Why hadn't she found someone else, another winery perhaps, to support her lofty ideals—why hadn't she gone directly to Vic Allison?

Defiantly she said, "I'm dedicated. I'm determined, and I'm not dumb," implying that it wouldn't have mattered. Going to Allison was out of the question. She had done the best that she could under the circumstances.

Niblack says the Washington wine industry should have put its money into improving its product and educating people, "putting wine on the table and teaching people how to talk about wine." She stated, "I believe Washington wines chose their direction, either consciously or unconsciously." With a heavy sigh she said, "You put your money where your heart is."

Old West Wines, and Chateau Merryl, made its last wines in 1969. Just before the winery closed, Vic Allison called her to express his sympathies. She recalls, haltingly, "I was really bitter . . . I can't say it. . . .

"The door had closed."

Chapter Sixteen

COMPETITION FROM CALIFORNIA

By the end of the 1940s, the California wine industry was convinced that Washington wineries would never be able to produce wines competitive in quality or quantity. California winemakers reasoned that Washington was simply too far north. They considered anything north of Ukiah, in Mendocino County, to be in danger of frost damage; Washington's primary wine region, the Columbia Valley, is more than 500 miles farther north. When California looked for new markets for its wine, it looked to Washington state.

Protective laws created during the first years after Repeal blocked California's ability to sell wine in Washington. In response, as early as 1935, California wine interests lobbied for relief against those protective laws. California's demands fell on deaf ears. The Washington wine industry was a huge success; it offered considerable employment in farm labor and in the distribution and sales of its wines. The Washington State Liquor Control Board was pleased at the industry's growth rate; it provided needed revenues to the state.

The Washington State Liquor Control Board had a vested interest in selling wine: the governor and state representatives increasingly looked to the board for increased revenues to balance the state budget. However, when the Washington wineries pulled their brands out of the state-run liquor stores to sell in taverns and retail stores, they created a schism between the Washington State Liquor Control Board and the Washington wine industry.

The board, looking for ways to further its sales of wine, turned to inexpensive California wine to sell to taverns. To arrive at a competitive price, inclusive of higher state taxes and markups, the liquor board, beginning in 1938, imported wine in bulk direct from California and then bottled it at its own warehouse. Suddenly the WSLCB, which was the regulator and enforcer, was in direct competition with the industry it was regulating, a most unfair and unparalleled situation. This led the Washington wine industry to argue for more protective legislation, including higher margins on California wines, to keep California wines out of the state, pointing out that Washington wineries couldn't compete with California without the protection of taxes and markups. The situation drew a battle line; the repercussions are felt to this day.

To counter their case, the director of the California Department of Agriculture wrote a letter to the liquor board in January 1942 hinting at possible retaliation against Washington lumber, apples, and beer. The letter also asked the board to reduce the markup on out-of-state wines to 53 percent instead of the average 75 percent.

William Bridgman, one of the chief advocates for the Washington wine industry and owner of Upland Winery, used his persuasive skills to defend the market share of Washington's wineries, while the Washington Liquor Control Board policies wreaked havoc. Bridgman was able to stop the California wine industry from restricting the use of the popular Washington pint bottle, but he couldn't stop the liquor board from importing California wine during the war years.

During the war, Washington wineries could hardly keep up with the huge demand created by the new influx of people into the state. The industry was crippled during the war by the fruit, grape, and sugar rationing policies established by the War Production Board and the Office of Price Administration (OPA). Sugar rationing especially affected the Washington wine industry, which depended upon sugar for the wines to reach even modest alcohol levels. Many in the Washington wine industry saw this as the result of manipulation by Californians, whose wineries dominated the committee set up to advise the OPA regarding policies affecting the wine industry. Californian board members knew that California winemakers could rely on raisins to boost the alcohol of their wines, whereas calling for a reduction in the availibility of sugar would affect northern winemakers.

When the Washington wine industry was unable to keep up with the demand of the taverns, the California wine industry, recognizing a golden opportunity, made several moves to increase its market share. It persuaded the OPA to lower the taxes on California wine in Washington state, a most unusual move by the OPA, as taxes were

virtually never lowered. Also, in a position paper presented to legislators (in 1965), William Bridgman states: "(The California wine industry) secured an OPA order which permitted—in Washington state
alone in the Union—a differential in price of wines sold by the glass
between California wines and the local wines." The California wine
industry thus got the price of its wine by the glass raised. California also
convinced the Washington State Liquor Control Board to make direct
deliveries of California wines to taverns, instead of making them buy
from state stores, based on the rationale of saving gasoline and rubber.

The California industry also began using 1-gallon bottles, effectively lowering their per-ounce price to the tavern owners. Bridgman
lamented in his 1965 position paper, "Of course, nearly every bartender
became a booster for California wines and told his customers that
California wines were superior in quality." Washington taverns asked
the liquor board to bring in more California wine. The liquor board
responded. Washington wineries began to lose market share immediately; Washington wine production decreased by nearly 15 percent in
1944, after annual increases the previous three years.

The liquor board's tenth annual report, for the fiscal year of
October 1, 1942, to September 30, 1943, proudly describes its actions:
"This combing of the wine markets has resulted in the board being able
to buy 54 percent more wine than it formerly purchased, when no
shortage existed." The board did make some disastrous purchases,
including 25,000 cases of Mexican wine, which remained in inventory
for many years. But the real damage to the wine industry occurred
when the liquor board began buying wine in bulk from California and
bottling it in Seattle. The board increased its sales by 54 percent during
1944; sales of Washington wines decreased by 21 percent. The liquor
board was competing directly with the Washington wine industry.

Bridgman was furious. Notes to the liquor board and to the legislature show his strong opposition to the board's policies. Bridgman had
spent many years pressing for protection of the Washington wine
industry, arguing that it was an important source of jobs and taxable
income for the state. He also pointed out that the industry for the most
part was agriculture-based. Earlier, in the '30s, prior to the great
buildup of the cities, these arguments carried weight with the rural-
based legislature, but no longer.

Besides, for most of the 1930s and 1940s, America was caught up
in a tangle of protective trade barriers. Even Bridgman encouraged protective legislation as part of the competitive scenery. Howard Somers

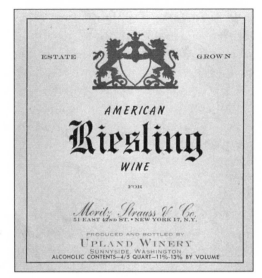

Riesling label from wine made at
Upland Winery, sold to wine store in
New York, possibly in the 1930s.
—*Photo courtesy of
Erica Swanson Steenborg.*

told me of a conversation he had had with Bridgman during the '60s, concerning competition from California wines. Bridgman, showing his legislative acumen, said, "Why don't you do what Boeing and the timber industry does and go down to the legislature and ask for enough to make yourselves rich rather than just asking for enough to keep yourselves in business?" Somers, thinking back reflectively, said to me, "Most of us just wanted to get a fair shake—a chance to stay in business and compete."

Bridgman didn't realize that his welcome was wearing out in Olympia. He had been so used to influencing the liquor board and persuading it to promote the state's wines that it took him awhile to realize the liquor board had its own agenda. As the wine industry matured, the Washington State Liquor Control Board aligned itself with California wine. Washington winemakers should have argued for a free competitive market in which Washington and California wines were available for sale on the same basis, either through the state stores or direct to the retailers. On the other hand, in a free market California would have crushed the Washington wine industry, as it did the fledgling Oregon wine industry when the laws were changed in that state to allow open and direct competition in 1955.

By 1948 the Washington wine industry's share of the state market had plummeted to 39 percent, down from the high of 65 percent in 1942. Meanwhile, the number of wineries in the state had dwindled to about 20, the result of increased consolidation within the industry as well as natural attrition. Bridgman counteracted the losses by lobbying for new regulations, in the form of higher taxes on California wines, which allowed Washington wineries to garner 53 percent of the wine business by 1958. It was clearly a dramatic turnaround.

By 1963 California dessert wines were paying a hefty 66.3 percent markup on delivered cost to the liquor board, and 53.6 percent on table wines. Additionally, the Washington wine industry continued to seek minimum prices and restrict the sales of out-of-state wines through the liquor board.

During the 1950s and '60s, the Washington wine industry was profoundly changed by several simultaneous developments. First, the Washington wine industry's rivalry with California affected not only the type of grape varieties that were planted, but also the protective liquor laws that remained in place since Prohibition; the resulting California Wine Bill paved the way for varietal wines. The second development was the sheer competitive drive of American Wine Growers and its refusal to be outdone by California or any Washington upstart. Third, a remarkable group of home winemakers eventually established Associated Vintners, the first Washington winery to sell only premium *vinifera* varietal wines. Fourth, the Wine Project linked winemakers with grape growers through the extraordinary research efforts at the Irrigated Agricultural Research and Extension Center in Prosser. The story of these developments is one of intertwined people and events that spanned several decades of Washington state history.

Part III

THE WINE PROJECT

"I think the Washington state recovery is one of
the greatest human stories in the wine industry."
Leon Adams, *The Wines of America*

Chapter Seventeen

THE CALIFORNIA WINE BILL

Somewhere there is a picture, taken in March 1969 at the conclusion of the Washington state legislative session, that shows four men seated on a sofa in the marbled walkway known succinctly as "ulcer gulch," which runs between the two legislative houses of the capitol dome in Olympia, Washington, the state's capital. The four men who sat for this photo were Syd Abrams, a wine broker for the E. & J. Gallo Winery; Tom Owens, a lobbyist for the California Wine Institute; Ivan Kearns, executive secretary of the Washington Wine and Grape Growers Council; and Victor Allison, general manager of American Wine Growers.

The picture captured in one frame all the genius behind the battle for the Washington wine market. The Washington State Senate and House had just passed into law House Bill 100, known derisively as the California Wine Bill, ending in one fell swoop all of the protectionist legislation enacted and piled up since the end of Prohibition. At the end of the battle, here were its warriors sitting together, overwhelmed by the process and symbolically in the same boat. Abrams, understanding the historical significance of the moment, asked a young man who was taking pictures of the capitol dome to take a picture of the four of them. Giving him his business card, Abrams asked that the picture be sent to him. He never received it.

House Bill 100 was a political and economic war. The battle was tough, nasty, and divisive, and sometimes comical, a struggle that went far beyond the issue of competitive fairness in the marketplace. The final vote mirrored a dramatic shift in the persona of Washington voters, a population torn between its frontier beginnings and its urbane future. The Senate and House voted to dismantle the barriers of the past and to adopt the credo of the future: open markets without tariffs and special interests.

There are two remarkable stories here. Besides the story of wine production and the change in consumer taste toward dry table wines, there is another, equally fascinating story about the changing legislative climate. In a sense, the California Wine Bill helped usher in a new openness in the legislative process by changing the political landscape.

—IVAN KEARNS—

The war years, the mid-1940s, were a critical time, when California and Washington wine interests were constantly sparring over war-rationed items such as sugar and glass. In 1946 the California Wine Institute hired Ivan Kearns as its Northwest representative. Kearns, who at thirty years old had started in 1936 as a clerk for the Washington State Liquor Control Board, rising to assistant store supervisor by 1945, was instructed by the California Wine Institute "not to undertake any educational work in the state of Washington which would be harmful to Washington wine or Washington wine growers." These instructions were a clear indication of the California wine industry's fear of the power of the Washington Wine Council and its stranglehold on the laws of the state.

The California wine industry sought and received some major concessions in its dealings with the state of Washington. The effect on the Washington wine industry was an immediate drop in sales. California had outmanuevered the locals. It is not clear how much of a role Kearns, as a representative for the California Wine Institute, had played in any of these developments. He may have been hired merely to soothe ruffled feathers.

In 1949 Kearns jumped ship and was hired as secretary of the Washington Wine Council, a position he held, off and on, for twenty years. At the same time he became the manager of Pommerelle. Carl Kroll, who worked for Pommerelle for thirty-two years, remembers Kearns fondly: "Under him new wines were added, chain-store outlets [were] negotiated, and there was, all around, more activity." Kroll recalled that Kearns was so successful that J. C. Sams, manager of National Wine Company (Nawico), engineered a merger of the two companies. In 1954, Kearns was replaced by Victor Allison.

In 1956, Kearns came close to buying the Upland Winery from William Bridgman. Kearns and Kroll visited the winery and decided not to buy it. Instead, Kearns fell back on what he did best: he brought producers together and forged a strong voice for the wine industry. During the '50s and '60s, he shaped an effective consumer education program about the advantages of Washington wines. During the late '50s, the Washington Wine Council, under the leadership of Ivan Kearns, stated that its purpose was "to promote better types and quality of grapes and fruit, develop closer cooperation with the Washington State College Experiment Station and to solve problems for growers and processors." Kearns understood very well that, to be competitive, Washington wines would have to strive to be the very best—whether the wines were specialty wines or table wines.

The Washington State Department of Commerce and Economic Development published a report in 1959 entitled "The Grape Industry in the State of Washington," under the direction of H. Dewayne Kreager. Included in the report was a section specifically on wine production and market data. It is a wonderful snapshot of the industry:

"The wine industry in the State of Washington shows every indication of being well over its 'Birth Pangs' and is fast reaching the age of maturity. An evaluation of its prospects should take place in the very near future. This industry has a true growth potential and could double its sales volume in the next ten years."

Further on the report states: "A projection of future population related to the present Washington per capita consumption shows almost a 650,000-gallon increase in 1970 over the 1958 consumption in the state.

". . . At present, the per capita consumption stands at 0.83 gallon. If, through an increasing standard of living and future promotion, the per capita consumption could be brought up to a full gallon, it would be a 17 percent increase in gallonage."

[A decade after this study, production levels were below those of 1959. It wasn't until 1984 that production doubled.]

A key section of the report offered some interesting criticisms of the wine industry:

1) As Fergus Hoffman stated in the *Seattle Times* on January 10, 1958, "One fault of (Washington) state wine is that it is not romantic."

Grape growers, winery owners, winemakers at the Wahluke Slope viewing soil profile.
Left to right: Martha Niblack (Old West Winery), William Lewis, John Molz (American Wine
Growers), William Barnard (Upland Winery), Victor Allison (American Wine Growers),
not known, Ed Mack, Vere Brummund (Aide at IAREC), Lester Fleming (American
Wine Growers), Jim Cole, George Thomas (Upland Winery), Don Wilson (Werberger
Winery), George Carter (Chemist at IAREC), not known, Robert Fox, Jake Holland, and
Ronald Tukey. Others not pictured: Walter Clore, Ray Milne, Lowell Quinn and Otis Harlan
(both of Alhambra). —*Photo by Walter J. Clore, May 17, 1967.*

To put it in stronger terms, Washington wine does not have "Beau
Monde."

2) A program for new types of bottles, corks, pricing, and label
designs is needed.

3) Develop brand names with romanticism—Gallic or Italianized or
authoritative connotation.

4) Request and partly finance Washington State University to make
studies of soils, climate, cultivation methods, land use, control, etc.,
and varietal development.

Also of interest, the report mentions that the *Seattle Times* "com-
piled and published the '1959 Consumer Analysis Findings.' Of the
195,400 families in the Seattle area, 3,600 were surveyed (1.84 percent)
for their buying preferences. Of the 15 brand names mentioned, only 4
were Washington-made brands. Only 26.6 percent showed a preference
for Washington wine by brand name. However, it is known that 54 percent of the wine made in Washington is consumed in this state.
Therefore, the assumption can be made that Washington wines are not
reaching the home consumer or the type of consumer on which the
Times based its study."

The report included a list of the consumer preference of leading brands in Seattle for the years 1955 to 1959. In 1959 the leading brands were, in order of preference: Christian Brothers (18.4 percent), Mogen David (12.7 percent), Manischewitz (9.2 percent), Pommerelle (9.1 percent), Roma (8.5 percent), Italian Swiss Colony (5.3 percent), Alhambra (4.5 percent), Petri (4.0 percent), Nawico (3.6 percent), and Gallo (2.4 percent).

The report concluded with a series of graphs and charts showing how wine grapes were utilized by the industry and showing their growth pattern. In 1959 there were approximately 500 acres of wine grapes in the state. As of 1957 the industry was processing 6,900 tons of grapes utilized for wine. There was also a good section on start-up costs and production information.

During the '50s, California's generic wines (with names like chablis or burgundy) still accounted for most of its table wine sales. Only a very few wineries were producing what today is called a varietal wine, a wine made from a single variety. Napa Valley was still a sleepy little backyard playground, a mix of rural farmland with a few premium wineries. There were less than 1,000 acres of premium wine grapes in the valley.

In the '50s the Grenache Rosé wines from California came out. Gallo began moving away from the very successful fortified-wine market into the table-wine market, although it still sold an equivalent amount of Thunderbird, an inexpensive, fortified specialty wine. Gallo produced an excellent table wine, Gallo Paisano Red, dry and flavorful, capturing the interest of an adventurous consumer. Gallo was spending money to educate the consumer, using clever advertising to appeal to the mass market. In one television ad, a man who looked much like Julio Gallo rode his white horse into a dinner party, admonishing guests to drink table wines—much like the Man From Glad commercials of the '70s.

Other California wineries also cast their marketing and winemaking efforts to the table wine industry. Some of the big players of the day were Almaden Vineyards, the California Wine Association (creators of the Eleven Cellars brand), Italian Swiss Colony, Paul Masson Vineyards, Mont La Salle Vineyards (a Christian Brothers brand), and Petri Wine Company. According to records from the Washington State Liquor Control Board, the best-selling table wines of the day were Almaden Grenache Rosé (6,050 cases), Le Domaine (Almaden)

Extra Dry Champagne (13,400 cases), Almaden White Chablis (4,650 cases); Eleven Cellars Vin Rosé (11,500 cases), Eleven Cellars Vino Fino Red (7,675 cases); E. & J. Gallo Paisano Red (25,650 cases), Gallo Vin Rosé (44,650 cases), Gallo Rhinegarten (25,275 cases); Guild Vino Da Tavola Burgundy (21,150 cases); Italian Swiss Colony Special Reserve Grenache Rosé (11,475 cases); and Christian Brothers Napa Rosé (5,300 cases).

In Washington, Ivan Kearns worked closely with American Wine Growers manager Victor Allison, a tough, no-nonsense competitor who continually found his company on a difficult course. The road he was on was lucrative; protective state measures made it easy to sell strong fortified wines to the taverns, and there was good money in it. But he could also see the California wine industry slowly approaching with its light table wines. Allison knew that if the Washington wine industry was going to remain a viable business, his company—and the rest of the industry—was going to have to experiment with table wines, especially table wines made from *vinifera* grapes.

Allison was no stranger to *vinifera* grapes. He had had a long relationship with grape growers in the Yakima Valley and further east into the lower Columbia Basin. Allison's dilemma was deciding what kinds of wines to make and, more to the point, who was going to drink Washington state table wines.

Allison watched with interest Upland Winery's efforts to produce and sell *vinifera* table wines. He knew that their sales represented less than 10 percent of the winery's volume. Even though indications were that the wine market was slowly turning away from the sweet fortified wines of the late '40s and early '50s, it wasn't clear what kind of wine the customers wanted.

The tendency for most Washington wineries was to blend in whatever *vinifera* grapes they had with the more readily available, and cheaper, *labrusca* grapes. But Allison and company (with help from Kearns) were quick to copy the Grenache Rosé wines from California. In 1956, under the Granada label, American Wine Growers put out one of its first *vinifera* wines, a Grenache Rosé.

Washington wineries were quick to see the trends; unfortunately, they were slow to respond. As long as the state's protective legislation remained in place, there was little incentive for them to change too drastically. Rather than respond quickly to the competition, they chose to gradually phase in the new table wines. Most Washington wineries were beginning to present a complete line of table wines that included a burgundy, a chablis, and a rosé. American Wine Growers led the pack. In 1965 AWG, led by Allison's vision, hired Howard Somers, formerly of St. Charles Winery, to begin making traditional table wines. That same year it planted White Riesling grapes on Hahn Hill north of Grandview.

Plantings of *vinifera* grapes had begun to expand in the mid-'50s. Nawico had planted Grenache grapes in 1950—it also bought Bridgman's Vineyard #6, which contained a mix of wine grapes. Meanwhile, W. B. Bridgman's main farm was growing Semillon. In 1957 Alhambra Winery of Selah planted Cabernet Sauvignon and Pinot Noir, while American Wine Growers planted Grenache, Pinot Noir, and Semillon. In 1963, AWG planted its first Cabernet Sauvignon vineyard at Benton City.

Other growers followed: Clarence Rush, a Kennewick barber, planted Riesling, Cabernet Sauvignon, and Pinot Noir in the lower Columbia Basin (Finley area); nearby, Doc Mercer planted 10 acres of Chardonnay, 6 acres of Riesling, and 4 acres of Pinot Noir; and Jim Blankenship put in 30 acres of Zinfandel and 6 of Semillon. In 1963 Associated Vintners, a group of home winemakers, planted its Harrison Hill vineyard on 5 acres purchased from W. B. Bridgman. Varieties planted included Cabernet Sauvignon, Pinot Noir, Grenache, Chardonnay, Semillon, White Riesling, and Gewurztraminer.

These plantings became an important new beginning for table wines in this state because the winery owners were committed to making dry table wines. They were a complete break from the immediate past. This effort played a major role in convincing state lawmakers that Washington state was capable of producing quality wines that could compete with the wines of California.

—LEON ADAMS—

Howard Somers told me of the agony of watching his family winery get squeezed by the changing times. It became clear to him that in order for St. Charles Winery to succeed, the family should move their entire operation to eastern Washington. But his father was happy with his life; if the winery wasn't particularly profitable for a few years, it seemed like the real estate business would tide them over. His father could run both businesses out of the old farmhouse on Stretch Island. Howard's older brother, Bill, was pretty settled in. Howard, with younger children, and his wife tired of being wed to the winery, wanted change.

Howard's father's death in 1961 forced the brothers into a decision. Like most decisions in life, Howard got some outside help: American Wine Growers began to talk to him about the possibility of buying out the St. Charles Winery. This forced them to consider the inevitable: Somers recalled, "My brother wasn't interested in that. We went on for a couple of years—I could project things getting worse and worse. So I finally got my brother to set a price for which he would sell his share of the operation. He didn't really want to sell." However, they didn't sell the winery to American Wine Growers.

In 1965 Howard Somers left the St. Charles Winery to work for American Wine Growers. At the same time, he brokered a sale of St. Charles Winery's inventory and brand names to the Alhambra Winery in Selah, located northeast of Yakima. At American Wine Growers, Somers was anxious to begin producing table wines.

Somers was one of the few trained winemakers in the state. He hadn't attended a wine college but he was a trained chemist. He was the winemaker for St. Charles Winery and had become familar with some of the great winemakers of California. Somers had been a founding member of the American Society of Enology and Viticulture. His friends included many of the great California winemakers: Carl Wente, Louis Martini, and Myron Nightingale. And he knew well Jules Fessler of the Berkeley Laboratory. All were carrying the table wine banner, pointing California wines in a new direction.

Somers was also well acquainted with journalist Leon Adams, writing then for the various newspapers in the Bay Area. Adams had visited the St. Charles Winery prior to the second world war and fell in love with it. Somers remarks fondly, "He was really impressed that we could grow oysters and grapes, and make wine, at the same property." It was Adams's ideal winery: producing wine from primarily its own locally grown grapes, the Island Belle. He felt it was the quintessential American winery using a grape propagated to match the climate and growing conditions of Puget Sound. Somers recalled that Adams was convinced it would be good for the entire wine business if there was a wine industry in as many states as possible.

Adams became a very important beacon for many of the wine industries outside of California. As a founding member of the California Wine Institute, his voice carried far. His philosophy was shaped around the European model: each area strives to make wines unique to its soil and climate. Adams was no wine snob; he understood the virtues of *vinifera*, but he could also appreciate the practicality of *labrusca* and other American species, or even hybrids: as long as the grapes were used, and allowed, to express the wine's climatic situation, with flavors uncorrupted by huge doses of residual sugar or euthanized by the addition of brandy. He argued for drier-styled table wines that express the true character of the grape. He wasn't alone.

Adams and Fessler and the new cadre of California winemakers were pressing for the new-style table wines, taking advantage of the latest developments in stainless steel tanks and filtration to make dry table wines, or even slightly sweet wines that at least showed the varietal flavors of the wine.

Somers knew that with this same technology, Washington state could begin producing top-quality table wines. When he was hired by American Wine Growers in 1965, he was greeted with a commitment from Vic Allison to produce table wines. Allison expected Somers to guide AWG to the realm of table wines.

That first year was very tentative, as Somers began to explore what varieties were in American Wine Growers' vineyards. It wasn't until the 1966 vintage that Somers really began to make his first table wines.

That same year, in the spring of 1966, Leon Adams visited Washington state to research material for his book *Wines of America*, published in 1973. In the book he writes, "I visited the Yakima Valley and saw several vineyards of such pedigreed varieties as Cabernet Sauvignon and Pinot Noir. I was amazed to find the wineries were wasting these costly grapes, mixing them with Concord in nondescript port and burgundy blends. The only fine *vinifera* wine I tasted on that trip was a Grenache Rosé made by a home winemaker in Seattle."

When Adams visited Howard Somers at the American Wine Growers winery down on East Marginal Way in Seattle, Somers had no wines made yet from the 1966 vintage because harvest was months away, and he could only offer Adams to taste wines from the previous vintages. Even his own wines that he had made that first year in 1965 were not ready, nor had he begun to work with individual varieties. Adams was disappointed in the wines, having seen the potential in the vineyards in eastern Washington. Adams wanted to know if anyone was making *vinifera* wines. He had tasted some of the first wines produced by Chas Nagel at the Irrigation Experiment Station in Prosser, and he was impressed to learn that the research had been funded primarily by American Wine Growers. Although the experimental wines were youthful and unfinished, Adams was sophisticated enough to understand the significance of their chemical analysis; the wines were perfectly balanced in acids and sugars, with bright, assertive flavors.

Somers had the good grace to call Dr. Lloyd Woodburne to see if he had any wines that Adams could sample. Somers had had a continuing dialogue with Woodburne over the previous year, Somers had helped Woodburne's group (Associated Vintners) get grapes, and they compared notes on winemaking. Somers, a soft-spoken man, was often disappointed in his dealings with Woodburne; he felt that Woodburne didn't respect him or his efforts to make premium wines—Woodburne was so full of his own efforts toward that goal. Somers recalled that Cornelius Peck and others in the Associated Vintners tended to be more tolerant.

Woodburne came over to the winery and brought a bottle of his Grenache Rosé, a wine that he had made in his garage. Adams liked it. There is some irony in this: Woodburne had made this wine out of grapes he had bought from Vic Allison, the very grapes over which Fleming had mused, "They just seemed like they was being fussy."

Adams then recommended to Vic Allison that if American Wine Growers wanted to improve the quality of its wines, it should invite a good California enologist to consult with AWG. Adams recommended that AWG talk to a number of enologists, including André Tchelistcheff, the winemaker at Beaulieu Vineyards.

A year later, Tchelistcheff visited American Wine Growers. Before this, Tchelistcheff knew little of Washington state except that his nephew, Alex Golitzen (who now has his own winery, Quilceda Creek, near Everett), lived there. In Tchelistcheff's heavily accented words, "I knew that the Concord was well known as a fruit, an industrial fruit, in Washington state and many of us, including Gallo, were deeply involved in the production of grape juice and fermenting some wines for aromatic reasons. Concord was a big thing. My first impression of the wines was really negative."

When he tasted the wines at American Wine Growers with Vic Allison and Howard Somers, he was very disappointed. Tchelistcheff recalled, "The wines had no charm. There was very little academic knowledge involved with the winemaking then at the winery." Tchelistcheff was about to return to California that evening, closing the door to Washington wines behind him.

Woodburne, knowing that Tchelistcheff was in town, called him and asked him if he could stop by the new Associated Vintners winery in Kirkland. Here Tchelistcheff was to meet the academic side of the wine industry. He stayed for dinner at Phil Church's home and was astounded by the Gewurztraminer that Church had made.

He had found the charm that he was looking for. Shortly afterward, Vic Allison wrote him requesting that he become a consultant to American Wine Growers. Tchelistcheff accepted and later that year he came back to Seattle. Vic Allison and Howard Somers drove him over to eastern Washington to visit their vineyards. Along with Les Fleming, they visited the research center at Prosser. There they met with Dr. Clore and sampled wines made by Chas Nagel and George Carter. Dr. Clore's notes indicate they were most impressed by the Grenache and Cabernet Sauvignon, and noted that the Pinot Meunier and the Barbera showed promise. It was noted that the Gewurztraminer and the Riesling were too low in alcohol.

This laid the groundwork for American Wine Growers. Now, with Tchelistcheff's help, it had made the intellectual leap in an attempt to make premium table wines. That fall in 1967, Howard Somers made his first commercial batch of vintage-dated varietal wines under AWG's new brand name, Ste. Michelle Vineyards: Semillon, Pinot Noir, Cabernet Sauvignon, and Grenache.

In 1969 Leon Adams accompanied Tchelistcheff to Seattle to taste these first wines from the Ste. Michelle label. He wrote in the second edition (1978) of his *Wines of America*, "We tasted separately, scoring them as unfinished wines, and then compared our notes. Tchelistcheff gave the 1967 Cabernet Sauvignon seventeen out of a possible twenty points, sixteen to the 1968 Semillon, and fifteen and sixteen to the two Grenache Rosés. The Pinot Noir wasn't ready to be tasted. I scored the Cabernet a point higher and my other scores were close to Tchelistcheff's."

A year later these wines were tasted by the San Francisco Sampling Club. They showed very well. The club's newsletter editor, W. H. Peterson, asked rhetorically, "Is the supremacy of California's quality varietal wines challenged?" His answer: "The quality of three wines tasted at the San Diego conference of the American Society of Enologists in June promises a serious challenge in the near future." He then gave a general background to these wines, giving credit to the WSU research center at Prosser. He credited Vic Allison with development of the wines, with assistance from Lester Fleming as manager of the Grandview winery and vineyards. He also credited Howard Somers, citing his academic achievements and his twenty years' experience in the Washington wine industry.

He then went on to share his tasting notes:

The wine is labeled as "Ste. Michelle Vineyards—Semillon—produced and bottled by bonded winery number 8." The wine has a pleasing brilliance and is a pale yellow. The aroma is very generous, with a flowery perfume and aromatic scents. The flowery fragrance has the sweetness of honeysuckle but without its heavy redolent qualities; the aromatic quality suggests a gossamer touch of a grapefruit's zest. In the background is a crisp green accent that contains the mossy freshness of a mountain stream tumbling over granite boulders. There is a slight amount of sulfur dioxide.

With the first sip, the perfume scents intensify, as does the pungency of the sulfur dioxide. In the mouth the floral qualities, while still delicate in composition, become heavier in character and dominate the flavor. The taste is fresh and clean but not tart.

With a bigger mouthful, the wine is unexpectedly round and full for a wine of such elegant and refined flavor. It has a slight sweetness that is balanced by a proper amount of acidity. It is not astringent, but there is a slight earthy-humus quality in the taste that is characteristic of wines made from Semillon grapes.

After swallowing, long lingering flavors remain on the palate. At first the flavors are the heady floral perfumes with a slight resinous quality; these taper gradually into an aromatic, faintly citrus-like taste. Throughout its changes the finish maintains a clean freshness. A slight bitterness develops that is very pleasant, and very late a clean straw-like flavor remains.

This wine is unusually generous in delicate fragrance and flavor for a Semillon. It is a full wine with excellent balance and moderate complexity. The resinous and citrus scents and flavors that are so attractive now will probably not last beyond eighteen months. It is an excellent wine to enjoy now but not one to lay away.

This wine placed second behind the dry wine, 1965 "Y," made by Chauteau d'Yquem, priced at $2.40 a bottle. Ste. Michelle's Semillon listed at $1.89 for the 1968 vintage. Immediately following was Tchelistcheff's own Beaulieu Vineyards' 1966 Semillon, followed by wines from Concannon, Martini, and Charles Krug.

The San Francisco and San Diego tastings were a perfect launching pad for these first wines from Ste. Michelle Vineyards. The wines were spotted by retailer Darrel Corti of Corti Brothers in Sacramento. Darrel Corti began importing the wines into its huge Sacramento delicatessen, with its sprawling wine cellar in the basement. Corti judged the wines as more European than Californian and praised their fresh acids and flavors.

In four short years since Adams had first glimpsed the potential for Washington wines in 1966, the wines were making headlines in California. It appeared that Vic Allison had perfected the magician's hat trick, pulling out of his hat the genius of varietal wines. Posed alongside Associated Vintners' first wines, written up that same year by Stan Reed of the *Seattle Post-Intelligencer*, Washington wines definitely fit Leon Adams's pointed appraisal: "It's a miracle!"

—SYD ABRAMS'S STRATEGY—

In 1967, Washington State House Bill 635, which attempted to remove protective wine regulations, was presented by Representative Dave Ceccarelli, Seattle Democrat. It failed by one vote, cast by the Speaker of the House, Republican Don Eldridge, who cited "outright vote buying and bullying" as reasons for defeating the bill, referring, I assume, to attempts by the California wine industry to buy the vote. During the following legislative off-season (in those days, the legislature was in session every other year, not every year), Syd Abrams, a wine broker for the E. & J. Gallo Winery, began to draw up a battle plan to pass new legislation in the 1969 legislature.

Abrams first became involved with the wine laws in his work for a Seattle advertising agency that handled the California Wine Institute account. In 1968, Abrams sent a memo to the E. & J. Gallo Winery, California's largest winery and largest voting member of the California Wine Institute, suggesting that "the time was right" to change the protective wine laws in Washington state. He was invited to the Gallo winery, where he presented his plan. He then sought a Washington state lobbyist for the California Wine Institute. He asked people from both political parties to recommend someone.

Ultimately he settled on Tom Owens, a young attorney known for his appreciation of fine wine. He was one of those odd sorts who actually drank wine with his lunch. Owens was married to Angela Pellegrini, daughter of noted food and wine lover Angelo Pellegrini.

Owens, who was then working as a lobbyist for the billboard industry, was known as an effective power broker. He was young, smart, and aggressive, a perfect complement to the soft-spoken, cerebral Abrams.

Convincing state lawmakers that Washington state was capable of producing quality wines that could compete with the wines of California became part of the strategy of Syd Abrams and the California Wine Institute. They had decided sometime in 1968 to broaden the appeal of the California Wine Bill. The California wine industry had failed to pass its original legislation in the 1967 legislature because it so brazenly tried to buy its way through the political process. Obviously another tactic would need to be tried.

For the '69 legislature, if legislative action was going to be successful in changing the wine laws of the state, the California wine industry had to make a public issue of the campaign. Abrams and Owens knew that the wine bill could win on its merits but were doubtful that they could get the bill through the powerful committees. Merely tossing money at the legislators hadn't worked in '67 and wouldn't have worked in '69 (although that didn't stop them from spending a lot of money). Instead it was decided to launch a public campaign and to organize a grassroots effort to change the law.

In the 1969 legislature, House Bill 100 was sponsored by Republican Representative Hal Wolf, a supermarket owner from Yelm. There was little doubt that the bill would pass once it got to the floor for a vote. But there were many hurdles the bill had to pass before the members of both houses voted. The most powerful were the Ways and Means Committee and the Rules Committee of both houses. Committee chairs could rule the legislature by keeping a close rein on committee members. The Rules Committee also met in secret, a situation made ripe for power brokers—the perfect setting for Ivan Kearns.

In the old-school legislature (1969 was one of its last years), vast amounts of power were vested in committee chairs, and legislation was often handled in closed-door meetings. Those were the days of concentrated power—if not corrupt, then certainly venal. Legislation was made or died at the committee level. It was a much more streamlined process. It wasn't necessary to go through time-consuming consensus building. Of course, some legislation never made it out of committee; there was never a question of consensus. And rarely did a legislative action get voted on based purely on merit.

That is why Ivan Kearns was so sure that he could control the process. As executive secretary of the Washington Wine and Grape Growers Council (the restructured Washington Wine Council), he had instituted a two-cent-a-gallon slush fund assessed from members of the council. By 1968 Kearns convinced growers, who sold to wineries, to pay the council a dollar per ton of harvested grapes. Much of these funds were distributed to legislators in both houses who were allies of the Washington wine industry. Foremost was Senator Robert Grieve, Seattle Democrat and Senate Majority Leader. Grieve was the point man and distributed money to various supporters. But Kearns didn't just go through Grieve. He went directly to various legislators and contributed to their political campaigns either with outright donations or by purchasing campaign materials.

Kearns believed that he could also stop the California Wine Bill in the Senate Rules Committee. He had a powerful friend in Lieutenant Governor John Cherberg, a Democrat, who also chaired the Rules Committee. Cherberg was considered a fair and impartial person but he had reason to support Kearns. For one thing, he had just finished a tough challenge to his office from the Republican Party's candidate, Art Fletcher. Kearns had supported Cherberg, and Cherberg probably felt beholden to him.

Kearns, however, had misjudged the mood of the legislators on two important counts. First, he may have worn his welcome thin. Throughout the '67 campaign he indicated that it would be his last battle and that he would retire. The rallying cry had been "one last one for Ivan." During the '69 campaign, his rallying cry changed. It became "just give the Washington wine industry a few years to make the change;" and during the last stages of the campaign, "a few years" became "ten years." Second, Kearns, so sure that he could kill the bill in committee, lost sight of the issues.

Meanwhile, Abrams and Owens clearly stated, "The merit of the issue is trade barriers." They argued forcefully that there was no longer any justification for barriers, that barriers were part of the past. They argued the quality issue. The relatively recent, and drier, California table wines were clearly superior, and a very vocal minority of wine drinkers who wanted access to these exciting new table wines were beginning to be heard.

Among the vocal minority of wine drinkers who made themselves heard was Dr. Belding Scribner, a renowned professor of medicine at the University of Washington credited with helping develop the kidney dialysis machine. In 1969, while Scribner and his wife were away on a medical conference in New Jersey, their home was raided by agents of the Washington State Liquor Control Board acting on a tip from the disgruntled wife of one of Scribner's best friends. The liquor board, upon raiding Dr. Scribner's home, found a large cellar of imported and California wines. When Scribner returned home, he found an inventory list of confiscated wines "left conspicuously on the coffee table."

The next day Scribner turned himself in at the county jail, where he was photographed, booked, and fingerprinted. In court he was found guilty and received a six-month suspended sentence for "possession of illegal alcohol," and fined $250. As part of the negotiations, he was allowed to buy back his collection by paying 76.654 percent of the original retail purchase price. He bought what he could of his beloved Bordeaux chateaux and contacted friends to buy the rest.

In a *Seattle* magazine article that he authored entitled "A Wine Smuggler Spills All," he noted the considerable bad publicity that he received and lamented about having a "mug shot" and fingerprints on file with the FBI. Then he says, "These things resulted not from my having done anything which I consider morally wrong, but rather from my having broken a state law designed to protect Washington 'wines' which, to my palate, are undrinkable." He stated that the laws should be changed so that "Washington might well become as famous for its wines as it is for its apples and its airplanes."

Scribner was a part of the university crowd that included Dr. Angelo Pellegrini, Dr. Lloyd Woodburne, Cornelius Peck, and others. Pellegrini had written his wonderful book *Wine and the Good Life* in 1965, a rallying call to the intelligentsia (the new upper middle-class) to explore the pleasures of wine. It was a wonderful collection of anecdotes, vignettes, and lectures about the enjoyment of fine wine and food. In the book, Pellegrini praised California wine and the movement toward table wines. In a chapter entitled "Is There an American Wine Fit to Drink?" he noted, "In our own state, a group of dedicated wine men have planted several acres of choice hybrids. As wine drinkers, we wish them luck, for the success will be our pleasure. Meanwhile we must look to California for most of the dinner wines in our cellars."

It was Pellegrini who counseled Dr. Lloyd Woodburne in making wine at home in 1951. This led Woodburne to seek out a group of home winemakers. Initially they used California grapes, primarily Zinfandel, that came by train into Georgetown in south Seattle. One year, they had difficulty getting all the grapes they needed and Woodburne, who was interested in making white wines, began to explore vineyards in eastern Washington, around Sunnyside. This led his group, later known as Associated Vintners, to W. B. Bridgman, who supplied them with their first Washington grapes. Bridgman, once again, was about to pass along the wine torch.

The efforts of Associated Vintners were not lost on Syd Abrams. He had been introduced to its wines through his Mercer Island neighbor and friend, Alec Bayless. Bayless had befriended some of the vintners in Woodburne's group and he became interested in the idea of grape growing himself. Abrams remembered traveling to eastern Washington and visiting Dr. Walter Clore at the research center in Prosser. There they tasted some of the first experimental wines made by Dr. Chas Nagel in Pullman. These wines were to affect both men, in slightly different ways: for Bayless, it was motivation to start a vineyard; for Abrams, it was proof that Washington wine could indeed compete against California wines, without trade barriers.

—LEGISLATIVE HEARINGS—

Prior to the '69 legislative session, a joint Senate and House committee of the Commerce and Agricultural Committees held two important hearings—one in Yakima, the other at the University of Washington—to collect information about the implications of the changes in the wine laws. Abrams recalled that Cornelius Peck, one of the partners in Associated Vintners, said at the University of Washington hearing that the protectionist laws were the only thing that were keeping Washington from producing quality wines. Peck stated in a provocative voice, "I'm not afraid to compete; we can. If we can't, we don't deserve to be in business."

Records of the hearing in Yakima make fascinating reading; tension hung in the hearing room. Robert Grieve was greatly annoyed that Tom Owens brought a court reporter to record the hearing. Included are testimonies from Dr. Clore and Dr. Nagel of Washington State University, Victor Rosellini (noted Seattle restaurateur), and Ivan Kearns. Rosellini spoke about his restaurant needing to be able to offer his customers good quality wines. He pointed out the difficulty of ordering special wines through the liquor board, complaining that "we in the business have to wait anywhere from two weeks to a hundred days on special orders to get them." Continuing, he said, "I think, furthermore—I am very proud of our state, and I wish they'd do something about producing a better table wine, and I would love to serve it. I have no objection to the product that we produce in this state, but I can truthfully tell you that I would love to serve Washington wines if they were the type of wines the public would buy."

Robert Grieve, chairman of the joint committee, wanted to know how the state was going to make up the $5 million in lost revenue from profit and taxes that the state collected through the sale of wine in the liquor stores.

Rosellini shot back, "We could increase sales, number one. I think, number two, if you are going to have distributors you are certainly going to license them, aren't you?" Grieve responded: "Five million dollars' worth?"

Rosellini then explained to the joint committee how a system of wholesalers would provide better distribution of hard-to-find wines because the wholesalers would tend to specialize and be more willing to carry unique brands to keep their customers happy.

Then Dr. Clore was introduced to the committee by Dr. John S. Robins, director of research at the College of Agriculture at Washington State University. Dr. Clore testified, "About four years ago, through the efforts of the Washington Wine and Grape Growers Council, we were encouraged to increase our research on the adaptability of certain grape varieties for wine production. We have been working since 1937, at least I have, on grape varieties and grape problems in the Yakima Valley."

Dr. Clore continued his testimony: "At the present time there's somewhere between 10,000 and 10,500 acres of grapes. Approximately 800 acres of these go into the production of wine, and approximately 50 percent of those that go into wine are of the *vinifera* type of grape. This is the European type of grape. This is for the past five years including 1967—the state has an average production of 61,200 tons. Last year's production was 72,500, I believe. About 90 percent of this goes for Concord juice concentrate and jelly.

"We do not feel that we can compete favorably with California in table grapes or in varieties of table grapes that are used in producing the sweet wines. So we have investigated the varieties of wines that are known around the world for their high quality in producing premium wines, such as Chardonnay, Semillon, White Riesling, Chenin Blanc, and others. Red wines would be Cabernet Sauvignon, Pinot Noir, Grenache, and others.

"We have found thus far through our research that many of these varieties seem to be well adapted here from the standpoint of producing good yields and wine of good to excellent quality. Many of these grapes here are more productive in our climate than in California, particularly when compared to the fine areas of the Bay region around San Francisco. We have more light intensity, we have a longer daylight period during the growing season, while they have fog early in the season and in the mornings and also late in the season, and then some cloudy weather. When we get hot weather, they get hot weather, and we can grow a grape up to a certain sugar content; 22 percent is considered quite acceptable with a good balance of acid, and it is this kind of grape that makes a high-quality wine. We feel, if our research continues to prove this point, that we can compete very favorably in producing top table and varietal wines with any other region in the United States, and we can do it with California, and we can do it with other parts of the world.

"The states of Washington and Oregon, and the province of British Columbia, are in the latitudes of the fine wine regions of Europe—France and Germany. The one thing that we do have against us that California doesn't usually have [is] subzero weather. About every eight years we'll get temperatures below zero, and this means that it is very difficult for the *vinifera* varieties or the top wine varieties of the world to survive. However, we do not have all of the insect and disease problems that California has, so we can grow grapes on their own roots; so if [the vines] do kill back (because of cold), they come back within the following year and you lose (only) one year's crop.

"Our work at the research center at Prosser is to develop cultural practices that will allow us to grow a good crop of grapes every year. We are studying different methods and also covering the grapes, where we cover the base part of the vine so if the upper part gets killed back, we have the lower part to depend on for production.

"So far we have not had wines of any age to give out for evaluation, but the wines that have been evaluated by Dr. Nagel in Pullman through his taste clinic—and I wouldn't say this if we didn't have favorable comments from California—show considerable promise."

After Dr. Clore testified, Dr. Robins introduced Dr. Charles Nagel, a food scientist in the department of horticulture at Washington State University at Pullman. Nagel made some introductory comments about his research, pointing out that he was involved with testing up to 50 different varieties of wines and then subjecting them to taste comparisons based on a scoring system developed by the University of California Davis. Chairman Grieve went right to the point: "How do the Washington wines compare?"

Dr. Nagel said, "In my opinion, quite favorably with certain varieties of any produced in the world, according to our taste panel."

Senator Joel Pritchard asked, "Is it your opinion that we could have first-class table wines from the grapes grown here?"

Dr. Nagel replied, "Well, again, as a scientist I would like to accumulate more data, but I personally am convinced; yes, we can."

Representative Stu Bledsoe asked, "Would it look like there's a real possibility for the wine industry in this state?"

Dr. Nagel responded, "We are convinced of it. Incidentally," Nagel added, "there is another reason why we are looking into it that may not have been made clear. Those of you who are in Concord grape production realize that you are producing about as much as the market can take and yet you have the competence to grow grapes. Why not have a second crop, a varietal wine grape that you can grow next to your Concord?"

Then Ivan Kearns requested to testify. He was not on Grieve's list of people to testify.

Kearns said, "I thought I was on that list."

Vice-Chairman Wolf replied, "Ivan, somebody took you seriously when you said you were tired."

Ivan Kearns testified to the nature of trade barriers, and how barriers are erected all the time by various industries. He then pressed his point that HB 635 (the 1967 version of HB 100) should definitely be considered a "California wine bill." Kearns detailed how the state of Oregon ten years earlier had passed similar legislation and as a result no vineyards remained and there was no longer an Oregon wine industry. He further pointed out "that two California wineries sell 78 percent of the wine that is sold in Oregon and the complete amount of California wine sold in Oregon is 92.4 percent. Now this leaves for all foreign wines, all other states, including the state of Oregon, 7.6 percent of sales within that state. We feel the very same thing would be applicable to us in this state should such a bill as HB 635 go through."

Senator Pritchard then asked, "I am trying to, in my own mind, come up with the reason why we are not competitive. California and, I see, New York and some of these other states are starting to come on here in a competitive way. Why have we [in] just the last few years started to...why haven't we done more in this field of research, which any other industry does? I'll bet the beer industries spend thousands of dollars in research."

Kearns responded, "I, many times, would have liked to have that answered for me also, Senator Pritchard. We have been late. I admit that we are tardy in getting started. I think we are making good progress in that area now. I think maybe the good doctors have left you thinking that the only wine that has been produced from these grapes was in the experimental stage, and this is not true. We have today wineries with Cabernets, Chardonnays, and other types that are now aging and under control and will be marketed one of these days."

Senator Pritchard then questioned what Kearns meant by "one of these days."

Kearns responded, "I would say that probably some white wines will go on the market this fall. The red wines are slower in aging, and it took us of course some time to get enough plantings to give us a volume of wine."

Senator Pritchard continued to press Kearns, asking why the Washington wine industry hadn't spent money on research. Kearns stated that the Washington Wine and Grape Growers Council contributed about $1,250 per year to the research center for grape research. Another $25,000 came from the state for processing and production research. Pritchard asked why we couldn't be competitive with California. Kearns replied that Washington could never compete because of higher grape costs, without access to raisin grapes for blending and sweetening and without access to a large surplus.

Then Representative Bledsoe pointed out to Kearns that sales figures from the Washington State Liquor Control Board showed a dramatic increase in table wines. He singled out rosé wines, noting that there was a 56 percent increase in one particular wine, with sales increases from 6,000 cases to 9,000 cases.

Kearns shot back, "But they have been doing it longer."

To which Bledsoe replied, "Well, we are not going to argue peanuts, but it looks like that's the way to go. And—I don't know—as long as you have a protective setup, the rate at which you get there is going to be just about as slow as the rate you have gotten there so far. That's the way it looks to me. I could be wrong."

For Abrams and Owens, the battle lines had been clearly drawn. At issue was how the state was going to make up for lost revenue if wine sales were going to go to private stores, a point pressed repeatedly by Senator Grieve. Abrams and Owens hoped to show that the increase in sales would make up the difference, and also that the liquor board would have to impose a tax on the sales of all wines to make up for the shortcoming. Eventually, this tax was set at 25 percent.

Abrams's and Owens's efforts were directed to showing that there was a change occurring in the wine industry, led by the California wine industry, toward lighter and drier wines. They argued persuasively that Washington wines were stuck in a rut of sweet dessert wines sold mostly in taverns; they reasoned that the protective laws that had accrued since the repeal of Prohibition made it nearly impossible for the industry to change.

Abrams used as his weapon Boddewyn's 1964 UW doctoral thesis entitled *The Protection of Washington Wines: A Case Study in the State Regulation of Business.* His thesis shows how the protection of Washington wines became a complicated pattern of competing interests. This pattern of protection outlined by Boddewyn was to change slightly over the years. Increasingly, the board felt less inclined to support the Washington wine industry because of its own vested interests in California wines. The board shifted responsibility for protecting the Washington wine industry to the legislature and, to a lesser degree, the governor's office. Throughout the '50s, most of the work of the Washington Wine Council had been directed toward the legislature.

This continued into the '60s, with Ivan Kearns at the helm of the council. In 1960 Kearns helped reorganize the wine council into the Washington Wine and Grape Growers Council, a much more powerful lobbying group that would be used effectively during the campaign against the California Wine Bill. Kearns understood well the need to associate the wine industry with its agricultural roots, and he targeted some of the more powerful legislators who, at that time, were from eastern Washington farming communities.

The California wine industry continued to keep pressure on the Washington State Legislature and the governor's office by continued threats of retaliation on Washington's beer, apples, and lumber. In 1958 the state of California brought suit in the United States Supreme Court against the state of Washington in an effort to open up the wine market. California charged in the suit, "The Washington laws here challenged are not intended to and do not have the effect of promoting the cause of temperance; they do not in design and effect make use of the police power of the State of Washington to protect and promote the public health, safety and morals of the people of that state; nor do they serve the legislative purposes which the Twenty-first Amendment was enacted to promote." And, further, California stated that the single issue of substance was, "Can a state, which does not prohibit the use and consumption of wine by its citizens, prescribe a wholly different economic system for the distribution, marketing, pricing and sales promotion of wine produced elsewhere...and thereby confer economic and competitive advantages upon locally produced wine, which are denied to wine produced elsewhere?"

The U.S. Supreme Court refused to rule on the case. In essence, the Supreme Court reaffirmed that the state power to control liquor commerce was freed from most of the restrictions imposed by the Constitution on other areas of commerce. Kearns was able to forcefully use this ruling to keep legislators on his side, telling them that California's continued threats of retaliation were meaningless because even though Washington state could erect wine trade barriers, it was against federal law for California to erect similar barriers against the threatened products.

The California wine industry could stand it no longer. In 1967 it brought its full weight against the Washington State Legislature in an attempt to pass Substitute House Bill 635. It poured huge sums of money into the campaign—openly buying legislators' votes. But to no immediate avail.

By 1969, using a concerted grassroots effort (and considerable money) choreographed by Abrams and Owens, the California Wine Bill defeated Ivan Kearns. Kearns, in a last-ditch effort, had tried to gain time for the industry by arguing, "Just give the Washington wine industry a few years." Kearns, and Vic Allison at American Wine Growers, had given the legislators bottles of Ste. Michelle Vineyards' new varietal wines to show that Washington could indeed make varietal table wines, and argued that they just needed more time.

Time had run out, however. The final tally in the Senate on March 24, 1969, was thirty-six yeas and twenty-four nays. Of that final vote, Grieve and Abrams had very different interpretations. According to Grieve, during the final vote a California representative was sitting up in the gallery above the Senate floor signaling to senators that he would give them more money. Abrams laughed at this; he said, "That was me. I was counting the votes."

What is clear, however, is that the final vote for House Bill 100, which was signed by Governor Dan Evans on April 2, went far beyond the merits of the bill. It represented a dramatic power shift in the legislature, as Grieve's grip on power was overturned by the young new upstarts. The battle of House Bill 100 left plenty of spilled blood (and wine). And Washington's wine industry was turned upside down.

The full story of what went on will remain behind closed doors. In 1978, at Vic Allison's funeral, Syd Abrams approached Ivan Kearns and said, "You know, Ivan, we owe it to Victor to tell our stories."

"Never," said Ivan Kearns.

Chapter Eighteen

ASSOCIATED VINTNERS

William Bridgman and Lloyd Woodburne, a home winemaker who later started Associated Vintners, began communicating as early as 1954. In one of the first letters to Woodburne, Bridgman the patriarch lent his support and encouragement to Woodburne, stating, "I welcome any constructive criticism of the wine industry, such as you have given.

"I wish you would try some of my 'vin ordinaire,' namely a quite dry Zinfandel wine, or my semi-sweet Concord, if you like Concord flavor, as many do.

"I have made and marketed fine dry wines, Riesling, sauterne, and burgundy, which the best group of wine connoisseurs I know of preferred to all others."

Continuing, he wrote, "But the demand for such wines is so small that a winery cannot make any profit on them. The public demands the heavy, sweet wines, and that is what we must make and sell if we are to remain in business. I have discontinued the Riesling and dry sauterne for that reason."

Then, poignantly, he wrote, "While our state wineries have not developed the best types of fine dry wines, whether the public will in time learn to appreciate them is the question."

Woodburne's letters reflect an inquisitive and suspicious personality: there is a sense that he was unwilling to accept the status quo and was trying to fathom a vision of the future—the professor sorting through information to weigh fact against fiction.

Bridgman, however encouraging, still harbored a sense that the market was too difficult to develop. He said in a letter to Woodburne that he would like to someday invest in the winery: "I have been thinking about your group someday making fine dry wines. I believe you could do that by contacting some clubs, such as the Rainier Club, letting them sample the wines, and also get Pellegrini's endorsement. And get the support for a Washington-made wine of highest quality. Probably do the same with two or three high-class hotels like the Olympic and New Washington and Edmund Meany.

"Some day I hope to be able to take some stand in your corporation myself, if you do branch out. I'd really like to see some of the wine grapes I have sponsored go into commercial wine in this state."

—LLOYD WOODBURNE—

Woodburne, now deceased, recalled in his memoirs that he first learned about wine while lying in a hospital bed in August 1951. He was then a professor of psychology at the University of Washington, vacationing in Oregon when he accidentally brushed some poison oak. This put him in the hospital for three days with his arms in epsom salts. While in bed he began reading a book on winemaking. This piqued his curiosity. He called his colleague, Angelo Pellegrini, an English professor also at the University of Washington.

Pellegrini told him, "It's as easy as boiling an egg." To this Woodburne wryly responds, "He was quite wrong, as I was to learn over the next three years, but I was hooked and made my first batch of wine that fall. It was pretty poor stuff. My wife refused to drink it, and I used it mostly with ice and soda water." By the next harvest Woodburne recruited friends to help him.

They began by getting their grapes from the California grape train that delivered grapes to Georgetown in south Seattle. Since Prohibition, Italian-Americans had been getting grapes sent up from California, mostly Zinfandel, Alicante Bouschet, Muscat, and Petite Sirah. Woodburne's early sources for grapes were Anthony Picardo—who at ninety years old in 1993 was still bringing grapes into Georgetown from sources he had in Lodi—and the DeSanto Brothers, also still offering grapes in the 1990s.

Encouraged by the excitement of making wine, Woodburne and his friends bought a hand grape crusher and a screw press. All of the wine grapes went to Woodburne's garage. The white grapes were crushed and pressed into juice; each winemaker took his allotted

Lloyd Woodburne of
Associated Vintners.
—*Photo by Lawrence J. Allen.
Courtesy of Elizabeth
Purser-Hendricks.*

amount home to ferment and finish. The red grapes were usually divided amongst the home winemakers—to be fermented and pressed at their homes.

Some years, only eight winemakers would choose to make wine; other years that number would double. It became cumbersome. Woodburne early on wanted a more formal winery structure, and circumstance was pushing the group toward that. But it was really this amazing sharing that kept them going. For a number of years, even after incorporation, they continued to make wines in their own homes and then get together and compare wines. There was no single winemaker; all delighted in discovery.

By 1956 Woodburne was joined by Cornelius Peck, a professor of law at the University of Washington. Phil Padelford, a downtown businessman, came in around 1957; Lew Leber joined in 1958; and later Lew's brother, Ted, came in, both of whom were in the printing ink business. Also in 1958 Charles Sleicher, a professor of chemical engineering, joined them. In 1959 Allan Taylor of Boeing got involved, as did Phil Church. Church was then head of the meteorology department at the University of Washington. In 1960, Warren Bierman, a child allergy specialist, joined in. Rounding out this group was Don Bevan of the fisheries department at the University of Washington. Here were the basic ten. What a marvelous group of professionals, each able to contribute in some important way. One witty *Journal American* writer quipped, "Among them they have enough Ph.D.s to launch a mini-university." And Peck suggested they use the name Academia Winery.

In Woodburne's original notes, he identified some interested people he wanted to get involved in the winery. It was an impressive group: John Hauberg, a renowned Seattle arts patron; Ed Carlson of United Airlines fame; Victor Rosellini, the great Seattle restaurateur; Ivan Kearns, head of the Washington Wine and Grape Growers Council; and W. B. Bridgman.

In 1960 Woodburne met with Bridgman at the Roosevelt Hotel in Seattle. Notes from that visit revealed Bridgman told Woodburne that Ivan Kearns was very intent on making fine wines; Bridgman also said that Vic Allison was very reliable and would give Woodburne grapes and cooperate with him; and Bridgman said that Allison had no Semillon (as Bridgman, who planted the grapes, would have known) and the white that Allison called Semillon might have been White Pinot or White Chardonnay. This was the beginning of an intense correspondence and dialog that continued through the next five years.

In the very beginning, when Woodburne thought things were going well, his friends began to drop out. Next, he couldn't get any white grapes from the Georgetown connection, so he was forced to go over to eastern Washington to find grapes. On one trip to Sunnyside, he found a 2- to 3-acre vineyard of Delaware grapes owned by William Bridgman. Delaware is not a *vinifera* grape but rather an American hybrid grape grown extensively in New York for making champagne-type sparkling wines. Not exactly pedigreed grapes.

But most important from Lloyd Woodburne's perspective was that these grapes were really going to be there at harvest. He was further committing himself to eastern Washington grapes, learning what grapes were available and what problems were unique to eastern Washington.

Bridgman believed that this group was possibly the hope of the future for Washington wines. He tried to relay his knowledge to them as best he could. Unfortunately, by the mid-'50s, Bridgman had become ambivalent about *vinifera* wine grapes. Though Bridgman remained an enthusiastic supporter of Woodburne and his group, he was more and more inclined to look for new varieties, either French hybrids or new grapes being developed at UC Davis. In January 1961, Woodburne's group contracted with Bridgman to get Ruby Cabernet (one of the new grapes bred in California) and Semillon for ten years.

Associated Vinters saw the 1959 Washington State Department of Commerce and Economic Development report, "The Grape Industry in the State of Washington," as a vindication of its own aims. The group knew that they could produce a wine better than any of the top wines, and definitely better than the leading Washington wines. And they were convinced that the market was going to go toward dry table wines. Looking back, it is a bit hard to understand their audacity, but this group felt that they could answer the pent-up needs of other potential wine drinkers.

The budding amateurs sent wine samples out to a number of people and waited for comments: Angelo Pellegrini was encouraging; he liked their Pinot Noir and Chardonnay. They also sent wines to Vic Allison, and later to Howard Somers. And though encouraged by Allison and Pellegrini, Woodburne was suspicious of them. Pellegrini was on some kind of retainer to American Wine Growers as a consultant. That is probably why Pellegrini never got involved with Woodburne's group, even though he, as a university colleague, would have been a natural shareholder. And Allison, Woodburne felt, couldn't be trusted. Woodburne later said, "Peck and I have no interest in doing the testing and experimentation for Pommerelle. In fact any connection with any of the present wineries would make the distribution of a quality wine nearly impossible." And Woodburne blamed Allison for the loss of two potential investors in Associated Vintners.

Woodburne was probably justified in spurning Allison. Allison wore his competitive spirit like a red bandana. But the record tends to show that Allison was truly interested in helping Associated Vintners and was quite generous in providing grapes to the group. It is hard to believe that he would let Associated Vintners do all the research and testing of *vinifera*-based wines for him. He would have been more hands-on. Allison was so convinced that there wasn't a market for table wines that he must have felt that he had nothing to lose in helping these amateur winemakers.

Wines were also sent to a number of California vintners, including Louis Martini, John Daniels Jr. of Inglenook Winery, and André Tchelistcheff, the highly respected winemaker at Beaulieu Vineyards. John Daniels wrote back to them, "I am afraid that I can't be too encouraging about your plans to raise Cabernet Sauvignon in the Seattle area, since there is a distinct question whether you have enough degree days of heat during the growing season to mature this variety."

In 1961 they sent bottles of Chardonnay, Pinot Noir, and a pink sparkling wine (made from the 1960 vintage Grenache) to Beaulieu Vineyards. Tchelistcheff liked all of the wines and declared that the champagne was as good as Beaulieu Vineyards'. It was very encouraging. [And also very interesting, because it conflicts with the accepted history of interaction between Tchelistcheff and Associated Vintners, which tells of Tchelistcheff first tasting AV's wine in 1967 (six years later).]

A lot took place between 1961, when Tchelistcheff first tasted AV's wine, and 1967, when he later sampled the AV Gewurztraminer. AV found it increasingly difficult to get wine grapes, because both Vic Allison of American Wine Growers and George Thomas of Upland Winery grew more reluctant to share *vinifera* wine grapes with the group. This put pressure on the founders to plant their own vineyard.

Woodburne, in his memoirs, said, "The ten regular winemakers, after a lengthy discussion of grape supply, discovered that we could have our own vineyard if each of us could invest as much as a good golf club membership would cost."

Obviously, this winemaking group was getting more serious about becoming commercial. Peck recalled, "I think the group was thinking different things. Lloyd, Phil (Church), and I thought that this was a chance to have a small commercial winery. I think the others thought that this was our chance to get a vineyard and have a source of grapes in eastern Washington." If they bonded as a winery it would also allow them, legally, to make wine in one place.

In 1962 Woodburne and his group began to look for a vineyard, and Cornelius Peck began to draw up incorporation papers in preparation of buying vineyard land. Prior to incorporating, Woodburne met with Vic Allison of American Wine Growers and Ivan Kearns. Both were delighted to have a new small winery in the state. They thought it would benefit all.

Woodburne's memoirs suggest a sudden surge toward incorporation. But Woodburne's more detailed archival notes, which include minutes from the stockholders' meetings, memos between stockholders, and various letters, show a much greater tentativeness and a very thorough plodding in their approach to commercial status. Finally, in 1962 Cornelius Peck incorporated and bonded Associated Vintners.

Bridgman, an enthusiastic supporter of this group, wanted to be a partner. Sadly, Bridgman was essentially broke except for his land holdings, which by then were tied up by bank liens. When Associated

Vintners bought its first vineyard on Harrison Hill, the group had to get the bank to agree to allow Bridgman to sell them the property.

They first looked at the vineyard that supplied them with Delaware grapes, but rejected it because it was valley bottom land and was particularly prone to spring and fall frosts. It was Bridgman who finally showed them an ideal site on Harrison Hill, a 5.5-acre piece well above the valley floor with good air drainage. Its south to southwest exposure maximized the sunshine, and the slope provided optimum conditions for irrigating. The land had never been planted in table or wine grapes.

What grapes to plant? Phil Church, the meteorologist, undertook a comparative study of the climates of famous wine regions of middle Europe and Sunnyside. Church had been assigned to the Hanford Bomb Project back in the '40s and was very familar with the weather patterns of eastern Washington. According to Woodburne's memoirs, Church stated, "The averages of twenty-seven years showed Beaune in the middle of the Burgundy district had 2400 degree days whereas Sunnyside had 2397. In the cooler summers, our vineyard temperature resembled Burgundy climate, while in warm summers it resembled Bordeaux (2553 degree days)." Based on his study, they decided to plant the noble grapes of Europe.

They were familiar with Philip and Jocelyn Wagner of Boordy Vineyard of Riderwood, Maryland. The Wagners were pioneering hybrid growers and early advocates of cool-climate viticulture. Philip Wagner's first book, *American Wines and How to Make Them,* published in 1933, pointed the way for America's winemakers to produce European-type table wines. Bridgman knew of Wagner personally because he was experimenting with some of Wagner's recommended hybrid grapes in the mid-'50s. In a telephone conversation, Wagner cautioned Peck to "not be guided exclusively by California wine tasters."

The group ordered their first grapes from Curtis J. Alley, of the Foundation Plant Materials Service at UC Davis. Included were Gewurztraminer, White Riesling, Semillon, Chardonnay, Grenache, and Cabernet Sauvignon. All the grapes were planted in 1963, with all of the work being done by the stockholders. Vic Allison offered grapes from a Grandview vineyard that was owned by American Wine Growers, originally planted by W. B. Bridgman; starts included Semillon, Pinot Noir, Grenache, Delaware, and French hybrids Seibel 13053 (Cascade), and Seibel 10096.

A chorus of volunteers and investors now had their opportunity for sweat equity. With the planting of the vineyard in 1963, the day of reckoning for the stockholders occurred. Putting up money was one thing, putting down roots was another. Vines have a way of growing on their own. They don't care who owns them or what the growers' intentions are. Those vines are going to grow—unless dug up or exposed to prolonged cold.

In December 1964 a prolonged warm period occurred. Temperatures shot up to 60° F in the vineyard for nearly a week before suddenly dropping to -9° F. Woodburne recalled, "Everything above the ground froze, and since sap had begun to flow at about 60° F temperature, the canes were split. So we got no crop and no wine in 1965, but the roots were still good. Practically all of the vines came back and in 1966 we had a partial crop."

—REMARKABLE WINES—

According to Woodburne's memoirs, "In the summer of 1966 I received a call from Howard Somers of American Wine Growers. Leon Adams of California was visiting them. He did not like any of their wines and asked if any varietal wines were being made in Washington. In response to this invitation, I took over a bottle of Grenache Rosé made in my garage. Adams liked it, and suggested that if American Wine Growers wanted to make good wine, they should invite a good California enologist to consult with them on how to do it."

Woodburne then related how André Tchelistcheff of Beaulieu Vineyards agreed to come up the following year to visit American Wine Growers: "He was not interested because of the poor wines they were then making. We got him to come to our small winery for a short visit. He made a number of suggestions, but it became evident very quickly that he expected to stay with us until his plane took off about 8:30 p.m. for California." Woodburne then called Phil Church, the treasurer of Associated Vintners, and asked him to prepare a meal: "Phil was a good cook and he had a nice poached salmon ready for us when we arrived. With the salmon he served a '66 Gewurztraminer he had made at home. Tchelistcheff liked the salmon, but became very excited when he tasted the wine. He exclaimed, 'Where did you get that wine?!' Phil, like André, had a short fuse and was about to start an argument, because it was his own homemade wine. I was watching André and finally I said to Phil, 'Take it easy. He likes the wine.' It was then that André made the much-quoted remark: 'This is the best

Associated Vintners' shareholders at winery. Left to right: Charles Sleicher, Ted Leber,
Alan Taylor, Willard Wright, Lloyd Woodburne, Neil Peck, Peter Rawn, Phil Padelford,
Don Bevan, Warren Bierman. Wright and Rawn became shareholders in 1970.
Not pictured are "original" shareholders Lew Leber and Phil Church.
—*Photo by Lawrence J. Allen. Courtesy of Elizabeth Purser-Hendricks.*

Gewurztraminer made in the United States.' Phil bathed in the glow of
that praise for weeks."

That same year, 1967, Associated Vintners harvested its first commercial crop, fermenting Gewurztraminer, Riesling, Pinot Noir, and
Cabernet Sauvignon at its first winery, at the Parmac Industrial Park in
Kirkland. The group initially fermented their wines in 100-gallon
open-top fir barrels and aged the wines in a variety of barrels, including 50-gallon American oak barrels from Sweeney Cooperage, a
Canadian firm with a branch located near Seattle's ship canal. They also
used a number of 70-gallon Portuguese brandy barrels for the second
year of aging of the reds. To further age the whites, some of these barrels were sprayed with hot paraffin—a bizarre but effective method to
prolong the use of the barrels and to keep the white wine away from the
residual red wine (or brandy) in the oak.

Early on the group had decided that they would do whatever was
necessary, within monetary reason, to produce a superior product to
distinguish themselves from previous Washington wines. Thus they
made a policy to age white wines one year in tank or barrel and one year
in bottle—two years before release. The reds were to be aged two years
in barrel and two years in bottle—four years total. In 1969 the white
wines from the '67 vintage were released, a Johannisberg Riesling and
a Gewurztraminer.

The timing of the release of Associated Vintners' wines was impeccable. The ink had hardly dried on the California Wine Bill and a flood of California wine was beginning to pour into Washington. Washington wineries were dropping like fruit flies into their tanks of fortified wines. Out of this vinous murk, Associated Vintners' wines emerged, a beacon on the hill.

Stan Reed, the *Seattle Post-Intelligencer*'s noted food columnist, wrote in the July 11, 1969, edition, "A new industry has been born in Washington. Its name is Associated Vintners, Inc. Its total aim is the production of fine varietal wines from fine grape varieties grown within the state. That last sentence makes AV more than a new industry. It qualifies the firm as a revolutionary industry within this state."

Although Reed played the role of midwife, when you read this and subsequent columns, you might think him to be the proud papa. He was beside himself. He was honestly ecstatic over the wines and what they represented. These were wines made in Washington state that rivaled the great European wines Reed knew from his travels to Europe. His enthusiastic reviews caused a stampede at the University Village QFC supermarket, the only retail outlet for the wines.

Continuing, he wrote, "And, to add to the wonder of that wondrous situation, the state's fine-wine industry that now is a reality was created by ten dedicated vintners who started out eighteen years ago not knowing winemaking from carpentry.

"Amateurs bore the torch for the professionals, and we hope that the light has been seen.

"Associated Vintners just recently put its first wines on the market, two whites of the 1967 vintage, a Johannisberg Riesling and a Gewurztraminer.

"What do I think about them? I think they're of a stature so high that a Washington Wine Month should be proclaimed in their honor.

"They are wines that are the equal of the very best California Rieslings and Traminers. Among their German cousins, they match all but great growths. They're the peers of the finest Alsatians. They're...

"But I could go on for two Washington Wine Months and not run out of praiseful words for those superior wines grown in a state hitherto without any vinous achievement."

Stan Reed did go on for three more columns, all within a week. In the following week he even got the toughest competitor on earth, Vic Allison of American Wine Growers, to compliment Associated Vintners:

"With its excellent wines, Associated Vintners dramatically

demonstrated that superior wines can be produced in this state. The firm has put Washington into the fine-wine business. It deserves our gratitude."

Stan Reed was, more accurately, dumbfounded. The quality of the AV wines caught him by surprise. He couldn't believe that Washington could produce wines of that caliber. This was only a few months after passage of the California Wine Bill. It proved that Washington could produce quality table wines.

Reed's description of Associated Vintners' first two releases marked the historic occasion:

"The Riesling charmed me immediately. It was flowery, had a beautiful balance, an engaging bouquet, and was a delightful merger of strength and delicacy. It recalled to me at least a dozen Moselles I've known.

"The Gewurztraminer was even more impressive. The typical spiciness of this wine was generously present, but along with it was a special...of the soil. I thought, the volcanic earth in the Yakima Valley where the wine grapes were grown.

"This taste of its native earth, if that is what it was, subtly emphasized the elegance of this perfumed wine. This subtle essence was present in the Riesling also."

In romanticizing these wines, Reed was overlooking faults that the average consumer would have gotten hung up on, like high acidity and higher-than-normal levels of sulphur dioxide. But the reality was, these wines were impressive against the landscape of other Washington wines.

The wine sold out within one week. The winery was completely out of its first batch and, keeping to its aging policy, would not have wine available until the following June. Thus it went for the next few years.

—A Commercial Reality—

The group's dream had become reality. The stockholders regularly helped in the winery, dividing their talents into three different areas: finance, winery, and vineyard. They bought a new vineyard in 1972. Called the Church Vineyard, it was an 80-acre vineyard located on Arrowsmith Road just north of Sunnyside, planted in Cabernet Sauvignon, Pinot Noir, White Riesling, Gewurztraminer, and Chardonnay. This vineyard helped fuel Associated Vintners' expansion.

Lloyd Woodburne became the winery manager and winemaker in

1975, continuing to direct the winery with his strong vision. The winery was in the throes of growth. The early arrangement of selling out the wines by Thanksgiving was no longer working. They were losing some customers who felt slighted.

In 1976 the winery operation moved to a larger space in Redmond, not far from the original winery where Associated Vintners began its expansion. In 1976, AV produced 9,000 gallons of wine (less than 4,000 cases). To do this, AV also bought a truckload of Cabernet Sauvignon from Sagemoor Farms. For the next three years the group increased production by slightly over 30 percent a year. In 1978 the winery hired John Albin, a trained enologist from the University of California Davis. This didn't work out as expected. The winery was beginning to experience financial pressures, because it was difficult to finance this kind of growth, and Albin left in 1979 out of frustration. Woodburne wrote, "He thought a rough red wine, a combination of Petite Syrah and Merlot, was the best wine we made. So I was ready to let him go on that count alone."

In 1979 Associated Vintners hired David Lake as its new winemaker. Lake, a Master of Wine, brought to the winery—and the Washington wine industry—experience culled from his years in the British wine trade. The Master of Wine program is a grueling sensory and oral test; only a very few people pass. It also requires the participant to have worked in the wine trade. Lake, though knowledgeable about wine and winemaking, was not an expert winemaker. Yet here he was, thrust into making wine during what was to be a difficult time.

The 1979 harvest was affected by one of the coldest winters in twenty years. The winery was forced to rely heavily on other grape sources, and this was the beginning of its relationship with Red Willow Vineyard, and a cementing of its purchases from Sagemoor Farms. That cold winter experience affects AV to this day. It now buys grapes from a wide circle of vineyard sources, including Red Willow Vineyards (in the extreme western portion of the Yakima Valley), Sagemoor Farms (to the east, twelve miles north of Pasco along the Columbia River), the Otis Vineyards and the Wycoff Vineyards near Grandview (in the lower portion of the Yakima Valley), and in southwest Washington north of Vancouver.

In 1980, AV produced 25,000 gallons, supplementing its grape needs from the above vineyards. In 1980 a new management team came into the winery. To satisfy loan payments, both the Harrison Hill vineyard and the Church Vineyard were sold. Enter Willard Wright, a prominent Seattle attorney, as president, and Peter Rawn, an accountant, to help the winery through this difficult period. Additionally, Langdon Simonds and Associates, a consulting firm, determined that AV needed to get to 50,000 gallons to be profitable. They also found a new group of investors. The most important was Dan Baty, who took over direct management of the winery in 1981, when Dr. Woodburne retired.

The winery was in new hands. In 1983 it produced 96,000 gallons of wine. The group had moved the winery again, beginning with the '81 vintage, to a still larger facility in Bellevue. In 1983 the winery changed its name to Columbia Winery, as it is still known today. In a few years it moved to Woodinville, across the street from Chateau Ste. Michelle, at the former Havilland Winery, where it continues in operation today.

During my most recent visit to the winery, I was handed a business card by Max Zellweger, vice president of operations. It wasn't until a few days later that I noticed that the front and back sides of the card were different. The side Zellweger handed to me read COLUMBIA WINERY. But the other side read ASSOCIATED VINTNERS.

I smiled with a warm feeling inside. The company had come back to using the name Associated Vintners as its corporate name. The Columbia Winery is now a brand name. This corporate umbrella would allow it to include the Paul Thomas Wines brand as well, which Associated Vintners had recently purchased. In 1996, it also purchased Covey Run Wines. Part of its current strategy is for the Columbia Winery brand to focus more on the premium level of wines, while diverting the everyday table wines and less expensive wines to the Paul Thomas Wines label, and, I assume, the Covey Run Wines will fill in the middle.

Lloyd Woodburne, who died in 1987 of complications resulting from a stroke, would be proud of the current Associated Vintners. He would be astounded by its growth since that pivotal year in 1980 when it chose to become larger. From the winery's lobby, he could overlook the massive stainless steel tanks and rows upon rows of small oak barrels. He might shake his head in wonder as he walked through the new winery. He would laugh at himself, reminded of how his original vintner friends used "a real Rube Goldberg device (as a wine press). It was built on an aluminum base, was both hydraulic and pneumatic, with a basket about three feet across built by Schleicher."

The winery vision had grown remarkably since those first home-made wines in his basement back in the early '50s. In 1960,

Woodburne, Peck, Church, and fellow vintners believed that Washington could produce wines as well as those out of California. In 1983, when they had proved this to themselves, Woodburne said, "When Northwest wines are carefully made and properly aged, they can compete on equal terms with the best wines in the world. This is especially true of Associated Vintners, where the attempt has been to make the best wine in the state. The emphasis has always been on quality, as the awards have indicated."

Chapter Nineteen

THE WINE PROJECT

Though Associated Vintners was on its own track to achieving fine varietal wines, its progress prior to its initial wine release was largely unremarked within the industry, perhaps because the group were amateurs, perhaps because they worked out of a garage. In any case, immediately following the ferment of the California Wine Bill, like a wine that has finished its violent initial fermentation, there remained a fine sediment, an as yet unanswered question: Can Washington state grow *Vitis vinifera* grapes in a consistent quality manner to make fine table wines and varietal wines?

Looking back over the entire history of wine and grapes in Washington state, the answer would seem to be a resounding yes! But each succeeding generation, pioneers in their own right, were unaware of preceding efforts; they simply inherited an accumulated knowledge of grapes and wine, through a non-verbalized history.

Hints to the answer came from many directions. Clues had been planted in those first grapevines at Fort Vancouver, at Tampico in the Herke Vineyard, near Wenatchee by "Dutch" John Galler and Philip Miller, by Frank Orselli (and Philip Ritz) of Walla Walla, by Robert Schleicher at Lewiston, Idaho, and even by Adam Eckert at Stretch Island. And later, by Elbert Blaine of Grandview and William B. Bridgman of Sunnyside. And into the '50s and '60s with Vic Allison, Lester Fleming, and Howard Somers of American Wine Growers; Martha Niblack of Old West Winery; Otis Harlan Jr. of Alhambra Winery; as well as Associated Vintners.

It seemed no one had yet answered the question conclusively, nor had they really even stated the question. It took a group of people at Washington State University to bring the question forward.

It started with Dr. Walter Clore, the horticulturist at the Irrigation Experiment Station (IES) at Prosser. Up until 1959, all contacts between the Washington wine industry and the IES research staff had been on an individual basis. People like Lester Fleming of American Wine Growers were comfortable working with Walt Clore, seeking advice and providing guidance as well. In 1959, the Washington Wine and Grape Growers Council had officially invited the research staff at the Irrigation Experiment Station to attend its annual meeting; this was the first time that the Washington wine industry as a group had come to the research staff to get help.

In 1964, when Dr. Clore asked for help from his colleague Dr. Cyril Woodbridge, also a horticulturist, Dr. Clore was looking for someone to make wines from the grapes he had at the research center, to formally prove that premium wines could be successfully made from Washington-grown wine grapes, primarily *vinifera* grapes.

Dr. Clore pulled together a loosely knit community of winemakers, producers, growers, and researchers; 1964 marked the first year that wines were made by Washington State University (WSU). That year, WSU-IES received funding from the Washington Wine and Grape Growers Council and an agreement to conduct "Studies of Wine Grape Varieties, Cultural Methods, Wine Production and Quality." The council granted $1,018.80 that first year and then went to $1,250 annually from 1965 through 1969. American Wine Growers funded an additional year in 1970. The industry finally recognized that if it was to adopt a *vinifera*-based wine industry, it needed help with all aspects of wine production, from site selection and grape selection to production methods.

By this time the WSU administration was fully supportive of the Wine Project, and the project was able to obtain matching funds to continue these studies from 1971 to 1973 with the USDA-ARS, Western Regional Laboratory, at Albany, California. From 1974 to 1976 the project also obtained a technical assistance grant with the Economic Development Administration of the U.S. Department of Commerce in Seattle.

It is fun to think back to those first heady days of the Wine Project. It had all the drama and excitement of another more famous project just east of Prosser at the Hanford Project, where work was conducted to build the atomic bomb that eventually ended the war with Japan. Although the Wine Project was much less profound, its results helped revolutionize an industry that was on its deathbed in 1969. Dr. Clore was the unlikely director of this effort; he was truly a wine neophyte. He had only recently begun his journey into the enjoyment of wines.

—*DR. CLORE'S MOTIVATION*—

Dr. Clore's family background would have suggested that he avoid wine. None in his family drank alcoholic beverages. He grew up a Methodist and his mother was active in the Woman's Christian Temperance Union.

But in Prosser, far from his Oklahoma roots and put in charge of developing horticultural crops, he found that he was challenged to improve the grape and wine industries in the state, among other things. His résumé in these efforts is impressive. In 1937 Dr. Clore was assigned project leader of an eight-year research program regarding vegetable crops at the Washington State Penitentiary in Walla Walla. Under supervision of a prison guard, prisoners worked the vegetable row crops, experimenting in crop varieties, fertilizer use, and management practices. Dr. Clore was also active in other research that resulted in his publishing on a wide variety of subjects, ranging from irrigation studies to fruit and vegetable fertilizer studies.

His education into grapes began upon his arrival at the research center in 1937 with his first planting of 27 grapevines, a mix of *vinifera* and *labrusca* grapes as well as hybrids. He continued planting grapes and investigating their potential uses to the juice and wine industry, planting 4 varieties in 1938 and 13 in 1939. This led to his meeting with W. B. Bridgman, who had encouraged him to study European wine grapes. In 1940, Clore, at the insistence of Bridgman, planted 27 grapevines: 3 *labrusca* and 24 *vinifera*, of which 11 of the latter were from Bridgman.

In 1947 Dr. Clore finished his Ph.D. thesis, "Root Distribution of Apple Trees as Related to Moisture and Tree Response," and was awarded his doctorate in pomology. It was the culmination of his work he had begun when he first arrived at the center in 1937.

In 1950, Dr. Nelson J. Shaulis, the viticulturist at the New York Agriculture Experiment Station in Geneva, New York, spent a six-month sabbatical at the Prosser research station studying the culture of the Concord grape. Dr. Clore states matter-of-factly, "Dr. Shaulis's

Dr. Walter Clore in vineyard. 1977.
—*Photo by Lawrence J. Allen. Courtesy of Elizabeth Purser-Hendricks.*

enthusiasm for investigating the culture of the grape inspired me to spend more time researching this crop. Dr. Shaulis was impressed with the fruitfulness of the basal buds on the canes (one-year-old shoots) of the Concords in Washington, which was not the case under the lower light conditions in the grape areas of western New York state. As a result of this response, he started investigating ways to trellis and train vines to improve light conditions on the basal leaves of shoots. Eventually he became famous for developing the Geneva Double-Curtain trellis for New York conditions, which allows the basal shoots of the grape canopy better exposure to sunlight, resulting in a remarkable increase in fruitfulness."

During the '50s Dr. Clore was prolific in his research, with publications on a wide range of subjects, including zinc deficiency of Concord grapes; sensitivity of the grape to 2,4-D injury; growing lima beans in irrigated central Washington; hardy early-blooming chrysanthemums for central Washington; effects of certain insecticides in the soil on crop plants (which involved the residual effect of DDT); grape varieties for the home vineyard; tolerance of asparagus to 2,4-D; irrigating Concord grapes in south-central Washington; response of Concord grapes to cold injury; effect of certain climatic factors on the growth, production, and maturity of the Concord grape; growing and handling asparagus crowns; Columbia, a new disease-resistant field bean; the response of certain crops to 2,4-D in irrigation water; some effects of the 1958 growing season on Concord grape production; fertilization and fruit quality of grapes; factors affecting yields of Concords; grapes and petiole composition in some vineyards in the Yakima Valley; the use of green manure and cover crops in nutrition control in vineyards; and some responses of Concord grapes to the 1959 growing season. During his first twenty-three years of research, Dr. Clore authored fifty publications. Of these, eighteen involved grape studies.

After Dr. Shaulis's visit, Dr. Clore began to limit his research increasingly to two crops, asparagus and grapes: "Commercial cropping of grapes and asparagus was common because of the compatibility of farming these two crops. Asparagus was spring harvested and laid by, and grapes were a late summer- and fall-harvested crop. Also, much of the equipment required in the culture of these two crops was the same." Dr. Clore's extensive work in these two crops helped to propel these crops into the national limelight. Eventually, Washington state became the nation's outstanding leader in quality and production of asparagus and Concord grapes.

—VERE BRUMMUND, CHAS NAGEL, AND GEORGE CARTER—
Dr. Clore may not have initially had any particular enthusiasm for wine, but he was definitely excited about the possibilities of grape culture and its many uses, including wine. His primary focus was to develop and improve the grape crop in Washington state. Clore has often intimated that his work on wine grapes was a direct result of his initial work on Concord grapes. Once, when I questioned his detailed tracking of the grape juice industry, he looked at me and said, "Well, they make wine out of grapes, don't they?" I now understand what that means: without his work and the work of the agriculture industry—with all types of grapes—the wine industry would not have developed so rapidly in this state.

During the 1950s Clore continued to maintain the varietal vineyards at the research center and maintained a working relationship with a number of people in the wine industry. In 1957 WSU hired Vere Brummund to work with Clore as a technical aide. Brummund turned out to be an enthusiastic sidekick of Dr. Clore. Brummund says that his first taste for wines developed in France when his army battalion overran a German occupation of a French country estate with an enormous wine cellar. Victory was toasted with aged French wine; Brummund recalls that it was unbelievably mellow and soft.

In Prosser, Brummund learned winemaking from John Chiara, an Italian native who also worked at the research center. Chiara, then nearing seventy years old, had long made wine in the Yakima Valley, having arrived in Prosser in 1921 to form a small nucleus of Italian families that settled there. John's son, Joe, recalls that his father made about 150 gallons of wine per year, selling 50 gallons and using the rest. Joe Chiara gives a good description of how his dad made wine in those days: "As best as I can remember, our winemaking consisted mainly of crushing the boxes of grapes in an old cider mill and press. Fermenting was done in open-ended 50-gallon wood barrels (with 18 million vinegar flies supervising the entire process!) in the basement.

"Pressing was followed by storing the wine in other closed 50-gallon barrels. Clarifying was done strictly by gravity, moving the wine from barrel to barrel and, when finally clear, it would be eventually settled in the barrel with an air-water vent in the bung of the barrel. The next spring it would be jugged in gallon glass bottles."

In his singsong voice, Brummund remembered, "So I asked John one day, 'John, how do you make wine?'" Chiara said it was easy: "You go down there to the variety vineyard (at the research center) and you get about half of the Concord kind and half of those other kind—for every gallon of juice you add a pound of sugar, and add some yeast." With those simple instructions, Brummund began his first efforts to make wine; they weren't so good. Brummund recalls, "The first year was a total disaster." He says, "I think the first book I turned to was by Hedrick out of New York. It was mostly about grape growing, with a small section on winemaking." It wasn't too much help. But he continued to improve his techniques, turning to winemaking textbooks out of the University of California Davis.

Brummund says he found out that "we had a better opportunity for growing wine grapes than California had. We retained our acid content, and our sugar content was right up there. We had a better ratio of sugar to acid. I began reading *Wines and Vines*, which was subscribed to at the research station, and occasionally it had an article on winemaking. I began to make wines in small batches from individual varieties to see if we could make a wine as good as or better than California's." He then began to buy wine to compare to his own. This led to trips to California's wine country, visiting wineries: "In those days you had the whole damn winery to yourself."

Continuing, he said, "I'd buy a couple of cases—at that time wine wasn't very expensive—and I would compare my wine to what came out of California. I found we could produce a really outstanding wine." Later, when he and George Carter attended a winemaking shortcourse in 1966 at UC Davis, he remembered Vernon Singleton telling his group that "Washington will never grow wine grapes. Singleton said it rains too much." This incensed Brummund and he asked Dr. Singleton where he was born. He replied, "Longview, Washington," located along the Columbia River in western Washington.

In pretty short time, by 1960, Brummund was making palatable wine. He got really excited about a Chardonnay that he made: "We had two vines down there at the station and every year there were enough grapes that I could make a 5-gallon batch. Besides Chardonnay, I made Chenin Blanc and what I thought was Riesling, which turned out to be Scheurebe. I thought I was making a Gewurztraminer, and I was playing around with some Pinot Noir and this one variety called Blue Burgundy, for want of a better name. It came down from Canada; it was blue, there was no question about it. The juice was even red. Anyhow, I was making about seven to ten varieties a year in my basement at home." Pausing, he continued, "When I first came here to Prosser I didn't even dare mention an alcoholic beverage."

Brummund says he became interested in wine "because the grapes were there and nobody was doing a darn thing with them. I hadn't really developed a taste for wine but I wanted to find out what could be done with those grapes." He had convinced himself that Washington state was capable of growing *vinifera* wine grapes as well as or better than the Californians. Brummund became attached to the varietal vineyard and guarded it closely, taking personal responsibility for its upkeep. He claims that soon after he began working at the center, he was directed by Dr. Clore and the director of agriculture at Pullman to pull out the *vinifera* grapes because they didn't believe that at that time there was enough commercial interest in *vinifera* wine grapes. Dr. Clore does not recall this. Brummund, forever combative, says that he refused to follow their directive and "just never got around to it."

That the varietal vineyard survived is a tribute to the hardiness of the vine—in the vineyard were vines originally obtained from William Bridgman. After the terrible back-to-back freezes of 1948–'49 and 1949–'50, the research center's vines survived, while many of Bridgman's were torn out due to winter damage. Again, the vine had been passed along on its journey. Now it was being discovered by Brummund.

In 1961 Walt and Irene Clore and their daughter Judy went on a sabbatical to Japan. While there, Dr. Clore studied the grape and horticultural practices of the Japanese. He made numerous new Japanese friends, and both Walt and Irene grew as people, expanding their personalities and global outlook beyond the confines of a small eastern Washington community. Walt's reputation as a horticulturist grew in international proportions.

While Dr. Clore was in Japan, Vere Brummund was asked by the research center's Superintendent Singleton to make a presentation to the Washington Wine and Grape Growers Council during their annual December meeting in Yakima. Brummund was reluctant to address the group. He felt there was nothing he could tell them that they didn't know: "They've been talked to all the time about growing Concord, how to grow Concord, they've been told that." Singleton was insistent: "You are going to be on the program."

This got Brummund busy looking at data on areas that had the mildest winters in the state: "It turned out to be all along the Columbia River." Brummund figured that he had collected enough data about sugar/acid ratio, maturity dates, and weather patterns that he could make a decent talk to the council. Brummund says, "So I decided, why not go up to Yakima and tell them about wine grapes?"

Thus, in 1961, Brummund challenged the growers to begin growing wine grapes based on his experience and study, pointing to a future premium wine business. The speech fell on deaf ears. Brummund reported the response to his speech: "Vic Allison said, 'You can't do it here, you can't sell table wines in the state of Washington.'" Brummund went back to Prosser determined to continue to take care of the varietal vineyard.

Then Dr. Clore came back from his year's visit to Japan. Brummund noticed an immediate change in Clore's demeanor. Clore was well aware that Brummund was making wine at his home, because he had given Brummund permission to use the grapes. One day Irene Clore called Vere and asked him if he had a bottle of homemade red wine that she could use in cooking. This shocked Brummund, for he had known Irene as only a teetotaler. Shortly after, Brummund was further surprised when he and his wife were asked to join the Clores and Bill Barnard, who was Bridgman's nephew, and his wife for dinner. Brummund was asked to bring a table wine.

Brummund recalled, "I took along what I thought was the Gewurztraminer; it had a little bit of a spicy character to it, but it wasn't really a Gewürztraminer. It was a good wine, though. Bill Barnard was quite impressed, although I don't think he was a real wine drinker. But what really surprised me was Walt and Irene Clore bringing out wine glasses, a set of fancy cut wine glasses. This was just shocking to me; I had always thought of Irene as a prohibitionist."

Walt, whose early interest in wine grapes had been piqued by William Bridgman, was being exposed to Brummund's wines at the same time that pressure was building in the wine industry to do something with wine grapes. Brummund remembered when the director of agriculture and a group of politicians came over to the research center and he served them some of his homemade wines. They were impressed. Brummund was excited: "The ice was being broken. This is what I was after, to get the state interested in the production of good table wines. And I always said this, 'If you don't produce quality, stay out of it.'"

Again, Brummund bided his time. In 1964, the first wines were made at Pullman by Dr. Nagel. Two years later, George Carter, a chemist, was hired to make the wines at the research center. Brummund said when Carter was hired on, it was "my job to teach George Carter how to make wine." Brummund continued to work in the vineyard, tending to the varietal vineyard and working with interested growers.

Brummund recalled Carter and he making a Grenache Rosé wine like the California rosés (especially the Almaden Grenache Rosé) that were popular at the time. The idea was to leave the skins in contact with the juice just a bit to extract some color. Carter got a little too excited and took it off the skins and killed the fermentation. Brummund recalls fondly, "It was just like making soda pop. Dr. Clore couldn't leave it alone. I don't think he got tipsy but he was just delighted with that Grenache Rosé." Later, Chas Nagel recalled playfully that Walt probably made the first wine cooler when he would add a glug of Seven-Up to the rosé.

I think of the tasting at the research center that reunited Brummund, Carter, Nagel, and Clore. Images flash back and forth in time of the four of them tasting wine together. Quite a group: Vere Brummund, acrimonious and combative, but committed to *vinifera*-based wines; Chas Nagel, skeptical and absorbed in his scholarly work but helpful, encouraging, and curious; George Carter, eager, methodical, committed (and a little playful); and Walt Clore, dedicated, resourceful, and inquisitive. I think they were all drawn into the Wine Project by their complementary personalities and their mutual respect and agricultural roots. I try to imagine them sitting together at the research center slightly affected by the alcohol in the wine: I can hear Carter's laughter, telling elk hunting stories, and Clore's cackle at hearing the story for the thirteenth time. And Nagel, always trying to get a word in, spoken in his high, almost whining voice, reassuring the group that the wines were really good. And Brummund, the cynic, challenging the group to move forward. It is a picture of four satyrs—historically represented as part human and part goat—attendant on Bacchus, the Roman god of wine.

These men had met Bacchus (Dionysus to the Greeks) in those first wines that they drank—imbued by the moderate consumption of alcohol, and the sense that they were part of something new and exciting—wine that may have played a subtle role in helping them to socialize and share in this camaraderie. These are all fine men, hard working and dedicated to their professions. In many respects they are all innocent men, born in the country, unsullied by the social trappings of urban life. They are family men, Carter with seven sons and one daughter, Nagel with three daughters and two sons, and Clore with two daughters and a son. Brummund did not have children.

I believe that, for Carter and Clore especially, their initiation into wine was viewed by them as a gift; if God provided such a delicious beverage with the ability to lighten their minds and loosen their tongues, from such beautiful vines and grapes, it must be good.

—THE RESEARCH CENTER ATTRACTS ATTENTION—
These scientists were being inundated by people interested in vineyards in eastern Washington. There were requests for information from all kinds of people, including investors; wine enthusiasts visited, California wineries snooped around, and the political battles in Olympia brought politicians to Prosser. One investor who proved important in the early days of the Wine Project was Alec Bayless, an attorney from Seattle. Alec visited the research center a number of times in the late '60s as he planned his eventual vineyard, Sagemoor Farms, along the Columbia River just northwest of Pasco. This became the most important vineyard planting in the Pacific Northwest; with 466 acres of vineyard and no winery, it became a crucial supplier to many of the small wineries throughout the Pacific Northwest for quality *vinifera* grapes.

A frequent visitor from California was Julio Gallo of E. & J. Gallo Winery in Modesto. Dr. Clore recalled one visit by most of the wine-

George Carter at winemaking lab IAREC-Prosser. 1977.
—*Photo by Lawrence J. Allen. Courtesy of Elizabeth Purser-Hendricks.*

making staff of the Gallo Winery, including Charles Crawford and Paul Osteraas. They were favorably impressed with the wines. Julio Gallo—who once called Washington's wine-growing region "acid country"—referring to Washington state's ability to overcrop and still get high soluble solids and high levels of acid in the grapes—was particularly taken by tasting the Limberger (or Lemberger) wine. He said he preferred it to the Cabernet Sauvignon he tasted. Dr. Clore asked him if he would be interested in buying Limberger from Washington. Julio Gallo replied, "Sure, if you can supply me with a whole trainload of tank cars, not just one." Continuing, Gallo impressed Clore by saying, "A million gallons of wine is needed to market a new variety."

At that time it was out of the question; the only Limberger was planted at the research center. Besides, Gallo was too busy buying Concords by the trainload to ship to California. It was the mainstay of the immensely popular Cold Duck, a champagne-like wine marketed in the late '60s and early '70s. Gallo Winery had purchased Concord juice and apple juice from Washington state since 1949. With frequent visits to the area, there was often speculation that Gallo was going to invest in vineyards in Washington state. Julio Gallo was quoted in the *Tri-Cities Herald:* "We are keeping in touch there and we are going to make more frequent trips up to watch those experiments—to see the experimental vineyard they have there. Dr. Clore has some very good experiments going on."

Additionally, Gallo pointed out "that California can grow all of the lesser-quality grapes it will need in the foreseeable future (except Concords)." But, he said, "If Washington up there happens to produce the quality, for example, of our North Coast counties, then I think you have a tremendous potential."

Sweet, well-spoken words to Dr. Clore and his colleagues at the research center. This idea that Washington wines should stick to the thin and narrow path of premium varietal wines was born in reaction to the poor quality of Washington wines and a fear of competing directly with California's inexpensive table wines.

This whole notion of quality was addressed by Dr. Ray Folwell and John Baritelle in a thorough study published in 1978 entitled *The U.S. Wine Market.* Folwell, then an associate professor of agricultural economics, and Baritelle, an agricultural economist with the U.S. Department of Agriculture, conducted a comprehensive study of wine consumption and wine-buying habits gathered from 7,000 households. The report analyzed a number of important aspects of the market, including demographic characteristics, market penetration, market share of wineries in a given region, prices of wines, brand preference, changes in wine purchases, market demand functions regarding pricing, and motivational factors in buying wine. Through a maze of statistical analysis, the bottom line of the report came to the same conclusion as Julio Gallo—Washington must produce high-quality premium wines. It was a sentiment echoed by Clore.

But how would these researchers at the center know how to recognize and promote quality? This burden fell on Chas Nagel's shoulders. To help him discover the best wines and the best grapes being produced from the experimental vineyards, he assembled a group of forty wine tasters in Pullman. Hardly professionals, this group consisted of friends and colleagues of Nagel. Nagel would whip them into shape: The tastings would start at 1:00 in the afternoon and go until about 5:00 p.m. Tasters were given instructions on scoring and what to look for in the wines. Tasters would be required to taste sometimes up to two weeks straight to get through all of the wines. There was never any lack of tasters; it was a job well liked.

It was also fortuitous that this group was basically inexperienced; they brought an innocence to the tasting panel that was probably more experimental, and less demanding of the wines. A more sophisticated group might have been too critical or, a greater danger, not able to relate to the general innocence of the wine consumer in Washington state. Nagel kept good records of the tastings and relied on the University of California Davis scoring system for evaluating wines.

Nagel immediately understood the potential for Washington wines that first year that he made the wines. Nagel was born in St. Helena, California, the very center of the Napa Valley wine country. His father had been a cellarmaster at Louis Martini Winery, and Chas had helped put himself through college working in wineries. Nagel, trained as a microbiologist at the University of California Davis, was not terribly interested in wine. He was first and foremost a food scientist; his research varied from investigating prolonging the shelf life of poultry to metabolic effects of moisture stress on the development of potatoes.

When he had been approached by Dr. Cyril Woodbridge to help Dr. Clore, he was hesitant. He told me, "I was brainwashed by Californians to believe that Washington state could never make wine." But when he tasted those first experimental wines, he knew immediately that Washington state could produce exciting wines equal to or better than the wines he knew in California.

Chas Nagel's wife, Beatrice, tells how Chas suffered a heart attack just before getting involved with the Wine Project. He was not an old man, about forty-eight years old. This made him stop and think. He decided that he would pursue the Wine Project, devoting 10 percent of his time to it, thinking it might be kind of fun to take his mind off the continual pressure of academic publishing. Besides, he liked his contact with Dr. Clore and George Carter. They were honest, real people on the firing line, in direct contact with the growers. And he found that he liked wine, the romance of wine, and all that it brought back of his childhood. The first wines that he made were rough. He still has the data on those first wines. He read the results from his data: "We had things like Chardonnay. Funny, we did not have a Riesling, we had a Riesling-Sylvaner, which scored really well. We had Limberger, Pinot Noir, Pinot Meunier, Royalty—all grapes grown at the research station."

I asked Chas Nagel if they had any notion of what kind of wines they were trying to make. Were they trying to make wines comparable to French or California wines, or was there any ideal that they were trying to achieve? His reply: "Originally we were just trying to find out if we could (make wines); that was the idea behind the (Wine) Project. It didn't take very long before we realized that we could. As we accumulated the data, it became apparent to us that we could make good quality wines."

But I pressed Nagel. I asked him what criteria they were using to judge the wines. These guys were scientists; they were documenting the numbers on the wines. I wanted to know when they knew that they were making good wines. Chas responded, "Well, we were using a standard procedure to make the wines, trying to make the wines in a consistent manner. We were looking for varietal characteristics. Therefore, it was difficult to evaluate the red wines because they were so youthful. But the white wines were ready much earlier because the standard procedure was much closer to the procedure used to make white wines. We could really tell immediately that we were on to something."

Nagel was the only one of that group who had been raised in a wine environment. Like Brummund, he made frequent trips to Napa Valley. Nagel would visit his family and bring back a case of mixed wines. Bea, Chas's wife, also was from Napa Valley, brought up in a culture of wine. She was horrified when she first came to Pullman; it was so distant and unsophisticated. She recalled with great inflection, "It was so rural." In time, she appreciated the remoteness of Pullman and her ability to raise her children in a healthful environment. She learned to love the openness of the people of Washington, an openness that matched the landscape.

Nagel remembered the time that Walt Clore took him up to Bridgman's vineyard at Upland Farms, and he was impressed with the age of the vines, the thickness of the trunks of the vines. Walt took me on the same tour, a reminder that Washington has been growing quality grapes for a long time. I wonder how many others have accompanied Walt up the slopes of Sunnyside to regard the potential of the wine industry. For Walt it was almost a Dionysian rite of passage—hardly the hills above Athens, but nevertheless a hill looking down on the valley below through ordered rows of vines.

Bea Nagel talked of the wonderful cooperation that occurred between Walt Clore and Chas Nagel, a kind of male bonding, a fairly rare occurrence in academia. They weren't competing with each other. She said, "They both saw the excitement in this. They had such great vision. They saw that Washington wines were going to be able to compete with the world."

Chas idolized Clore. Bea found their relationship interesting. For her Dr. Clore was "rural," an Okie, she recalled fondly. "His mannerisms, his gait, his way of talking—all seemed so rural. I imagined him in bib overalls." Chas enjoyed the cooperative spirit that Walt possessed, and his sensitivity. Bea said, "They laughed at the same things. There was just some magnetism there. Chas felt that he could visit with Walt anytime that he wanted." Bea talked about the sense of family when Chas, George, and Walt would get together.

—PIVOTAL TEN-YEAR STUDY—

As the Wine Project began to unfold, other disciplines were brought in. The family began to expand. It would never be as close as Nagel, Carter, and Clore were, but this core family would accept into its nucleus other scientists and field workers. In 1966 Clore, Carter, and Nagel began an ambitious study entitled "Ten Years of Grape Variety Responses and Wine-making Trials in Central Washington." Known as Bulletin 823, it was funded through the technical assistance grants from the Economic Development Administration. It became the framework for answering the question of whether Washington state could produce a quality table wine, as well as the blueprint of the Wine Project.

Completed in 1976, it was an exhaustive study that became the guiding light of the emerging industry. Although it was published in 1976, its content was well known much earlier within the agricultural community in eastern Washington. Couched in scientific jargon was a simple statement: high-quality premium wines could be made from grapes, especially European wine grapes, grown in eastern Washington. There was one caveat: winter injury; about one year in six, there was the potential for severe cold that can cause damage to the grapevine. The thirty-two-page report contained sections on climate, with records dating back fifty years; adaptability of different varieties, with data on yields and must analysis; and a section on the evaluation of different varieties of wine based on records kept by Nagel's wine-tasting group, with data showing the wine's components. The study involved 149 varieties, of which 88 varieties were fermented and evaluated.

Contributing to this milestone study were scientists from other disciplines: Dr. Cyril Woodbridge (horticulturist), Irving Dow (soil specialist), Dr. Wyatt Cone (entomologist), Drs. Calvin Skotland and Gaylord Mink (plant pathologists), and Drs. Raymond Folwell and Richard Dailey (agricultural economists).

Additionally, Clore worked closely with the various county agents who got the information out to the growers: John Keene and Don Chapman in Yakima County, Frank Anderson in Benton County, Ray

Hunter in Adams County, Wayne Stambaugh in Walla Walla County, and Edward Forester in Klickitat County. Clore also worked closely with Dr. Robert Norton, horticulturist and superintendent of the Northwestern Washington Research and Extension Unit in Mount Vernon, on the west side of the Cascades.

It was truly a team effort brought together by the grace of Dr. Clore. If Nagel, Carter, and Brummund were the brothers of the family, these others were close relatives. All of these scientists shared the same basic motivation: help develop a new agricultural crop. Wine made it fun.

Wine, because it is appreciated as a cultural beverage with its historical roots, aesthetics, and intellectual properties that encourage people to compare its qualities, brought this family together. Dr. Clore, in his no-nonsense approach, kept the family focused on its mission—to answer the question: Can Washington state produce quality wine from premium wine grapes? A sense of purpose was made more immediate by the political atmosphere surrounding the California Wine Bill. Additionally, Prosser and the research center were drawn into the national wine network. They were visited by distinguished people: doctors, lawyers, politicians, and investors wanting to know what they were doing. All of it contributed to a sense of purpose and reinforced their efforts.

These ardent researchers had never before seen such interest in an agricultural crop. Rarely would people of such stature come to Prosser to talk about the quality of alfalfa, or even apples. If they did, it was more a discussion of either dollars and cents or growing practices. But with wine it was a clearer discussion of quality based on an international standard: Washington wines would be compared to the wines of the great wine-growing regions of the world: Bordeaux, Burgundy, Rhone in France; the wines of Germany; Italy; and particularly the wines of northern California's Napa and Sonoma Valleys. Tiny, isolated Prosser set in the alluvial sands of the Yakima Valley became intellectually closer to the world.

In 1974 Dr. Clore and George Carter were visited by Nancy Davidson-Short and Dorothea Checkley, both social sophisticates from Seattle. Nancy Davidson-Short was then editor for *Sunset* magazine and was researching a piece on Pacific Northwest wines. She brought along her friend Dorothea Checkley.

Before their trip, over lunch at the Space Needle, they had dreamed up the idea of a wine study group. They had been solicited by the

Pacific Science Center board to develop some kind of supportive activity that might align itself with the Science Center. That is when they thought about wine: a society of people who would come together and appreciate wine, the social, scientific, and aesthetic qualities of wine.

At the research center, in the stark institutional lab, they were treated to wines made by George Carter. Dorothea recalled, "There was no air-conditioning, though the windows were open, and this was my first time to have a Limberger wine. Limberger is a great thing to have on a cold winter's day with a leg of lamb, but when the temperature is 109 degrees—it's a marvelous way to put people on the road to abstention.

"We tasted nine different heavy red wines. It was fun because Dr. Clore was so full of himself. He was almost seeing visions of what was going to happen over there: changing from grapes for grape juice to grapes for wine."

Nancy and Dorothea found Walt to be a very impressive and attractive man. He was slow speaking, though enthusiastic and serious about his vision of wine. Nancy recalled, "It was the fall of the year: melons, tomatoes, peppers, and an abundance of fruit. It was tremendous."

Nancy wasn't new to the Yakima Valley. She was born in Yakima, then raised on both coasts, as her father was a naval officer. Yakima was her emotional home. Her maternal great-grandfather, William Parker, was one of the earliest settlers to the region. Her grandmother was a Moran, born at The Dalles, at the end of the Oregon Trail. And her grandfather, Harry Scudder, had come from Boston in 1888 to manage the Moxee Company.

For Dorothea, the Yakima Valley was a cornucopia of wonderfully fresh foods. When she was growing up in Connecticut, her parents were known to drive miles in search of the best food ingredients. She fell in love with the landscape and the people of the Yakima Valley.

On their drive home, Dorothea took out a pencil and paper and sketched out their vision of a wine society. They would have a big party in the fall, a festival of wine. They would have monthly dinners. They would take tours in the wine country of Europe, California, and the Pacific Northwest.

All of which came to pass. Thus was born the Enological Society of the Pacific Northwest. Their first official meeting was held in May 1975. The first festival in the fall of that year attracted 700 people to the Pacific Science Center in Seattle. With Dr. George Taylor as the society's first president, Dorothea helped guide it through its first years. The society became the largest consumer and "non-commercial" wine society in the world, with a membership of well over 2,500 members. Monthly dinners, called regional dinners, often sold out to 400 people, with over 50 volunteers.

Special were the trips to eastern Washington where the society picnicked on the lawn of the research center or in the orchards of Sagemoor Farms. Dorothea talks lovingly of the rapport with the people from eastern Washington, calling them educated agrarians. She says, "It was almost as if it were magic because of the fruit trees, that feeling of abundance. An abundance of such wonderful things. I had never been in a cherry orchard when the sun was hot, and the cherries were hot, and they were so incredibly good.

"I brought good cheese and specially baked bread. And all the wine in the world. People got sloppy with the sun beating down on us, so much wine."

And so much fun.

Prosser was no longer detached from western Washington. This was a major phenomenon that brought these scientists together. They had an audience, at first local, then national, with connections that spread to other parts of the wine world. This audience took on the quality of a cult following.

Washington wines deserved to be followed because they were distinct and promising. They also were an alternative to the overwhelming attention given to California. Washington state was a respite from the frenetic pace that was carving up Napa Valley. Napa Valley's wines had been discovered and declared equal to the world's greatest wines; Washington's wines were still in the discovery stage; the excitement of discovery was genuine.

For California, wine had been a continuous part of its agricultural community since the mighty gold rush that engorged that state. For Washington, even though wine's roots can be traced to the first Euro-American settlers, the development of the wine industry took on a sense of revolutionary proportions; change occurred seemingly overnight. It was a phenomenal circumstance of timing: Washington's consumers were weaning themselves off California's soft wines and discovering the potential of Washington wines; the wine industry, laying prone on the canvas after the fight of the California Wine Bill, gained consciousness; and the Wine Project was reaching out to the agricultural community, encouraging it to plant *vinifera* grapes.

This was probably the Wine Project's greatest accomplishment: its ability to convince skeptical and wary farmers to plant wine grapes. Those in the wine industry at the time, basically American Wine Growers and Associated Vintners, didn't need convincing; they knew that they could grow *vinifera* grapes and make quality wines. Foremost, they needed to know that they could sell the wines. Ultimately, they and other producers would need more grapes. The Wine Project planted the affirmative seed, propagated the vines, and nurtured the expanded interest in wine grapes and wine.

Because Dr. Clore had been involved in agriculture since 1937 with some of the first studies of irrigated agricultural practices, farmers were receptive to Clore's advice. They had listened when he taught them new strategies for farming asparagus, increasing yields and quality. They had listened when research improved their cultural practices, and yields, with the Concord grape. Now he was taking them to a new level of sophistication: wine grapes and wine; it required them to learn about grape varieties and the complexities of wine.

As receptive as they might have seemed, they still needed to be convinced. That's where Vere Brummund excelled. His hard-earned knowledge of wine and grapes had broadened. Dr. George Stewart, a former Mississippian, a well-respected surgeon, and an early wine grape grower on Harrison Hill in Sunnyside and on the Wahluke Slope, recalled how he met Brummund. Stewart's property on Harrison Hill, incidentally, was part of William Bridgman's original vineyard, including some of the first grapes planted by Bridgman. One of the grapes still grows in his backyard, the Csaba of Hungary. His own interest in wine began when he made his first batch of wine from the Catawba grape, also growing on his property. He said, "It was wonderful, with a bit of a sparkle to it." He had been bitten by the wine bug. Curiosity led him to Dr. Clore.

One of the physicians he consulted with worked out of Prosser. The physician's nurse was Irene Clore. In casual conversation, Stewart mentioned that he needed help managing his small vineyard. Irene Clore knew just the right person. Dr. Stewart began to make trips out to the research center to visit with Clore. There he met Vere Brummund. Dr. Stewart recalled, "He has to be given a lot of credit, he trained at Cornell, and he was Dr. Clore's assistant. In those days, Dr. Clore was mainly involved in Concords and Vere was the *vinifera* man. He was on a mission: he called them the noble wine grapes. I remember four grapes that he was particularly interested in: Chardonnay, Cabernet

Sauvignon, Riesling, and Pinot Noir." He recalled how adamant Brummund was about wine grapes and wine. The fact that Dr. Clore was backing him up gave him even more credence. Dr. Clore was the farmer's federal reserve. He gave added weight to Brummund's mission.

Stewart recalled visiting the research center and tasting the wines being made by George Carter. Stewart had bought his property in 1965 and made his first wines in 1966, when he began to visit the center. He remembered George Carter: "He was dedicated to three things: wine-making, chess, and elk hunting. Nothing would interfere with his elk hunting. In fact, I once thought about getting him as my winemaker but Dr. Clore pointed out that nothing could get Carter away from the elk season." Recalling his visits to the research center, Stewart said, "Those were wonderful times. We didn't know that we were necessarily on to anything. We had been brainwashed to believe that Washington would never be able to make good wines. I remember that I once asked Santa Rosa Winery to make a special wine for me out of the Catawba grapes that I had on the property. Marie Christensen was the winemaker then and the wine she made didn't work out. I think it was because the barrel she used had been contaminated by a previous bad wine."

Stewart, recalling that early excitement at the research center, continued: "We were all thinking about trying to make something special." And they had fun. Soon, Chuck Henderson of Bingen would join them in tasting the center's wines. Then Les Fleming, vineyard manager at American Wine Growers, would show up and start telling stories. Add Vere Brummund, George Carter, and occasionally Chas Nagel, and suddenly there were enough people for a party. Here was a serious group, some scientists and some growers, about to have a good time. Together they forged a vision of the wine industry's future.

They were undaunted by potential marketing problems. How were they going to convince the wine-buying public that Washington wines were good? Wines, unlike other commodities, tend to appeal to a highly educated and select group. The biggest hurdle would be to convince wary consumers in Washington state, because Washington wines were largely undrinkable. Ignorant of these potential marketing problems, these enraptured researchers and early wine growers forged merrily ahead.

By 1968 Dr. Raymond Folwell, an agricultural economist at Pullman, entered the scene and began a lengthy study of the marketplace. And although the results of his study would not be published until nearly ten years later, he published smaller articles early on. Most important, he would make a sometimes icy drive down from Pullman to the monthly meetings at the Fireside Inn at Grandview to meet with grape growers and present his information.

It is probably the unique nature of Washington state, severely divided by the Cascade Mountains, that creates a cultural split in the state's population. Eastern Washington is primarily drier, higher, and agricultural-based. Western Washington is moister, lower, and industrial-based. Sometimes the two sides never seem to meet: the east side tends to be more conservative and actively pro-individual rights; the west side is liberal and more concerned with public rights. There are few gentlemen farmers in Washington state, crossing both sides of the state. Rather, the farming community is set off by itself. And this is where the Washington wine revolution would begin. It is a very different situation from that in California, or even Oregon.

In California, the north coast counties are the playgrounds for the rich and famous. Even though not all wineries that grew out of the '70s were started by wealthy owners, the consumers were close by in San Francisco and its rapidly expanding suburban communities. In Oregon, the first wineries were begun mainly by transplanted Californians born into the culture of wine. Later, Oregon wineries would be dominated by artisans.

But the first Washington wine grape growers were primarily farmers. Dr. Clore and Vere Brummund had convinced them that if they would just plant *vinifera* grapes, quality wines would eventually be made, and the marketplace would respond.

Chapter Twenty

NEW VINEYARDS AND WINERIES

Of all the decades of Washington's wine history, the decade of the '70s was by far the most exhilarating. It was the decade of the wine grape; there was a huge increase in plantings of wine grapes and an explosive growth in viticultural knowledge. By the end of the decade there were over 3,000 acres of wine grapes planted.

Fortunately, it was also a time of an incredible upsurge in consumer interest in wine, a decade when the baby boomers came of wine-drinking age. With the accumulated wealth of their parents, along with disposable income, the growth potential was extraordinary.

This fact had not been lost on Bank of America, based in San Francisco, a short drive from the vineyards of northern California. The world's largest bank forecast in 1970 that by 1980, U.S. consumption of wine would rise from 250 million gallons to about 400 million gallons, a projected increase of 60 percent. Bank of America noted that the annual per capita disposable income would rise from about $3,200 in 1970 to about $5,600 in 1980, and that 40 million young adults would reach drinking age during the 1970s.

Based on those rosy forecasts, a massive dose of investment capital radically transformed the sleepy wine valleys of California, taking them from basically farming communites to the playgrounds of the wealthy and the byways of corporate industry.

Washington state's entry was much more humble. It grew acre by acre—5 acres here, another 10 acres somewhere else—built slowly by individuals and families, or by firms generating enough excess operating income to grow ever so slowly. In 1970 Washington state had less than 400 acres of premium wine grapes planted. That same year, 16,000 acres of wine grapes were planted in California.

—*STE. MICHELLE VINTNERS*—

Wally Opdycke, a young man of thirty-two, was managing fixed-income portfolios for Safeco Insurance Company. He was also in charge of the bank lines for the company. Opdycke had lived in San Francisco and knew a little about wine. He had visited the Napa Valley numerous times and taken an interest in wine. His interest in Washington wines was piqued in 1969 by Stan Reed's series of articles in the *Seattle P-I* about Associated Vintners.

As a person interested in investment and finance, he found the wine industry appealing. He had read the glowing reports of the financial promise of the California wine industry. He had been working with a core group of people, including Mike Garvey, a Seattle attorney, who had already done a couple of business deals. He clearly saw an opportunity to get into the Washington wine business at its very beginning.

In 1970, Opdycke had written Dr. Clore of the Irrigation Experiment Station in Prosser to tell him that he was interested in wine and wine grapes in Washington state. He wanted to know more about the wine grape trials, about varieties of grapes and where they were growing. Having asked these questions, Opdycke hadn't heard back from Dr. Clore. Then one day Opdycke's secretary came into his office and said that there was a Dr. Clore there to see him.

Opdycke recalled: "I said, 'What? *The* Dr. Clore came to see me?' He had his wife with him. He came in and we had a great visit. Walt is a true gentleman. He gave me a lot of information about the potential for investing in grapes and wine. He said, 'Look, someone should really do something here.'

"I said, 'Would you help me? This is something that I have decided to do.' He said, 'Absolutely.'"

Visits to the research center in Prosser furthered Opdycke's appreciation for Washington's potential. He saw firsthand what they were doing, tasted their wines, and knew that he wanted to make an investment (in vineyards, a winery, or both). Later in 1970, with his good friend Joe Ramseyer, he visited a number of *vinifera* vineyards in the Yakima Valley. They also looked at the Santa Rosa Winery (the former Upland Winery) in Sunnyside. They stopped at the Prosser research center and tasted the wines being made by George Carter.

It was during this trip that Wally Opdycke really got excited about the possibilities for wine grape growing. He recalled, "It was one of those days, it was beautiful; everything just seemed to fit." He and Ramseyer were impressed with the valley's abundance, with the variety and quality of flavors, not just with wine grapes but with all the fruits of the valley. And even though they were seeing hills lined predominantly with Concord grapes, it wasn't hard for Opdycke to envision wine grapes as he had seen in California. Opdycke says, "The country was different, but it was spectacular.

"The vision, for me, was really there. I could see it, almost taste it. Driving around the valley, there were only several hundred acres of *vinifera* planted at that time. Most of it was owned by American Wine Growers. I remarked to Joe that if we were going to invest here, we needed to acquire someone who was already in the business. It takes so long to start from scratch.

"I did a little research and found out that American Wine Growers was the only operating winery outside of Associated Vintners at that point. Everybody else was out of business or close to being out of business. So that was the impetus for me."

Opdycke called American Wine Growers and set up an appointment with Joe Molz. Molz, the leading partner in the winery, was the youngest. And Wally recalled that he was probably in his early sixties. The other partners were even older. Opdycke recalled thinking that these men were from an era when being in the wine business was not at all glamorous or respectable; it was the kind of thing you didn't talk about. The winery was still making primarily dessert wines. Opdycke recalled, "They were very low-key and nobody knew much about them. They had the Nawico label and the Pommerelle label and several others; these people were reticent, because of the nature of the business, to make much of an investment, to grow, and to be contemporary in the AWG product line."

Continuing, he said, "In fairness to them, they did make an attempt with the Ste. Michelle label, which represented maybe half of 1 percent of their sales. They did plant some *vinifera*—Cabernet Sauvignon, Semillon, Riesling, and Pinot Noir—so they did make a start. But they didn't have the patience, the capital, or the will to go beyond that."

Wally did his homework. He started with a Dunn and Bradstreet report on the company. He set up a meeting with Molz and found out that they wanted to make a change but weren't sure how to do it. Molz and partners wanted to sell; the time was right.

Victor Allison at American Wine Growers in Seattle about 1954.
—Photo courtesy of Lester Fleming.

Joe Molz called in a professional investment banker to help with negotiating the deal. Opdycke was concerned that the banker might quickly learn that Wally and partners didn't have any money and the banker might learn how they planned to do this deal. Wally was used to engineering leveraged buyouts, although nobody called them that at the time. The idea was that he and his partners would go to a bank and borrow the money needed for the acquisition.

Opdycke, a lean man with a distinctive, etched, round face framed in dark black hair and bushy eyebrows, was insistent, shrewd, and forceful. The investment banker thought that the winery partners should present the deal to someone else, to get another viewpoint. But they quickly found out that there was no one else interested, either locally or out of California. The Californians were too busy with their own vineyards and couldn't conceive of making table wines much north of Napa Valley.

In 1972, Opdycke's group made their offer. Molz and partners accepted. Opdycke quickly formed a new company, Ste. Michelle Vintners, that acquired all the assets of American Wine Growers, including brands, equipment, and land. The acquisition had been a lot of fun for Wally. He was able to do this in his spare time while still working full-time for Safeco.

Now he owned a new company and would have to manage the

business. That was far different from managing investment portfolios. His plan was to run the company off of its operating capital. This meant that he had to continue to sell the very wines he wanted to change. His new winery was stacked to the ceiling with wines that he abhorred. They were producing over 300,000 cases of wine, and Opdycke faced a terrible dilemma: How were they going to continue selling the Pommerelle and Nawico wines and increase their production of the Ste. Michelle brand? They couldn't afford to dump all of that wine; that was their bread and butter.

Opdycke relied on Vic Allison, who continued on as the general manager, and Les Fleming, who remained in charge of the vineyards and the Grandview plant—two seasoned veterans of the wine business. Without them, Wally would have been up a creek. Not only was he trying to finance the operation and the transition to table wines with cash flow, but he also had to finance new vineyard plantings. He knew that he had to act fast, for a couple of reasons.

First, there was the lead time necessary for the grapevines to produce grapes: three to four years. Secondly, they had to line up to get planting material out of California. Quality grape plants were in short supply because of the rush of plantings in California. But being in a hurry would backfire on them later.

In 1973 Ste. Michelle Vintners bought 500 acres of land at Cold Creek, three miles west of the Hanford Project and considerably north of most of their other vineyards, based on information given to Wally by Dr. Clore. This was a drastic change in direction for the company. Nearly 100 acres of Cabernet Sauvignon and 100 acres of White Riesling were planted. Les Fleming and Vic Allison had been used to planting 5- and 10-acre lots of different grapes. Suddenly they were told to plant, ultimately, 500 acres, in effect doubling the state's total wine grape acreage.

At the winery, Wally was trying to decide how to expand the premium wines and focus on quality. He thought that it was important to bring in a California winemaker. He still had André Tchelistcheff acting as consultant, but he felt that he needed a full-time winemaker from California. He reasoned that Howard Somers had been in the Washington wine business too long to make the change to *vinifera* wines.

One of the winemakers he met was Mike Grgich, a protegé of the company's consultant, Tchelistcheff. Opdycke invited Mike to come to Ste. Michelle. Grgich was already familiar with the wines because he had tasted samples sent to Tchelistcheff by Allison of American Wine Growers. Grgich was very interested in the potential for quality wines in Washington. He had visited the vineyards in eastern Washington with Wally. Grgich indicated that he was very interested in moving to Washington and being a part of what Ste. Michelle Vintners was trying to do.

But Vic Allison cautioned against bringing in Grgich, because it might create friction with Tchelistcheff, with whom Vic got along well. By this time, Wally trusted and appreciated Allison's insights, and relied on Allison heavily. Opdycke, remembering that difficult decision, said, "I wasn't going to (be able to) have them both. André clearly had the stature and the knowledge and the voice in the industry that would be more beneficial to us than Mike, even though Mike was willing to come up full-time. André would still be just a consultant. Mike would have invested in the future; it wouldn't have been the cost thing. Mike said he would like to do this, but he didn't want to be under the shadow of André. That wouldn't work.

"I thanked Mike for his encouragement."

Today Mike Grgich is one of America's preeminent winemakers producing wine under his own name in Napa Valley.

"We stayed with André, and he was really helpful to us over the years."

—MARKETING—

In 1973 Ste. Michelle wines were selling better in Washington, D.C., than they were in Washington state. The wines were being sold nationally by a young company out of Houston named Bon-Vin, owned by two young Oklahomans, Robert Conley and Charles Finkel. Conley, tall, slender, and handsome, had the sweet drawl of a southerner. Mild in manner, he handled the administrative side of the business and managed most of the marketing of their young company. Charlie Finkel was the consummate salesman—bowtie, curly blond hair, and round, expressive face. His Oklahoman twang added resonance to his sales pitch.

Charlie had worked for Monsieur Henri Wines out of New York. It was typical in those days for large wine brokers like Monsieur Henri to represent brands nationally. Most of the brokers were based in New York: Warren Strauss, Frank Schoonmacher, and Frederick Wildman. They tended to sell their wines to big retail stores and restaurants in the important metropolitan areas of the United States. On one visit to

Tulsa, Charlie called on one of his customers, Sidney Matless, a retailer. Matless knew that Charlie was on his way out to San Francisco and suggested that he visit with his uncle, Leon Adams.

Charlie and his wife, Roseanne, traveled to San Francisco in 1968 and looked up Leon Adams at his home in Sausalito. Finkel recalled, "Adams was very hospitable. I learned a lot from him. What we learned was that in his opinion—and his opinion was the Dorian of California wine writers, having written the most successful wine book, the first wine book in the Book-of-the-Month Club—'if you are interested in good wine, the potential for the Yakima Valley'—he didn't say Washington state—'is ready. That is where I think you should seek out wines of quality because it has unlimited potential.'"

Charlie didn't think much more about that conversation until a year later. Charlie was aware of Washington state from a stint at Fort Lewis in 1966. He recalled being interested then in wine and going to a local grocery store and purchasing either a Nawico or Pommerelle burgundy. He says, "It was horrible."

But a series of events led him back to Washington, beginning with his visit with Leon Adams. He went back to Tulsa and started his new company, Bon-Vin, with Conley. They had no money and relied on Charlie's wife's income as a dental hygienist. Bon-Vin began with a few wines out of California, small, unheard-of wineries like Sutter Home, Dry Creek, Fetzer, Kenwood, and ZD. He and Conley would try to work the slightly smaller businesses that were bypassed by the big New York wine brokers. They slowly built up their business until even the big shops and famous restaurants wanted to talk to them.

On one of Charlie's visits to California in 1969, he called on Darrel Corti of Corti Brothers in Sacramento. Charlie was impressed with Corti's selection of wine. It included wines from around the world: great sherries, ports, Madieras, and Italian wines—"every specialty you can imagine. Included in that was a multiple case stack of 1967 Ste. Michelle wines." Corti had floor stacks of the wines, 5 cases of each varietal.

When Charlie asked Corti what he thought of the wines, Corti politely suggested that he taste them for himself. Charlie recalled that "the reds were suspect; the whites were wonderful. I called Victor Allison from Darrel Corti's office. I said, 'Mr. Allison, I am Charles Finkel and I have a company that is distributing wines nationally.' That was more or less true; we had aspirations."

Charlie recalled that he didn't know the scope of Allison's company, only the Ste. Michelle wines that he had tasted, and he didn't realize that Allison's American Wine Growers was the company that produced the Pommerelle burgundy he had tasted three years earlier. Charlie told Vic Allison that Bon-Vin wanted to be AWG's national agent.

Charlie remembered: "He said, 'Why?'"

"I replied, 'What do you mean, why?'"

"'Why would you like to represent our company?'"

"'Because the wines are delicious.'"

"He said, 'I can't give this goddamn stuff away.'"

Shortly after, Charlie went to Seattle and met Victor Allison. Vic took him to a Holiday Inn on East Marginal Way, in the industrial area of Seattle close by the winery, where the wines were being served. In the late '60s, Charlie figured, there were maybe two or three restaurants that carried the Ste. Michelle wines. Charlie signed a contract with Allison that allowed him to be the sole agent for AWG wines through-out the United States, excluding Washington and Oregon.

Bon-Vin hit the road. In New York, Boston, Washington, D.C., Chicago, and Denver, Charlie Finkel and Bob Conley would take the Ste. Michelle wines to the best restaurants and the best retailers and ask them what they considered to be their best wines. Then they would have them taste the Ste. Michelle wines next to their choices. In every instance, the buyers were taken aback; the Ste. Michelle wines were so fresh and distinctive.

Charlie recalled that it wasn't difficult to compare wines in those days. Usually the restaurateur would offer a Wente Brothers Grey Riesling to taste. It was a very popular wine at the time, but it is not a true Riesling. Ste. Michelle's Riesling was concentrated and fruity. Charlie recalled, "Washington wines were superior to California wines. Chardonnay was no big deal. If 5 or 10 wineries made Chardonnay in California at the time, I would be surprised. It wasn't until the '70s. There was no Gewurztraminer or Merlot."

Bon-Vin was allotted 3,000 cases of Ste. Michelle wines to sell that first year. Using its comparative tasting technique, the brokerage was able to sell out the wines that first year and all the years up to 1974, when Bon-Vin was allocated 25,000 cases.

—*U.S. Tobacco's Capital*—

This increase in the Ste. Michelle brand was encouraging to Opdycke, but he was quickly running out of capital to expand the Ste. Michelle brand. André Tchelistcheff was asking him to outfit the winery with stainless steel tanks, newer oak, and costlier equipment. All of this was being financed by the company operations. But Opdycke could see that Ste. Michelle was on a collision course with the company's former brands, Pommerelle and Nawico. Their sales were dropping off dramatically, while the Ste. Michelle wines were shooting ahead. The difference was that the Ste. Michelle wines were far more capital-intensive: new equipment, new vineyards, and higher distribution costs.

In 1973 Wally wrote up a new business plan. There was nowhere to go but up. By 1973 there were effectively only two remaining active wineries in the state: Ste. Michelle Vintners and Associated Vintners. It was Wally's idea that if he could just secure some venture capital through selling stock options, maybe they could advance to the next level. But Opdycke recalled, "The stock market kind of peaked then. There were lots of excesses in the marketplace. And the market was soft on deals. We didn't have much luck.

"Here we were, still trying to make berry wines. I was still at Safeco. Vic Allison was in charge and I would come down each day and try to bolster the distribution of the existing stock. How much port and muscatel could you sell? Costs were high and getting higher. It was a tough thing, trying to raise money. We found that the corporate route was the way to go."

Through a corporate agent, Opdycke and partners attracted a nibble from Labatt's Beer out of Toronto. Labatt's was trying to get into the wine business in a bigger way. It owned several operations back east in Canada and had a winery locally in Victoria. Labatt's vineyard manager knew Washington grapes very well. He understood the potential. The company also understood some of the financial advantages of wine production in Washington state, and the risks. It had also looked closely at investing in California.

Opdycke and Garvey, on behalf of their partners, went back to Toronto to negotiate a deal. Labatt's let them know that it was very interested. Wally recalled, "That had to have been the summer of '73. Then I came back here and had a minor hemorrhoid operation; I was in the hospital. And the president of Labatt's was out here in Seattle and he wanted to meet me.

"So here I am in bed at Providence Hospital, I believe, and this guy is trying to do a business deal. That meeting went pretty well. Labatt's wanted me to run the company for it. That sounded pretty good. I had never managed a business before. If the deal was right, I would do it. I liked the people, not only the wine division people but the president and the people managing Labatt's. I was all set to do it."

Then he got a call from a representative of the United States Tobacco Company out of Connecticut: "Couldn't you just take some time to talk to these people? They have read your report and they are quite interested in talking with you."

Opdyke replied, "Well, ok, but I don't want to blow this other deal because we are real close. If these guys are interested and can make a decision quickly, I will meet with them."

A couple of people came out. They had a couple of good meetings, and Opdycke remembered that things escalated very quickly. He found himself attracted to U.S. Tobacco. For one thing, it was an enormously successful company, selling primarily smokeless tobacco, one of America's oldest consumer products. They were also down-home people; they had never done an acquisition before. It was an old-fashioned company that just happened to be very profitable, and it was market-savvy. This market angle was what most interested Wally. He was aware that to expand his company, two things would be necessary: cash and market penetration. He liked the way U.S. Tobacco was committed to the long term and how it understood that, to be successful, one had to build a brand. It also understood what was necessary to build a brand, from image to distribution. But it didn't know wine.

Labatt's did.

Both deals were about the same in value. In the end, U.S. Tobacco won out because Wally believed the future was in the company's ability to build recognition. Also, Opdycke really liked the people and he believed that they really liked him.

The offer was fantastic. U.S. Tobacco was willing to give the partners shares in U.S. Tobacco (UST) commensurate with their ownership in Ste. Michelle Vintners. Additionally, Wally would be retained to implement his original business plan. Opdycke recalled, "I thought, 'In the long run, here is a company that doesn't know the wine business and they are going to rely on me, and here are the other guys and they already know the wine business.' UST was a U.S. company and I thought in the long term it might be a better deal than Labatt's.

"I thought they really had the conviction to stick with it and that really mattered to me."

In 1978 Washington experienced one of its coldest winters. The Cold Creek Vineyard, planted five years earlier, was hard hit. The entire vineyard was nearly completely destroyed; in its haste to get the young plants into the soil, the company hadn't bothered to rip the soil deep enough or plant the young vines as deeply as they should have been. Opdycke pointed out that U.S. Tobacco "didn't even blink." For UST, it was a question of whether in the long term Washington state could grow fine wine grapes.

U.S. Tobacco had deep pockets. Wally estimated that they invested over $150 million in the wines of Ste. Michelle. That had a profound impact on the fledgling modern industry. Ste. Michelle Vintners dominated the wine landscape in the vineyard and in its sales efforts, nationally and locally. That is why Walt Clore is so appreciative of what Opdycke accomplished; the money that U.S. Tobacco pumped into the industry was the needed primer.

In October 1974, Ste. Michelle Vintners' 1972 Johannisberg Riesling won the top ranking in a tasting of Rieslings by a panel organized by Robert Balzer of the *Los Angeles Times*. It was a stunning announcement to the world that Washington-produced wine was as good as or better than comparable wines from around the world. It was described as a "flowery, delicate, sweet-edged wine with a wonderful fragrance." It really shocked the wine communities in both California and Washington.

But the tasting's real value was its effect on the growers in eastern Washington. Charlie Finkel and Bob Conley were out convincing the rest of the United States, and Wally Opdycke and partners had convinced the corporate world, but the farmers—the people who had to make that initial planting—were still skeptical. Sure, they trusted Dr. Clore when he told them that premium wine grapes could grow in eastern Washington. And, yes, Vere Brummund was right; they should be planting *vinifera*, now, for the future. But they remained unconvinced. Hadn't many of them watched in horror as Hinzerling Vineyards and Preston Vineyards, then the Sagemoor Farms, and finally Veredon Vineyards all got blasted by arctic air a couple of years earlier?

The tasting results sent a ripple though the valleys of eastern Washington like a chinook out of the north. Growers perked up. The *Los Angeles Times* tasting was in October. Effectively, the 1974 season was behind them, but the next two years, 1975 and 1976, were the true turning point in the Washington wine industry.

Growers were ready to plant; they were only limited by the availability of plant material, especially strong, certified virus-free vines.

Chapter Twenty-One

INVESTING IN WASHINGTON'S WINE FUTURE

U.S. Tobacco's entry into the Washington wine industry in 1974 was a major development—by its sheer economic presence it dwarfed the efforts of all the other vineyard plantings at the time. In 1976, U.S. Tobacco built an amazing estate in Woodinville at a staggering cost of $6 million. The winery, with its French chateau styling, appeared to be staking claim to its territory; its fiefdom would be all the vineyards of Washington.

What would it have been like if Chateau Ste. Michelle had not involved corporate money from the vast resources of U.S. Tobacco? What might have happened if Opdycke had been unsuccessful in recruiting capital to his new Ste. Michelle Vintners?

If Ste. Michelle had been unable to continue, it would have been a crushing blow to the fledgling industry. Yes, there were numerous small wineries just around the corner: Hinzerling Vineyards, Preston Wine Cellars, Manfred Vierthaler Winery, Salishan Vineyards, Bingen Wine Cellars, Leonetti Cellars, Puyallup Valley Winery, and Snohomish Valley Winery. All of these wineries, and the many vineyards that went in around 1975, got caught up in this frenzy of optimism.

Had Ste. Michelle gone under, it might have dampened the hopes of these start-up wineries. Remember, these were small businesses. They often relied on bank notes for funding. If Ste. Michelle had gone under, there might have been a crippling ripple effect throughout the banking community. There is no doubt that the industry would have grown much more slowly and it would have likely remained a cult industry, known to only a devoted few.

No doubt, U.S. Tobacco saved Ste. Michelle Vintners. More difficult to answer is whether its entry helped fuel the dynamic plantings and wineries that began to spring up by the mid-'70s. I doubt it. Those plantings and wineries were the result of a hardy group of independent individuals. They were well aware of Ste. Michelle's expansion, but I doubt that they made market or production plans based on the fortunes of Ste. Michelle.

—BOORDY VINEYARDS—

Just as UST was immersing itself in the Washington wine industry, another corporation was thrashing in deep water, trying to remain afloat, trying to find its place in the Washington wine market.

Boordy Vineyards was owned by the Seneca Foods Corporation, then called the Seneca Grape Juice Company, in conjunction with Philip and Jocelyn Wagner of Baltimore. Seneca built a 250,000-gallon winery and with the 1971 vintage began production of 130,000 gallons of wine. That was a huge commitment, considerably greater than Ste. Michelle's and Associated Vintners' output of premium wines at the time.

Philip Wagner, the east coast equivalent of Leon Adams, was a newspaper editor for the *Baltimore Sun* and a student of the grapevine. On the side, he and his wife took an active interest in wines and began planting grapes on their estate in Riderwood, Maryland, relying chiefly on French hybrid grapes. In 1945 they began selling commercial wines from their estate winery. Additionally, he published two books: in 1933, *American Wines and Wine-Making,* and in 1945, *A Wine-Grower's Guide.* Both books were well written and directed toward the winemaker interested in producing table wines. Boordy Vineyards, in partnership with Seneca, later opened a second winery in New York.

Philip Wagner came to know about Washington through his association with Seneca Grape Juice Company and the company's president, Art Wolcott. Seneca was already using Washington Concord for its juices. Wolcott convinced Wagner to go into partnership with him and to expand the Boordy Vineyards brand to include Washington-produced wines.

Today, Wagner is in his nineties. His original winery in Riderwood celebrated its fiftieth anniversary in the fall of 1995. Wagner recalled that Wolcott was a large-scale producer. He was used to entering a market in a big way. Wagner said, "I favored an extremely modest beginning because an established market, a real market, had first to be realized in Washington."

The Boordy Vineyard Washington wines were unique in a number of ways. First, its entire production was devoted to dry table wines. It released four wines: a 1971 Pinot Chardonnay, a Yakima red table wine, a Yakima white table wine, and a Yakima rosé table wine. Second, the proprietary table wines used Yakima as part of the wines' titles, a daring move, but consistent with Wagner's philosophy of identifying the region where the grapes are grown (and the wine is made).

Wagner, who believed in using French hybrid grapes but without direct experience in Washington state, assumed that French hybrid grapes would fare better than *vinifera*. Through Wolcott's direction, Seneca entered into a three-way partnership with Pete Taggares and Mogie Spiegel, of the Spiegel Corporation in Chicago, in a vineyard development east of Pasco called the Snake River Vineyard. In 1971, the partners planted 500 acres of Concord alongside smaller amounts of *vinifera* and French hybrid grapes. A year later, they planted 1,700 more acres of Concord to become (and remain) the world's largest Concord vineyard. Besides Concord, they eventually planted about 100 acres of wine grapes: 70 acres of *vinifera* and 30 acres of French hybrid grapes.

This was an ambitious commitment of grapes for the winery. In addition, by 1974 the winery held contracts with growers for over 238 acres of hybrid grapes. It calls to mind William Bridgman's parallel efforts with grower contracts at the repeal of Prohibition, when he advertised that he had 165 acres of grapes under contract with seventy farmers. Both were grand undertakings in untested markets.

Unfortunately, the wines were not liked by consumers. One of the problems was that Wagner was no longer directly involved with the winery operation. Had he been more hands-on, he would have recognized the potential for *vinifera*. It wasn't until later, after the winery had failed, that he accurately described the Yakima and Columbia Valleys as "the Mediterranean turned upside down." By that he meant that Washington combined the qualities of Europe's southern wines—warm and generous—with the qualities of the northern European wines—intensely flavored with balancing acids. But even wine-wise Wagner could not overcome his east-coast prejudice and enthusiasm toward French hybrid grapes.

Additionally, Andy Tudor, the winemaker, had come from California and was ill prepared to deal with Wagner's vision of wines

made from both hybrid grapes and *vinifera*. In an interview with Helen
Willard, he admitted, "I am learning along with others how to grow
wine grapes." He also noted, "It is just beginning here. It may take ten
to twenty years to learn the varieties most suitable for this climate and
soil and how to produce these efficiently in order to obtain premium
wines from them."

Tudor wasn't used to working with the tart (often one-
dimensional) flavors of the hybrid grapes. When they were added to the
slightly acid *vinifera* grapes, it caused the wine to be out of balance,
resulting in wines that were Washington wine's worst nightmare: thin
and acidic.

Nate Chroman, a respected writer for the *Los Angeles Times,* tasted
the first wines from Boordy Vineyards in 1973. He kindly called them
"interesting wines" and said they were making "a good beginning, particularly Boordy Vineyards' Yakima Valley white, 1971, a blend of
Semillon and Chardonnay grapes." In that same article, Chroman
noted some of the difficulties Washington wines would encounter outside of the state: "Washington's biggest hurdle may be its image as an
apple-producing state. Few wine drinkers or writers have waxed
eloquently over a glass of Washington state wine. Getting the wine
drinker to try the first glass will be more difficult than getting him to
taste the second."

Tom Stockley of the *Seattle Times* was much less enthusiastic about
the Boordy wines. In one of his rare departures from his glowing wine
reviews, Stockley actually suggested the wine was maybe better poured
down the drain.

The Boordy Vineyards never established a market for its wines,
stung as it was from the poor quality of its initial wines. Finally, in a
tragic ending, in 1976 Andy Tudor was found dead in his winery office.
Presumably he fell and struck his head on the corner of his desk.

The winery was finished. To Wolcott and Wagner's credit, they
pulled the wines off the market rather than risk hurting the
Washington wine industry.

Boordy Vineyards' trials had not been in vain. Other growers
and budding winemakers saw that the future was in *vinifera*—not
in hybrids.

But one has to wonder about the other modern pioneer growers at
that time. Could they be so enthralled by their own visions that they
couldn't see the hazards that confronted them? What were Mike
Wallace, Bill Preston, or Alec Bayless thinking when their first vineyard

plantings were frozen? What kind of people were these?

These were not people who had deep financial wells.

More importantly, these were people who had staying power.

Chapter Twenty-Two

NEW PIONEERS

—HINZERLING VINEYARDS—

Today, Mike Wallace of Hinzerling Vineyards is a man at relative peace with himself. At fifty years of age, he can look back in wonder at the last twenty-five years. His life in the Washington wine business has been as exhilarating as driving a four-wheeler up a sagebrush hill. He laughs a wonderful, high, carefree laugh that spreads the wrinkles in his sun-worn face. Wallace is an interesting study in character. His almost southern accent and manner of speaking belie his intense, well-chosen words. His insights are direct and colorful.

His path to the wine industry began while he was in the army, stationed in California. He had befriended the father of a girl he was then dating. The father, also in the service, had taken to collecting wine while traveling in Europe and the United States. He initiated Mike's journey into wine with a taste of a Louis Martini Reserve Cabernet Sauvignon. Cost: $3 a bottle. Mike then bought his first case of wine. He was twenty-four years old.

When Wallace, who grew up in Seattle, returned in 1969 after his stint in the army, he happened upon the series of articles in the *Seattle Post-Intelligencer* by Stan Reed. Mike remembered that Reed wrote about tasting the wines made at the Irrigation Experiment Station in Prosser and about Clore's and Carter's work.

Wallace began to explore wine through Emile Ninaud's Champion Wine Cellars, then located down on Third Avenue a few blocks north of the Seattle police station, where Mike's dad, Jerry Wallace, was a beat cop.

Mike called Dr. Clore and made arrangements to visit eastern Washington in the summer of 1969. Mike recalled, "Walt was overly enthusiastic about the whole thing." Wallace was familiar with eastern Washington. When he thought about it, he envisioned a vast area of rolling wheat fields, or the Grand Coulee Dam, and the inland cities of Wenatchee and Spokane. He recalled, "I had to look up on a map the area called the Wahluke Slope that Walt had talked about. So I went out there. It was unirrigated. It was a windy day. It looked like the most desolate, god-awful place that you would want to look at. There were tumbleweeds rolling down the road. And you couldn't see because it was so dusty."

His next visit was quite different. It was one of those beautiful clear days when the sky is bigger than the horizon. He visited the research center and one of Ste. Michelle's vineyards. He didn't know what he was looking for; his wine vision hadn't yet taken shape. He was attending the University of Washington at the time and reading articles about wine. Everything he read pointed him toward the University of California Davis. After graduating from the University of Washington, he then enrolled in a two-year master's program at UC Davis in 1969 and was basically allowed to write his own course of study in agricultural management.

Mike remembered seeing Dr. Clore at UC Davis a couple of times making presentations, and he was even more excited because by then Ste. Michelle Vineyards had a couple of vintages of wine on the market; these were the wines that were gathering attention in California wine tastings.

When asked what the people at UC Davis thought about him making wine in Washington state, Mike replied, "They were interested, but nobody knew much about it. They always thought it was an interesting idea. They looked at you kind of funny. If I told people that I was going to go back and plant some vineyards, they would say, 'Uh-huh,' and that would be all I would get out of them.

"Early on at UC Davis, I was in the library and a lady came in. She was from the Philippines, taking winemaking classes because her father had a winery in the Philippines, making fruit wines. I asked her why she was over here. She said their wines weren't very good. And I said, 'Uh-huh.' Making wine in Washington state was just a whole other set of circumstances—like making wine in the Philippines."

After graduating from UC Davis, Wallace went directly to Prosser. He and his father had already bought land in 1971, under a corporate

Mike Wallace in Hinzerling Vineyard. 1977.
—Photo by Lawrence J. Allen. Courtesy of Elizabeth Purser-Hendricks.

umbrella with partners. They ordered vines for planting the next year.

Mike recalled, "I wasn't talking about it. I was doing it. I had moved up here as soon as school was out; so, not too long after that, we planted a vineyard in June of '72, kind of late. My folks moved over a couple of months later." His idea had gone from dream to reality within three years of reading Stan Reed's wine columns.

Toward the end of that summer, Mike visited Dr. Clore again. Clore told him about a grant that he had just received; it was in the same academic area that Mike had just studied. That's when Mike began working for the research center. Mike remembered, "It was a good deal because I learned a great deal from Walt. He was pretty open to my doing some other things as long as I did the things that I had to do."

I wanted Mike's perspective on the Wine Project. Was Walt in charge?

He answered, "Walt ruled with an iron hand. But that is so ridiculous because Walt is the kind of guy who is really easy to get along with. He has always been very progressive in his thinking. There are obviously other people who had ideas about the wine industry, other investors, and other people—the Lloyd Woodburnes, the Alec Baylesses—but in my own opinion there isn't anyone who acted as much as a catalyst as Walt. He was always encouraging people to go out there and try things. He is so enthusiastic about stuff!"

In November 1972 the newly planted Hinzerling Vineyard was destroyed by unseasonably cold weather. The partners had lost 65 percent of their vines on their 23-acre vineyard. Wallace says they made a few mistakes: they shouldn't have planted greenhouse plants, especially so late in the season; they planted too shallow in the soil; and they should have irrigated later. But how were they to know?

"I kind of got discouraged. But Walt kept saying this happens. The chance of it happening back to back is one in twenty and if you want to be in business you have to accept that. Also, one of my friends, an investor and one of my college professors, a plant scientist, said, 'That is agriculture; get off your butt and plant it again. Maybe it will happen again.'

"I said, 'Yeah, you're right.' So we did replant, in 1973, and it worked."

Mike recalled, "You go in and you think, hey, this is easy. You don't know, nobody knows. Easy or not easy, you see a vineyard out there and you think it can't be that hard. Once you've done it, you find out it is not that easy."

Continuing, he said, "A lot of things are out of your control. There is nothing you can do about the weather."

In 1975 Mike was able to make a small batch of experimental wines from his own grapes. His first commercial vintage was in 1976, 100 cases each of four wines: Cabernet Sauvignon, Gewurztraminer, Chardonnay, and Riesling.

—WINES AND AGE—

In 1993 I tasted the 1976 Hinzerling Cabernet Sauvignon at a wine tasting sponsored by Pike and Western Wine Shop. After tasting a number of wines from the '81, '85, and '87 vintages, I asked owner Michael Teer if he didn't have something older. That is when he brought out a bottle of 1976 Hinzerling Vineyard Cabernet Sauvignon.

What a treat! I had just that morning been listening to my interview with Mike Wallace, taped the previous year. As I tasted the wine, his reminiscences echoed in my head. The wine smelled of ripened fruit, cherries and raspberry. It had a deep garnet color, only slightly hinting at being nearly twenty years old. On the palate it was tart, the fruit slightly diminished by bottle age, but the flavors were bright, like tart, unsweetened raspberry. It was a bit awkward, like the other aged Washington Cabernet Sauvignons that we had tasted that evening.

I read the label: 110 cases, 9 bottles. His label notes suggested aging the wine until 1981–1982, and he signed it *Mike Wallace, Enologist.*

The wine was definitely tired and probably on a downward spiral, but I was amazed at the bright inkling of fruit in the middle, like a twinkle in the eye of a nursing home resident. Consider also that the wine was made from three- and four-year-old vines (common wisdom suggests that older vines produce richer wines), and from a hot year, when there tends to be less concentration of flavor, acidity, and tannin.

I thought about the other wines, mostly Cabernet Sauvignons, we tasted: an '81 Columbia Winery "Red Willow," the '85 Woodward Canyon "Charbonneau" (70 percent Merlot, 30 percent Cabernet Sauvignon), the '85 Columbia Winery "Otis Vineyard," the '85 Leonetti Cellars "Seven Hills Vineyard," '87 Columbia "Red Willow," '87 Woodward Canyon, and '87 Leonetti Cellars "Columbia Valley." For comparison we tasted a bottle of '92 Woodward Canyon Cabernet Sauvignon, recently released from the winery.

These were stellar wines from generally accepted great vintages. Michael Teer noted, "Prior to the '87 vintage, these wines were our little secret," meaning that it was with the '87 vintage that national wine writers discovered these wines and their makers.

Thinking back to the tasting, I have two mixed thoughts. On the one hand, none of the wines jumped out at me as being better than when I first tasted them, either out of barrel or when they were released. In fact, I was greatly disappointed. I had recently drunk a bottle of 1985 Chateau Gloria, a St. Julien, Bordeaux, that was really marvelous. Its flavors had just turned into a perfumed rose with that wonderful complexity of crushed leaves and vibrant rose petal aromas, old enough to be showing some of its rich, mature qualities. It reminded me of the 1970 Chateau Gloria that charmed many of my colleagues in the late '70s.

But the Washington wines didn't have that quality, nor could I envision them developing it. It seemed like they were losing the intense wood and fruit flavors that were so beautifully framed in the '92 Woodward Canyon. The question is: Is that the best that we will ever see?

My other thought: These wines are still very young; they still have plenty of acidity, tannin, wood flavors, and fruitiness. They are awkward and singular. Maybe they haven't even begun to really age. We might have been tasting these wines too early; rather than aging them ten years, we may need to age them twenty or thirty years. For one thing,

Washington wines are made from grapes grown on their true own-rooted vines. The plants are not grafted onto American rootstock as in the vineyards of Bordeaux or California to protect against phylloxera, a burrowing parasitic plant louse that kills the grapevine by eating the vine's roots. It is thought that the sandy soils might play a role in inhibiting the phylloxera; maybe even that one-in-six years freeze might discourage the little pests.

Second, we just don't know. The oldest wines—those first vintages of Associated Vintners, Ste. Michelle's first Cabernet Sauvignons, and some of those first wines made by the research center—give an inkling. And we know that those wines are still kicking nearly thirty years later. But the winemaking and viticultural techniques have advanced remarkably since those first wines were made. And the vines are much more mature. And we expect more.

Mike remembered that first commercial vintage vividly: 2,500 gallons off the partners' own vineyard: "I remember seeing the first grapes coming in the door. And thinking, 'Oh geez, this is it. What do I do now?' (He laughs.) It is a whole lot different than the abstract, or making it in small lots, experimentally. Now it is commercial. What style is it going to be and where is it going to fit? Here it goes."

Mike recalled Vere Brummund's Veredon Vineyards: "Just about everything that could go wrong did go wrong; he was pretty savvy and knew what he was doing, but he had never done it before in those particular circumstances. That was how everybody learned: what not to do.

"Brummund had a good idea down there, he just had bad timing that had nothing to do with anything he did. They were things that anybody could look back and say were stupid things to do. Nobody could have told you how to do that. Cold, 2,4-D, soils that were hard to manage, and conflicting partners. The fatal mistake he made, I think, is that he put in a vineyard that was too big. In fact, I went in too big. I should have gone in much smaller."

Like Brummund, Wallace was not a farmer. He recalled that the farmers used to come around and laugh at them at the research center. "They still do," he said. "They refer to the research station as the play farm or the funny farm. It was always funny because everybody did things their own way, some of which worked and some of which didn't work. But on the other hand, the first place they came to was the research station.

"I think another thing about Walt is, even though he is a research-oriented person, he is also practical. He was always going out and looking at what farmers were trying. And evaluating that with what people knew about things. There was a lot of respect for each other."

I wondered how farmers looked at wine grapes.

Mike said, "Apple growers would ask, 'Hey, how much do you make on wine grapes?' And I'd say, 'You're going to get 5 to 6 tons to the acre of some varieties.' And they'd ask, 'How much do you get for that?' I'd say, 'Oh, I get maybe $300 a ton. So maybe we get $1,800 (an acre).'

"The apple grower would say, 'When I can get $2,800 (an acre), why would I want to do something like that? Who you going to sell them to? There is no established marketing system like there is with apples.' They always looked at it from that standpoint: too much uncertainty."

Besides starting the winery and working at the research center, Mike teamed up with fellow research aide Bob Fay to consult to vineyardists. Fay had for a while managed Associated Vintners' Stout Farm (also known as the Church Vineyard). Additionally, Wallace and Fay began selling wine grapes to home winemakers. At first they started hauling grapes over Snoqualmie Pass in their pickups, then trailers, then U-Hauls, and eventually they graduated to semi trucks. They were selling a large portion of Sagemoor Farms' grapes. They used to deliver the grapes to Associated Vintners, where the grapes were disseminated by boxload.

Eventually Gerry Warren, who had helped form Western Washington Winemakers Association, took over distributing the grapes in the Seattle area. Mike had worked with Gerry at the University of Washington; Warren had been his professor in the department of medicine. Wallace credited Western Washington Winemakers Association with expanding the wine industry in a couple of important ways: It connected amateur winemakers to the growers and fledgling wineries in eastern Washington; home winemakers would buy his wine just to compare his style and quality with their own. Also, a number of these home winemakers struck out on their own with commercial wineries, such as Gene Foote of E. B. Foote Winery.

It was like a dust devil, one of those little twisters, a swirl of dust on a freshly tilled field. Excitement ran deep. Wallace knew that he was on to something exciting and pioneering. He was at the ground floor of a new industry; much of the design work had already been done.

Mike tells of tasting experimental wine on one occasion at the research center with Walt and George. They were tasting wines with the folks from American Wine Growers: Wally Opdycke, André Tchelistcheff, Mike Grgich (who was then just visiting), and Howard Somers; Tchelistcheff tasted a lot of the experimental wines and made comments about them, and Opdycke talked about building another winery and invited the research center staff to visit their winery in Seattle.

Wallace liked their enthusiasm and their apparent willingness to invest in the wine industry. It must have validated his own dream. Shortly after this visit, Wallace remembered meeting Charles Finkel and Robert Conley, the two marketing geniuses from Bon-Vin. Wallace recalled, "I remember thinking that this is going to be interesting because these guys have a whole different outlook on marketing." Their enthusiasm was infectious; they were young and bright and they were able to articulate to Wallace and others just starting out the importance and the possibilities of the national market.

Wallace pointed to the significance of Ste. Michelle's grand entrance into the wine industry. He recalled meeting Vic Allison, then the manager of the company. Wallace said, "He was a very conservative guy. Nice man. He was one of those hard-nosed manager kind of guys: 'Tell me why this is going to work,' that kind of guy. You needed some of that." All the tension of the wine industry seemed to locate in Allison. He represented the past thirty years, but he also represented the future because if he could be convinced of its viability, anyone could. Wallace continued, "I'm kind of amazed that he took a venture into the (table) wine thing in the first place. Maybe they were forced into it; knowing Vic Allison, it is really hard to imagine him venturing into this; he acted like he knew nothing about it."

Then Wallace answered his own thoughts: "Their other business was pretty profitable. I can't believe that there was more money in this business than in what they were doing. But on the other hand, the companies that didn't make the change are no longer in business. Call it luck."

With U.S. Tobacco's grand entrance, first with the Cold Creek Vineyard planting, then with the construction of the Woodinville winery, Wallace began to clearly see the future. He liked it. The '70s were the beginning of an ocean's wave that would eventually reach the far shore in the '80s. The trick for Wallace, and other modern pioneers, was how to survive when the wave hit the far shore.

Throughout the '70s, Wallace's winery excelled. His wines were available in all of the best shops and restaurants. His picture graced the *Seattle Weekly* and in 1983 splashed nationally into *Time* magazine. Wallace and his mom and dad, Dee and Jerry, were a hot commodity: a small winery growing its own grapes and making exotic, full-flavored wines. Especially noteworthy were Mike's Cabernet Sauvignons. They were big, sometimes tannic wines that shouted "here we are" to consumers just discovering Washington wines, and wines in general. Mike also made a delicious dessert wine called Die Sonne, made from Gewurztraminer grapes that had been infected with the mold *Botrytis cinerea,* causing the grapes to dehydrate and concentrate the sugars, the acids, and the flavors in the wine—a whimsical wine during a fanciful time.

Wallace was a busy winemaker. As his own winery grew, he cut back on selling grapes. He was busy as a consultant to a number of wineries and hopeful vineyardists. He made Salishan Vineyard's first wines under the brand name Timmen's Landing, and eventually under their own name, Salishan Vineyards.

—PRESTON WINE CELLARS—

In January 1976, Bill Preston called Mike Wallace and asked him to come by his winery. Preston was in a pickle; his recently hired California winemaker, Darryl Delavan, had just given five days' notice that he was going back to California. Preston needed someone to oversee his first vintage, wines made from the '75 harvest.

Bill Preston asked Mike Wallace, "Do you do any consulting and what do you charge?"

In classic Mike Wallace style, Mike replied, "Is the pig's ass pork?"

Bill then asked him if he was interested in doing some consulting.

Mike responded, "Is the Pope Catholic?"

Preston had found the perfect ally. Basically, he wanted Wallace "to put his wines to sleep" until he could go find a new full-time winemaker. Mike accomplished this by allowing some of the wines to finish fermentation; others were given a good dose of sulphur dioxide, the winemaker's anaesthetic. Preston recalled going out to the winery one morning, and on the way passing some outdoor tanks. "Here was this stuff shooting out of the Gewurztraminer. It had been left on the lees (the spent yeasts and solids) and was refermenting. It blew the breather out of the tank and was shooting thirty feet in the air. It smelled like a fresh-cut grapefruit. So Mike racked it off the lees and cleaned it up, and got it to stop fermenting.

That Gewurztraminer geyser was symbolic of Preston's entry into the wine business. His personality, like the tank of wine, was explosive. He recalled planting his first grapevines: "I'll never forget this if I live to be 500 years old." Beginning to laugh, he told me, "The grapevines came in on the third day of July 1972. We planted those late, a little late in the season for little greenhouse plants." His hearty laugh is now in full swing. "I told McCormick, 'Boy, oh, boy, somebody is going to guarantee these things.'"

Preston had bought their cuttings from McCormick Nursery in Yakima. He had tried to get cuttings the year before but the demand on *vinifera* plants was overwhelming. McCormick had gotten hold of a supplier out of California that had greenhouse plants. This was the same supplier for the Bayless group and Mike Wallace.

It was 104° F the day they planted those grapes. Preston recalled that he had shared plants with Sagemoor Farms. "The plants came in those goddamn little ol' milk cartons. We were hand planting them. I'll never forget; that goddamn truck went over to Sagemoor. The plants were sitting on these bricklike things. That truck would go over a bump and the vines would get all mixed up. Is this a Cabernet? Or is this a Riesling?"

Preston roars in laughter, his tanned, round face creased with lines. In 1993 I talked with Bill at his kitchen table while Joanne, his wife, worked in the kitchen. She served me a glass of Muscat wine made by a neighbor. It was dark and sweet, a delicious sipping wine, a wine right out of the '30s. Preston looked tired and reflective. Normally he was animated and busy. In his sixties now, he was pensive and slightly bitter. The wine business has been tough and I guessed that he was mad, more than anything, that he wasn't young enough to start over.

Preston comes from a line of farmers. His parents arrived in the Tri-Cities area in 1927 from Wyoming, where they had farmed sugar beets and grain. Bill says, "They basically loaded everything and shipped out here. Moved down by Finley. That was wine country back in the '30s. They farmed big. Then they went broke in the '30s."

Preston recounted how his father lost everything and how the family regrouped, working as hired hands, buying an acre here and there until they were back in the farming business. Bill was born in Kennewick. He grew up amongst potatoes, sugar beets, and grain crops.

Then in 1939 his father sold the farm and moved the family to

California. In Bakersfield he got the idea to farm peppermint. They moved back to Washington, where he introduced peppermint to the fields of eastern Washington. The Prestons became big peppermint farmers, distilling the mint into oil. Preston recalled that his dad also had beans and potatoes; he was a basic row-crop farmer and he did well the next time around. Whenever his dad went into an area to farm, he would pull out grapes or fruit trees to make way for his row crops. Bill remembered that near their farm there had once been hundreds of acres of grapes, mostly owned by the Church Grape Juice Company that was later sold to Welch's.

In 1948, when Bill was in high school, his father bought a Ford tractor franchise with the idea that his boys might need something to do when they got out of high school. The Columbia Basin was just getting started. It represented a great opportunity.

After Bill got out of the service in 1952, he went to work for his dad. Irrigation was really important at the time, especially aluminum piping. Preston took some irrigation courses at the Columbia Basin College in Richland and got into the irrigation business. He said, "I did very well in it. As that ran out, I took over the tractor business from my dad. That was in '56. We took another franchise up by Othello. By then I was running the whole show, irrigation and tractor. Church's was a big customer. Other customers that we had were in Finley and they were wine-grape people."

Preston's franchise was very successful and Bill Preston served on the dealer council. Meetings alternated between Pasco and Portland. In about 1969 the meetings moved to Oakland. There he began traveling in the California wine country with other tractor dealers. In Madera, he saw the wine business in its raw form, where it was more akin to farming than the quaint wineries in Napa where he also visited.

Like father, like son. His father had seen mint; Bill saw grapes, wine grapes. He became interested in wine. He visited wineries in both the San Joaquin Valley and in Napa. Through the local Ford franchise dealer, he got a close-up view of how the wineries operated. He became friends with the Papagni wine family and watched as their company expanded greatly in the late '60s and early '70s.

Back home in Washington, Preston had a ranch that he rented out while he was operating the dealership. He had options on the property that allowed him to use portions of it if he chose. That is why he planted only 17 acres that first year, 1972. As each option opened up, he replanted his property in grapes. Soon he had 70 acres planted in grapes.

In January 1976, with Wallace watching over his wines, Bill told Joanne that they were going to California to get a winemaker. In March they set out in their Mercury Cougar and drove straight to Napa Valley. The next morning Bill called out to Joanne, "How many hundred dollar bills did you bring?" To me, Bill said, "She likes diamonds, but she likes hundred dollar bills, too."

To Joanne he had said, "I'm going into the wine country and I'm going to pirate me a winemaker." Back to me, Bill recalled, "I put on my shiny shoes. The first place I walked into was Chateau Montelena. I said, 'I want to hire a winemaker.'" He remembered he got a nice reception but no winemaker.

Bill told me how the word got out in the Napa Valley that he was looking for a winemaker. Eventually he thought he met his winemaker, Tom MacRostie, at Hacienda Winery in Sonoma. But MacRostie never showed up. MacRostie did happen to mention the winemaking job to Rob Griffin, a young winemaker at a neighboring winery, Buena Vista.

Griffin flew to the Tri-Cities the following year, in March 1977. It was a terrible, nasty day; dust descended on the Columbia Basin in great gusts of wind from the wheat fields on top of the Horse Heaven Hills to the southwest. Joanne recalled, "We had one of the worst storms I've seen; we couldn't even see the hills."

Soon after he'd returned to California, Rob called the Prestons. Joanne remembered how enthusiastic he was: "He said, 'I really want to come to work for you.' I told Bill, 'Anybody who could come up during that storm and say they want to come up here and work must be O.K.'"

Soon Rob was finishing off and bottling the wines Wallace had "put to sleep." Griffin made some interesting wines that first year, but it was the next year that established his reputation. In 1977 the Prestons produced about 42,000 gallons, each year adding to their original acreage. Griffin was developing his touch with the fruity, white wines, producing beautifully concentrated wines from Chenin Blanc, Gewurztraminer, Johannisberg Riesling, and Chardonnay. At the 1979 Enological Society of the Pacific Northwest's annual Northwest Wine Festival, the 1977 Preston Chardonnay won that organization's first Best of Show award. Judges and consumers were taken by its concentrated and fresh Chardonnay flavor.

Griffin continued to make outstanding wines, garnering awards and setting the standard for most of Washington's wines in the late '70s

Bill and Joanne Preston at Preston Winery. 1977.
—*Photo by Lawrence J. Allen. Courtesy of Elizabeth Purser-Hendricks.*

and early '80s. Preston's vineyard was Rob's proving ground. The vineyard grew in size until 180 acres were planted with over a dozen varieties. Production ballooned to over 100,000 cases of wines.

Joanne poured a fresh glass of wine for me. It was the 1991 Preston Reserve Cabernet Sauvignon, aged in white oak. It was a stunning wine; it was remarkably balanced and full-flavored, with an incredibly soft texture. It reminded me of a modern classified Bordeaux, beautifully balanced with soft tannins. I smiled. I was happy for the Prestons. This was a truly great wine.

I was happy for them because I have a sense that the winery fell on hard times in the mid-'80s. Rob had left after the '83 vintage to go to work for Hogue Cellars. After seven years he and the Prestons parted ways. It had not been an easy separation. Rob appreciated the family atmosphere. He and Bill got along well. Sure, they had occasional blowouts, but there was always a respect for each other.

The final break occurred when Rob approached Bill with the idea of producing his own wine under a different name. That fall, in 1983, when Rob was ready to make wine, Bill Preston told him point-blank, "Let's follow up on that. Let's say you've got Chardonnay and I've got

Chardonnay. They both need racking; same day, same time. Who is going to get first choice?"

Preston answered his own question, "This is mine. You better start looking for another job."

It was unfortunate for Preston because Rob was hitting his stride. The Preston winery went into a long slide. The industry changed quickly; new wineries opened and Preston got buried in backed-up inventories. Rob looked back at that time and shook his head. He thought Bill Preston was too pig-headed to change his label to meet new industry standards, and his brand suffered in the market.

I was glad that the Preston winery was back. It, like Hinzerling, Salishan, and Mont Elise Vineyards, truly pioneered those first small estate wineries at great human and financial cost. I want to see them rewarded. I think most of the industry has a warm feeling in their hearts for the Prestons. Bill's gregarious personality and Joanne's warmth match the openness of the country. Customers and industry people can recall the Prestons' great hospitality in hosting large parties in their expansive front yard, overlooking their vineyards, often in conjunction with the annual Tri-Cities Wine Festival.

I still recall vividly some of those parties. The Preston winery is located north of Pasco, along State Highway 395, the road to Spokane. About five miles outside of Pasco, Prestons' vineyard and winery appear, with a huge sign, of course. Turning right onto McGregor Road, the road goes straight east between his neighbor, Balcom and Moe Farms on the left, and the Preston vineyard on the right. In a quarter mile the football-field-length entrance to the Preston winery beckons. On the night of a party, cars usually parked the entire length of the driveway.

The Prestons' front yard, literally in front of their home and contiguous with the winery, is at least an acre of west-sloping lawn. Usually their parties would start in the very early evening. Other Northwest wineries were invited to pour some of their wines, and would set out cases of wine and chill their white wines in large buckets of ice. Usually a barbecue was arranged and the best parties in the world would proceed. Often the swimming pool was open and excitement ran in the air.

It was a wonderful meeting place that brought together the wine industry and consumers alike from western and eastern Washington, as well as other Pacific Northwest states. Those were truly remarkable evenings and we toasted our good fortune as we watched the breathtaking sunsets, a huge yellow-red ball descending beyond the greenness and pastoral Prestons' vineyard, the lower Columbia Basin, and the Yakima Valley to the west.

Part IV

SNIFFING, SIPPING, AND TASTING HISTORY

"The writer, knowing the possibilities of fine wine grapes in this area, is convinced that some day it will produce and export to other parts of the United States as much fine dry wines as our entire present production of State grape wines."
William B. Bridgman, 1946

Chapter Twenty-Three

THE VIEW FROM RED MOUNTAIN

In 1979, 16 wineries in Washington state produced about 1 million gallons of wine (or about half of what was produced annually by wineries in the '30s, '40s, and '50s). By 1990, 92 wineries produced over 7 million gallons of wine, an explosive growth not seen since Repeal. Following the harvest of 1986, the wine industry finally out-produced its previous best year of 1947.

Beginning in 1980, Washington wines were mostly enjoyed by Washington natives who proved to be enthusiastic and loyal supporters. It helped that Washington state's population grew at a robust rate and that the economy soared during the early '80s. The baby boomers discovered wine, as had been predicted by Bank of America.

This fueled a phenomenal expansion of new vineyard plantings and new wineries. The Yakima Valley was quickly transformed from a forgotten farmland to Puget Sound's backyard garden. The Columbia Valley, which includes the Yakima Valley and Walla Walla Valley appellations, was the marketing genius of Chateau Ste. Michelle. Someone brilliantly designed a back-label map depicting Washington state, and the Columbia Valley, being on a parallel with the famed wine regions of Europe. Wineries filled in the parallel lines.

In Spokane, there was Arbor Crest Winery with its sumptuous Sauvignon Blanc; Latah Creek Winery produced a smooth, mouth-filling Merlot and crisp Chenin Blanc; Mountain Dome Winery made true-to-type sparkling wines; and Worden's Washington Winery produced fresh and fruity, honest table wines. Walla Walla saw L'Ecole No. 41 producing rich Merlot and Semillon; down the road,

Waterbrook Winery made rich Chardonnays and Cabernet Sauvignon; Woodward Canyon was about to stain the scene with its bold Cabernet Sauvignon.

In Puget Sound, wineries sprung up like mushrooms in the Cascade (and Olympic) foothills: from Lost Mountain Winery, in Sequim, with poetic reds, to Salishan Vineyards, north of Vancouver, with graceful Pinot Noir and Chardonnay. Bainbridge Island led the way with cool-climate grape wines, followed by Vashon Winery making barrel-rich Semillon and Cabernet Sauvignon. In the north, Mount Baker Vineyards was pioneering westside viticulture, working closely with the WSU research center at Mount Vernon.

Meanwhile, neighborhood wineries were sprouting in the Seattle area: Vernier Wines (later renamed Salmon Bay Winery) had crisp white wines; Daquila Wines in the Pike Place Market made austere table wines; Newton and Newton (later to become Whittlesey-Mark, then DiStefano) made a fresh sparkling wine using Oregon grapes. In south Seattle, E. B. Foote Winery quietly made austere yet fruity table wines with Riesling and Gewurztraminer.

Woodinville began to look like Napa Valley with its convenient wine touring, with the likes of Haviland Cellars audaciously facing the grand entrance to Chateau Ste. Michelle, offering bold reds and whites. French Creek Cellars made a run with barrel-aged whites. Facelli brought his Idaho history to Washington with his perfectly balanced whites and soft Merlot. And Tagaris Winery tried to make a go with Washington Pinot Noir. Nearby, in Kirkland, Cavatappi Winery made tentative Nebbiolo.

Close by, in Bellevue, Paul Thomas Wines defined dry fruit wines and, later, perfectly balanced red wines. Snoqualmie Winery, above Snoqualmie Falls, struggled to remain afloat with delightful wines, while Hedges was heading over Snoqualmie Pass, first starting out in Issaquah with bold blends of Cabernet Sauvignon and Merlot. Near Everett, McCrea Cellars pioneered Syrah and backed it up with bold Chardonnay.

In the Yakima Valley, vineyards and wineries tripped over one another to get established in time for the next spring barrel-tasting. Out of the desert farms grew Hogue Cellars in Prosser, with its fresh, fruity whites. Tucker Cellars in Sunnyside made farmhouse whites to buy with the fruit and produce of the valley. Also in Sunnyside, Cascade Estates splashed on the scene with fresh white wines, only to be replaced by a bigger winery—Washington Hills—which defined wines for the table. In Hogue's back yard, former Chateau Ste. Michelle employees married their strengths at Chinook Winery, where they focused on crisp, full Sauvignon Blanc and structured Merlot. Yakima Valley Winery focused on bold reds and whites, and delicious dessert wines. North of Prosser, Pontin del Roza marketed its fresh white wines with bold, award-winning labels.

Zillah, home to the classic El Ranchito Restaurant, nurtured a covey of wineries: Quail Run Winery (later named Covey Run Vintners) produced bold reds and whites that captured the valley's flavors. Hyatt Vineyards joined the fun with a range of well-made table wines. Then Bonair Winery took Chardonnay to its fullest conclusion, while nearby Portteus Vineyard explored its favorable vineyard site for bold red wines.

In the Columbia Basin wineries popped up like jackrabbits in the sagebrush. Gordon Brothers made bold fruity wines from its Snake River vineyard, while Champs de Brionne, at George, went from wine to music (music at the Gorge simply made too much money). In Othello, Hunter Hill Winery made a perfect Riesling. Quarry Lake north of Pasco started out with red and white table wines from vineyards it planted in 1971 (and today make even better wines under its new label—Balcom and Moe Vineyards). On the Horse Heaven Hills, Mercer Ranch Vineyards defined Limberger, brickish Cabernet Sauvignons, and a delightful Muscat.

At first, in the early '80s, wineries could barely keep up with the local demand. Then in the mid-'80s the saturation point set in. There was too much wine, and not enough people drinking wine. By 1987 the baby boomers traded in their wine cellars for mortgages and growing families. Grapes were left hanging on the vine. Pioneer wineries from the '70s were being forgotten.

But an amazing thing happened. Washington wines began winning national awards alongside America's best wines. Along with awards came recognition from the wine journals. Washington was, if not on center stage, at least on the same stage. Walla Walla Valley wines were mentioned next to Napa Valley wines. In a modern world of instant gratification, Leonetti Cellars wines were a phone call away. Washington wineries got calls from restaurants in Chicago and New York demanding their wines.

It took the power and resources of the California wine industry to wean America's big East Coast cities off European wines. This paved the way for Washington wineries, themselves hanging onto the pants leg of Chateau Ste. Michelle. America found Washington.

Grocery chains dramatically expanded their wine selections, with Safeway leading the way. Seattle's University Village Safeway, especially, had a truly amazing assortment of wine; wines from every conceivable wine area in the world were represented, including the wines of Washington.

Other grocery chains leapt into the fray—wines were everywhere. Every newspaper had its wine specialist. At the *Seattle Times,* Tom Stockley wielded power with great acumen; a good word from Stockley could sell hundreds of cases of any wine. Stockley became an important ally of Washington wine, taking readers into the vineyards, and to the retailers' shelves, through his weekly columns. Wine writers regularly met together to taste and report on Washington wines—guiding consumers through the thick forest of wine.

Seattle and the rest of Washington state, spurred on by its alarming growth, was a hot commodity. Seattle was no longer a sleepy outpost, home to Boeing and Weyerhauser. And Microsoft was about to blast off. Overnight, Seattle became a big-league city with all of the many problems and glitz of large American cities. At the same time, Northwest cuisine was being molded and formed, and touted across the nation. Washington wines went along for the ride.

—KLIPSUN VINEYARD, AUGUST 1994—
From the back side of Klipsun Vineyard, there is an expansive view west into the Yakima Valley. The blue sky in August provides a huge dome in contrast to the brown, baked hills to the north and south. South, the Horse Heaven Hills rise up, hiding the persistent flow of the Columbia River. To the north, the Rattlesnake Hills frame the northern perimeter of the valley floor. It is about twelve miles from the top of Rattlesake Mountain (at 3,524 feet) to the Horse Heaven Hills (1,975 feet). This is the eastern end of the Yakima Valley. From here the valley spreads west about eighty miles. On a topographic map, it looks just like what it is: a former lakebed, spreading ever wider until it is blocked by the rugged Cascades. The Yakima River cuts a small opening through Ahtanum Ridge at Union Gap toward the west end of the valley, and through the Rattlesnake Hills on the east. These two ridges form the northern border of what's known as the lower valley. On the north side of Ahtanum Ridge, the city of Yakima is about five miles north of "the gap," in the upper valley.

Looking west from Klipsun Vineyard, the Rattlesnake Hills slope gradually and obviously to the south. It is a slope of averaging 3 to 4 percent, providing excellent air drainage for most of the crops that grow in abundance in the valley. Looking again at the map, it is clear that over half of the valley floor is sloped, predominantly to the south. At the west end, the valley flattens out as it bumps up against the foothills of the Cascade Mountains.

Red Mountain itself is dwarfed by the nearby hills. It is one of a series of small ridges that rise up, like stepping stones in decreasing size, and lie in a southeasterly direction toward the Tri-Cities: Richland, Kennewick, and Pasco. To the north and to the east is the great Columbia Basin, a flat, broad landscape where the Columbia River flows down and south around the Saddle Mountains to the north, about forty-five miles away. At the Tri-Cities, the Yakima River and the Snake River meet the Columbia River, a remarkable convergence of nature's power concentrated in this wide-open basin.

Below is the town of Benton City. The Yakima flows past. Orchards dominate the landscape. Walt and I surveyed the countryside from a wood pergola, shading us from the afternoon's bright sun. Looking at Rattlesnake Mountain, there is a road that curves its way up the hillside. It is one of those inviting roads that make you to want to drive to the top. This one, Walt informed me, leads to an observatory at the highest elevation on Rattlesnake Mountain.

Walt talked about the movement of air. I realized that he sees the world much differently than I do. He sees an air mass in constant motion over a landscape, rivers of air, alive to wind and temperature fluctuations. Cool air movement, like water, will seek out the lowest level, cascading down the southern slopes of the valley.

"When you are in the vineyard, and you can see out all around you, and you know that there is a gentle slope—that is a perfect place to plant," he said.

Red Mountain is a perfect place to plant. The cool winds of the north move downhill across the vineyards, moderating the summer temperatures, moving on before settling. Even here, though, vine-yardists must be cautious in their plantings. Where there is a depression in the vineyard, even a slight one, there is an increased danger of frost or freezing cold, from standing cold air.

Klipsun Vineyard is about 240 acres; 80 acres are planted to grapes, with 60 acres bearing this year. It is owned by Patricia and David Gelles of West Richland. David Gelles works as an engineer at the nearby

Hanford Atomic Works. The vineyard is Patricia's hobby. Patricia is English-born. Together they wanted an investment that they could enjoy. Their vineyard is managed by Fred Artz.

At the time of our visit, Artz was about forty years old. Dressed in Levi's, with boots and grain cap, he looked the part of a young farmer. He helps manage another, nearby vineyard on Red Mountain, owned by Tom Hedges of Hedges Cellars. Artz grew up in Richland, working on farms as a kid in high school. He got an agriculture business degree at the Columbia Basin College in Richland. He has always wanted to farm. Besides managing these vineyards, it is his hope to plant a vineyard, and build a home, on Red Mountain.

Walt wanted me to see a well-managed vineyard. In many ways, Klipsun Vineyard is a direct descendant of research conducted at the research center at Prosser. This vineyard usually gets premium prices for its grapes, often 30 percent above the average market price. In the midday sun, the Cabernet Sauvignon grapes hung elegantly. Close by, rows of Sauvignon Blanc had already been picked. It was an early harvest. Picking began in this vineyard about August 17.

The vines were neatly groomed. The uniformity of the rows and the green lushness of the vines clashed with the vastness of the horizon—the broad blue sky and the soft brown soil. These vineyards were planted as Dr. Clore would approve: they were grown using a double trunk, unilateral cordon trained. This means that two of the stronger shoots were selected and brought up from below the surface of the soil. The shoots were then trained singularly in opposite directions on a wire, which extended the length of the row, to form cordons, shoots that remain on the vine. Sixteen inches above the cordon wire was a twenty-four-inch-long "T" at the top of a steel stake, with catch wires on each end that extended to the end of the rows. These catch wires supported the shoot growth that rose up from the cordon. This supported vigorous growth and provided a method to manage the canopy. Both Clore and Artz like this system of trellising because it works as a protection against frost and cold damage. In years like the freeze of 1990, this vineyard stood an extra chance of survival because of the double trunks.

I asked Artz what it costs to set out a vineyard: planted, staked, and irrigated, ready to go. He said it runs between about $10,000 and $12,000 an acre. A 40-acre piece runs about $450,000. Then there is the irrigation. If a well is drilled, it can run $100 a foot. At a depth of 650 feet, water can cost more than gold: $65,000. Typically, this cost is amortized over twenty years or longer, and this beats paying out money over time to the water utility. In a desert subject to water shortages, that's an unpopular option.

Forty acres will produce about 30,000 gallons of wine (or 12,500 cases), figured at about 750 gallons per acre. A new winery to make that amount of wine will cost about $2 million.

—THE GLOBAL MARKET—

Across the Cascade Mountains, in the suburban sprawl of the greater Seattle area, Tom Hedges planned for the future. Hedges, a man of about forty with sand-colored curly hair, brown eyes, and a handsome, direct face, thinks about the future. With his newly planted vineyard at Red Mountain, Hedges was about to build a new winery at the vineyard site.

Hedges represents the future. He is youthful and articulate. Born and raised in Richland, he went to the University of Puget Sound in Tacoma to study marketing. He then attended Thunderbird College in Arizona, where he met his French-born wife, Ann-Marie. He learned the marketing business of food, working for years as a food broker for Castle and Cook, sellers of bananas and pineapples. He developed a taste for red wine while stationed in Argentina.

"Everything you ate there was beef, essentially, and they always served lots of red wine," he recalled.

Hedges is an entrepreneur. He is convinced of the existence of a global economy. And he plans to market to it. He produces both a red and a white wine, although his specialty has been a tasteful blend of Cabernet Sauvignon and Merlot, released under his label, Hedges Cellars. His first vintage was 1987. It was bulk wine that he shipped over to Sweden to be sold by the Swedish liquor monopoly. All he had to do was provide the wine and a label. His first label, designed by Sebastian Titus, was a direct but elegant label.

The Swedish monopoly maintains its own bottling facility. It bottles about 60 percent of all the wine it sells. With his new label and 10,000 cases of wine, Hedges was in business. Five years later, he found a partner in Mats Hanzon, a resident of Sweden. He plans to build a winery over at Red Mountain that will handle about 40,000 cases.

Hedges sold his wine in seventeen states and ten foreign countries, including Norway, Denmark, Belgium (where his wine was marketed by mail order), France, England, Mexico, and Japan. He was most excited about Europe. While many wineries are trying to market to the Far East, Hedges prefers to work with the Europeans, who have a great tradition of wine consumption. He finds that their economies are more similar to ours.

With the '89 vintage he started using his own grapes as well as other grapes. He hopes to always be able to buy sufficient grapes to complement his own source, using about two-thirds purchased grapes and one-third his own. Hedges likes to hedge his bets.

"Insurance," he said.

Hedges poured me a glass of wine. It was dark red. It was the 1991 vintage made from grapes purchased from Klipsun Vineyards. Hints of oak blended beautifully with crisp cherry and freshly-sharpened pencil aromas. On the palate it was young but not harsh. Red wine, Red Mountain. The flavors captured perfectly the sense of the vineyard, the rich loamy sand soil, the baked quality of the grapes in the hot eastern Washington sun.

Hedges's Issaquah office looked east across the Cascades. A large Rand McNally world map adorned the wall behind his desk. Sweden, and markets beyond, were just outside his door.

Chapter Twenty-Four

INTO THE VINEYARDS

Harvest '94 had begun. It had been a hot growing season, both in eastern and western Washington. Grapes were coming in earlier than usual. This was in great contrast to the previous year when everything was late, the harvest season extending into late October. It seems that in a hot year all the grapes ripen at the same time, which presents a serious challenge to the winemaker. Crush, a word used to describe the process of crushing the grapes, takes on added significance. The '94 season was the winemaker's worst nightmare, when everything happens at once. It means long days, and oftentimes long nights, as growers and winemakers rush to bring the harvest to conclusion.

David Lake, the winemaker at Columbia Winery in Woodinville, more than anyone in America, has consistently preached the importance of working with the vineyard, working directly with the grower to express the optimal flavor distinction from the vineyard's site—its soil, its slope, and its location. Sometimes he is forced to work around the grower to get what he wants. It may be that the vineyard owner is removed from the day-to-day operation of the vineyard, or that the vineyard manager is new. Regardless, David Lake knows what he wants from the vineyard. He regularly visits the vineyard, especially during the weeks leading up to harvest.

David Lake is a Master of Wine. Only a handful of Masters reside in the United States and there are fewer than two hundred Masters of Wine in the world. Most Masters of Wine end up in the English wine and spirits trade. Lake is especially versed in the wines of Bordeaux but his knowledge of all wines is nearly complete.

As a result he values the European concept that a wine is a product of its place, expressing the *terroir,* a French word meaning soil, but also meaning the location of the soil. It is not a notion that sits well with Americans, at least Westerners. Westerners feel that our wines are just fine, thank you, without this overbearing worry about a particular site. We suspect, I assume, that this is just a way for the Europeans to over-value themselves and their wines.

For Lake, I believe, it is an expression, an artistic expression, the ultimate distinction to be made between wines, like an artist who captures the light intensity of a certain landscape. David Lake has assorted some of the best vineyards in the state to reside on his palette.

Lake works for Columbia Winery, formerly Associated Vintners. At the time Columbia Winery owned no vineyards; all of its grapes had been contracted. It has purchased grapes from various locations throughout the state: Sagemoor Farms northwest of Pasco; Wycoff Vineyard northeast of Grandview; Otis Vineyard north of Grandview; Red Willow Vineyard six miles north of White Swan; and vineyards in western Washington near Vancouver. It is a lot of territory that represents an astounding variety of climate and topography.

I agreed to meet David Lake at Gilman Village, in Issaquah, at 6:00 a.m. It was dark but warm, the sky ablaze with stars, and a nearly full moon beckoned on the horizon. By the time we settled in his rented Park Avenue Buick, the sky began to lighten. It was an eerie feeling driving east up Interstate 90 toward the summit of the Cascades: my brain was waking up like the world around me. Issaquah was left behind in a shroud of fog, visible in the morning light. The sky was clear up ahead of us, the morning sunlight turning the sky yellow-green. The greenness of the trees was delicious, dark green, almost primordial.

—EASTERN WASHINGTON, SEPTEMBER 1994—

Lake announced that he planned to visit all of the vineyards in eastern Washington under contract with Columbia Winery. We headed toward Sagemoor Farms. We were to travel along Interstate 90 to Vantage, on the Columbia River, then turn south along the river on State Highway 243 until we reached the Wahluke Slope, where we would turn east to Mattawa and State Highway 24. From there we would drop down over Radar Hill south to Sagemoor Farms.

David told me that he spends about three days out of seven in the vineyard, caring for nearly 350 acres. This was his sixteenth vintage; he is a veteran of Washington wine harvests like his colleagues Gary Figgins, Rob Griffin, Chuck Henderson, Mike Wallace, and Joan Wolverton. He talked about the importance of continuity, knowing the vineyards and the wines that they produce.

He was intent on the road, his body was still and straight, but I could tell his mind was moving quickly. Lake was about fifty years old. He was a big man. His round face, with a smallish nose, was handsome and distinctive. He squinted at the road and small creases fanned out from the corners of his eyes. His hair was sandy with a reddish tinge. He looked and spoke like a Brit.

Just before reaching the Snoqualmie Summit, he received a call on his mobile phone from Gordy back at the winery. It was 7:30; I was impressed by how early work got started. David was accessible in his traveling office. I could tell he liked this role. He can be out in the vineyard but still a phone call away from the drama of the grape crush.

David Lake grew up in Toronto and attended McGill University in Montreal, a protestant and English enclave in a sea of French-Canada. This interested me because so much of the early history of our region involved the early exploration by French-Canadians. The French-Canadians were known for their fearlessness, their adept trapping skills, and their ability to commingle with the native populations. I told David that so far the earliest known grape planting in this area occurred at Fort Vancouver but that I believed, without any verification, that French-Canadians (and Scots) probably would have planted grapes prior to Fort Vancouver in settlements along the Willamette River, near Champoeg, Oregon. David pointed out, however, that many of the French-Canadians originated from Brittany and Normandy in France and thus were less likely to have a strong interest in wine and grape culture.

At Vantage we crossed the Columbia River. The land was generally barren and carved by the flow of the river. The blueness of the river was spectacular in the morning light. I think both of us envisioned early explorers as they must have paddled canoes up the river and seen native settlements along its banks. What is amazing is that little has seemingly changed in the physical environment in those 150 or so years. It was a good setting in which to reflect on history.

Lake received multiple degrees of history and political science from McGill University. Lake is fascinated with this history; he shocked me when he told me that he recently learned from his uncle that part of the

Lake family actually began the Hudson's Bay Company in the 1700s. Part of David's family had come to America, landing in New England in the 1600s. Apparently, the head Lake of this delegation was killed by natives and the rest of the family went back to England to regroup. The other part of the family was busy laying plans for the development of one of the world's greatest companies.

Sitting next to me was a direct descendant of the Hudson's Bay Company. I wasn't on a full-day jaunt with just the winemaker from Columbia Winery but, rather, a link to those first grape plantings. Dreamily, my mind felt the downstream movement of the Columbia River, the present pouring out of the past.

Lake said that his grandfather homesteaded in Saskatchewan in the late 1800s but that his father made his way to Vancouver Island. This is what brought Lake to the Pacific Northwest. After graduating from McGill University, he enrolled at the University of California Davis in 1977. Prior to beginning his coursework he traveled up to British Columbia to check out the possibilities of producing wine. But he was dismayed by the political situation; most of the wine industry was protected by the provincial government and all sales went through the B.C. liquor control system.

Traveling through Oregon and Washington, however, he saw a new industry emerging, tentative and embryonic. This was exciting; it was exactly why he had chosen to come to the University of California: knowing that the West Coast was an exciting new frontier.

David studied at UC Davis, doing coursework to round out his education as a Master of Wine. He was thirty-four years old when he finished at UC Davis. He set out for Oregon, where he worked with one of the great Pinot Noir pioneers, David Lett, at Eyrie Vineyards. During that time he went through Washington state, visiting Mike Wallace, whose Hinzerling Winery was just getting going. He also visited Mont Elise Vineyards (then called Bingen Wine Cellars). Though David wasn't aware of it, the owners of Bingen Wine Cellars came close to offering him a job, but bickering among the partners in the winery never allowed Lake to be hired.

Instead he happened upon Associated Vintners and the venerable Dr. Lloyd Woodburne. It was a meeting that reminds me a little of the meeting between Steenborg and Bridgman. Lake joined Associated Vintners in the harvest of 1978 and took over the winemaking duties from Woodburne in 1979. It was a fortunate marriage of talents for scrappy Associated Vintners.

David Lake provided a continuity to Associated Vintners that would help it through a most difficult time. The 1979 harvest was a particularly difficult vintage for the winery. Extremely cold temperatures, in the range of -8° F, in December 1978 caused widespread damage to the vineyards in eastern Washington. Nearly half of the vineyards sustained damage, causing a scramble for grapes during the harvest of 1979.

Associated Vintners had at this time two vineyards of its own. Because AV was in a significant growth phase, these vineyards with their reduced crop couldn't supply AV's needs. Luckily it had already begun to purchase grapes from Sagemoor Farms and Mike Sauer at Red Willow Vineyards. Later, when growth requirements put a strain on the winery's finances, it was forced to sell its vineyards. This clearly put it on a path of developing new vineyard relationships.

Enter David Lake. David Lake is fond of using a word that sounds a bit stuffy—but a word I particularly like: providential. David Lake's entrance to Associated Vintners was providential. He helped guide them through a major transition as a group of zealous amateur winemakers into a professional corporate entity. He took what was a strong foundation, based on the firm vision of the original stockholders, and helped build a solid house on top, adding to it his vision of healthy vineyard relationships.

These thoughts percolated through my mind as we headed east on Highway 24 up the Wahluke Slope through the dusty town of Mattawa. Mattawa is home to the former Langguth Winery, the aborted German enterprise about twelve miles east, and the accompanying Weinbau Vineyards. Today Weinbau is part of Sagemoor Farms, and the winery is now owned by Stimson Lane Vineyards and Estates, which produces excellent budget table wines under its Saddle Mountain brand. Columbia Winery doesn't buy any grapes from this site; there is no need to. But it is a terrific site, high above the Columbia with its gentle but pronounced southwestern slope down from the Saddle Mountains to the immediate north.

This reminds me of a picture that Dr. Clore has, taken in 1967 during the early battles of the California Wine Bill. It is a picture Walt especially treasures. The picture shows a group of winemakers, field workers, and grape growers standing over a large hole in the ground, a hole dug out by a backhoe by the local soil specialist to expose the soil profile of the ground. Pictured are most of the important players in the Washington grape and wine industry, peering into a deep hole in the ground, set high above the great expanse of the Columbia River gorge. It is as if they are being dared to jump across an abyss to the promise of premium wines. By 1971 only a few survived the challenge; the rest fell victim to the effects of the California Wine Bill.

I am aware at this time that no one is in the picture from the Associated Vintners group. Perhaps they had already made it to the other side.

Driving almost directly east, we were high above the Columbia River. It made the Yakima Valley, directly south, seem like it was considerably below us. I was made aware of the drainage of the air and the advantage of the Wahluke Slope, and how the Yakima Valley must be the repository for the cool air that flows down over and around the hills. It was a wonderful way to experience the region.

Near the end of the Saddle Mountains, we turned south. Lake said we were going to cross over Radar Hill. Located near the top of the hill are 120 acres of wine grapes planted and owned by Mike Taggares. This is a slightly cooler site planted in primarily Chardonnay with Cabernet Sauvignon, Pinot Noir, Sauvignon Blanc, and other *vinifera* varieties. The Taggares family is enormously successful. Most of their success has been in potatoes, alfalfa hay, and onions, but Pete Taggares, son of the original pioneering P. J. Taggares, also controls the nation's largest Concord vineyards; Snake River Vineyards are fourteen miles east of Pasco, and bisected by Highway 124. Today that vineyard is managed by Pete Jr., grandson of P. J. Taggares.

From on top of Radar Hill, there was a pronounced slide down the hillside as we entered the Columbia Basin driving parallel to the Columbia River. We were driving due south on a high plateau entering the great drainage for the Columbia River. To the west is the Hanford Site. The Hanford plateau is considerably lower and flatter, covering a vast area between the Rattlesnake Hills to the west and the inverted "L" shape of the Columbia River on the north and east.

To the east, within ten miles, is US Highway 395, which bisects the basin north to south out of Pasco. Nearby were vineyards and wineries that grew out of the '70s, including Preston Wine Cellars and its neighbor Balcom and Moe. Close by and northwest of these vineyards was the Moremon vineyard.

Turning west toward the river, we decided to first stop at Bacchus and Dionysus Vineyards, part of Sagemoor Farms. As we descended the hillside down into the vineyard, the view was breathtaking. Lush green foliage spread down along the gentle slopes to the Columbia

River. It was a forest of vineyards, neatly maintained. Nothing stirred but the occasional rustle of a grapevine leaf in the warm, undulating breeze. Across the river was the Hanford plateau with a view of the space-age nuclear plants—gray and isolated—in a broad field of desert brown. The Columbia River, the water giver, framed it all—reflecting back the fullness of the baby blue sky.

David parked his car near the top of the vineyard. He wanted to check on some Merlot grapes. The blue-black grapes hung in large clusters from the dark green foliage of the vine. Lake changed his dress shoes for Gore-Tex hiking boots. On a plastic sandwich baggie, he marked in black ink the grape variety, the vineyard block, and the date that he was picking the grapes. We then proceeded to walk down the rows of vines. It took me a bit to understand what he was doing. After about fifteen paces, he stopped and tasted a grape from a cluster, then he dropped a few grapes into his baggie. Another fifteen paces, he stopped and did the same, this time on the other side of the row. We continued like this for a couple of rows, the rows running southwest about sixty feet. Lake had about fifty to seventy-five berries in the baggie and was thus assured of getting a representative sample of the vineyard. These were to be taken back to the winery for analysis, measuring the sugar content, the T.A. (the grapes' total acid content), and the pH level of the grapes (a measurement of the grape's acid stability).

We then drove down to Sagemoor Farms, where Lake did the same thing on more grapes. Whereas Bacchus and Dionysus Vineyards was all wine grapes, Sagemoor Farms represented a more diversified development, including tree fruits and alfalfa.

—*SAGEMOOR FARMS*—

Originally Alec Bayless, an attorney in Seattle, asked a real estate agent in Sunnyside to find a suitable parcel of land. Bayless, a distinctive man with a crown of flowing white hair and his characteristic bowtie, was a man of action—used to making things happen.

Winslow Wright, Bayless's partner, recalled in exacting detail, "In early May 1968, the real estate agent called Bayless and said, 'I've got just the place you are looking for; come over this weekend.' Alec said he couldn't think of any good reason not to go. He and Sydney Abrams flew over to Sagemoor and it was, in fact, what he had been looking for." Alec then contacted Walt Clore at Prosser. Clore told him he thought it an ideal site. Clore knew the site from earlier work in the

Alec Bayless —*Photo courtesy of MacDonald Hoague & Bayless.*

Columbian Basin. It had already been partially planted in fruit.

Win Wright also told how the property became available. The former owner of Sagemoor went berserk, killing his family and himself. The man's brother called a friend of his who was then living nearby and asked if he could go by the farm and check on it for him. The friend was John Pringle, who later directed and managed the original plantings by the Bayless group.

Bayless acted quickly. He wrote his friend and business partner, Albert Ravenholt, who was then in the Far East. Ravenholt gave the go-ahead and Bayless began raising $100,000 through limited partners. The original investors included quite a cross section of people, mostly social and business contacts of Alec Bayless and Al Ravenholt. These people tended to be cultural sophisticates and trusted Bayless completely. Raising money was not a problem; much of it was word of mouth and evidently many of this group were capable of chipping in $5,000 or more at a moment's notice.

That first year, the partners laid out some experimental vines that they got from the research center at Prosser, and some grape plants out of the foundation block at the University of California Davis. They were encouraged not only by the vigor of the vines but by the vigor of the debate over the potential change in the wine laws. I wonder now what must have been going through Syd Abrams's mind—the man who was the mastermind of the California Wine Bill—as he alternated between destroying (although he wouldn't think of it in that fashion) the "old" Washington wine industry while helping Alec Bayless (as a partner and friend) plant new vineyards of premium *vinifera* grapes to nurture the next generation of premium wines.

There was no doubt in Alec Bayless's mind that the Pacific Northwest would someday become a great and unique wine country. Again, Win Wright recalled, "Alec had a vision: growing grapes and making wine." Those words ripple through the past.

In 1972 Sagemoor Farms was planted in 85 acres of grapes. Additionally, Bacchus Vineyard, consisting of 195 acres, was planted at the same time. It was a very ambitious undertaking; that was a lot of grapes to be planting without a contract.

In 1972 there were only a few operating wineries in all of the Pacific Northwest. The largest, Ste. Michelle Vineyards, was busy expanding its own vineyards. Associated Vintners was in the process of planting its new 80-acre vineyard, Church Vineyard, north of Sunnyside, on the Roza Irrigation District. That year, 1972, was a kind of watershed year for vineyard plantings, but nearly all of those vineyards were directly connected to emerging wineries: Preston Wine Cellars, Hinzerling Winery, Kiona Vineyards, and Ste. Michelle's Hahn Hill Vineyard. It didn't seem that wineries would need grapes.

Just getting the grapes had been an ordeal, as grape plants were then in great demand in California as well as locally. Win Wright recalled the first heat-treated and virus-free plants arriving from California, each plant individually planted in a milk carton. John Pringle was then in charge of the farms. Apparently the grape plants finally arrived in July after numerous delays, the nursery telling them that it would just be another week, then another week, and another, and so forth. Pringle, upon receiving the plants, set them out and turned on the sprinkler system to help them recover from the hot transit out of California. Win Wright was amazed at how many of the young vines survived. Planted, the vineyard was now a realization of that vision.

In December 1972 a crushing freeze devastated the young vines planted in Washington's new vineyards, as if in challenge to the new growers. At Sagemoor Farms and at nearby Bacchus Vineyard (also organized by Alec Bayless), the vineyards were hit hard. Win Wright said that 76 percent of the vines planted at Bacchus Vineyard died. Undaunted, the managing partners went back to their investors for more money and replanted. It was as if they had decided that the worst had just happened; they figured another freeze like that would never again occur.

In 1973 they replanted the vineyards, replacing the dead grapevines. Dionysus Vineyard, which lay contiguous to Bacchus Vineyard, was planted and consisted of 180 acres of grapevines. Dionysus was a separate partnership with Winslow Wright as the general partner. Together, the combined 466-acre vineyard was then the largest block of varietals in the state. This large vineyard holding was managed by John Pringle, then twenty-eight years old and a recent horticulture graduate of Cal Poly. However, Pringle had never been trained in viticulture. Reflecting back, Win Wright said of Pringle, "To his everlasting credit, he laid out those vineyards, and he not only replanted Bacchus, he planted Dionysus in the same year, with no experienced personnel. At the time we didn't realize what a feat this was. As we got involved ourselves, planting grapes and watching others—in retrospect, it was an incredible feat. How he did it, to this day I don't know."

It is still a mystery why this group never built a winery. Win Wright has suggested that the time was never right. Sagemoor Farms consistently produced some of the best grapes in the state. It can be said that Sagemoor Farms and its companion vineyards truly became the mother vineyards for many of the first wineries that emerged in the '70s and '80s. Even Oregon's first wineries relied on Sagemoor fruit to get established, including stellar wineries such as Adelsheim Vineyards and Tualatin Vineyards. But for some reason, the Bayless group never could take that next step and realize a winery.

Win Wright said the time was never right. I call it bad timing. After the freeze in 1972, Alec had to go back to the partners for additional money to fund the replanting. Then it took a couple of years for the grapevines to bear fruit. By the mid-'70s, the combined vineyards of Sagemoor, Bacchus, and Dionysus were in full production; all 466 acres of vineyards were capable of producing at least 2,300 tons of grapes (that's an average of 5 tons to the acre) or the equivalent of 150,000 cases of wine. That is about the current size of Columbia Winery. That is a lot of wine. I'm sure they had grapes that they could not sell, and logic would dictate that their own winery could have used these extra grapes, but they could not convince themselves that starting a winery would make good economic sense. In 1973 they hired a consultant, Jim Carter, to help plan a winery. But nothing came of it.

Sagemoor Farms' current manager, Erick Hanson, said that after 1976 the partners no longer considered building a winery. Win Wright described a chaotic situation. Nobody was in charge. All of the partners were busy with their own careers. Finally in 1979 Win Wright sold his portion of his door manufacturing company and Alec suggested that Wright take over management of the farm. Wright took over then when the farm was deeply in debt to the John Hancock Insurance Company. They were way overextended.

About the same time they got involved with Wolfgang Langguth, from Traben-Trabach, Germany. Langguth had contacted Alec Bayless about growing grapes in Washington state. Bayless went out of his way to show Langguth around, taking him to eastern Washington to visit the various vineyards. Langguth was determined to make an investment in the United States. Along with fellowship with Alec Bayless and his partners, he felt that Washington state offered the best opportunity for producing German-styled wines.

Win Wright recalled caustically how Alec extended himself to Langguth to offer help in establishing a vineyard as a source of grapes for the eventual Langguth Winery. Again, bad timing. Langguth had put up 30 percent of the money needed to establish the Weinbau vineyard and Alec helped to raise the remaining money by going back to his faithful investors.

Win Wright remembered when Langguth offered to pay his and Alec's way over to Traben-Trabach on the Mosel. Wright recalled it was around Christmas and Langguth's family was at his home on the Mosel, and his managers and he announced that he would finalize the deal with the Americans.

Langguth Winery went under within a few years and the Bayless group got tangled up in litigation connected to the winery and the Weinbau vineyard. It was a bad situation and the Sagemoor group had just about hit bottom. Win Wright recalled ruefully, "I don't know why we did this except that it was just like the hill; it was there and we wanted to climb it."

Wright's voice softened, "That was a very unhappy experience, I'm sure you have heard." Continuing, he said, "He turned out to be a real tough guy. He couldn't make any kind of a compromise. If you didn't see it his way it was wrong."

In 1983, when Langguth Winery was going through bankruptcy, the Bayless group flirted with the idea of taking over the winery. But in the fall of that year, before they could act on taking over the winery, they had another dilemma; they had over 500 tons of grapes still hanging on the vine and unsold. They must have wished they had a winery to process the grapes, but, on the other hand, didn't this portend that the wine industry was growing too slowly? Here was evidence hanging on the vine that the industry couldn't even use all of the grapes that Sagemoor could produce. Additionally, the tree fruit portion of the operation was losing incredible amounts of money. Win Wright recalled that during the early '80s there was some discussion by the partners that they might just have to give up the farms; they could no longer afford the losses.

—SUCCESS FINALLY COMES—

In 1996, the farm was under the daily management of Erick Hanson. Win Wright was still the managing partner but relied on Hanson to run the vast operation. Hanson was youthful, slender, and energetic. He had flowing, shoulder-length brown hair and dressed in blue jeans. I noticed that he wore beads. Appearances suggested that he was a misplaced hippy. Earlier, during a meeting with Erick and Dr. Clore, I told Erick I thought he looked rather hip. He said that since winning the Winemaker of the Year award for 1992, he has loosened up his lifestyle, now that he has nothing to prove. His office was in the north end of a trailer with a window looking out over the shipping plant.

Hanson oversees the operation of all of the holdings of the farm, including fruit grown at Sagemoor, Bacchus, Dionysus, and Weinbau. All totaled, this includes 750 acres of wine grapes and 250 acres of tree fruits. Today 95 percent of the grapes are under contract and the operation of the farms is guided by a committee that includes Win Wright, Al Ravenholt, and Hanson. Alec Bayless passed away in 1992. With his passing there has been a noted lack of enthusiasm from the remaining partners, as Bayless was such an energetic spark. Hanson credited Bayless with his earlier success at setting up contracts that have led to the current stability of the operation. Somewhat ironically, today the farms are operating smoothly and efficiently. Cast aside are the aesthetics of the '70s.

Win Wright recalled, "We hadn't looked at this thing as a business. Alec wasn't interested in running a benefit for Washington wine, but more interested in the doing of it. He didn't want it to cost the partners money, but it wasn't to make money. That was very secondary." It is now a business, and it appears to be profitable. Win Wright brings to the table a business attitude honed sharp from his door manufacturing business. Struggling in business, he said, helped prepare him for the habits of the farm: "You've got to look at it as . . . is it cost-effective? And try to find a more cost-effective method of running the operation and try to stop waste. Look at prices."

He works closely with Erick Hanson. Hanson began in 1976. He had graduated at Northern Arizona University in biology and had come to work at Batelle in nearby Hanford Works. Instead he hired on at Sagemoor Farms as a tractor driver and within three months fell in love with the area and the work. A year later he was made foreman. Between 1977 and 1983 he learned farming from John Pringle and Jerry Bookwalter.

In July 1983 Jerry Bookwalter told Win Wright that he was quitting. Wright and Bayless were in a tough situation. The cherry season was about to begin and they didn't have anyone in charge. Formerly, when they needed someone, they went down to California, but that hadn't worked out well. In the middle of this dilemma, Hanson approached Wright and Bayless and asked directly, "Damn it, why haven't you considered me?"

Wright told him that they didn't think he had the stuff to run the farms. He was too intellectual, too nice. Wright was convinced that Hanson could never fire anyone or make a tough decision. Besides, Hanson looked and acted like a hippy. Wright and Bayless told Hanson that he could have the job through November and they would re-evaluate him then.

Eleven years later, Hanson has been a huge success. Win Wright spoke affectionately about his relationship with Hanson, almost father to son. Now that the farms are operating efficiently, the lines of communication are much better and Wright feels like Hanson has control of the management of the operation. This allowed them to divvy up the responsibilities and appreciate the other's strengths. Wright said that Hanson has become much more sophisticated in his knowledge of the farm, and of business. Wright manages the marketing of the grapes and payments from customers. They can talk in total confidence.

Today, the Weinbau's grapes all go to Stimson Lane. Columbia Winery is the largest buyer of Sagemoor, Bacchus, and Dionysus grapes. Sagemoor Farms still caters to a large number of customers, from small wineries to large grape-buying co-ops such as Western Washington Winemakers Association. Nearly all the grapes have a home.

—COVENTRY VALE WINERY—

Back on the road again with David Lake. Without stopping for lunch, we were off to our next destination: Coventry Vale Winery, northeast of Grandview. Coventry Vale Winery is owned by the Wycoff family. It is one of the largest wineries in the state, but you will rarely see wine under its own label. Rather, the winery specializes in custom crushing and wine production for other people.

The winery was not imposing. Beige metal buildings with brown trim were set off by a sloping green lawn in front. It was surrounded by hop fields and vineyards. Inside, we found our way to the lab, which was busy as technicians moved among laboratory equipment. Lake grabbed a few beakers and a hydrometer used to measure the sugar content of the fermenting grape juice. We stopped by the office of the winemaker, Jurergem Grieb. He directed David and me to the tanks containing Columbia Winery's wine.

Downstairs in the cellar, huge, jacketed, stainless steel tanks towered over us. Walking between the rows of tanks, we stopped at one enormous tank. It held 6,302 gallons (enough to make close to 2,700 cases) of White Riesling from grapes grown at Sagemoor Farms. Other tanks held about 3,000 gallons. David offered a taste. It was still quite sweet. It tasted like exotic grape juice at that point, but it was possible to pick out the smells that would remain after fermentation and aging was complete.

David Lake was checking on the new wine, monitoring its progression. He prefers to manipulate nature's process by inoculating the juice with a known yeast and then slowing the violent fermentation process by cooling the juice in the stainless steel tanks. I made sure to register the flavor of the wine so that I could compare it later to the finished wine.

Lake measured the wine's sugar level with the hydrometer and recorded it in his mind. He noted the concentrated flavors. David Lake's wines are always well balanced, capturing the delicate fruit flavors of the grapes while maintaining their acid, making wines that express the growing conditions of their vintage.

—WYCOFF VINEYARD—

We drove out to the Wycoff Vineyard, located on the Roza, to look at the Chardonnay grapes. Planted in 1976, it slopes gently down toward the Yakima River, between the towns of Prosser and Grandview, from high up on the slope toward the Rattlesnake Hills. The vineyards butt up against the grasslands to the north. Much of the vineyard is furrow irrigated, a bit out of sync with the latest in drip irrigation. Lake talked on his mobile phone to the vineyard manager. He was concerned that the grapes should all be picked—that maybe the harvest crew had overlooked a few rows. I overheard David tell the vineyard manager, "Please do your own calculation—you know the vineyards better than I." I wondered if this was true. Later, Lake got a call back. David was right, those vineyards should have been picked.

—OTIS VINEYARD—

Our job done, we headed out to Otis Vineyard north of Grandview. In all the years of being in the wine business, and with various trips to eastern Washington, I had never visited this vineyard. It was one of the earliest vineyards planted to Cabernet Sauvignon, planted in 1957 with commercial heat-treated vines. It is about 75 acres—by today's standards, a modest-sized vineyard. The Otis Vineyard has always struck me as producing wines that are powerful and full of raspberry flavors.

The vineyard was planted with roses at the end of the rows. Most of the vines were fan-trained; three or four of the vine's trunks come up out of the ground and are spread out, like a stretched hand, along the wires. Most modern vineyards are spur pruned; the vine's main trunk comes out of the ground and then canes are selected and trained horizontally; from these, shoots are selected that run vertically up to the next wire.

At the entrance to the vineyard were boxes full of Cabernet Sauvignon waiting to be hauled to the winery. We were going out to the vineyard to check on the Chardonnay. Again, David selected samples of grapes. It was getting warm. I opted to stay in the car. I was getting tired. It was about 2:30 in the afternoon. The September sun was hot, in the mid-'80s, I presumed. Samples collected, we headed for Red Willow Vineyard.

—RED WILLOW VINEYARD—

Red Willow Vineyard is located thirteen miles west of Wapato, situated against the foothills of the Cascade Mountains. Red Willow is on the northern bench of a natural basin between Ahtanum Ridge to the north and Toppenish Ridge to the south. This flat basin makes up a bulk of the land mass that is considered the lower Yakima Valley; it is about thirty miles east to west and about fifteen miles north to south. The closest town is White Swan, along an ancient Indian trail, later used by the first settlers, to reach the Columbia River. Red Willow Vineyard benches out from the base of Ahtanum Ridge, not far from one of the state's first grape plantings at Tampico, just over the ridge. To the southwest is Mount Adams, about thirty-five miles distant.

As we drove up to the vineyard, I saw that a lot of work had been done since I last visited the site two years before. Most noticeable were the new rows of vines that came right down the hill as we entered the property. Atop the orderly rows of vines was a small chapel in the process of being built.

As we pulled up to a stop in front of the machine shed, Mike Sauer greeted us. Mike's smile in his round face was genuine. He enjoys people. He also is proud of his vineyard. He is a smallish man, then forty-seven years old, with ruddy round cheeks. His eyes are steel blue, his hair blondish brown. His neck was reddened by the sun. Mike is a farmer. He helps oversee the 2,200 acres of farmland owned by his wife's family. They farm primarily alfalfa and wheat. They also have about 180 acres in grapes: 75 acres in Concord and 105 acres in wine grapes. This is Mike's responsibility.

He began experimenting with grapes over twenty years ago. He was then twenty-three years old. Sauer said, "I was just a kid out of Washington State University. I married into the family." He was working for his wife's family, the Stephensons, and their family corporation: The Latum Corporation. The Stephenson family's involvement goes back three generations, when the family first arrived in the 1920s with the advent of irrigation in this area. They had a 30-acre plot of land. Stephenson thought they ought to figure out an experiment with either orchards or vineyards.

Mike said, "I really knew nothing about grapes. But with his encouragement, they were looking for a new project on the farm for the new son-in-law." Sauer said he relied a lot on the County Extension Service people in the valley. He worked closely with Don Chaplin, a young extension agent working with Walt Clore. In his first year, Mike started into Concords. He recalled, "I was really intrigued in the early '70s with the wine boom that was going on in California. But I knew nothing about wine. I was just a farm kid, raised in Toppenish on a farm of field crops. But I was intrigued by the wine names. Also, there was quite a bit of talk at that time about the potential for wine grapes. I was young, enthusiastic, and willing to cooperate; the researchers were always looking for people who would cooperate."

In 1972 Dr. Clore asked Mike Sauer to plant an experimental vineyard at his site as part of a site study that Clore was conducting. Among those who planted the vineyard were Mike Wallace and Bob Fay, field aides at the research center. Clore was looking for different sites to put the same varieties on and see how they did. Sauer also put in a weather station in cooperation with the research center at Prosser. Then they planted about 20 different varieties. Grapes from this vineyard were sent down to the research center and made into wine by George Carter. These wines would then be tasted by Chas Nagel's wine evaluation group in Pullman to see if there were noticeable differences.

Sauer said, "I remember being so enthusiastic that every night, after work, I would hop on my Honda 90 trail motorbike and check on the various reset thermometers set around the farm. I could have done that once a week but I was so enthusiastic. I had about seven or eight of them and the round trip was about seven miles." After a couple of years Mike studied the scientific weather data maintained by the research center at Prosser, and he began to realize that he had a particularly good frost-free site. He recalled, "At that time the talk wasn't so much about what grapes made the best wine, but rather the whole emphasis was on winter survival."

Mike recalled putting in his first vineyard. He was in the National Guard at the time. He had experimented with a handful of varieties, not knowing whether they were red or white grapes. He was in the guard with a fellow who was caretaking the old Harrison Hill vineyard site for Associated Vintners. On the side, this person took cuttings and grew a nursery and had a bunch of Cabernet Sauvignon plants. They were two years old, and because they were so big he was having trouble selling them. One day at a guard drill he offered to sell some to Sauer at twenty-five cents apiece. Mike laughingly recalled, "I honestly didn't know if that was a red or a white wine grape." Mike bought a truckload.

Sauer recalled planting that first vineyard in 1973. They did everything wrong. They didn't break up the soil; rather, they hand-dug the holes for each plant for a total of about 3 acres. The vines struggled and the vineyard was far from pretty. Mike reminded me that this was an after-hours project. After a couple of years, weeds started to come in. Sauer remembered, "One writer then described the vineyard as languishing." In fact, the vineyard didn't produce for a couple of years after it should have.

Mike said that he didn't have a home for the grapes either. At that time white wine was in vogue. That first year they didn't even bother to pick the grapes. In '75 or '76 they should have been in production. Then Bob Fay came around. He was hauling grapes over to Associated Vintners on a flatbed truck. Sauer met Lloyd Woodburne. Woodburne signed a contract with him for his grapes.

Mike recalled one of the first vintages for which they sold grapes to Associated Vintners. It was for the 1979 Millenium, which incorporated some of his grapes from Red Willow Vineyard. The grapes were extremely overripe; they looked like shriveled-up huckleberries. The next year was 1980, the year of the Mount St. Helens eruption. Associated Vintners used the grapes and blended it into its Cabernet Sauvignon.

Beginning with the 1981 vintage, Red Willow grapes were kept separate and bottled as a separate wine with the Red Willow Vineyard designation. Mike Sauer said that David Lake recognized that the grapes from Sauer's vineyard were unique. They were slightly more tannic, producing a wine that is more slow-developing and backward. Sauer credited David Lake with creating the Red Willow reputation and credibility as a quality vineyard site. Suaer stated, "I really think it took his vision to see that there was something worth keeping separate, because Red Willow is always young and it would be tempting to want to blend it in with something to make it more drinkable." Thanks to Lake, there is now a continous vertical of Red Willow Vineyard-designated wines going back to 1981.

Mike Sauer, David Lake, and I went up on top of the vineyard to the new chapel. The vineyard that falls off below the chapel is designated Monsignor, to honor the local priest, and was planted in Syrah. Today Red Willow Vineyard is planted in a host of grapes, including Merlot, Nebbiolo, Sangiovese, and Tempranillo. The vineyards are planted on steep hillsides.

As we stood high on the knoll next to the chapel, the heady smell of ripe Concord wafted through the air, from the Concord vineyard just below us and next to the Monsignor vineyard. Mike explained how the Monsignor vineyard was carved out of the hillsides: "Before we could plant we had to level off the land. We brought in a big cat and cut through the hillside with a twenty-foot trough, leveling the sagebrush hillside. It was uneven and irregular. Even now as I look at it it gives me history goosebumps. Standing at the top here, it is about 1,150 feet elevation; 10,000 years ago, when the Bretz Floods came through here, the water washed up to about 1,100 feet. It means that the top of this vineyard is made up of extremely old soils and below it is a complex variety of soils caused by the flooding. When the cat cut through the hillside, it revealed some of the varied soils here; there was gravel below the sandstone and clay to loam."

It was late afternoon and the sun was beginning to set in the Cascades. The sky was beginning to turn color and the lightness of the air felt exhilarating. Lake and I were ending our remarkable day. We still had to drive back to the coast, as eastsiders call it, but emotionally I was finished, wallowing in the historical goosebumps Mike Sauer mentioned. By the time we got on the road and started climbing over Umtanum Ridge north of Yakima, the sky was spectacular. The sun had set. High above, the sky was a pale blue with the western horizon ablaze in a wash of yellow. The Cascade foothills were chocolate brown. Behind and below were the verdant fields of the Yakima Valley.

Chapter Twenty-Five

IN THE CELLAR

—*CANOE RIDGE ESTATE, NOVEMBER 1994*—

At the invitation of Mike Januik of Chateau Ste. Michelle, I joined him to taste wines at their new facility at Canoe Ridge Estate. The purpose was to taste the Merlot wines from the '93 vintage from grapes harvested at Canoe Ridge. Januik had already driven over to the winery, and I agreed to arrive the next day in the morning. He said he would begin at 6:00 a.m. and suggested I arrive at 9:00 a.m.

I was a bit anxious about driving over Snoqualmie Pass during the winter. The weather report warned of winter storm conditions, calling for considerable snow and suggesting that travelers carry survival kits with them. With that in mind, I rented an Isuzu Trooper four-wheel-drive vehicle and headed out for eastern Washington the evening before my appointment. It snowed as I approached the pass area and continued snowing until past Cle Elum—but it was hardly dangerous as I sailed through in my rented Trooper. I ended up driving to Prosser to spend the evening.

The next morning I drove up over the Horse Heaven Hills using the Ward Gap Road out of Prosser—the same road Walt Clore and I had taken a year before to visit Canoe Ridge Estate. Miraculously, I remembered to make the correct turns and found myself heading toward the Columbia River. At the river I turned east toward Paterson. Nearing Crow Butte Island, I looked for the entrance to the vineyard and winery.

The vineyards were barely visible from the highway but there was no mistaking the winery, perched on the hill about 500 feet above the river. I pulled alongside the winery and went around the building. I parked on the east side of the building in a gravel parking lot, remembering that a year ago this area had been covered with large stainless steel tanks lying on their sides. Below the gravel had been the fine dust of soil that makes up most of the soil profile of this area. I remembered kicking up the light soil as we walked.

I entered through an open door. It was impressive. Here was a working winery; a year ago it had been merely a shell, and now construction workers were replaced by winery workers. To my right was a tower of case goods of Columbia Crest wines being stored temporarily while new storage was being built at the Columbia Crest winery. Along the wall on the west side was a series of offices and a lab. There were few windows in this winery, and what windows there were all faced south.

I found Mike Januik out in the winery. He escorted me back to the office. This was the office of Charles Hoppes, the winemaker at Canoe Ridge Estate. The office was austere with ceiling-length windows looking out at Oregon and the magnificent Columbia below. Charlie's desk was on one side of the room. There were cots and mattresses in the corner. Toward the door was a round table.

Seated at the table was Mike Januik's assistant winemaker at Woodinville, Erick Olsen. Mike and Erick are responsible for all the wines produced under the Chateau Ste. Michelle label, some 600,000 cases of wine. Mike was forty-one years old then. He was soft-spoken and gentle. His laid-back, casual style belied his intense nature. He was just short of six feet and of medium build, reminding me of his Polish heritage; he looked like Lech Walesa with his brown hair, brown mustache, and round face.

His rise to head winemaker at Chateau Ste. Michelle was mercurial. Januik graduated in food science from UC Davis in 1984. He accepted a job for Dr. George Stewart of Stewart Vineyards in Granger, making some of Stewart's first wines from the '84 vintage. It was his first winemaking job; he was hired with no experience. He recalled fondly his first interview with Dr. Stewart, who had flown down to San Francisco to meet with Januik: "We talked over lunch and he decided that he liked me, that I was a good person."

Januik came to Granger and inherited some difficult wines that were doing weird things in the bottle and in the barrel. It became a proving ground for his winemaking ability. Soon Stewart Vineyards was producing exciting wines with bold, fresh fruit flavors. Januik's style began to emerge. His wines were soft and drinkable and always captured the grape flavors. He enjoyed working with the grapes from the Stewart vineyard located on the Wahluke Slope. Stewart also had grapes at his home vineyard on Harrison Hill in Sunnyside.

After three vintages, Januik moved to the Snoqualmie Winery, with a short stint in Idaho at Spring Creek Winery. The Snoqualmie wines were initially made at the Saddle Mountain facility, the former Langguth Winery east of Mattawa on the Wahluke Slope. It was a huge step: going from a winery that handled 150 tons to one that used 5,200 tons. A series of ownership changes thrust him fast-forward into the hands of Chateau Ste. Michelle. After three vintages at Snoqualmie Winery—'87, '88, and '89—the winery went through bankruptcy and into the hands of Chateau Ste. Michelle. In July 1990 he took over from Cherl Barber as winemaker, where he has excelled, leading the winery in its efforts to concentrate on the very best quality.

Mike now oversees the various wineries under the Chateau Ste. Michelle label, yet each winery maintains its own staff and resident winemaker. At Snoqualmie Winery, Joy Anderson is in charge. At Canoe Ridge Estate, Charles Hoppes is the resident winemaker.

Charlie Hoppes and his assistant, Kendall Mix, were at the table as well. Kendall Mix had brought back to the office beakers of red wine, Merlots from the '93 vintage. None of these wines were made at Canoe Ridge but they were transferred here once the winery was completed. The first wine that we tasted was the '93 Cold Creek Vineyard Merlot. It had seen fifteen different types of wood treatment. Its color was brilliant blue-red. Oak and young fruit aromas jumped out of the glass. On the palate the wine was very intense with ripe Merlot flavors.

Next we tasted the '93 wines made from the Merlot grapes picked here at Canoe Ridge. Although the wine was made from grapes grown here, they cannot call it an estate-bottled wine because they ended up having to ferment the wine at Columbia Crest. The '94 vintage will be the first estate-bottled wines from this facility. One had been aged exclusively in French oak, although there were ten different types (and/or treatments) of oak.

The oak varies considerably, depending upon the barrel maker and the source of their oak. The barrel may also vary according to how the oak is dried or whether and how the oak is charred; often the inside of the barrel is put over a flame and the inside is toasted. This helps caramelize the sugars in the oak, which in turn adds a toasty and sometimes sweet component to the wine.

The other wine was a composite of wine aged mostly in French oak but with some American oak; the actual percentage was about 76 percent French and 24 percent American.

The first wine, the all French–oaked wine, was very youthful with intense, almost tart flavors. The aromas were very perfumed. The second wine was more tannic and less round. Mike and Charlie talked about the wines. It was obvious that both of them particularly liked the wine aged exclusively in French oak. They made a decision. The first '93 Canoe Ridge Estate Merlot would be the wine aged in French oak. The other, the American aged, would go to Columbia Crest.

This winery was strictly a wine production facility. It was intended to be only a red wine facility for all of Chateau Ste. Michelle wines. Out in the cellar, there were two major components to the winery. On the northeast corner of the building were fermenting tanks. Each tank was about 6,000 gallons. They were about fifteen feet high and probably about ten to twelve feet wide. They looked like gigantic cleats sticking up out of their cement pads that keep them off the floor about four feet. They were state of the art, efficient, and convenient. One tank is designed to take a truckload of grapes, about 22 tons pre-fermentation. At the end of fermentation, the wine in these tanks is combined.

Once the wines have undergone the second fermentation, or the malolactic fermentation where the sharper malic acid is converted to the softer lactic acid and settled, then the young wines are put into barrel. The barrel room was on the northwest side of the winery and was very impressive. On the floor there were markings that identified the barrel lots according to their original tanks. Thus the wines are easy to track and work with. The barrels were stacked on double-barrel racks 6 high and 6 deep, or about 72 barrels in one row. Each lot was about 120 barrels.

We next went into the barrel area and tasted some wines from barrel. The first wines that we tasted were the Lot 1 Merlot from Canoe Ridge aged in Margaux barrels (a type of barrel produced for the Bordeaux wine trade). It was sinewy; the wine was sharp to the tongue but finished with a long fruit flavor combined with cedary oak and tannin. The next wine was the same source of grapes, Canoe Ridge grapes, and the same type of oak but a different tank: Lot 2. The wine was remarkable. First, it was so different from Lot 1. But, also, it tasted so wonderful. It was very soft and full on the palate. The third lot was a different type of barrel, still French, but a different producer. The wine was different again but without the quality of the second wine.

I didn't realize we were tasting different lots of the first wine that we had tasted earlier in the office. They were trying to decide which portions of that wine they would bottle separately as Canoe Ridge.

Mike and Erick walked me through the tank room and outside to show me the massive machinery that handles the grapes as they come in from the vineyard. A huge screw pulls the grapes into the crusher where the grapes are de-stemmed and crushed. The red juice, along with skins, is carried into their respective fermentation tanks.

Januik said that Canoe Ridge was already producing at capacity. They can produce 150,000 cases of wine. His intent was to make only red wines here. "I want to focus on red wine," he said.

Back at the office I was left with Erick Olsen while Mike went off to talk with Charlie. Olsen was a tallish young man, a recent graduate of the University of California Davis. He had an ever so slight accent. His parents are Danish but he was raised in Davis, California. Before coming to Washington, he worked in the cellar at Simi Winery in Healdsburg in the Sonoma Valley. Simi is a venerable winery with a rich history and a very good reputation. I asked Erick what the biggest difference is between California wines and Washington wines, especially during winemaking.

He said, "The wines up here have pure fruit flavors. The wines I was used to working with had lots of different things going on in the wines, especially with the presence of brett." *Brettanomyces* is a wild yeast often found in the vineyard or in the winery, often times in oak barrels. *Brettanomyces* imparts a distinct flavor component to wines. It is present in many Bordeaux wines and often this quality is viewed as positive by most wine drinkers, because it adds another dimension to the wine. *Brettanomyces,* however, is very unusual in Washington wines. Olsen hypothesized that it may be too cold for the yeast to survive.

Olsen got up out of his chair and paced the room. He said that it was cold. I thought about Davis, California, and how warm and hot it generally is there. I wondered how someone could get used to this weather. Outside it was cold, although being from the west side, I found it very pleasant because the air was so crisp and light. There was very little dampness.

Januik came back into the room. He was wearing goggles, mandatory out in the cellar. I noticed that his hands were covered with ink-black stains from working with red wine, like a mechanic's hands covered with grease. Charlie and Kendall returned. They had just brought in a new blend from the Lot 2 barrels that we had tasted individually out in the cellar. Mike said that this will be the final blend for the '93 Canoe Ridge Estate Merlot. It was very aromatic with lots of berrylike fruit and smells of fresh-cut cedar boughs. Its flavor was rich and round with youthful tannins grabbing at the sides of the tongue.

I was amazed at its softness. I asked if they filter their wines. Mike said they do a rough filtration. He said that he doesn't use any pumps to move his wine. Everything is moved under gravity. Each morning the crew siphons the wine that they are going to move into one of the hoses and then they maintain that suction all day. The only time the wine is mechanically pumped is from the final blending tank to the bottling line. Then the wine is pumped through a rough filtration system on the way to the bottling line.

—COLUMBIA CREST WINERY, JULY 1995—

Walt and I visited Columbia Crest. I was particularly interested in seeing the vineyards that Columbia Crest was using as part of the irrigation study with the research center, under the guidance of Bob Wample.

We stopped to talk to Doug Gore, the winemaker at Columbia Crest. He is a very accomplished winemaker and his wines are considered some of the very best wine values in America. The wines consistently win awards and are liked by judges for the balance of fruit flavors and fresh acidity—with pinpoint varietal flavors. The Columbia Crest Merlot is the best-selling Merlot in America.

Walt knows the winery well. The setting is spectacular. It is high above the Columbia, just north of Paterson, and Umatilla to the east. The mission-style winery resides comfortably in its setting. What it doesn't reveal, until you enter, is the vast underground winery. It is like a huge underground parking lot, over 9 acres in size (recently expanded to 11 acres), the size of Seattle's entire Pike Place Market Historical District.

Walt led me through the reception area and entered an unmarked door, where we descended a stairway. We went past impressive and seemingly endless fifty-foot-high stacks of barrels, stacked nearly to the ceiling, a new shipment of barrels still wrapped in plastic. Past the clinking bottling line, past the gigantic, glistening, stainless steel tanks, and up a metal stairway to Gore's office. It was a small, cramped office, a functional office with Gore's desktop perched on metal file cabinets.

On the north wall was a large world map. Columbia Crest thinks global and sells wines in the Far East and in Europe.

Gore, a young man, had brown hair and direct brown eyes, and wore gold wire-rimmed glasses. He was dressed comfortably and casually; he was at once intense but relaxed. Gore began at Columbia Crest in 1982 as assistant to Kay Simon. Then the winery was known as River Ridge. Gore took over red wine production in 1984. He worked with Cherl Barber and Peter Bachman. Today, Bachman is vice-president of operations, working out of the corporate offices in Woodinville. Bachman is the operational link between Gore, Januik, Hoppes, and Anderson, but has little to do with the day-to-day operations of the various Stimson Lane wineries.

In 1987 River Ridge was rededicated and renamed Columbia Crest Vineyards. Today Columbia Crest includes 18,000 acres; this includes acreage in corn, alfalfa, and grapes. Of this, slightly over 2,000 acres is in *vinifera* wine grapes, or 18 percent of the state's total *vinifera* grape crop. Originally most of the vineyards were under circular irrigation, but that has slowly been replaced with drip irrigation. Gore estimated that he makes about 2,000 tons of red wine alone at Columbia Crest but he doesn't know what their total wine production is. He was anxiously awaiting four new stainless steel 150,000-gallon tanks. The large tanks will allow Gore to better assemble his final blends, allowing him a more consistent bottle-to-bottle product.

We walked through the vastness of the concrete cave. Everything was so large. We gazed at the stainless steel tanks that are used to make the wines from the Sauvignon Blanc grapes grown by Columbia Crest for Bob Wample at the research center. It is impressive; there are twenty-eight 3,000-gallon tanks to a cement pad. Sixteen of the tanks are being used to make four different lots from each section of the vineyard; with four different sections, that gives a good replicated sample from the entire vineyard using different experimental water treatments. Eventually the wines will be bottled separately from the sixteen tanks.

From the cellar, Walt and I found our way up to the offices upstairs, where we met Charlie Hossom. Charlie is Stimson Lane's viticulturist. His domain includes vineyards at Columbia Crest, Canoe Ridge, Cold Creek, and various other holdings of Stimson Lane. There are 12 vineyards in all for a total of 3,370 acres. Assuming that the average yield per acre is 5 tons of grapes, that means their total tonnage is a whopping 16,850 tons.

Hossom, with blond hair and brown eyes, was a big, burly person with a boyish face. He was sitting behind his desk, back upstairs in an office just off the receptionist's desk, hands behind his head, looking out the south- and west-facing windows. On the wall was a poster map of the Columbia Valley, a reminder of the importance of this winery, its name, its location, and its wines trying to create a marketing name to one of America's northernmost wine areas. This is a very intentional effort by Stimson Lane to fashion a sense of place for the wine consumers of America. It is very smart. I recalled once that Bob Betz, vice-president of education and varietal research for Stimson Lane, told the story about doing a tasting back in Washington, D.C., for some knowledgeable wine drinkers. One of the tasters asked, "What side of the Potomac did you say these grapes were grown?" At that, Betz knew that educating America's wine drinkers was going to be a long, long uphill project.

Charlie's affable persona was deceiving. He was well educated; his book shelf was complete with scholarly works on grape physiology, grape growing, and grape disease. He studied for his master's degree at UC Davis in viticulture. He, so much like many of the other Stimson Lane professionals, was casual yet intense, well educated, up-to-date and comfortable with technology. Charlie grew up in Cheney, Washington, home of Eastern Washington University, where his father was a professor in political science with an expertise in Latin American politics. As a child Charlie spent a number of years in Mexico. He speaks fluent Spanish, even street Spanish, and this has proven advantageous in the vineyard where much of the work today is performed by Hispanic Americans.

Chateau Ste. Michelle had been the focal point for a boycott of its wines called by the United Farm Workers, which had singled out the most visible winery in the state to push for needed reform. Unfortunately, it seemed the UFW was picking on the wrong people; Chateau Ste. Michelle's record on workers' rights was one of the best in the Washington agricultural and wine industry. It had made everyone at the winery a bit jumpy and nervous. Prior to our visit with Hossom, the workers had requested a vote regarding union representation. At issue, and unresolved, was how that voting was going to be carried out.

Hossom called himself "the point person." He said, "Much of the problems with the laborers is a problem of communications." He thought that problems developed in 1986 with the passage of two federal legislative acts: the immigration act and the credit act. The immigration act upset everyone, but it was the tax credit act that caused the company to instigate new austerity measures that fell unfairly on the farmworkers.

Hossom's real contribution is his advanced knowledge of plant physiology. He loves working in eastern Washington. He particularly likes growing grapes at Paterson, calling the Paterson Ridge site one of the best sites that Stimson Lane owns. Hossom said that, from his standpoint, working with grapes in eastern Washington is the viticulturist's dream. Nature is so benign that the viticulturist is generally in charge of the growth of the vine. And he described growing grapevines in the sand as being nearly hydroponic. Hossom has great respect for the grapevine, saying, "it is very resourceful. Grapevines have a mind of their own—they regulate themselves." He was working closely on the Wample water experiment and succinctly described the experiment: "The concept is to control water to affect quality."

Continuing, he said, "It is not the quantity of water that is important, but rather the timing of when the water is applied to the vineyard. That's what this experiment is about." He explained in quick one-liners: "Never allow the vines to go into stress. Don't irrigate a grapevine until it's thirsty. Accelerate the maturation of the fruit by reducing the water."

His enthusiasm for the experiment was obvious. He pointed out that nobody has ever done this experiment on this level, quantitatively or statistically. He gets regular computer printouts of water availability to the grapevines in the vineyard through probes that measure the moisture content in the soil; the probes go down to between three and five feet. The water treatments were Low Low (LL), Low High (LH), High Low (HL), and High High (HH), referring to how much water was added during an early and a late treatment. He was convinced that the final analysis was going to lead them to a low-moderate water application. He said the high-high vineyard has led to vegetative wines, while the low-low is an intense wine.

From his office telephone, Hossom called Kevin Corliss, the vineyard manager, and asked him to accompany Walt and me out to the Clore Vineyard. Corliss, youthful with moderately long red hair stuffed under his baseball cap, was wearing shorts and hiking boots. We jumped into his company truck and went out into the vineyard, located just south of the winery.

He parked his truck in the middle of the vineyard. From this vantage point we could see the different sections of the vineyard that were receiving the various water treatments. The low-low application had orange markings on the posts at the end of the row of one section. The low-high were marked with green. The high-high were marked in yellow, while the high-low were marked in blue. In July it was not easy to see the differences in the vineyard sections, except in the extreme: the orange-tagged low-low section showed some stress with reduced foliage and smaller berry size, and this contrasted with the yellow-tagged high-high section with its larger clusters and much more foliage.

We then visited the vineyard nearby, formerly called Circle 102, now known as the Nagel Vineyard, named after Chas Nagel. The sign at the row end identified the vineyard as a Chenin Blanc vineyard. I laughed to myself, thinking of the arguments that I used to have with Chas Nagel when we were both judges at the Tri-Cities Wine Festival. To Nagel, Chateau Ste. Michelle's Chenin Blanc was the definition of the variety. Personally, I found it too fruity and perfumed, as if sweetened by a Muscat-based sweet reserve, and we would argue strenuously over how a Chenin Blanc should taste. Now Nagel might get the last word. However, now I recalled that Januik listed the Chenin Blanc as one of the wines that Chateau Ste. Michelle is phasing out. A pity I think—no doubt Nagel would agree.

—BOOKWALTER WINERY, NOVEMBER 1994—

Leaving Columbia Crest Winery I turned left, and north, toward Prosser. I thought about Vere Brummund's vineyard, located about ten miles away to the southeast, a mile outside of Plymouth. Brummund, Walt's assistant, had early on advocated planting grapes along the Columbia River based on his own study of the weather in the Columbia Valley. His own site had been planted in grapes early on. Brummund passed away in 1994, but I am sure he took some pleasure in seeing the developments at Columbia Crest and at Canoe Ridge. He advocated planting *vinifera* along the Columbia in his initial speech to the Washington Wine and Grape Growers Council in Yakima back in 1961.

Thirty years later, here was this massive vineyard owned by Columbia Crest and Stimson Lane, descendants of American Wine Growers. Recent plantings along the river at Canoe Ridge further vindicated Brummund's foresight.

Even President Thomas Jefferson would be pleased. He spent a lifetime trying to establish *vinifera* grapes in this country. Through Lewis and Clark's pioneering travels, he unwittingly discovered a premier wine-growing region.

I dropped Walt off at his home and decided to travel east toward Walla Walla. Along the way I stopped at Bookwalter Winery in West Richland, owned by Jerry and Jean Bookwalter. Jerry had been the horticulturist at Sagemoor Farms from 1976 to 1983, and is well known in the wine industry. Bookwalter's enthusiastic sales of Sagemoor Farms' grapes to the fledgling wine industry helped establish many of the early wineries of the 1980s.

Bookwalter's own efforts at managing a winery have been less successful. I learned why: He likes to dabble in a little bit of everything. The backbone of the winery is crisp, fresh white wines—Riesling, Muscat, and Chenin Blanc. It was wonderful to see a small winery make these kinds of wines, but it was hard to imagine that, as a small winery, he can afford to make these kinds of wines. I noticed that he had a '93 vintage Muscat for sale in the tasting room, $48 for a case. There was no way he could be making money on that wine. He said that he was selling it cheaply to raise money to help buy bottles for his '94 vintage, which he planned on bottling and releasing immediately— hardly two months after the harvest.

In the winery we tasted the '94 Muscat of Alexandria. It was divine drunk very cold and fresh from the stainless steel tank. This is one of the world's great wines for flavor purity and balance of sweet flavors and acidity. It tasted like a perfectly ripened Crenshaw melon with hints of lime and honey.

Jerry and Jean came to Washington from Atwater, California, in California's Central Valley. They farmed peaches, almonds, and Thompson Seedless grapes. A local headhunter out of Fresno had heard that Sagemoor was looking for a horticulturist and he mentioned it to Jerry, then twenty-six years old. Jerry went up to meet with Alec Bayless and Win Wright in the dead of winter. He noted that there were a lot of poplar trees planted but didn't think much of it until he had accepted the job and moved into a trailer at Sagemoor Farms.

Jean told him, "You go up and see if you like it." She remained at Atwater and tried to sell the farm. Then on St. Patrick's Day in '77, Jerry found out why the poplar trees were planted around the perimeter of Sagemoor Farms. He said a windstorm came up and he thought for sure he was going to be blown across the Columbia Basin like a piece of tumbleweed. It was cold and miserable—-then the septic system backed up and remained plugged up for a long time. To him it was like some kind of living hell.

But then spring came, one of those early springs; the cherry blossoms broke and Jerry was hooked. Jean had been successful in selling the farm and suddenly there was no reason for Jerry not to stay.

Jerry continued as the farm manager until 1983 when he left Sagemoor Farms to start his own winery. Bookwalter Winery opened in 1984. He was also involved in a number of orchard investments with his ex-partner, Bill Broich, from Idaho. Broich was then the winemaker at Ste. Chapelle Winery just outside of Boise. Broich relied on Sagemoor Farms for about a third of his grapes. He made gorgeous wines and helped establish Idaho (and Washington) for Chardonnay with his big and buttery-styled Chardonnays.

Eventually Bookwalter teamed up with Broich in a number of land investments. They became very good at developing orchards and selling them to tax-credit customers. It also was Bookwalter's undoing. In 1987 he declared bankruptcy and he and Jean had to basically start all over. For many years their winery was located in an industrial park north of Pasco. After the bankruptcy they sold everything they had and put together their new winery on the north side of Badger Mountain, just outside of Richland.

The new winery, located close to Interstate 82, is a model of efficient winery living. The winery and sales area are connected directly to their apartment-style house. From the tasting room you go left through a door to the winery, or right through the door to their home and office. They are determined to make it go.

Jean and Jerry are in their early fifties. Their children have grown and moved away. The Bookwalters are clear on what they want to do. Both are scrappers. Jean is ebullient, with a wonderful soft smile. Jerry could be a frazzled Santa Claus. His nature is warm and friendly. What you see is what you get. He is slightly portly and disheveled, his pants sag not unlike some of my son's friends, the current fashion among teenagers. Jerry poured me a taste of '93 Chardonnay Reserve. It was nicely made with fresh, balanced flavors and a hint of oak. We also tasted the '91 Cabernet Sauvignon, the '92 Merlot, and a generic red table wine. Jean clutched a computer printout of each of the wines. She charts all of the various costs associated with the wines. She is determined that they are going to make it. Jerry admitted, "If it wasn't for Jean I wouldn't be able to do this; she keeps us going." Jean beamed in satisfaction.

I left them and drove east on Interstate 182. East of Pasco, Highway 12—the highway I wanted to take to reach the Walla Walla Valley and taste the wines made there—merges with I-182, and at the Wallula junction, Highway 12 swings east through rolling wheat fields toward Rick Small at Woodward Canyon and Gary Figgins at Leonetti Cellars. Small helped locate the siting of the Canoe Ridge Vineyard, which is a separate development from the Canoe Ridge Estate. I also wanted to taste Gary Figgins's wines at Leonetti Cellars from the '92, '93, and '94 vintages. Walla Walla is about an hour's drive from Pasco. With luck I would get there at about 10:00, find a motel, and then visit with Small and Figgins in the morning.

—WOODWARD CANYON WINERY, NOVEMBER 1994—
I made arrangements to meet with Rick Small in the morning at his winery just outside of Walla Walla at Lowden, also the home of L'Ecole No. 41. Lowden is extremely small. The roadside narrows at the Small grain elevator that dominates the skyline. Ramshackle buildings, a former store, a gas station, and warehouses run along the roadside. Then a sign: WOODWARD CANYON WINERY. The setting reminded me of recent television commercials for pop or beer, tight jeans, or a sporty car. I half expected a beautiful woman to walk out of the door of one of the neglected buildings, holding a bowl of deep red wine and enticing me to come into the cellar.

Actually, no one appeared. I got out my camera and took a picture of the the entrance to the winery; next to the door was a picturesque stack of wooden grape bins stenciled WOODWARD CANYON WINERY. Just as I snapped the picture, Rick Small walked into the frame. I hadn't seen Rick for awhile. Other than the new white hairs, he looked the same. Wiry and energetic, he has a handsome, strong, thin face. Intense—that's Rick. His glasses framed his intense eyes.

We went into the building on the side where he maintains his office. I asked Rick how Canoe Ridge Vineyard was founded. He leaned back in his chair and thoughtfully tried to recall how he got involved. Small himself began making wines with friend Gary Figgins. Gary had already gone commercial with his '78 vintage Cabernet Sauvignon. Rick started soon after when he introduced his powerful 1981 Cabernet Sauvignon. Like Leonetti wines, they were big and powerful Cabernet Sauvignons. It helped that there were two wineries making super-premium wines in Walla Walla. They helped each other get attention from the Seattle market. In 1983 they were joined by Baker and Jean Ferguson at L'Ecole No. 41 with their lush Merlot. A year later Eric and Janet Rindal began crafting wines at Waterbrook Winery.

Walla Walla was now on the Washington wine map. Rick and Gary were about to be on the American wine map. In 1992 the *Wine Spectator* chose three of Woodward Canyon's wines in its review of the world's top one hundred wines. Pretty heady stuff. But so are Small's wines.

At a dinner one evening in Seattle, Phil Woodward and Dan Duckhorn, on a marketing tour of the Pacific Northwest, were dining at Rosellini's The Other Place. Their wine steward, Steve Burnell, suggested they try a Woodward Canyon Chardonnay. Phil Woodward was an investor, and CEO of Chalone Wines. Dan Duckhorn was one of his clients and made excellent wines in the Napa Valley. Woodward was surprised, maybe shocked, and said, "I didn't know they were doing this here." Meaning, making great wines. Phil Woodward immediately contacted Rick Small.

Rick recalled, "Through that connection I knew Phil Woodward was looking to get involved with Washington. He asked Dick Graf and his vineyard manager, Corky Roach, to visit eastern Washington. I was their tour leader and took them on a one-day driving tour of the area. We started with my vineyard nearby, then drove up to Mercer Ranch.

"We came down the paved road and stopped to visit a piece of land known as the Sandpiper Farms, a portion of which had recently been purchased by a group of Walla Walla investors. I drove them to the top of the hill, the northeasterly edge of Canoe Ridge. Dick Graff said, 'This is a great place. Can we find out who owns this?' We then met with the owner and found out that he wanted to sell the whole lot."

Rick said the Chalone group wasn't interested in the entire parcel. Instead Phil Woodward talked to the Walla Walla investment group about buying some additional land and planting some more vineyards. They already had 40 acres planted. Woodward wanted to know if they would become half partners in a new winery and additional vineyard plantings.

Today there are slightly more than 100 acres planted in Merlot, Cabernet Sauvignon, and Chardonnay. The original site located on the Sandpiper Farms next door eventually became Canoe Ridge Estate, owned by Stimson Lane. The Chalone development became Canoe Ridge Vineyards, which has led to some confusion. Rick showed no animosity toward Stimson Lane. He thought that the farmer then went to Stimson Lane after the Chalone group only purchased a portion of his land. Stimson Lane jumped at the offer—especially with the chance of being next to the development by Chalone; it was a simple marketing decision.

The '92 vintage was the first harvest from vines that were three years old. Rick described the soil characteristics of the site: it is a very fine, sandy soil, very light. Rick was sure that the wines would be very distinctive but found it too difficult as yet to see their style.

I told Rick I was interested in tasting the '94 wines from Canoe Ridge Vineyards. He retrieved a glass wine thief and we went into the back of the shop behind his office. This was a new barrel space devoted strictly to his red wines. All the barrels were on the floor or on 4x4s on top of the first row of barrels. Rick explained that his is a working winery, meaning, I supposed, that he didn't put his money into bricks and mortar—but rather into oak and winery equipment. His winery had grown considerably since I last visited. He was now close to 8,500 cases. The red wine facility is in his family's old machine shop. It is a narrow building, maybe about 60 feet across by about 100 feet long. It reminded me of some of the small Bordeaux wineries I have visited, except that there were a lot of new oak barrels at Woodward Canyon Winery.

Rick drew some Cabernet Sauvignon out of a new American oak barrel. The wine was still cloudy and unsettled, but it smelled grapy and of raspberry. The raspberry quality was evident on the palate too, with a direct grapy finish. It was so young it was difficult to know what to think. I believe that I just wanted to revel in tasting the wine that came directly from the site. It made it so immediate. That is one of the great pleasures of wine. It brings to an exacting moment the character of the climate and soil of a particular site.

We then tasted some other '94 Cabernet Sauvignons out of barrel and tank. Tasting wines at this stage is almost hopeless because the wines are so young and undetermined. It is like tasting a soup's broth after the vegetables and spices have just been added; all the spices are kind of obvious, they haven't yet melded into the overall flavor. We tasted a wine from a French barrel, from the center of France, that was made from old block vineyards at Mercer Ranch and a third from a new vineyard nearby called Pepper Bridge. Rick liked the Mercer Ranch and was fascinated by the thought that the vineyard soils are ancient soils undisturbed by the Bretz Floods because they are so high up in the

Horse Heaven Hills. The wine was bigger and broader with more structure.

Then we sampled a '94 Sagemoor wine with less than 20 percent Canoe Ridge grapes. This wine was a big mouthful. Rick nodded his head. He was so earnest, so intent on making the best wine. It is like an artist mixing paint pigments from naturally derived sources, struggling for the right hue. Rick, at forty-six years old, was more philosophical than when I first met him. He said that he has no timetable for himself anymore. I think the market has been good to him. I remembered visiting with him years ago and I'm sure he told me he probably would never grow beyond about 1,500 cases. That was a while back, but I don't think he anticipated the demand on his wine. He sells about two-thirds of his wine in the Pacific Northwest. The rest is sold through Chalone along the I-5 corridor.

—LEONETTI CELLARS, NOVEMBER 1994—

My next appointment was with Gary Figgins. I wanted to revisit Leonetti Cellars because I realized after reading my notes from two years previous, when I had last visited Gary, that I got so caught up in the winemaking that I didn't keep good notes on the wines we tasted out of barrel in the cellar. Besides, I wanted to taste the '92 vintage that he had crushed during my last visit.

Gary, like Rick, was running out of room. His fermenting room was full of barrels. Gary laughed his hearty laugh: "I'm getting ten letters a day asking for our wine. We have far more people who want our wine than we have wine." The previous day Walt had given me a reprint of an article in the *Wine Spectator*. It was a feature article by Jim Laube about Gary Figgins entitled "The Merlot Master." It claimed that he was making the best Merlots in the United States. Accompanying the article were tasting notes on both his Cabernet Sauvignon and Merlot, going back to his first commercial vintage Cabernet Sauvignon in 1978 and his first Merlot in 1981.

Gary takes the recognition in stride. His wines are expensive, ranging from $30 a bottle up to $40 for his reserve bottlings. He sees himself moving toward a Leonetti blend, one wine made up of component parts. Gary buys from a number of vineyards for a couple of reasons. One practical reason is insurance against a vintage like '91 where the grape crop was reduced significantly. The other is aesthetic, relying on various sites contributes different flavor characteristics.

We walked down into his cool cement cellar. First we tasted the '94 Sagemoor Farms Merlot aged in American oak. It was soft and velvety. I thought about Jim Laube tasting wine with Figgins and being seduced by the ambiance of the cellar and the beauty of the wines. Then we tasted a '94 vintage Cabernet Sauvignon from the Seven Hills Vineyard in Oregon aged in a barrel that used an interstave of Oregon oak. The wine was spicy and smooth. It was surprisingly clear and approachable.

Interstave is the latest rage amongst wineries. The interstave is new oak that is added to the inside of a barrel so that the winemaker can get longer use out of the barrel. In theory the interstave needs to be replaced each year. It costs about a fifth of a new barrel. The Oregon oak was assertive and spicy.

Gary is fascinated by oak and is growing his own oak. He also gets staves of Oregon oak from a friend in Oregon and then air-dries the staves himself. Figgins was in the process of writing a book on oak and barrels. He is almost as enamored by the oak as by the grape and the grape's source.

Next we tasted another '94 Seven Hills Cabernet Sauvignon, without the interstave. It was ripe and smooth with distinctive raspberry fruit flavors. Then another Cabernet Sauvignon, '94, made half from grapes grown at Portteus Vineyard in the Yakima Valley and half from grapes grown on the Wahluke Slope at the Connor Lee Vineyard. (Flash to Walt's prized picture of winemakers at the Wahluke Slope looking at the hole in the ground in 1967. I was tasting the past in the present—to be drunk in the future.) This wine had a deep color, bright red, with ripe, complex flavors. The softness of Portteus Vineyards' grapes was balanced by the crispness of the Connor Lee Vineyards.

Then we tasted some '93 vintage Cabernets: first a blend made of primarily Portteus Vineyard grapes, then a wine predominantly of Sagemoor Farms, each with distinct vineyard flavors: Portteus with cherrylike flavors and Sagemoor with a softer, almost strawberry character.

Figgins then poured from his long glass thief a '93 vintage Merlot from Sagemoor Farms grapes. It was aromatic and full with a strikingly smooth, silky grape flavor and feel.

My palate was beginning to reel, not from palate fatigue but from just too much: too many wines that were different but the same; too much wine that caused me to focus all of my senses in analyzing it (yet wanting just to drink it!); too much wine from too many vintages and from too many barrels. But—it was too much of a good thing. I knew that this is what the winemakers like to do: taste their new wines to watch them evolve from grapes that generally all look the same. I tried to imagine doing this with any other fruit product, maybe apples; possibly one could compare vintage ciders made from the same apple variety grown in different locations, but I doubted that the differences would be as significant as the wines I was tasting. It was truly amazing to taste the Cabernet Sauvignon grown at the Wahluke Slope and contrast it with the Cabernet Sauvignon from Portteus Vineyard. The vineyards are only forty miles apart, but separated by Umtanum Ridge, Yakima Ridge, and finally the Rattlesnake Hills.

Then Gary's face beamed. He related a wonderful story that he knew would please me. His dentist introduced him to the dentist's eighty-year-old uncle, who has a vineyard in Walla Walla. The uncle continues to make his house wine from grapes whose vines were planted thirty-five years ago. Gary remembered tasting the wine: "It was horrible; it was thin. The uncle was adding sugar and boosting the alcohol." The uncle told Gary that the grape was the Black Prince. This was the same grape grown by Frank Orselli in Walla Walla back in the 1800s. And it was the same grape grown by Bert Pesciallo at Milton Freewater. Gary said it is the same as the Black Malvoisie, which is another variety cited as being grown in the 1800s. Something more exciting: Gary's brother, Rusty, has done some ampelography (the study of grape varieties) in the past and has identified the grape as Cinsaut, the workhorse grape of southern France. Gary, with Rusty's assistance, then went out and found some other locally grown grapes, also grown in the Rhone valley: Grenache and Syrah.

Gary withdrew from barrel a sample of the '94 vintage. Only two barrels were made, enough for about 50 cases. The wine was 35 percent Cinsaut, 50 percent Grenache, and 15 percent Syrah. The wine was young, undeveloped. It was light in color and in weight. It was way too early to tell what kind of wine it will make. Compared to the Cabernets and the Merlots, it was much lighter and more acid.

That Cinsaut taste treat turned out to be a short respite. It was like having a sip of Normandy Calvados (a high-proof apple brandy), serving the purpose of burning a hole in one's stomach to make room for the rest of a heavy Norman meal.

We then tasted more of the '94 vintage Cabernet Sauvignons. Blam, blam, blam: the '94 Portteus, very soft; the '94 Sagemoor, berry-like; the '94 Pepper Bridge, very concentrated; '94 Pepper Bridge aged with Latvian oak interstaves, spicy and concentrated; '94 Sagemoor aged in Latvian oak interstave, again spicy and soft. We also tried some '94 Pepper Bridge blended with Connor Lee Vineyard; I could tell by Gary's voice that he liked this wine. I agreed; it was incredibly concentrated. Next we tried the '94 Merlot from Connor Lee, a big tannic wine. That was followed by a '94 Cabernet Franc grown at Connor Lee on the Wahluke Slope; the wine was silky soft. I mentioned to Gary that Walt was really excited about this grape after seeing how well it survived the freeze in '91. Walt was even thinking it was hardier than the Lemberger.

We then tasted the '93 Connor Lee Merlot—a year older than what we had just tasted and it was already much softer; it had ripe grape flavors that were rich.

Figgins commented, "I really like to blend, to find the right combination. I feel like I am getting closer to doing just one wine. Eventually I would like to just have an estate wine. It would be our Leonetti Chateau. It would be made from estate-grown grapes: Sangiovese, Syrah, Cabernet Sauvignon, Cabernet Franc, Petit Verdot, and Merlot." All of these are grapes that Gary has planted on his property. I could tell that Gary was excited about the future of an estate-grown wine. I knew that he understands the risk too. His property is quite low in elevation and there are a number of frost pockets in his vineyard. But there is that artist thing, a provincial need of wanting something local, a wine specific to the soil and site.

Gary added, already wavering on a singular bottling, "Maybe there will be two select wines."

He said this because he realized the risk of an estate wine. It is better to buy grapes from a range of vineyards to make sure you get fruit in unfriendly years, and to use to advantage flavors resulting from different microclimates.

This led us into tasting the '92 wines. We tried two wines. One was the Leonetti Select. It was made from Walla Walla-grown grapes: 50 percent Merlot, 40 percent Cabernet Sauvignon, and 10 percent Cabernet Franc. Aged in a combination of three oaks, it was fat and aromatic with wonderfully rich, ripe flavors. A beautiful wine.

The other wine we tasted was the Columbia Valley appellation made up of mostly Cabernet Sauvignon with about 7 percent Merlot and 8 percent Cabernet Franc. The grapes were from Portteus, Sagemoor, and Seven Hills Vineyards. It tasted wonderful!

Gary asked, "Isn't that lovely? It is very elegant, very drinkable;

great vintages taste great from the very beginning."

Gary gave me a bottle to take home. I wanted to taste it later so that I could take better notes. This was, after all, the same vintage I had watched his family process two years ago. Here are my notes: "It is deep, rich red, blood red with a wide, distinctly red edge. It is all Cabernet Sauvignon grape smells, muscular and fruity, layered with sweet oak aromas, almost smelling of fresh-cut cedar. On the palate the wine is fat and round. The acid is perfectly balanced with the intense flavors of the Cabernet Sauvignon fruit. There are abundant tannins but they seem subdued or woven into the wine. The finish is chalky almost and the aftertaste is berrylike. It is truly a great wine made by an artist."

Frank Orselli, one of the original Walla Walla winemakers a century earlier, would be proud.

Chapter Twenty-Six

STRETCH ISLAND
ISLAND BELLE REVISITED

Dr. Clore has been concerned that I am giving the impression that Adam Eckert created the Island Belle grape. I have hit a sensitive nerve with Walt; he doesn't think that I appreciate the difficulty of creating a specific grape variety by cross breeding. Nor does he think I value the judgment of horticulturists like himself who have stated repeatedly that the Island Belle grape is synonymous with Campbell Early.

I do not mean to imply that the Island Belle was ever created by Adam Eckert or anyone else in his family. I would like to believe that there is a grape unique to the Puget Sound region. On Vashon Island, where I live, there are numerous small plantings of grapes in people's backyards. When I study the plantings, typically I find a row of vines about six vines long, trellised with cedar posts at the ends with wire holding up the canes. I can recall at least a half dozen of these plantings that are visible from the road. The granddaddy of them all is along Quartermaster Harbor in a vineyard called the Tsugwale Vineyard. This vineyard was planted to grapes by Paul Billingsley in about 1917. It includes the Island Belle and the Chasselas grape.

Whenever I stop to inquire about various plantings on the island, current property owners know little or nothing about the grapes. Often I estimate the planting to have occurred around the late teens, either by hearsay or by learning when the property was developed, or by comparing the size of the vine's trunk with other known plantings, such as at the Tsugwale Vineyard. Is it a coincidence that many of these plantings occurred at the beginning of Prohibition? I think it is likely that

A young girl (Priscilla Angle) sampling Island Belle grapes
—*Photo by Heckman. Courtesy of Mason County Historical Society.*

Walter Eckert, Adam Eckert's son, did an excellent job of selling the Island Belle plants, including instructions and materials, to small farmers throughout the Puget Sound region. I have seen pictures of similar plantings on Bainbridge Island. Eckert would have pointed out the advantages to raising grapes with the dawning of Prohibition.

In 1995 I got a phone call from Bob Allen on Stretch Island. Allen has a vineyard on Stretch Island called The Misty Isle Vineyard. He has been re-establishing his vineyard over the years and sells some of his grapes to the Hoodsport Winery where he is a board member, as one of the stockholders. He called to tell me that he had just received notice that the Bureau of Alcohol, Tobacco and Firearms (BATF) was no longer going to allow the use of the name Island Belle. Beginning in 1996 the grape would be recognized as the Campbell Early, which is considered its synonym.

I told Allen that I would help him pull together a group of people to talk about the Island Belle grape. I then called Peggy Patterson of Hoodsport Winery and together we called upon interested parties to meet at the old St. Charles Winery. It was a momentous occasion. Included were Howard and Bill Somers, Harley Somers (son of Bill Somers), Harry Branch (of Branch Vineyard on Stretch Island), Peggy Patterson and her daughter Ann, and Bob Eacrett (the grandson of Adam Eckert) and his son. Also attending were a photographer,

Lynn Saunders, and a writer, Jack Swanson, from the *Bremerton Sun*.

I showed slides that I had come across in Walt's and my research for this book, and gave a short talk using a chronological history I had accumulated. It meant that I was telling them about their history rather than being able to listen to them. I was quoted by Swanson as saying that I believed the Island Belle grape was developed around 1898 by cross-pollinating two other grapes. I intended to say that some people, including Bill Somers, had heard that the Island Belle was a cross between the Hartford Prolific and the Concord.

When Dr. Clore saw the article from the *Sun*, he immediately called me to register his displeasure. He suggested that we should do a replicated planting of the varieties and arranged to get me some Campbell Early grapes if I would secure some Island Belle cuttings from Stretch Island. I called Harley Somers and asked him to provide me with some cuttings. In return I told him that I would get some plants from Dr. Clore when I attended a seminar in Yakima later that week.

The seminar was sponsored by the Central Washington Wine Technical Society with assistance from Washington State University. Entitled "Winemaking in the Vineyard," it was a two-day seminar dealing with how decisions made in the vineyard affect the eventual quality of wine. I made arrangements with Dr. Clore to exchange our Island Belle and Campbell Early plants and cuttings. Clore handed me the Campbell Early plants covered in black plastic with rubber bands on either end. I don't recall how I had packaged the Island Belle. But I recall the symbolism of exchanging the plant material with him, a circumstance that occurs regularly in the propagation of grapevines. Plant material is handed on to someone else, the vine becoming the baton in a long relay race, handed to a new generation or a new group. This baton was living; its only requirement was to be planted.

In attendance at the seminar was John Vielvoye, a British Columbia horticulturist stationed at Kelowna, British Columbia. Vielvoye suggested that he could take wood material of each grape variety and subject it to DNA testing. He was willing to do this as a favor to Dr. Clore. About two months later I was told that the laboratory had done four probes and as yet no difference had been detected. However, he also said that that is not uncommon and more probes may be necessary.

At about that time Dr. Clore had made the acquaintance of Bob Tice, a young man from Tacoma. His fiancee's father was about to take over at Clore's Methodist Church in Prosser. While visiting Walt's home, he noticed grapes growing in his backyard and remarked that his grandfather planted a vineyard in the University Place area of Tacoma, stating that in the vineyard, planted side by side, are the Campbell Early and the Island Belle.

Walt was beside himself. He called me and we made arrangements to visit the vineyard, planning to visit when the grapes were ripened. During October Walt came over and we spent a couple of days together. The first day we planned to visit the Tice vineyard and then take the grapes up to Stretch Island to compare to the Island Belle grapes growing at the Somers vineyard.

We stopped by the Tacoma vineyard early in the morning. It was a beautiful day—clear and bright. Walt was wearing a hat and coat, expecting the weather to be cool and wet. He was pleasantly surprised and remarked a number of times how nice it was that it was clear. The vineyard is located at Bob Tice's mother's house. It was planted by his grandfather, Nick Alfonso, sometime during the 1950s. Prior to the vineyard, Alfonso grew vegetables in his front yard and operated a butcher shop in Tacoma's Hilltop area, or "Little Italy." Alfonso arrived in Tacoma in 1936 by way of Pasco. He had actually come to America before World War I. I wondered if he had known any of the Italians in the Tri-Cities area.

Walt recalled the Fred Pardini vineyard that was planted at the Richland "Y" near Kennewick. This vineyard was planted around 1933 to 15 acres of Zinfandel and 10 acres of Muscat of Alexandria, with a 5-acre mix of Tokay and Black Malvoisie. The remnants of the Pardini vineyard could still be seen years later along the freeway, a small triangle of vines surviving without irrigation. Pardini's son, Albert, told Walt that during World War II, trusted Italian prisoners of war were shipped to Pardini's vineyard to work the harvest. Apparently they liked that setup quite well. They liked his grapes and his homemade Zinfandel wine.

Alfonso might have known Pardini. But he didn't try to grow *vinifera* grapes in his own front-yard vineyard. Instead he turned to hybrid grapes including Delaware, Niagara, Campbell Early, and Island Belle. Bob Tice, Alfonso's grandson, provided invoices that showed that his grandfather bought 100 Campbell Early plants, but there was no documentation for the Island Belle.

I asked him how he knew that he had Island Belle grapes in his vineyard. He said, "Well, Grandpa would take me out into the vineyard and say, 'Here is the Campbell Early,' and point to it, and 'Here is the Island Belle.'"

Walt and I stopped at the vineyard to get some grape samples and we arranged to meet Bob Tice at his vineyard in the afternoon. Walt took a number of pictures from the road and from above the vineyard. The vineyard is situated in the front yard and takes up most of it except for the driveway along the side of the property. It is a normal-size front yard in a typical American middle-class neighborhood, and while neighbor's yards are planted to lawn with a few trees and shrubs, here stands this vineyard. There are about fourteen rows with about fifteen vines per row. Tice hopes to get about a half ton of grapes off the vineyard, although he says that Alfonso got quite a bit more.

Bob Tice has marked the Island Belle grapevines for us. Next to them are the Campbell Early. I had already been to this vineyard a couple of weeks before, so I could direct Walt to the vines and recall what Tice had said. During my earlier visit I met Tice's mother, Deleva. She had been kind enough to open up two bottles of wine. One was a wine she had made from the 1992 vintage, a mix of all the grapes in the vineyard. It was fruity and of medium weight and reminded me of a Beaujolais-styled red wine with flavors much like the Island Belle made by Hoodsport Winery; both had a telltale grapy quality, not foxy but of a sweet, fresh grape smell. Next she opened a bottle that Alfonso made twenty-five years ago. It was a golden yellow-brown color. The aromas were like a sweet, aged Muscat, like a perfumed yellow rose. The palate was fresh and fruity and very smooth. The wine was obviously aged but it tasted wonderful and didn't taste at all old.

Walt examined the various grapevines' leaves. Bob Tice had told me earlier that the vines acted much differently. The Campbell Early was a less vigorous grower and the cluster size was much more irregular; even the berries within the cluster varied in size. Also, the Island Belle berries were bluer in color, while the Campbell Early were blacker and slightly more oblate. Walt took out his red refractometer (a hand-held device used to measure sugar) to take a reading on the berries. First he measured sugar in the Island Belle. He took a berry and crushed it between his thumb and forefinger onto the glass plate on the handheld refractometer. Then, holding the refractometer toward the morning sun, he read the measurement: 18° Brix, which is a measurement of the sugar in the grape. Three other readings: 18.1°, 18.0° and 18.0°: very consistent. Then the Campbell Early. Walt noticed it was juicier when he squeezed it. It read 15.2°. Other readings: 17.6°, 20.8°, and 21.0°. Walt plucked a sampling of berries from different parts of the vine and noted that the tip berries were smaller and more concentrated.

There was clearly a difference. We then got into my Honda and drove up to Stretch Island. It was a beautiful, sumptuous fall day. We took Highway 16 out of Tacoma across the Tacoma Narrows Bridge until we could go west on Highway 302, which skirts first Carr Inlet, then Case Inlet, landbound among a perplexing series of peninsulas and islands that form the upper Puget Sound. I was aware of the geographic difference for Dr. Clore. All this water! In eastern Washington this water would be an irrigated valley floor. Here it was so laden with green, and a cobalt blue sky with billowing white clouds in the horizon. Throughout the day we had been blessed with dramatic views of Mount Rainier to the southeast. Now driving along the inlet we caught glimpses of the jagged Olympic Mountains to the northwest.

Walt asked me if I had seen the recent September '94 issue of the *Wine Spectator.* No, I told him; I hadn't been able to find it anywhere.

He said, "Well, it sure is a nice write-up on Washington wines."

He was right. Later, when I reviewed that issue of the *Wine Spectator,* I was impressed with its emphasis on some of the smaller Washington wineries. Receiving glowing reviews were Leonetti Cellars, Woodward Canyon Winery, and Quilceda Creek Winery. I was happy for them, but I was skeptical whether this newfound excitement for Washington wines would last. I thought of the Oregon experience during the 1980s when the wineries were discovered by the national wine writers, glowing in their praise, but just as suddenly dismissed. It devastated some Oregon wineries and they had only recently begun to re-establish themselves. I didn't want to see this happen to Washington wineries.

Then I realized that, from Walt's standpoint, it was a wonderful reinforcement of his life's work with grapes and wine. It is not an ego thing; rather it is a realization of his vision being played out. Driving along, I thought about when he first arrived at Prosser in 1937. I thought about the incredible progress that he had witnessed, and helped shape, in the farming communities of eastern Washington and in particular his work with grapes and wine. Although Dr. Clore is known as the "father of the wine industry" and is not at all comfortable with that flattering description, it took on new meaning for me; here was a father (Dr. Clore) looking at his child (the Washington wine industry) in appreciation.

At Allyn we turned south on Highway 3. From there we took the Grapeview cutoff. Harley Somers was there to meet us. He had just picked the grapes over the weekend and there wasn't much fruit left on the vines. Dr. Clore, Somers, and I walked through the same vineyard where I had picked Island Belles back in 1992, another warm and dry harvest. This vineyard is said to have been replanted in the 1940s. Walt noticed that the vines were much more mature and uniform in vine growth in this vineyard than in the Alfonso vineyard. The leaves were much more yellowed, a sign of early maturity, and there were fewer of them. Walt noted a much more uniform leaf shape than the vines in the Alfonso vineyard, of either the Campbell Early or the Island Belle. Of the few grape clusters that we found, they were less blue and darker than the Island Belle in the Alfonso vineyard.

Walt put the cluster on the trunk of my car along with a sample he brought of the Concord grape from the Prosser High School vineyard across from his home. Using the refractometer, it read in at 19.0° Brix. The Prosser Concord was very aggressive to the taste with a strong grape flavor and an aftertaste that was reminiscent of wintergreen. Walt told us that a common characteristic of the Concord is the pale green brush, which are the vascular strands that remain on the pedicel when the berry is pulled off the cluster. Also, the berries are medium to small and have an attractive blue color because of their waxy surface. The leaves are nearly entire, with very little lobing. The Campbell Early has a pink brush, and so does the Island Belle from the Somers's vineyard. The sugar reading on the Somers's grape was 18.2°.

Next we visited the Bartholet vineyard, also on Stretch Island, located higher off the floor of the island, owned by Ed and Olga Bartholet. They have about 4 acres planted to mostly Island Belle. When we arrived, Ed started out for his garage, where I could see from a scale for weighing grapes that he assumed we were going to harvest. Ed, a slender man light of foot, wore a blue feed cap slightly askew as he looked us right in the eye. Olga was the perfect grandmother, with light, wispy white hair and sky blue eyes. Both were direct and straightforward in their manners.

Their unpruned vineyard was heavily set with grapes. Generally, the vineyard looked very well maintained. Ed Bartholet had recently had bypass surgery and apologized for the slightly longer grass between the rows of vines. To me the grapes looked slightly bluer than the grapes at the Somers's vineyard. Walt noticed that the grape leaves were uniform except on vines in shallow soil areas. Each grape leaf was similarly trilobed with very little variation. The vines were vigorous and seemed more like the Alfonso vineyard. Walt took readings of the grapes: 17.5°, 17.6°, 17.0°. We gathered grapes into plastic bags, each marked according to the vineyard source and grape variety.

Next we drove up to Hoodsport Winery. Leaving Stretch Island, we got back on Highway 3 going south toward Shelton. We then turned off Highway 3, driving through various undeveloped prairies and valleys until we turned onto Highway 106, which runs along the southern edge of Hood Canal. We then joined up with Highway 101, driving north until we arrived at the winery. The winery was surprisingly busy considering that it was a weekday in October. Dick Patterson greeted us as we entered the winery. He is a scruffy sort of person, but also very sociable and friendly.

We walked outside to where the Island Belle grapes sat in bins ready for processing. There were only two bins from grapes picked on Stretch Island. The grapes were a gorgeous dark blue in the afternoon sun. Patterson complained about the low yield and available low tonnage—it would be only enough for about 25 cases.

For Walt it showed precisely why he prefers to work with grapes in eastern Washington, where annual yields are much more consistent. In eastern Washington, in the worst-case scenario—such as the cold weather in 1991—the vineyard yields were down about half. The Island Belle yield was down to a tenth of the harvest in 1992. The irony was that yields this year in western Washington, usually crippled by damp harvest conditions, were likely down because of a lack of water, it being a drought year.

Inside we tasted the Island Belle wine produced by Hoodsport Winery. Currently available were two wines. One was a blend of years; the other was from the glorious 1992 vintage. We tasted the blend. It was very smooth and light with a telltale grapy flavor and aroma. It was the same wine I had tasted two years before at the harvest meal served after we were done picking the 1992 vintage grapes at the Branch Vineyard, now the Harley Somers vineyard. We didn't sample the 1992 Island Belle, although I had tasted it earlier at the Island Belle meeting at the St. Charles Winery. The 1992 was a delightful wine with bursting fruit flavors, and perfectly balanced.

Since tasting it I noticed that it won a silver medal at the Western Washington State Fair wine judging. It sported a designer label with original artwork done by Bremerton artist Amy Burnett. The label shows an unidentified woman encircled by grapes, presumably the

Island Belle. Beside her in a square insert is a line drawing of Adam Eckert holding his grandson, Bob Eachrett. It is an especially attractive package combining history, art, and taste.

After our short visit, we then headed back to Tacoma to meet Bob Tice at his grandfather's vineyard. Walt, Tice, and I walked into the vineyard to look at the grapevines that Tice had identified as the Campbell Early and Island Belle. Returning to the vineyard, there was clearly a difference between the two varieties. Neither one of them looked like the grapes we had seen at Stretch Island. While Walt and Tice talked about the vines, I went back to the grapevines identified by Tice as Island Belle. I picked a grape or two and noted that the pedicel's brush was pale green, close to what I thought was translucent white.

I turned to Walt. "Walt, this is interesting—when I picked the grape, the brush is white."

He says, "That would indicate it is a Concord. I can't believe we didn't notice that this morning when I did the readings with the refractometer. And that explains why the grape leaves are so varied, some being well indented and others being more rounded."

My heart sank. I felt that all that we had done that day was wasted. The basis for our comparison suddenly had no foundation. Except—and this is a big exception—I was able to watch Walt Clore firsthand use his scientific skills in observation and scrutiny in the vineyard.

Chapter Twenty-Seven

THE IRRIGATION EXPERIMENT
PROOF IS IN THE WINEGLASS

—YAKIMA, APRIL 1994—

Four glasses of Sauvignon Blanc sat in front of me waiting to be tasted. Their strawlike yellow color twinkled under the glare of the overhead lights.

I was attending a two-day seminar entitled "Winemaking in the Vineyard," put on by the Central Washington Wine Technical Group with support from Washington State University. Toward the middle of the remaining day, we were tasting wines presented to us by Dr. Bob Wample. The four wines had been made at Columbia Crest Winery by winemaker Doug Gore.

Wample jumped up on the stage with the enthusiasm of a thirty-year-old, although he was likely closing in on fifty. He was fit and tanned and slightly balding with brown hair brushed to the side. He wore stylish clothes with reading glasses hanging on his chest by a strap. His demeanor was more coach than scholar.

Wample was about to accomplish an amazing feat. He was going to distill all of the detailed information that had been laboriously presented to us over the last day and a half into four glasses of wine. In taste, smell, and appearance, the four glasses of wine would be a powerful metaphor for his ongoing study about the effects of irrigation on grape and wine production. It is a classic (and forceful) teaching tool.

Long after the seminar was over we would all remember tasting the four wines. They spoke volumes. They were the end result of a study begun in 1982 when Wample joined with Dr. Sara Spayd and Dr. Bob Evans to establish a complicated monitoring system, in a vineyard located at the Prosser research center, to measure moisture use, establish water requirements of wine grapes at varying crop levels, and determine their effect on vine growth, yield, wine quality, and winter hardiness.

Wample had taken the study to the next level of refinement. With the help of Stimson Lane Vineyards and Estates and winemaker Doug Gore of Columbia Crest Winery, together they used a circular 64-acre Sauvignon Blanc vineyard near the Columbia Crest Winery overlooking the Columbia River on the lower Horse Heaven Hills slope. They divided the vineyard into quadrants. Within each quadrant, vineyard rows were treated with four varying levels of irrigation. Under this system, four different water treatments were replicated in four different locations. Wines were then made from each of these different treatments, beginning in 1992. Gore made sixteen different wines in batches of 3,000 gallons each.

The water treatments were Low Low (LL), Low High (LH), High Low (HL), and High High (HH). LL referred to a low water treatment applied throughout the growing season. LH was low irrigation early in the growing season, followed by increased irrigation from the point where control of canopy growth had been achieved through harvest. HL was high irrigation during the early season, followed by low irrigation from the point where the low irrigation treatments showed control of canopy development through harvest. This treatment was similar to standard irrigation practices. And finally, the HH treatment referred to high irrigation maintained throughout the growing season.

High and low levels of irrigation were defined as 2.2 and 1.2 inches of water per foot of soil, respectively, in the top three feet of the soil profile. Even at the high levels, not a lot of water was being added to the naturally occurring 7 to 8 inches of annual rainfall. Thus, in the high-level treatment, the soil received an additional 6.6 inches of water, or a total of less than 15 inches of water, including nature's addition. At low levels the total water, including treatment and rainfall, was less than 12 inches.

Wample provided an aerial photo of the vineyard on the overhead projector. It looked like a giant dartboard with concentric circles and lines. Originally named Circle 100, in 1993 the vineyard was renamed the Clore Vineyard, in honor of Dr. Clore. What a fitting tribute! The vineyard encapsulates all that Dr. Clore set out to accomplish so many years ago.

Wample also showed a number of graphs to highlight photosynthesis of the vine during different times of the growing season. He told how different water-level treatments affected the vine growth.

His talk had three elements of immediate importance to Washington growers and winemakers. First, by regulating a low irrigation treatment early in the season, the grower can better manage vineyard canopy, which reduces physical management strategies, decreases vineyard diseases and pests, and sets the vineyard up for better hardiness by limiting the growth of the wood on the vine. Second, the vineyard uses much less water than the standard irrigation practice has suggested. And third, the results of the various treatments could be easily tasted by growers and winemakers.

We tasted the four Sauvignon Blancs from the 1993 harvest. The four wines were from only one vineyard quadrant. Wample asked participants to indicate which wines they liked best. A clear preference was shown for the wines using the LL and LH water treatments, with roughly an equal split in votes. Wample smiled broadly; these were the same results he gets whenever he has people taste these wines.

I voted for the LH wine. It was fruitier in the aroma, highlighting melonlike fruit aromas with just a bit of the grassy character of this grape. On the palate the wine was rounder and fruitier, with a mouth-filling grapiness. The LL wine had a tarter, more austere finish. The HL and HH wines tended to be leafier and more austere, higher in acidity and more tart.

Literally, the proof was in the wine. It was there to taste. It was an exciting culmination of all the overwhelming data and input. The taste of the fruity, tart Sauvignon Blancs brought it to an immediate and powerful conclusion.

Clearly, Wample was excited. And the results of the work were exciting. The wine growers, faced with another year of drought, could use his study to better manage limited water resources by using less water at the beginning of the season and slightly more at the end to help the vine survive potential cold weather conditions. Beyond the drought conditions loom even greater water-use issues such as drawdowns of the Columbia and Snake Rivers, and more restricted water usages in the future are going to make Wample's work much more important.

As water becomes limited, only those crops that use less water and are of higher value will be allowed to use the available water supply. Clearly, we were tasting the future of wine grapes: it was bright and fresh.

The results of this promising study showed that the Columbia

Valley is one area in the world where growth, production, and quality can be manipulated by the grower to produce distinctive, quality wines.

Chapter Twenty-Eight

THE TASTE OF WASHINGTON WINES

I have tasted many wines in the last twenty years; now when I taste Washington wines, there is a much richer experience. The wine, the winery, and the winemaker touch a vein that often goes right to the heart of history.

Wine rose out of the southern valleys of the Black Sea at least five thousand years ago. This is the home of *Vitis vinifera,* or the European grapevine that is the basis for the world's greatest wines. This is also the basis for Washington state's premium wines. It is the standard by which all wines are judged today. It is a worldwide standard that has evolved over time from the world's best vineyard sites, and helps define what wine is; it is thick with tradition.

But it is only a standard. It represents a progression of tastes: the neophyte to wine first learns to enjoy sweeter wines, then learns to enjoy wines with other flavors beyond sweet, tasting perhaps the racy natural acidity of the wine or its fruit flavors, and eventually accepts even the astringent flavors and feel of the wine's tannin.

This progression is the world's history of wine. Before the standard of dry table wines was accepted, the most cherished wines of the Old World were very sweet. This progression is also the history of Washington state wine. And it is my and Dr. Clore's personal wine history, and I suspect it is each person's wine history. My first remembered experience with wine was drinking loganberry flips (loganberry wine and Seven-Up) in a tavern. Walt's first wine may have been that wonderful Grenache made by Dr. Chas Nagel. Our taste for dry wines developed slowly as our habit of drinking wine moved from drinking wine recreationally to drinking wine at the table. Ultimately, wine's role is found best expressed at the table. Wine, as a food, plays an important role in digestion, it dances with food with fancy gustatory footwork, it enlivens the senses and opens dialog, and it can extend the life of the imbiber when used in moderation.

But not all people progress in the same manner. Each comes to wine in his or her own time and under his or her own terms. That is why there will always be a role for sweet wines. For the beginner, often the most preferred taste sensation is sweetness, tasted at the tip of the tongue. Sweetness often dominates the taste sensation and covers up the acidic flavors of the wine. Slowly, the beginner tires of this sensation and demands a bit more interest. That is when he or she begins to taste the wine's acidity along the sides of the tongue, where acidity receptors are located. Acids provide the structure of the wine, the framework.

The flavors of the wine come from the variety of grape that is used to make the wine. These flavors are best expressed when the wine is made from adequately ripened grapes. The flavors are the result of a selection of grape varieties (or a single variety) from a particular growing area which, taken together, help to define the wine. That is why there is such a contrasting variety of flavors between a Cabernet Sauvignon grown along the Rutherford Bench in California's Napa Valley, or in the St. Julien district overlooking the Gironde River in Bordeaux, or the wines of Coonawara in South Australia, or Red Mountain in eastern Washington.

Even within Washington there is a wide range of taste differences when the same grape is grown in different areas. Contrast the flavors of the Cabernet Sauvignon grown at Red Willow Vineyards with those grown at Sagemoor Farms, or Paul Portteus Vineyard in Zillah, to those grown at the Mercer Ranch on the Horse Heaven Hills. Or compare the Pinot Noir grown at Salishan Vineyards to that grown at Bainbridge Island Winery, and for a real contrast compare those flavors to Pinot Noir grown at Radar Hill and made into wine by Taggares.

These same differences can also be found in Riesling, Sauvignon Blanc, Gewurztraminer, Chenin Blanc, Semillon, Chardonnay, Muller-Thurgau, Chasselas, Siegerebbe, Grenache, Pinot Noir, Cabernet Franc, and Merlot. And in other grapes that are just now starting to be used more extensively in winemaking: Syrah, Viognier, Pinot Gris, Nebbiolo, and Sangiovese.

This is what makes wine so fascinating; it is both an intellectual and sensory experience. By using all of our senses, it demands our acknowledging a geographic place.

Wine is a personal experience. One's taste in wines should never be dictated by the media or the merchant.

I am sensitive to the negative perception of the earliest wines made in Washington state. By today's standards the wines were probably poorly made, and often they relied on varieties that are not thought of as premium varietals. But they played an important role in the progression of the Washington wine industry, carrying the historical wine drinker along the way. There will always be a role for sweet wines, or even pop wines, that introduce the novice or, maybe, even an entire generation to wine.

The future is marked by the same cyclical forces that have affected its past: changes in the consumer base, overproduction, acts of nature, acts of government, and changes in the way that wine is distributed.

The world truly has gotten smaller. Walla Walla may still be an isolated region, far from the byways of transportation, but it is now a region accessible to information and capable of communicating with the outside world quickly and easily. Distribution is no longer a hindrance because the wines are as easily available in Chicago as Seattle.

—DELILLE CELLARS, MARCH 1995—

One of the more interesting wineries to have developed recently is the DeLille Cellars in Woodinville. It is the brainchild of two veterans of the wine industry in the Seattle area: Jay Soloff and Chris Upchurch. Together they teamed up with the Lille family to bring to market a concept in wine.

I was attracted to their winery because I had talked earlier with Chris Upchurch over a glass of Grant's Imperial Stout at Grant's Brewery in Yakima. Upchurch was then working for Larry's Markets as a wine clerk. He told me about his plans to open a winery in Woodinville to produce a very high-quality wine that would sell in the top price category. His friend Jay Soloff had his own marketing company, Wines and Spirits, and would handle the distribution and marketing. I suddenly got very interested when Chris told me that they had made an agreement with Al Newhouse of Sunnyside to obtain the grapes from the former Bridgman property planted to grapes by Associated Vintners.

Upchurch was aware of the significance of the old property and felt

Associated Vintners shareholders planting their Harrison Hill vineyard.
—*Photo courtesy of Associated Vintners.*

that it was one of the potentially premier sites in Washington state. Working with Newhouse, they have begun to replant and refurbish the old vineyard planted back in 1963. Of the original 6 varieties planted, only the Cabernet Sauvignon has been saved. DeLille Cellars is replanting the vineyard to classic Bordeaux blend varieties: Cabernet Sauvignon, Merlot, and Cabernet Franc. Upchurch told me that their intent was to produce a Bordeaux type blend because he and Soloff believe that a Bordeaux blend is potentially the best kind of wine for Washington state.

He also said that they planned to market the wine in the $30 to $40 price point. They were convinced that this was the price range that was most attractive. It would allow them to focus on high quality while permitting them to keep their production down to a manageable level. Upchurch told me, "We already have phone calls coming in from out-of-state customers who are interested in selling our wine. They can't get Leonetti Cellars or Woodward Canyon and they want a high-end product."

Upchurch told me in a matter-of-fact manner that they will probably be sold out of their wine before they even release the wine for sale. I thought to myself, "And before anyone even tastes it."

I was interested in tasting the wine made from the old Harrison Hill site. DeLille Cellars was still in the process of being built, so I made arrangements to meet Chris Upchurch at their temporary facility, located in one of those metal distribution buildings that sprawl throughout the suburbs. Upchurch had the roll-up door opened when I arrived, revealing brand-new barrels stacked against the walls and in the center of the tiny space. He was in the middle of racking wine and cleaning barrels. The familiar smells bit at my nostrils—it was winy, pungent.

Upchurch, forty-one years old, is the full-time winemaker. He was very approachable, wearing jeans, sweater, and tennis shoes. Upchurch was born in Washington, D.C., and raised in New Jersey. He went to the University of Colorado at Boulder. Most of his adult life he has worked in the wine trade.

He said, "I started in 1974, the same year that Ste. Michelle won its award. Jay hired me at the Thirteen Coins." The Thirteen Coins restaurants were part of the Ward Enterprises and included Lafitte's and El Gaucho in Seattle. Upchurch and Soloff became best of friends. Together they dreamed of being in the wine business together.

In 1979 Soloff started his own wine brokerage, Wines and Spirits, representing wineries nationally and locally in the Pacific Northwest. Jay was determined to make the wine business work. Jay, darkly handsome, was a natural salesman and marketing person. He sold even when he was not trying. He was confident and cocky. Together they considered opening a champagne winery in 1980. For awhile they ran the Grapeline, supplying grapes to home winemakers in the Seattle area with grapes from eastern Washington.

Jay's business forced him to move his office to Portland, Oregon, and he and Upchurch put their winery dreams on hold. Upchurch began working for Larry's Markets, an upscale grocery chain. After a few years, Soloff moved back to Seattle. As a member of Rotary Club, he met Greg Lille, a young businessman in north Seattle. Greg's father, Charles Lille, had a 10-acre farm in Woodinville and he and Greg were trying to figure out a use for the property. Charles Lille considered a bed-and-breakfast as a viable business.

It is a beautiful site; it is an old farmhouse that looks west out over the pastoral valley. Almost directly west, about two miles, are Chateau Ste. Michelle and Columbia Winery. A new addition to the neighborhood is the Red Hook Brewery, a large, modern, metal Gothic structure.

The Lille property has always been Charles Lille's therapy. He tends to the sheep that graze the pasture, and prunes and cares for the fruit trees that line the three ponds. Charles Lille, a French Huguenot whose family ended up in Czechoslovakia, emigrated to Canada in the late '50s, on his way to the United States. As an "enemy alien" he wasn't allowed to enter the United States until later. Lille made a small fortune in the insurance and travel business, catering mainly to the strong German community in the Pacific Northwest. After acquiring the Woodinville farm, it was Lille's intent to make it a paying asset to offset some of the taxes.

Enter Jay Soloff and Chris Upchurch. Through their contact with Greg Lille, they suggested a winery. That was in May 1992, less than three years ago. Charles Lille loved the idea. He felt that the winery would be a way to honor his European roots, especially his French Huguenot beginnings. With sufficient capital, he assured Chris and Jay that he was willing to spare no expense to produce a wine that satisfied these genealogical yearnings.

It was also a business that his son, Greg, was interested in; it was something he could pass on to his son. Greg, a young man in his thirties, I believed, was built like his father, squat and strong-looking with a muscular, round face and short-cropped hair.

Charles Lille, in his late sixties, looked fit and tanned with a crop of white hair. I met him later that evening at the actual winery site. He had stopped in to look after his sheep. One of them had just lambed the day before.

Back at the temporary winery, Chris drew out a sample of Cabernet Sauvignon from barrel. "This is produced from thirty-three-and-a-half-year-old vines." This wine drawn from barrel was 100 percent Cabernet Sauvignon from the old vines at Harrison Hill. It would in time be blended with other barrels of wines from other grapes and vineyard sources. However, Upchurch hoped that maybe eventually they would produce a wine solely from the Harrison Hill site. Steve Newhouse (son of Al Newhouse, viticulturist of the old Bridgman property on Snipes Mountain) was renovating the vineyard, pulling out the old vines of Riesling, Chardonnay, Gewurztraminer, and Pinot Noir and replacing them with Cabernet Franc and Merlot.

The wine was beautiful. It showed wonderful, berrylike fruit aromas and flavors. At that time it was dominated by youthful French oak tannins. It smelled of cedar and berries.

David Lake, of Columbia Winery, consults for Upchurch. It is an invaluable service. It was through David that Upchurch found the Harrison Hill site. Upon approaching the Newhouse family, they found out that the grapes were being contracted out to Stimson Lane for its

Chateau Ste. Michelle brand. Newhouse asked Stimson Lane president Allen Shoup if it would be all right to sell the grapes to DeLille Cellars.

"All I want is to make a top-quality wine," Upchurch insisted. At the temporary winery, he had all the right equipment: small upright fermenters, brand-new, expensive French oak barrels. Upchurch continued, "I have experience in tasting expensive, great wines. When we tasted our first wines against some of the best wines in Bordeaux, we blew them out of the water. We had, then, a model of wine that we were trying to make. It is a Medoc style of wine, I think reminiscent of St. Julien."

St. Julien wines are pretty wines. They tend to be less heavy than the wines from the neighboring commune of Pauillac, and not as soft as those from Margaux. I admired Upchurch's directness but questioned his use of such noble models. I thought to myself that comparing the wines of eastern Washington was a bit bold, especially comparing the DeLille wines that were still being defined. Differences in growing conditions between Bordeaux and eastern Washington are significant. Bordeaux is much more influenced by its maritime climate, and in Bordeaux, vineyards can vary greatly in a small distance according to the soil profile and the vine's ability to withstand the vagaries of climate. The Bordeaulais have worked with these differences for a long time.

In Washington we are just starting out. The 1990s will be dominated by discussions of vineyard differentials as new ways are found to market and appreciate the difference between the various growing sites. And there are big differences, as David Lake has clearly shown with his vineyard-designated wines at Columbia Winery.

I liked Upchurch's spunk, though. Why not use St. Julien as a model? I thought how proud Bridgman would be. Hadn't he said that his Sunnyside site was as good as any in Europe? I wondered if he ever went to Europe and saw the vineyards in Bordeaux or Burgundy.

Upchurch and I drove to the new winery about two miles south of the temporary winery. Evening was descending, but we were able to look out from the deck over at Chateau St. Michelle. Upchurch gave me a quick tour of the winery. The winery has grown out of the old farm estate house that was originally built in the '20s. They were still about four or five months away from completion. The old farmhouse was newly remodeled with a cellar downstairs and an entertaining facility on the main floor, along with accommodations for overnight guests.

Already they had sold out their first vintage, the 1992, to the wine trade, holding some in reserve for their anticipated opening in late summer of 1994. Their wine has been bottled under two labels. The best is labeled as Chaleur Estate. A second wine is called D2, which sells for a little less and is made up of the lesser wine selected throughout the winemaking process as slightly inferior to the Chaleur Estate. The 1992 Chaleur Estate sold for about $25; the D2, about $17.

Upchurch felt secure. His future is bright. Both he and Jay are each quarter partners in DeLille Cellars. They have found their winery.

"It is a dream come true," Upchurch said. I believed him.

—CLE ELUM, AUGUST 1994—

Passing through Cle Elum on my way to the Yakima Valley, I decided to stop and visit with Ernest Breznikar. Two years earlier I visited the town library to research the history of the town, trying to find some connection perhaps between Cle Elum and the early vineyards in the Yakima Valley and down at Columbus (later called Maryhill). I discovered that Cle Elum and its immediate neighbor, Roslyn, are towns thick in history. Both started as coal-mining towns: Roslyn in 1886 and Cle Elum shortly after. Most of the actual coal digging was done in Roslyn; nearly half of the state's coal came from this important mine developed by a subsidiary of the Northern Pacific Railroad. Roslyn's population was 40 percent foreign-born, while Cle Elum's was 20 percent foreign-born. Both had dynamic ethnic communities of Italian, German, Irish, and Slavic peoples—populations ripe for making homemade wine (well, maybe not the Irish).

The librarian suggested that I contact Ernest Breznikar. Breznikar, the former Superindent of Public Works, was known for his homemade wine. I called him and told him that the next time I was on my way through town, I would look him up. He said, "Make sure you stop by. You can have a glass of wine. I have a lot of visitors. I think they like my wine."

When I did visit, I went to Breznikar's small house in the residential section of Cle Elum, just off the busy commercial district that runs parallel to Interstate 90. I was directed to the backyard by his wife, Julie. Here I met Ernest amongst family and friends. I offered French bread from the local bakery (which began in 1906), and salami and cheese from the town's sausage maker, Glondo.

Ernest Breznikar was a small man, very European in appearance, with salt-and-pepper, sandy hair. His face was deeply etched with lines cascading from his nose and eyes. His sky-blue eyes were set in a round face. He was square-shaped and animated, swinging his short arms to make a point, or darting a quick gesture to measure a response to something he had said. When I met Breznikar, a Slovenian, he was sixty-nine years old.

"Would you like to taste my wine?" he asked.

He returned in a moment with two McNaughton's whiskey bottles filled with wine. He told me one was a Chardonnay and the other a Cabernet Sauvignon. He poured the Chardonnay into my glass tumbler. It was very smooth with a surprisingly golden color, normally an indication of oxidation (caused by exposure to too much air). But the flavors were generous and distinctly Chardonnay, with a buttery flavor that emanated more from the fruit than the evidence of oak. The Cabernet Sauvignon was also smooth and balanced, neither youthful or old, but with a berrylike flavor.

"Do you like my wines?" he asked.

"Yes, I do—but they are different. They are so drinkable," I told him. I asked what year the wines were from.

I was astonished to learn that they were from the previous harvest, 1993. He next served me a Merlot. It was really good, brighter and broader in flavor than the Cabernet Sauvignon. They were indeed incredibly smooth and developed for such youthful wines. Breznikar told me that the grapes came from Harold and Janet Pleasant's vineyard in Prosser. The Pleasants delivered to his backyard via the alley.

"I am one of the last," Breznikar said. "Everybody else is gone. Nobody makes wine here anymore . . . oh, Pasco, he still makes wine."

He laughed. The wine made him even more animated. He called his wine "happy wine." He said, "Nobody ever gets drunk drinking my wine but they always get happy . . . oh, maybe once in awhile someone that is new to wine will drink too much of the white especially, then it will creep up on them and they will get light-headed." Julie Breznikar laughed and said, "Sometimes they fall asleep."

I could feel the effect of the wine on me, sitting in the bright afternoon sun in the light, refreshing air, high in the Cascades. A nap sounded pretty good. Mrs. Breznikar told me to eat. I made a sandwich of onions and tomatoes along with the salami and cheese. On the table were olives and roasted red peppers. Julie Breznikar looked Italian to me, which she later confirmed.

While I ate my sandwich and tasted (at this point, drank) some more wine, Ernest told me a bit about how he made the wines. "My father came here in 1931 from Montana. He brought with him his barrels. I still use the same ones," he proudly exclaimed. And he added, "I don't add anything to the wines: no yeast, no sulfites, no nothing."

Breznikar invited me down into his cellar. To get there he lifted a wood cover from the wrap-around deck on his house. We descended steep, well-worn wooden steps. I stood in blackness while I waited for him to pull the light string. It was cool and damp. I could smell wine and the earthiness of the cement walls. Suddenly the light came on and lit up a lifetime clutter of stuff.

Along the back westerly wall of the basement cellar were three upright barrels of standard size. Along the southerly wall was a collection of four small 25-gallon barrels, and an assortment of smaller ones. Breznikar showed me his father's wooden crusher. It looked more like an apple crusher, with a metal drum of small teeth to crush the grapes. This was his only technology. He crushes all the grapes the same, red or white, into the upright barrels where the juice ferments from the grape's own yeasts. After fermentation is complete, he transfers the wine from the upright barrels to the smaller, horizontal barrels by bucket. He draws the last of the wine off of the sediment that forms at the bottom of the barrels through a spigot located about two and a half inches from the bottom. Nothing wasted.

Once the wine is in the small barrels, he watches and listens closely to the wine. When he is convinced that the fermentations, both the primary and the secondary (malolactic), are complete, he pounds in the plastic bungs, sealing them by slathering them with beeswax to keep air out.

At the bottom of each barrel is a spigot. When he wants to drink one of the wines, he just comes downstairs and grabs an empty bottle from a nearby stack of assorted clean bottles, and draws off the wine. He showed me by refilling my wine tumbler. He turned open the wooden spigot to the Merlot barrel. The wine dripped out, working against the vacuum of air created in the barrel as wine was drawn off. Before each drip the barrel let out a bong, bong. Slowly the glass filled: bong, bong, drip; bong, bong, drip. He said it is like milking a cow. I was hypnotized. It was all so simple.

Seeing his setup explained why his Chardonnay was so golden in color and why the reds were so easily drinkable at a young age. The Chardonnay was treated like the reds; the juice was fermented in contact with the skins which explained the wine's golden color. The Cabernet Sauvignon and the Merlot were not pressed after fermentation and

Gyro Club members tasting wine with Erich Steenborg in Upland Winery.
—*Photo courtesy of Erica Swanson Steenborg.*

therefore are less extracted and tannic. Thus they are more approachable at an earlier age.

And so simple. Anyone could do the same, even my generation, as impatient as it seems. This was wine at its simplest. Because the oak was so old, there was little wood flavoring to the wine, but the effects of using wood were obvious: the wood had mellowed the wine. Without sulfites the wine was rounder, smoother. The only stumbling block to making wine in this manner is finding well-used barrels, and in a size that is manageable.

Breznikar obviously likes to share his wine. He makes just enough to last a year, or until the next harvest. He said he has a spring wine tasting, and then a wine-ending party at the end of summer with his bowling buddies. I wondered, before or after the game?

On a pile of stuff next to me was an old cardboard poster announcing Jimmy Dorsey playing in Yakima. Breznikar told me that when he was younger he had a band called the Music Makers. It was the house band at the Playland in Yakima. He has played with the best: Tommy Dorsey, Jimmy Dorsey, Gene Krupa, and Harry James. Breznikar told me that most of the patrons drank beer, a lot of beer. And I forgot to ask him what kind of wine they drank.

Back outside, the sunlight was intense. I thanked Ernest and Julie Breznikar for their hospitality and said good-bye.

"Stop by again," Ernest offered.

—HEDGES CELLARS, MARCH 1995—

Walt and I went to Benton City to meet with Tom Hedges. Hedges had a new vineyard planted in 1991 by Fred Artz, his vineyard manager.

The same road that feeds into Hedges's new vineyard goes by other respected vineyards, Kiona Vineyards and Ciel du Cheval. Additionally there are vineyards and wineries nearby such as Blackwood Canyon Vintners, Oakwood Cellars, and Seth Ryan Winery.

Walt and I pulled into the vineyard, where we found Fred Artz giving instructions to his pruning crews. They were pruning back the four-foot-long canes and training them to support wires, alternating the direction of growth. The crew was all Hispanic. They were efficient. Artz walked with us through the vineyard to the winery site. He told us that the Hedges Vineyard is actually two vineyards divided by the road we were walking on. One one side is 18 acres of Cabernet Sauvignon and on the other 18 acres of Merlot. Between the rows the ground is covered with dryland crested wheat grass. It is an ideal cover crop. It takes its water from the natural six to seven inches of precipitation that falls in the valley. It is green in the spring and fall. During summer it is dormant, thus serving to hold the soil while not competing with the grapevines for soil moisture.

Near the top northeast corner of the vineyard we saw Tom Hedges. He was talking with the contractor. Brian Carter was there too. Brian Carter has made the wines for Hedges Winery since the 1988 vintage. Most of Hedges's wines have been made at Washington Hills Cellars in Sunnyside, where Carter reigns as the winemaker. Carter is one of the great winemakers in Washington state. At Washington Hills Cellars, Carter has excelled at producing reasonably priced red and white wines. His attempts to make super premium wines are under the Apex brand.

I arranged to meet Hedges out here because I considered him to embody a bold vision that will help carry Washington wines into the next century. He had clearly set his sights on a national and even an international market. In fact, this winery is in a sense the direct result of his European experience. There, when he has presented his wines to the European wine trade, they want to know where his vineyard is and that his winery is at the vineyard.

I like Hedges. He is of this land. His sandy brown hair and short-cropped mustache gave him the appearance of an army captain. Trim and handsome with leather jacket, cords, and stylish shoes, he proudly showed Walt and me his plans. The facade of the winery is a takeoff of the front of Chateau Montrose, a Bordeaux from the St. Estephe district. Hedges plans to have a billiard table and fully operating kitchen to entertain guests. The view west is stunning; it looks up the Yakima Valley, and on a clear day Mount Adams is impressive.

In 1993 Hedges Cellars produced nearly 70,000 cases of wine. In '94 its production was down to 55,000 cases. Eventually, he hopes to produce nearly 150,000 cases of wine out of this facility. Hedges produces an excellent Cabernet-Merlot blend. Expert winemaking by Brian Carter makes the wine amazingly accessible at an early age.

I told Hedges I was impressed by his market sense. He said, "It was just pure luck. I made a wine that my Swedish partner wanted, a Bordeaux blend of Cabernet and Merlot." He happened to make a very good wine, about the same time that red wine sales were beginning to take off. Combined with a reasonable price, his wine captured national attention with reviews in the *Wine Spectator*. His success tied in perfectly with the phenomenal sales of moderate-priced wines (what the industry has dubbed "fighting varietals") from Columbia Crest Winery, especially its Merlot.

Talking to Hedges, the future was bright. He talked about phylloxera devastating the vineyards of California and how that was going to increase the prices on California wines. "We're going to kill them," he said, confidently.

Hedges planned on attending Vin Expo, a wine exposition held in Bordeaux, in June. Over 3,000 wineries would present their wines. He was hopeful, and convinced, that his '91 Reserve would show well. He said that the last three or four vintages in Bordeaux have been bad. "We're going to tear them up," he said in his combat voice.

There was a bit of lightheartedness in his voice, as if not to take himself too seriously. He was truly having fun. I really was not sure how market savvy he is, and I took him at his word that his success has been more luck than design. I wondered to myself if his success hasn't also been achieved because he hasn't owned any of the financial trappings of the wine business: a winery and vineyard. Those are major commitments. I asked him whether this was going to change his situation considerably. He said, "No, my costs will remain the same." I'm skeptical.

Then Brian Carter chirped in, "I don't think he knows all the costs of running a winery."

Knowing that Hedges lived in Issaquah, I asked him where he was going to live once the winery is built. He laughed and pointed to his mammoth Chevy Suburban.

Later, at dinner, Walt served the '91 Hedges Reserve. The wine label stated only that it was a red wine produced from grapes grown at Red Mountain. It was a beautiful wine, deep garnet red. The aromas were focused and intense. On the palate it was muscular, yet not heavy. Slightly tannic and concentrated, it had a nice weight and body. The flavors were direct and fruity.

It will do well in Bordeaux. And Hedges's effort to market the wines outside of Washington will reward him. His goal is to sell a third in-state, a third in the United States, and a third internationally.

To myself I thought, "Lead the way, captain."

—HINZERLING VINEYARDS, MARCH 1995—

My next visit was to Hinzerling Vineyards in Prosser. I met Mike Wallace at his winery. Sitting next to the roadway, it was an old garage that the Wallace family had transformed into a winery. Next to the winery was a trailer that Mike had converted into his office.

The trim around the winery building was painted in almost psychedelic colors, hot purple and tangerine green. Mike emerged from the trailer and met me at the winery entrance. I have known Mike since he first began the winery with his first release. I have picked his grapes, and brought customers to his winery and vineyard to help pick the grapes. I can still taste the sweet Gewurztraminer plucked from the vine and hear the laughter of the rookie harvesters.

I remembered the robust red wines that Mike has made, big fat tannic Cabernet Sauvignons from his own grapes and occasionally from Mercer Ranch Vineyards. And I recalled the exquisite beauty of the black Cabernet Sauvignon grapes hanging on the withered yellow vine awaiting ideal ripeness and picking. A divorce rocked Mike's personal life, sending shock waves through the winery. Money had always been tight; now it didn't exist. Meanwhile, competition from new wineries started to eat into his base. While Mike and Hinzerling were on hold, other wineries were taking off in the early '80s, most notably Hogue Cellars nearby. It seemed Hogue Cellars couldn't do anything wrong. Its wines seemed so fresh and fruity; they showed the roughness of Mike's wines. It didn't seem like anyone was minding his barrels.

Mike is a very bright man and I regard him a friend. He is outspoken and direct. He has learned to keep some of his opinions private. His disdain for some of the larger wineries has hurt him in the political climate of the wine business. Mike is a scrapper, independent and tenacious.

Inside the winery I looked around at the small tasting room. It was cluttered with merchandise. Hinzerling Vineyards early on understood the importance of selling out of the winery's small retail shop.

Past a short hallway was the winery. It was dark and crowded with large tanks, shelves of barrels, and packaged wine. In the middle of the winery, against a post, was a jewelry display case.

I wanted to taste his wines. He offered me a Gewurztraminer. It was a combination of vintages, part '92 with some '93. It was okay. It was slightly heavy on the nose and lacked the spice and pearlike quality that I look for in a Gewurztraminer.

Then the Ashfall White, a white wine with a catchy name dreamt up after the Mount St. Helens volcano spread ash over the Yakima Valley. It was a combination of Riesling and Gewurztraminer. A fine sediment was on the bottom of the bottle, a protein haze I assumed, that looked like ash. The wine was smooth and fruity with a baked apple aroma and flavor. It was a nice wine.

Then the '92 Pinot Noir from Harold Pleasant's vineyard nearby. Pleasant also supplies grapes to Ernest Breznikar in Cle Elum, the home winemaker I had met a few years earlier. It was a nice wine, light with just the right acidity to frame the delicate flavors of Pinot Noir. A candied flavor detracted only slightly. Mike liked this wine and hoped to make more Pinot Noir.

A 1989 Lemberger was wonderful. It was very smooth, a combination of its age and oak treatment, and full. There was a peppery flavor on the back of the palate. This was very good.

Lemberger is bright in color, assertive on the palate with rich, juicy, berrylike flavors, but not always well balanced. It may be Washington's answer to Zinfandel. There is a slight gamey side to the grape. I recalled that Mercer Ranch Vineyards used to make its in a Cabernet style, lighter and oak-aged. They would celebrate this wine with a party at the winery, serving up the wine (labeled as Limberger) with grilled lamb burgers. One of the first producers of this wine was Kiona Vineyards at Red Mountain; oak-aged, it represented the fuller style with brisk tannins and dark red color. Also, today's Covey Run Wines, then Quail Run Vintners, made and still make a fruitier but rich-styled Lemberger.

Next I tasted an '88 Merlot. It was sweet and smooth but lacked the vibrant youthful Merlot character that consumers associate with the new Washington Merlots. Then Mike poured me two Cabernets: the '88 and the '83. The '88 was solid and a nice wine, although it had lost much of its youthful charm. The '83 was uninspiring. They were okay.

Then Mike served three port wines. The first I had had before: Rainy Day Fine Tawny Port. It was a lighter port, predominantly Cabernet Sauvignon. It was quite good. But I particularly liked the Three Muses Ruby Port. It was made from Cabernet Sauvignon, Merlot, and Lemberger. It had a straightforward and fruity flavor. The third port was the 1990 Wallace Vintage Port made from Merlot. It was very smooth and very much like a true Portuguese Vintage Porto. The final offering was an Angelica, a very sweet white wine, with concentrated fruit flavors that reminded me of peach and nectarine.

Later, I thought about these last four wines. They were a throwback to the wines of the '40s and '50s when the industry was dominated by dessert-style wines. They were good wines and they were very much like the wines of Portugal. But something about them bothered me just a bit. Were these wines indicative of a cynicism creeping into the Washington wine industry? Were we seeing the same cycle return that happened in the late '40s—as my parents aged, and got involved with raising their children, they became less discerning?

I don't know. The wines were good. And what is the difference between Mike Wallace making them and Dr. Wade Wolfe, who also makes port-styled wines under the Thurston-Wolfe Wines? Or Stimson Lane's Whidbeys Port? And not long ago I had been served a beautiful port by Bill Preston called Tenrebac (Cabernet spelled backward).

Was I witnessing a natural aging of the marketplace? That is part of it. Also, these producers are exploiting an area of the wine industry that has been ignored: after-dinner wines. What a good way to use up some less than sterling-quality wine: add brandy and sweeten it slightly. It just happens that the full, ripe flavors and acids in Washington wines hold up well to the addition of brandy and sugar.

Mike told me his plans for the winery. His partner, Frankie, has a farm in nearby Mabton. Mike hopes to raise various crops at her farm and sell them at the winery. He wants to reduce the amount of wine that he makes and just concentrate on a small selection of wines. I got a sense that he was thinking of making wines that are a little different from what others are offering—like the Pinot Noir or the ports—a way of distinguishing himself.

My thoughts about Hinzerling Vineyards were mixed. On the one hand, I was sorry to see his winery in such disarray and sad that his personal life intruded on the winery. I was really sorry that he gave up his vineyards and I assumed that he was forced to financially. I was upset that consumers haven't been nicer to him—abandoning him for the latest, the next, best winery. Which winery will fall next? When one light goes out, does it mean that another has just gone on?

Having visited with Mike I envisioned a smaller, more personable winery emerging. He will sell less wine, and they will be wines unique to his winery. He will also sell some fruits and vegetables unique to the valley. I see a Wallace who is more comfortable with himself. He's going to do it on his terms: reaching out and touching customers on a personal level.

—HOGUE CELLARS, MARCH 1995—

After lunch with Mike Wallace, I picked up Walt at his home and together we drove over to the Hogue Cellars. We had made an appointment with David Forsythe, director of winemaking, to taste wine made from grapes grown in Genesis Vineyard, the vineyard that Mike Hogue had pointed out to us as we flew over the Yakima Valley nearly four years ago. At that time the soil was just being ripped up and planted to grapes. Here now was the second harvest off that vineyard.

Over the phone Forsythe had told me that they had gotten a small crop off the vineyard the last two years and chose to sell the grapes the first year because there weren't enough grapes to produce a wine. However, in 1994 they got enough Cabernet Franc to make 4 barrels.

We met Forsythe in the winery lab at the new Hogue facility just off Interstate 82, a short drive, maybe a quarter mile, from the tasting room. This new facility was built to handle most of the winemaking chores as the grapes are brought in. There are only a few offices, used by people involved directly in winemaking or distribution. Thus, Wade Wolfe, the general manager of Hogue Cellars, had his office at the nearby tasting room.

With Forsythe was Anke Wildman, Forsythe's co-winemaker. Walt and Anke were pleased to see one another. Anke, a German immigrant, lived with the Clores when she first came to Washington State University to study. She never returned to Germany. An attractive, dark-haired woman with a bright face and a European twinkle in her eyes, she is from the Mosel district of Germany where her family's winery dates back to 1593.

When I heard this, I immediately thought of Erich Steenborg and his German roots. I wanted to tell Anke of all the Germans before her who had come to Washington: the Herkes, who may have planted the first vineyard in the Yakima Valley in 1871, or Dutch John Galler of East Wenatchee.

Anke married Ted Wildman, who has a master's degree in entomology, the study of insects. A young man, he is the main vineyard consultant to the industry right now, having taken over for Wade Wolfe.

Forsythe led Walt and me out to the barrel room. Sixty-gallon oak barrels were stacked five high. On the barrel ends were coded and abbreviated words about the wines in the barrels indicating the kind of wine, the vintage, and the vineyard source. I didn't see Genesis Vineyard on any of the barrels.

Forsythe pointed to the top. There were two barrels, coded CF, Heinz Vyds: Cabernet Franc from Heinz Vineyard. It was called Heinz Vineyard because that's what the vineyard was called when Mike Hogue bought the property. The vineyard is 17 acres, and planted to 6.5 acres of Cabernet Sauvignon, 9 acres of Merlot, and 1.5 acres of Cabernet Franc. Only Cabernet Franc was made from the vineyard in 1994; the rest, I assumed, was sold off.

Forsythe, a young man of about thirty-eight, sprang up the barrels. I asked him if he was a mountain climber, thinking I had heard that somewhere, and impressed with his agility as he climbed up the barrel racks to draw wine out of the top barrel with a glass thief in his hand.

"No," he called down in his deep, booming voice, "but I have done a lot of parachuting."

He released the young red wine into two glasses for Walt and me to taste. It was terrific. The red-purple color was vibrant and hinted at the weight and great richness of the wine. It was almost Merlot-like. Walt was impressed too. I know that he likes this grape, and having seen how this grape survived the winter freezes of both '78–'79 and '90, he is particularly partial to its use.

Forsythe said the Cabernet Franc vines were very vigorous and as a plant it can be difficult to manage. I asked (thinking of Chenin Blanc and Grenache), "But aren't vigorous plants usually less winter-hardy?"

Both he and Walt answered. Yes, that's generally true, but the Cabernet Franc is quick to mature its vine. This is important to winter survival, something that Grenache does not do.

I also asked if there are plans to make a wine called Genesis from Heinz Vineyard. Forsythe wasn't sure that the decision had been made yet and they really didn't have enough wine yet from the vineyard to make that decision. Regardless, I was thrilled to taste the wine, to come full circle with our book project. I could only hope that the book reads as well as the wine tasted.

The next morning I returned by myself to taste some more wines. I had asked Forsythe if he would allow me to taste a range of current releases from the winery. This time we met at the tasting room. Here are tasting notes of the wines:

1992 Johannisberg Riesling, Dry Reserve, Schwartzman Vineyard: This was a beautiful wine and could be easily mistaken for a well-made Alsatian wine. The aromas were so beguiling, of rose petal and orange blossoms layered on applelike fruit. These qualities carried through on the palate with just a hint of fusel oil, not unlike that mysterious flavor and aroma in many of Germany's Mosel wines. It was dry and beautifully balanced, with crisp acids holding up the intense Riesling fruit. This was truly a great Washington wine.

Schwarzman Vineyard was the first vineyard in the Hogue family. It commemorates their partner, Mark Schwarzman, from Chicago. Forsythe told how Andy Markam first made wine from this vineyard when he was Hogue Farms's comptroller. Forsythe said it was Markam's wine that first got Mike Hogue excited about the possibilities of wines. Forsythe also credited Markam with articulating the direction of Hogue Cellars. Markam later died when a train collided with his car at one of the numerous railroad crossings in the valley.

1993 Semillon: This was a Washington classic; its flavors are unique to Washington as it combined winy flavors with a concentrated fruitiness; it was simultaneously fruity and vegetative. It was crisp and fresh, smelling of green apples. It was vinous. It was a wine drinker's wine because it captured so perfectly what wine connotes: dry, light, and assertively tart. The fruit was abundant, tasting of honeydew with a lingering tart finish. The wine begged for a plate of tiny fresh Olympia oysters to accompany it.

1993 Chardonnay: A refreshing Chardonnay. Simple and to the point with delicate, round hints of oak and butter. The flavors were very mouth-filling, with a delicate pecan nut flavor. It reminded me of a French Macon-Villages made of the same grape, yet different. Its simplicity was its charm.

The style and flavor harkened back to when Rob Griffin made wine here. It was a style that he had developed at Preston Wine Cellars.

Griffin had begun work at Hogue Cellars the same year that Forsythe had started. Prior to that, the Hogue wines had been made by Mike Conway, now owner of his own winery in Spokane, Latah Creek Wine Cellars. Conway had captured the consumers' fancy with his brilliant Rieslings and Chenin Blancs. When Rob added the Chardonnay, it was a logical extension of the other fruity whites that Hogue did so well, including the beautiful Fume Blanc.

1992 Merlot: Deep red. The wine had a delightful black cherry nose that carried through on the palate. It had a terrific mouth feel, smooth and fruity. An addition of Cabernet Sauvignon added an element of complexity.

1990 Cabernet Sauvignon, Reserve: Garnet red. Complex aromas of cedar and concentrated fruit aromas pricked the nose. It was slightly stemmy and linear, restrained. The palate impression continued the elegant but restrained quality, hinting at leather and tart raspberry. It was slightly tannic. It impressed as a muscular wine.

Forsythe told me it was made to age. They highlighted the acids and tannins to help the wine age in the cellar. I asked Forsythe what the difference is between California Cabernets and Washington Cabernets. Like so many of the new winemakers in Washington state, he attended the University of California Davis. He had worked for a time at Vose Vineyards in Napa Valley.

"The California Cabernets tend to be more extracted, jammy. There is a separation of flavors. They taste processed."

California has been for so long the dominant standard of American wines that it is difficult to judge other wines. And California has so many different growing regions that it is hard to define one style. Yet there are differences. California wines tend to be softer. I find that their wines show oak treatment better than Washington wines because the grape flavors are lighter and meld better to the oak. Right now, oak flavors tend to be popular.

Washington wines can be aggressive to a fault; the fruit flavors can be too much. Washington winemakers have had to learn to extract less grape flavor either in the winery or by working with the growers to reduce vegetative flavors. In some wines the intense fruitiness works just fine, such as the Sauvignon Blancs, Semillons, Chenin Blancs, and Merlots.

But in other grapes such as the Chardonnay, the Cabernet Sauvignon, and Riesling, intense fruit flavors can actually detract from the more subtle flavors of the wine. Especially when compared to California.

Washington winemakers have to learn to abide by California rules but go out on the edge just a bit to make the wines slightly different. And differences there will always be, because the same grape grown at 46 degrees latitude is different from that grown at 38 degrees latitude. In Europe, the differences would be astounding. The 46th parallel runs through the middle of France, above Bordeaux and just slightly below Burgundy and Alsace. The 38th parallel crosses southern Spain at Cordoba, within easy reach of the Mediterranean. Further east it cuts through Sicily and Athens. It is even south of the Black Sea. And this is Napa, at 38 degrees parallel.

I have never looked at a world map so closely. It is a wonder that California wines are as good as they are. Napa and Sonoma Valleys are at the 38th parallel; that would put the rest of California viticulture in the middle of much of the world's deserts. No wonder, then, that those first northern European pioneers sought the northern areas of America, in climates they were familar with.

—BADGER MOUNTAIN WINERY, MARCH 1995—

I visited Rob Griffin at Badger Mountain Winery, located on the southwest side of Badger Mountain on the outskirts of Kennewick. It is about a thirty-minute drive from Prosser, my home base at Dr. Clore's.

Rob Griffin, forty-one years old, is considered by most knowledgeable wine people to be one of the best winemakers in the state. Upon his arrival in 1977, Rob made some of the best wines in the late '70s as the winemaker at Preston Wine Cellars. Today he is his own winemaker, producing wines under the brand name of Barnard Griffin Winery. Debra Barnard, his wife, has just resigned her position as a hospital administrator to take over the management of the winery. Barnard Griffin Winery produces about 15,000 cases of wine a year, selling almost exclusively in Washington state.

Barnard Griffin wines are highlighted by fresh, intense flavors. Rob's trademark wine is his Fume Blanc, or Sauvignon Blanc; it is intensely concentrated and shows concentrated fruit flavors. All of his wines are priced reasonably. He is a bit disappointed that the wine media tends to forget him when it searches out expensive wines, assuming that price somehow dictates quality. His reputation for making consumer-accepted white wines may affect his ability to draw attention to some of his other wines, especially his red wine reserves.

Rob Griffin makes his wines at Badger Mountain Winery, which is owned by Bill Powers. It appears to be a very suitable arrangement for both. Powers trades use of his winery for Rob's winemaking expertise and guidance. Badger Mountain Winery produces wines under two labels. About 2,500 cases of wine are produced under the Powers Winery label. Under a second label, Badger Mountain Winery, organic wines are produced from Powers's own vineyard that surrounds the winery near the top of Badger Mountain. Additionally, this remarkably industrious winery also bulk-produces nearly 100,000 cases of wines for a diverse client base including Keiichiro Yagasaki of Japan, owner of the Alps Company, Ltd. brand, and a friend of Walt Clore's.

In fact, much of Powers's winery can be traced directly to Walt Clore. Powers, a big man with thick glasses, is an Oklahoman like Walt Clore. He still speaks with a heavy Oklahoma accent. Back in the '70s he hit it big with apples, pulling in nearly $14,000 per acre, and decided to switch to cattle. In cattle he lost nearly $350,000 before he looked at another promising crop, grapes. In 1982 he moved from the Othello area to Badger Mountain and planted fruit and grapes based on recommendations from Walter Clore.

Between 1985 and 1986 the price of wine grapes dropped significantly due to overplanting and also a shift in the selection of varieties. Those were the same years that Powers's young vineyard was also hit by 2,4-D drift from construction along the new highway to Umatilla and the wheat farming along the Horse Heaven Hills ridge. Powers was in a difficult position: the value of his crop had depreciated so significantly that he couldn't show enough value to sue. That is when, overnight, he built a winery to process his grapes. Turning his grapes into wine made it possible to bring suit against the state, the wheat farmers, the applicators, and the chemical company. The state ultimately was removed from the defense because it was ruled that it could not be sued.

Powers's attorney called on Clore to testify. Walt recalled the trial with anguished memories; the defense had at least a dozen lawyers and he was intensely questioned for a number of days. Walt Clore is an expert on the effects of 2,4-D on wine grapes. I remembered attending a growers' and wineries' meeting at the Fireside Inn in Grandview where Walt brought along some young grape leaves from his own backyard vineyard to show the group his evidence of 2,4-D contamination. It distorts the grape leaf and reduces the grape crop.

Powers owes his existence in the wine business to Walt Clore and also to Powers's shrewd business acumen. He is cagey and durable. He is a farmer turned wine producer, not unlike Bill Preston or Mike Hogue, both former employers of Rob Griffin. Griffin is attracted to this native farming intelligence, as lovers are attracted to opposites.

Griffin is intelligent in a cerebral way and though he is comfortable in the farmlands of eastern Washington, he finds as his oasis the cultural benefits of wine and living in the town of Kennewick. Hogue, Preston, and Powers have no pretension of intellectual prowess but, rather, show their innate intelligence in their ability to manipulate their environment. Their manners are earthy and direct, qualities that Rob admires.

Badger Mountain hides the sprawl of the Tri-Cities from view as the mountain is approached from the west. It is a large hill, 1,208 feet high with broad, gentle slopes, mostly brown and bare on the northwest slope. Badger Mountain is one of a series of hills, so-called mountains, that include Red Mountain just to the west. These abrupt-rising hills, an easterly extension of the Rattlesnake Hills, change direction suddenly and step down southeasterly to Lake Wallula, formed by damming of the Columbia River by the McNary Dam about twenty-three miles south of Kennewick. It is here, in the Tri-Cities area, that the Yakima River flows into the Columbia River at Richland; and together they are joined by the Snake River slightly east of Pasco.

This series of seven or eight hills are like the tail vertebrae of a giant brontosaurus lying on the upper reaches of the Yakima Valley; the ridge top of the Rattlesnake Hills forms the upper outline of the dinosaur's massive body.

In stature Badger Mountain reminded me of densely populated Queen Anne Hill in Seattle. I tried to envision approaching Queen Anne Hill with one side nearly empty of development. On the east side of this hill, new housing tracts creep up the hill. Halfway up the mountain there are multimillion-dollar houses.

To get to Badger Mountain Winery, I drove through the neighborhood streets of new housing; vineyards arched gracefully toward the top of the mountain above the new homes. Apple and cherry orchards bordered the vineyard.

Because of the encroachment of housing, Bill Powers has chosen to farm organically, not wishing to expose his neighbors to pesticides. Thus he produces one of Washington's few (certified) organically farmed wines.

Rob Griffin still looked young. His brown hair was cropped short, his blue eyes boyish. His brown mustache had flecks of gray and he no longer was wiry-thin as when I first met him nearly eighteen years ago at Preston Wine Cellars. The wine life has been good for Rob, but he still seemed unsure of his role in the industry. In the '70s he made stunning wines for Preston. In the '80s he inaugurated the wines for Hogue Cellars and brought consistency and recognition to Washington's wines. He was at each winery for seven years. He has been at Badger Mountain since 1991. He has produced wines under the Barnard Griffin label since 1984.

Rob arranged for me to taste sample wines that he will blend. One is a Sauvingnon Blanc from the '94 vintage; the other a Merlot from the '93 vintage.

He poured me samples of Sauvignon Blanc from two vineyard sources, one from grapes grown at Maryhill by Gunkle Farms, just below Sam Hill's Stonehenge replica. Rob referred to it as being made "from grapes at the Stonehenge vineyard." The other wine was made from grapes grown at Sagemoor Farms and from grapes grown on the Wahluke Slope. The Stonehenge Sauvignon Blanc was assertive in citrus flavors and intensely melonlike. The other was more vegetal, hinting at spearmint with moderate grassy overtones.

Rob poured some of each wine into a metered beaker: 40 percent Stonehenge, 60 percent Sagemoor/Wahluke. The resulting wine was magnificent, combining the qualities of both wines. It was intensely aromatic and mouth-filling, with an explosion of tropical fruit flavors. This was classic Griffin wine. He will produce about 5,000 cases of this wine. Griffin offered, "This is my signature wine." It may also be Washington's signature wine, as it combines the power of the climatic conditions unique to eastern Washington: big, ripe, complex flavors that are mouth-filling and refreshing, with broad aromatics ranging from tropical to grassy. It is, in a single taste, what Washington wines do so well: capture that bipolar taste perspective in their ability to taste like cool-climate areas and hot Mediterranean wines, intensely fruity and yet balanced by a penetrating and racy natural acidity.

The next wines we tasted were Merlot samples and a sample of Cabernet Sauvignon. The first Merlot sample was from Sargeant Vineyard on the Wahluke Slope. It was intensely fruity but stemmy, reminding me of wood and crushed leaves. The second sample was from Caroway Vineyard in nearby Finley. This wine was much softer and rounder in flavor, tasting more fruity. This vineyard is located above an area that has been planted consistently to grapes since irrigation first arrived in the late 1800s. The third sample was a Cabernet Sauvignon from Mercer Ranch Vineyards.

It is said that the sense of smell is a powerful memory trigger because the olfactory bulb is located next to our memory depot. Little wonder then that memories spilled over me as I smelled the Mercer Ranch Vineyards wine that Rob offered me, then tasted it: the aromas were soft and full, reminiscent of soft blackberry and ripe cherry. But it was the mouth feel of the wine that was so unique to this vineyard, at once intense but soft, almost chalky. It was a quality I remembered about Mercer's Cabernet Sauvignons, the best made by his winemaker, Steve Redford.

Next Rob handed me a sample of the wines blended. It was a delicious Merlot with the addition of the Cabernet. Then he handed me a sample of the Mercer Cabernet with a small addition of the Wahluke Slope Merlot. It was a gorgeous wine. I must confess to my own preference for the Cabernet Sauvignon. It showed the qualities I best appreciate in a red wine. It is sensuous yet muscular. In the Cabernets and in this one made by Rob Griffin there reside a strength and sinewy character distinct from these kinds of wines made in other parts of the world.

Right now Washington Merlots are the darling of the nation's wine press, but I can't help but think that the media is trying to find a hook on Washington wines, something to distinguish the wines from the wines of California and Australia. The Merlots are wonderful. They are fresh and intensely fruity, with soft, round flavors. With judicious use of oak, they can be attractive. The Merlots are a jazz band; Cabernets are symphonic.

I asked Rob why he came to Washington. Here was a California boy with a winemaking career ahead of him. He could easily have been part of the growing wine scene in California.

Rob revealed that originally he had come up to Washington in the spring of 1975, a couple of years before joining the Prestons. He was still in school at UC Davis but he had heard that there was a possibility of becoming head winemaker immediately. He flew up to Yakima and went directly to a meeting with Otis Harlan Jr., of Alhambra Winery. I was surprised to hear this. I was under the impression that Alhambra Winery had by that time already decided it was going to get out of the wine business. Apparently not.

Rob chose not to make the move. With all the bad wine that the winery still had to sell, he just couldn't see its future. He must not have tasted the Otis Vineyard Cabernet Sauvignon. Likely it was blended into Alhambra's generic burgundies. Rob returned to Davis without even exploring the wine country that was just emerging. When he talked to his professor about his experience, he was told that Washington was too cold and that the long-term prospects were not good.

Rob laughed. Soon he will build a new winery and a tasting room at Richland. He and Debra have built a winery from scratch, based solely on Rob's ability to make outstanding wines, without a cash reserve or the intensive capital required of most wineries. Rob was looking forward to his wife's organizational skills, which will allow him to concentrate on doing what he does best: winemaking.

Chapter Twenty-Nine

APPELLATION PUGET SOUND

—BAINBRIDGE ISLAND WINERY, OCTOBER 1995—
Gerard Bentryn of Bainbridge Island Winery tends to his 6 acres of vineyards much like a mother tends to the constant needs of a child. Together with his wife, JoAnne, they have carved out a unique winery right in the middle of the Puget Sound area. Bainbridge Island is a wealthy community accessible by ferry from downtown Seattle. The island's demographics have changed profoundly since the Bentryns established their winery in 1981. Suburban wealth has made it difficult to find inexpensive labor to help them maintain the vineyard and winery. That kind of help can't afford to live on Bainbridge Island anymore.

Gerard and JoAnne Bentryn planted more than a vineyard; they planted an idea, a concept. They live a very conscious lifestyle. Their winery and vineyard are at the center of their lives. Gerard tends to the vineyard and the winemaking; JoAnne handles the winery's tasting room and sales along with the generous amounts of paperwork required of those in the wine business.

When I visited them, they were waiting for a decision by the Bureau of Alcohol, Tobacco and Firearms to okay the use of a new appellation: Puget Sound. It would encompass most of the Puget Sound growing region, including Mount Baker Vineyards to the north near Bellingham, and south to Olympia, the breeding ground of some of Washington's first grape nurseries.

In October 1995 the BATF approved the Puget Sound appellation. This was very exciting for the Bentryns; it validated so much of their hard work to produce wines of distinction, wines that mirror their microclimate and soil.

The Bentryns used as their model for a winery the tiny family wineries prevalent in Germany. Gerard was stationed there while in the army. He had always been interested in agriculture and geography. He had grown up in the farm communities of New Jersey, and received multiple degrees in history and physical geography. He had worked on farms as a child and a young man. He liked farming, well, agriculture, and knew that some day he would like to farm.

Gerard said, "In my mind we started the winery thirty-some years ago while living in Germany. I was working in the vineyards for free just to learn how to grow grapes. I was in the army the first time I went there, but I went back five more times. I learned wine at the village level, from people who drank wine at lunch with bread. They weren't out to impress people with how much they knew. They didn't hold their glass up and swirl it, and all the rest. If you told them people did that, they would probably die laughing. Wine was important to them; wine was a crop, it was food, it was a part of life, not something you impressed your friends with when you showed them your wine cellar. I really enjoyed that and it seemed so real to me."

He took a deep breath and then said, "I was twenty-three years old. I guess I have been chasing after that reality ever since. I am fifty-three now."

Gerard, a smallish man, was stocky, looking a bit like one of his shortened grapevines in his vineyard. His striking blue eyes contrasted with his wind- and sun-beaten face. I arrived as he was pruning his grapevines at the winery vineyard. The vineyard is about an acre rising gently but immediately above the barnlike winery and tasting room. The vineyard was swathed in sun, oriented in a southerly direction. The vines were severely but lovingly pruned to a lower-than-usual height to capture the warmth of the soil, a technique learned from other cool-climate growing regions.

Gerard and JoAnne planted their first vines in 1976 at this site. Today they have nearly 7 acres of grapes: "Six or seven depending on whether you include headland (turnaround space) at the end of the rows of vines." Initially they planted Chardonnay and Riesling. Gerard spent a lot of time commuting to eastern Washington attending grape and wine seminars. He talked to Walt Clore and Chas Nagel. He remembered sitting in seminars in which Dr. Ray Folwell would get up and show his marketing charts and tell how much money could be made selling a certain grape. Gerard said, "I got a little nervous because a lot of people listening to Folwell were not interested in wine nor had they been exposed to wine in a European, or Californian, manner. It was going to be grapes planted like soy beans and corn. And I just got a little frightened, and I said to myself, 'niche marketing.'"

The Bentryns decided to plant Muller-Thurgau, a German cross between Riesling and Sylvaner that yields well and ripens early. They had been impressed with Austrian wines made from this grape and felt that it would provide them with a distinctive wine, lighter and softer than the assertive Rieslings eastern Washington was about to mass-produce. They also planted Madeline Angevine and Madeline Sylvaner.

Looking back at those first years, Gerard shook his head and said, "Probably the silliest thing we did was bought grapes we didn't grow. At first we bought more grapes than we were growing. Then we were equal. Then we finally got to the point where we were using only our own. We still have people here who think we are buying grapes from the other side. We think it is something special about growing grapes where you live. It has taken an awful lot of advertising to tell them that it is an island wine; we don't buy any other grapes."

Today, Bainbridge Island Winery crushes about 32 tons of grapes and 8 tons of fresh strawberries, all grown on the island. It produces close to 2,500 cases of wines. Just recently the income of the winery equaled Gerard's salary as a government worker at 13-step 2, an income that pays the four salaries of those who work at the winery, including their son, Ian, who helps both in the vineyard and the tasting room, and their daughter, Betsey, with a master's degree in horticulture, who works the vineyard and does most of the winery work.

Gerard said, "It is not something you do to get rich. You never make as much money as you can sitting in an office."

Gerard and JoAnne work hard. It is back-breaking work. The winery is open Thursday through Sunday for retail sales and tours, including a one-hour vineyard tour by Gerard. It is all hands-on. The Bentryns are determined to carve a livelihood out of this soil. They have succeeded: they have never lost a crop, they are successful in viticulture and in business, and they don't rely on cheap labor (other than their own).

But they remain unfulfilled. For Gerard it is always worrying about the big picture, recognizing that whatever he wants to accomplish, it must be done in the context of his community. He remains an activist, fighting hypocrisy, seeking the truth in the way people around him live and in his own life: Socrates of the wine industry. For Gerard, and I am sure JoAnne as well, they are committed to giving back to the land what they have taken. They have tied themselves to the land, they grow like their tough, gnarled grapevines, casting aside rain, nurturing the afternoon sun. But around them the wine world is full of deceit. Customers clamor for expensive red wine; wineries, disconnected from their vineyards and removed from their customers, battle on the grocery shelves for recognition and market share. Never, never ask Gerard or JoAnne what numerical score their wine received in the *Wine Spectator*. And don't bother to ask where you might buy their wine in Seattle. All of their wine is sold at retail from their tasting room. Occasionally, they will allow some of the wine out to a few local restaurants.

Gerard was working on a climatic system that he hopes will be helpful to gardeners and grape growers. Most growing guides use a heat unit summation system based upon the hours in the growing season above 50° F. Thus Bainbridge Island Winery's vineyard receives about 1,780 heat units. Vineyards along the Rhine River are usually closer to 1,700. Much of eastern Washington is between 2,000 and 3,000: Yakima is about 2,100, while the research center at Prosser averages 2,400. Bremerton Airport records about 1,830 heat units, but it has more rainfall.

Gerard's new system would recognize that grapes do well in a very temperate environment. They grow best between 68° and 86° F and Gerard suggests that they do best at 77° F. Under his system a temperature between 68° and 86° F would be worth double the growing conditions between 90° and 96° F or 50° and 56° F. Heat units in the Puget Sound region vary greatly. Generally it becomes warmer as you go south but also wetter.

His system would recognize the value of rainfall and when it falls. He believes that rainfall below sixty inches a year can be okay as long as it occurs following harvest. At Bainbridge Island Winery he has recorded an average annual rainfall of between thirty-two and thirty-four inches of rain. Most importantly, rainfall is sporadic during harvest and usually the weather is clear in October when his grapes come in.

For Gerard, he is in complete balance with nature. He has struggled to find the right combination of grape varieties and customer appeal that also match the land that he has chosen. He is really irked when he sees advertisements by the industry that extoll the virtues of growing grapes in eastern Washington by pointing out that eastern

Washington's climate is vastly different from western Washington. The ads highlight the notion of rainy western Washington to contrast the drier conditions east of the Cascades.

Gerard said, "Puget Sound residents, Seattlites, have this profound climatological inferiority complex. It is bizarre. If you went to France, with our summer climate the farmers there would think they died and went to heaven—other than the lack of rain. The grass turns brown in summer.

"What I see endangered by corporate bad-mouthing is a whole way of life. It undermines agriculture in this region. It undermines what people see as special about it. As a climatologist, a geographer, I find it really strange that people think it rains all the time here. It does all winter. You've got to have a lot of moss on your back to get through winter. Summers are wonderful here.

"That is what bothers me."

Gerard was excited about the release of the 1992 Pinot Noir. And now they can use the Puget Sound appellation. I asked Gerard if I could sample the wine. I had tasted it a year earlier, out of barrel, and found it promising but quite tannic.

While Gerard went into the winery, through a door next to the tasting counter, JoAnne asked me if I wanted to sample their other wines. She was a perfect host with her buoyant, friendly personality. With her light brown hair tied back, she can work her customers beautifully. She had an ever so slight German accent and you might think that she stepped right out of the Mosel valley. Her mood was both serious and good-natured. The tasting room was surrounded by antique wine vessels and bottles that she had collected and sells. There was a wonderful bottle collection lit up under a glass case. One of the bottles was an old Church Grape Juice Company bottle out of Kennewick.

She served me the 1993 Muller-Thurgau, dry. It was clean and delicate with crisp acidity and a subtle apple flavor. It was a nice wine but hardly special...did I say that? Sure, it is special because of where it was grown, because of its delicate nature, because it matched the climatic requirements of the vineyard. It was lighter with less alcohol and the flavors truly were more delicate. But, I'm sorry, it was not an exciting wine. There are dozens of other wines that I prefer. It was interesting.

Then she served a taste of the traditional bottling of the same wine with 1.5 percent residual sugar. It was delightful. The residual sweetness brought out the grapy flavors and gave the wine more mouth feel. This was an exciting wine; it was both light and full flavored. I carried this wine into the winery room next to the tasting room. I thought about how Gerard had ranted about wine snobs. With their wine guides under their arms, they come into their tasting room. They might buy an expensive bottle of Siegerrebe, a delicious dessert wine usually sold in the half-bottle because of its rarity. Then they ask for a red wine, which the winery didn't sell yet, and then ask to taste a dry wine. Then they leave.

Other, less opinionated (and often less knowledgeable) wine people will say they like dry wines but invariably they leave the winery with the traditional style of Muller-Thurgau or the less dry Ferryboat White. Consumers have been taught to talk dry, but in taste they usually choose less than dry.

Gerard was excited about his new Pinot Noir. It will give his winery the red wine so many consumers want today. He poured me a small glass of the '92 vintage. A great year, a long and glorious, warm harvest. A true vintage, with all the meaning implied as used by the French and German, to note a special harvest, that one in five or even ten harvests when the grapes are fully and completely ripened, even overripened.

The color was a solid red, not at all light. The aromas were of delicate raspberry with just a hint of oak. It was medium weight. I was surprised that the tannins that were so pronounced a year earlier had diminished. They were still there but they were not harsh. The finish was wonderful; the aftertaste remained on the palate long after swallowing the wine; the balanced raspberry flavor lingered.

Gerard was clearly excited. Pinot Noir is a difficult grape to grow and its wines are difficult to make. As a grape it is very sensitive to climate. Its skin is thin-walled and the clusters are tight, inviting mildew problems. Without sufficient sunlight (not necessarily sunshine), it won't develop a very robust color.

But the rewards can be outstanding, as represented by his '92. The wine brings the winery into the mainstream and allies the winery to the wineries in the Willamette Valley in Oregon. It distinguishes his wine from the wines of eastern Washington and makes serious wine drinkers (read wine snobs, by Gerard) take notice. There were only 85 cases made of this wine.

Gerard said he wished he had recognized the value of Pinot Noir and Pinot Gris earlier. He claimed his late discovery was the result of his heavy German viticultural indoctrination and just plain time. It took him a long time to get around to planting the Pinot Noir.

Everybody said they couldn't grow it. First, they started with a few vines and they watched to see how they matured. Then they planted more vines and had to wait at least three years to get a few berries. Finally, in year five, they got their first commercial crop. And what a vintage. Gerard noted, "It takes a lot of time, and it takes a lot of money. This is a totally bootstrap operation here. There are no investors."

Gerard confided in me, "If someone drove in here and said, 'I want to do a little winery,' I would say, 'Do Pinot Noir in your garage. Put it in good French oak, and don't sell more than 500 gallons (about 210 cases) a year. Retail all of it at $20 a bottle, and make sure it is worth that. Don't spend vast amounts of money on equipment for whites.' I didn't know that then."

In fact Gerard and JoAnne have been instrumental in helping other wineries start up on Whidbey Island and on Lopez Island. Both wineries are working closely with the Bentryns to learn what grapes grow best in their vineyards. JoAnne researches and tracks down vineyards that currently exist throughout Puget Sound and tries to connect the vineyard owner up to a winery in hopes that they will make wine out of locally grown grapes.

It is close to religious zeal and Gerard could easily pass as a cult figure, except it would be antithetical to his own nature. No, I could see a special course that beginning wineries would take at Washington State University, or maybe Western Washington University in Bellingham, in their future wine program. The title would read, "Wine's Veracity: Professor Bentryn."

Chapter Thirty

WE'VE ARRIVED

—CHATEAU STE. MICHELLE, OCTOBER 1995—
Mike Wallace concluded an interview by telling me, "Washington wines will have arrived when there is a place in every wine shop, restaurant, and grocery store reserved for Washington." I thought about that statement as I drove onto the palatial winery grounds of Chateau Ste. Michelle in Woodinville, through the opened iron gate, past rows of pruned guardian vines, along the winding entrance roadway of the former Hollywood Farm, to the grand entrance of the imposing French-styled winery.

Though built in 1976, the estate and winery show few signs of age. If any, it is the patina that forms on the exterior plastered walls, just as in Bordeaux' chateaux. The winery is situated at the eastern base of a slight slope as the manicured estate meanders west up through curling footpaths, past the fish tanks and the beautiful lush gardens and broad evergreens.

Built at a cost of $6 million, it was a remarkable statement made by the winery to the rest of the Washington wine industry. Chateau Ste. Michelle's corporate backers, then called U.S. Tobacco (today, euphemistically, simply UST), said, "We are here for the long term."

It was also built at the right time. Woodinville, in a mere ten years, transformed into a sprawling suburban community. The winery became a symbol of the new suburban wealth, tasteful and adventuresome. Newcomers to Washington could taste the vibrant flavors of this state. The winery became an important tourist attraction, drawing upwards of 200,000 visitors a year.

To some in the wine business it seemed a bit bizarre to locate the winery 200 miles from the vineyards. It would be a little like Beringer Winery of Napa Valley being located in Marin, a wealthy suburb located north and just outside of San Francisco, trucking its grapes that distance rather than locating right next to the grapes. But this arrangement, which is somewhat unique to Washington, works particularly well. It recognizes that most of the population is in western Washington and that commuting to eastern Washington can be difficult, especially during the winter months. Many of Chateau Ste. Michelle's vineyard people work and reside in eastern Washington. Generally only the sales, marketing, and a portion of the winemaking staff work at the Woodinville winery and reside in the greater Seattle area.

Also, Stimson Lane's other wineries, Chateau Ste. Michelle-Grandview, Columbia Crest, and Canoe Ridge Estate, are fully staffed with winemaking and vineyard people right at those facilities. Thus Ste. Michelle's decision to build its facility on the west side of the mountains, though seen by some as folly, has proven prudent. And though the decision to locate in Woodinville seems wise now, one of the reasons for choosing the westside location was just a continuation of the old American Wine Growers setup. As the make-up of wines changed over the years, American Wine Growers increasingly relied on its Grandview winery to process its grape wines, continuing to ship grapes and wine over the mountains.

There are now nearly 20 wineries located in the Puget Sound region that rely primarily on eastern Washington grapes. And Woodinville has turned into a small winery community with Columbia Winery located across the street. Silver Lake Winery has recently relocated close by. In a warehouse/industrial park is Facelli Winery. Across the valley is the new DeLille Cellars.

Curiously, although this has worked well for the Puget Sound wineries, its correlate has failed; wineries whose main winemaking plants are located in eastern Washington have tried to maintain small sales facilities on the west side only to see these facilities languish. The logic of this would suggest that people are willing to support a winery on this side, as long as they can see the product being made.

I think of Gerard Bentryn laughing his cynical laugh, applauding the consumers, and asking rhetorically, "And just where is the reality in that?"

These were my thoughts as I walked from my car to the winery's entrance. The front doors are massive wood doors. Inside the lobby is a wonderful display mixing technical information about grape growing and winemaking with historical photos. Through the lobby I climbed the steps to the corporate offices upstairs.

I had called and asked to meet with Mark Jennings, director of communications, because I had a number of questions about Stimson Lane. I also wanted to taste some of its current releases. While waiting for him, I ventured into the hallway where a display case held a number of old bottles of wine. Also displayed were the first wine license held by the Pommerelle Company and one of the brass seals from one of its first brandy stills. The bottles, and labels, were rich in detail. There were bottles from the first apple wines made by Pommerelle, including a table wine, a sparkling version (bottled like a French Champagne), and even a dessert apple wine bottled in a Rhine half-bottle, tall and skinny, with a label that looked just like an expensive beeranauslese (a very sweet German-styled dessert wine). All of these labels were, graphically, very well done. They showed a high degree of sophistication on the part of Joe Molz and William Braicks, the originators of the Pommerelle Company.

There were also bottles of Black Prince. What a great name; until recently I just assumed it was a name made up by the Pommerelle Company. Instead, I have learned that the Black Prince is more likely to be the Cinsaut grape of southern France.

Additionally, there were the original bottlings of the Ste. Michelle Vineyards brand with their slightly gaudy labels, large awkward labels in pale yellow. Today's marketing team would scream if they had to sell that label.

—ALLEN SHOUP—

No, when those labels were produced, there wasn't a marketing team, nor a sales team. It was mostly production-driven, and it wasn't until Allen Shoup arrived in 1980 that the winery entered the marketing venue. Allen Shoup is the president of Stimson Lane Vineyards and Estates. He was hired by Wally Opdycke, then the president of Ste. Michelle Vintners.

Shoup, a soft-spoken man about fifty years old, is a marketing genius who has helped carry Stimson Lane Vineyards and Estates to its present position. Shoup, with a master's degree in psychology and a bachelor's degree in business, has a varied work history. He has done product development for Amway, been a financial analyst for Chrysler, helped in brand development for Gallo, did a stint in Los Angeles as the director of marketing for Max Factor, and just before arriving at Ste. Michelle worked at Boise Cascade in Boise, Idaho.

Wally Opdycke had originally interviewed Allen Shoup in 1978, but Shoup wasn't prepared to make a change. Wally had learned of Shoup through one of Opdycke's contacts at K2 Skis, a company then owned by Opdycke's investment company, who had worked with Shoup at Gallo.

Shoup liked Wally and the new winery at Woodinville. He remembered thinking to himself, "I could feel I was in a dream field. This is where I am going to retire. That was in 1978. I think it was fall; it was beautiful. I had never been to Seattle." It was so vastly different from L.A.—a refuge.

Instead of taking the job, he went to Boise Cascade, where he stayed for two years, hating it because there was very little decision making; his job was to comment, not to decide.

In 1980 Shoup came back. This time Opdycke told him that next year they were going to break ground on the brand-new Columbia Crest Winery at Paterson. It wasn't called Columbia Crest then. Rather, it was known as River Ridge, although it would produce wine under the Farron Ridge label prior to being renamed Columbia Crest. Shoup recalled, "Now, they had made the commitment to not just be a 250,000-case winery, but to be a 2 million-case winery. That year they were doing $5 million in sales.

"This was going to happen and it had the resources of UST and this was one of the major jobs in the wine industry. I took it. Certainly, every year has been a year of progress. Every year we have exceeded the previous year in growth, and also in terms of acceptance."

Shoup recalled being flown over to visit the construction site of the future Columbia Crest: "I can remember looking, standing at this cliff with this huge hole in the ground. There were these earth movers playing around down there in the ground. They looked like toys. The part that seemed crazy to me was that they were constructing a warehouse that was going to be 150,000 square feet."

It seemed crazy to Shoup because the winery was going to fill this warehouse up with wine, but it had no idea how it was going to sell the wine. Shoup saw that the Seattle market, which was buying up to 200,000 cases of its wine a year, was reaching a saturation point. He understood that his sales efforts were going to have to be beyond the state's borders.

In 1981 he argued with a UST budget executive that he needed $1 million for sales and $1 million for marketing. The exchange was quite heated. He asked the executive, "Do you know what a million-case brand looks like? It's ubiquitous; you see it everywhere. The only way that you will see it everywhere is to put a sales organization together that can stay on top of the distributors. And put a marketing program together."

The next day Shoup was given $1 million. He decided that it would be best spent in sales: "I said if it's only a million dollars, let's give it to sales. Because I have seen examples of companies that have succeeded with marketing but no sales. But I've never seen the opposite. Sales are your front line.

"That was one of the great challenges, convincing the parent company that this wasn't going to just happen."

Shoup continued, "We started hiring some of the best salespeople in the industry. We showed that we were a major player." The company could point to its sales program, to its wine quality, and to firm financial backing. This became important as Chateau Ste. Michelle sought and found the strongest distributors in the nation. Locally, it remained loyal to the Sid Eland Company, the same company that had first distributed Pommerelle and Nawico wines.

Shoup recalled, "We had a niche. The country doesn't need another Napa Valley Cabernet or a Sonoma Chardonnay, but every wine list in America should have one example of a Washington wine. We could say, 'If you have us, you have something that nobody else can compete with. We are a major Washington brand with national distribution.' That allowed us to get the best distributor in each market.

"That is a critical part of the success of the winery. Some of the wineries today just don't have that ability.

"The recession of the '80s caused distributors to consolidate among themselves and the number of brands that they were carrying. That is unfortunate because there are a number of wineries here that are producing excellent wines that still can't find good distributors. The solution for them is to make this a famous viticultural region so that wines from Washington kind of self-sell.

"It is frustrating for me that most of the wineries don't understand that phenomenon."

Looking at the display case, I thought about my interview with Allen Shoup the previous year, and about the remarkable changes that have occurred in the Washington wine industry over the last few years.

Shoup had said during that interview, "We've now had about three successive years of great acclaim and I believe that we are sort of where Oregon was, where people are going to try to push us over and try to show that we are not as legitimate as we think." The wines of Washington have taken a major step forward in national and international recognition. Both Robert Parker, of the influential *Wine Advocate*, as well as the *Wine Spectator* have consistently given high marks to wines from Washington state. The question will be: when will they and others try to knock the industry over?

Mike Wallace's voice resonated in my mind, "Washington wines will have arrived when there is a place in every wine shop, restaurant, and grocery store reserved for Washington." I think he and Shoup were saying the same thing. Washington wines are clearly on their way to fulfilling this challenge.

—JOEL KLEIN—

Mark Jennings joined me as I photographed a number of bottles, lifting them out of the display case with great deference. Jennings, a young man, watched as I gingerly set a series of bottles on top of the case. This must have seemed silly to him but, then, I doubted that he had any way of knowing how special these bottles and their labels were. Not many would.

Jennings led me through the winery's lab into a wine room reserved for technical tastings. It was the same room where probably ten years ago I had sampled some of the winery's first sparkling wines being made by Kay Simon, today of Chinook Wines. I had brought a group of tasters from Pike and Western Wine Shop and we were asked to taste different yeast treatments of four different sparkling wines. We each sat at our laboratory cubicles in this all-white room.

It also recalled to mind Joel Klein, who was the winemaker for Chateau Ste. Michelle from 1974 until 1981. Joel Klein, somewhat of an enigma, is bright, quick-witted, knowledgeable, and pompous-sounding. His tall stature, dark black wavy hair, and black trimmed beard belie his gentle nature. Today Joel and his wife, Karen, own and operate a chocolate factory in Issaquah, called Loveables, where they produce chocolates that are shipped nationally and internationally.

Joel Klein was hired in 1974 by Wally Opdycke. He was in his early thirties, working at the time for Geyser Peak Winery in California, helping to design and grow that winery. Joel had lunch

Joel Klein of Chateau Ste. Michelle in lab. 1977.
—*Photo by Lawrence J. Allen. Courtesy of Elizabeth Purser-Hendricks.*

every Wednesday with André Tchelistcheff. André was also the consultant to Simi Winery. Together Joel, André, and Mary Ann Graf, the winemaker at Simi, would share winemaking notes over lunch. One day Wally came by as they were having lunch and said, "André, we really need a winemaker." Mary Ann offered, "Joel's not exactly excited about where he is at Geyser Peak." André then recommended Joel.

Joel was slightly aware of Washington wines through his association with Chas Nagel in 1971, when both were working at United Vintners. They had become friends and Chas had spoken to him of the potential of Washington wines. Also, Joel's future father-in-law, Harold W. Berg, was in charge of enology and viticulture at UC Davis and he had counseled Joel that the future for premium wines was up north. Of course, Joel didn't realize at that time that Berg wasn't talking about Washington but, rather, Oregon, his home state.

Joel arrived in August, in time to direct the '74 harvest. Vic Allison and Wally drove Joel over to eastern Washington to show him the vineyards. He said, "I saw Cold Creek Vineyard just being planted. The soil type was completely foreign to me." And he remembered being struck by the absence of vineyards. He was used to the wine valleys of California where every hill was adorned by vineyards, where "within fifteen minutes you found grapevines." There might have been about 1,100 acres of wine grapes in eastern Washington at that time.

He said, "All very strange, very foreign, and very different to me. But there certainly seemed to be capabilities."

Afterward they returned to Seattle, to the winery on East Marginal Way. Howard Somers was there; Bert and Jerry Coombs, long-time cellar workers, were there; and Charlie Finkel and Robert Conley of Bon-Vin were there. Joel remembered tasting the wines in that first meeting. He saw great potential. Immediately he was at odds with the wines: The white wines were very good; the red wines were rough. He recalled, "The red wines were like brushing your teeth with a wire brush. The tannin levels were high, 3,000-plus parts per million of tannins, compared to California reds in the 1,000 to 2,000 range. The pH was low, which exacerbated the problem." He said out loud to his fellow tasters, "We've got to get malolactic in these reds."

That led to his efforts to introduce Washington red wines to the malolactic bacterium that helps to soften red wines by changing the sharper malic acid into the softer lactic acid. Joel recalled that he had discussed the malolactic with André in February or March. He told André that he hadn't been successful in getting the malolactic started. André advised him to be prepared to forget it. Joel described his next effort, "So I took two 5-gallon batches of Merlot from the '74 vintage, put them in the lab, and added some sodium hydroxide to raise the pH, then I added the malolactic starter. When André came up, there were little-biddy bubbles on the sides of the glass carboys. Then I personally took them out into the winery where we had a small 1,000-gallon tank. I lowered the two carboys'-worth of wine onto the surface of the wine in the tank. We had complete malolactic in about ten days. Then I took that 1,000-gallon tank and blended it into a 3,000-gallon tank." Eventually, everything went through malolactic.

This was a major breakthrough for Washington red wines, especially Cabernet Sauvignon and Merlot. With improved viticultural practices, the pH factor in the wines was raised and it became easier to inoculate the wine with the malolactic starter. The result has been softer, rounder red wines. And they were more stable once bottled, as the malolactic was capable of starting in the bottle given the right conditions.

Joel helped introduce a number of innovations to the red wines, in particular, such as pumping the juice over the skins, and fermenting the wines at higher temperatures. Joel worked at Chateau Ste. Michelle until his last harvest in 1981. He had seen the company through its most tempestuous years and decided it was time to start his own company.

In 1983 he organized his own winery, Snoqualmie Winery, with partner David Wycoff. After two years Wycoff wanted out and Joel was forced to reorganize the company in an unwieldy holding company with too many investors. It got worse: in 1986, Snoqualmie Winery purchased Langguth Winery. This eventually led to some nasty court battles. In 1987 Joel Klein relinquished control of his dream.

—TASTING—

I was seated at a round table with a lazy susan in the middle crowded with about eighteen bottles of wines. Mike Januik, Chateau Ste. Michelle's winemaker, joined us. Each of us had about fifteen empty glasses in front of us, a glass of mineral water, and water biscuits. I wanted to taste what the winery was currently making, to show the flavor range of Washington wines. Here are my notes:

1993 Sauvignon Blanc, Columbia Valley: This wine was clean and spirited, wonderfully fresh-tasting. It highlighted the melon flavors of the grape with only a hint of grassiness.

1993 Chardonnay, Columbia Valley: Also fresh and fruity and, except for the rich texture, I would have had difficulty distinguishing the first two wines. It reminded me that one of the criticisms of Chateau Ste. Michelle in the early days was that the white wines all tasted the same, as if they had been back blended with a muscat-based sweetening reserve.

I tasted three vineyard-designated Chardonnays and a Reserve, a blend of vineyard sources: Januik's pride, wines crafted from grapes harvested from single vineyard sites. Their labels were beautiful, with a line drawing of a cluster of Chardonnay grapes with subtle and coordinated colors. All the wines had intense fruit qualities to them, tasting of melon and apple with a mouth-filling fruitiness. The oak flavors were very subtle and seemed to frame the fruitiness rather than tasting of oak.

1993 Chardonnay, Indian Wells Vineyard: This vineyard is located a quarter mile south of the turn to Mattawa on the Wahluke Slope. It was fresh, fruity, and clean, with a soft coating of oak. Beautifully balanced.

1993 Chardonnay, Cold Creek Vineyard: This wine was more focused and fresh, lively, with a great roundness of fruit. A stellar wine.

1993 Chardonnay, Canoe Ridge Vineyard: A lighter version of the Cold Creek. More delicate and pointed but with a long finish.

1993 Chardonnay, Chateau Reserve: This wine was much broader and richer, with a more complex mouth feel. The flavors suggested the longer sur lees contact (where the wine remains in contact with the lees, dead yeasts, and gunk that settle to the bottom of the barrel).

Next we tasted two Rieslings and a Gewurztraminer.
1993 Dry Riesling: Lots of melon and apple flavors. Moderate fruitiness with a dry, actually off-dry, finish. This wine needed a bit more fruitiness. Winemaker Januik thought that maybe age will give the wine more richness. I am only slightly disappointed in this wine because I have tasted other, better examples from Washington and I think this kind of wine will someday far surpass the popularity of Chardonnay.

1994 Gewurztraminer: Fruity aroma, mostly grapefruit with some delicate lychee fruit flavors. It was slightly sweet. Another grape I think could do better, but who will spend the time to improve it when it attracts such a low price?

1993 Johannisberg Riesling: Floral with fresh apple and pear flavors in the background. Fruity and balanced on the palate. A classic Washington wine and still Chateau Ste. Michelle's cash cow. Chateau Ste. Michelle has found that other producers are abandoning this grape, thus leaving a void to be filled by Chateau Ste. Michelle.

Next, the heavyweight reds.
1992 Cabernet Franc, Cold Creek Vineyard: Assertive tobacco-leaf aromas, almost smoky, with a soft, round mouth feel. An interesting wine that is just a bit funky. This wine would have been better in a blend. As a grape it has adapted well to Washington state. The difficulty is controlling its vigorous vegetative growth, which can often translate to an herbaceous quality in the wine.

1992 Merlot, Columbia Valley: A near-perfect wine and a reason that

Merlots from Washington are the rave. It was focused, with round, berrylike fruit flavors in the nose and on the palate. Its weight was moderate, concentrated, and yet incredibly soft.

1992 Merlot, Indian Wells Vineyard: Hard to improve on the previous Merlot. This was similar and maybe more power-packed with slighty more distinctive flavors, with a dusty, chalklike quality in the aroma and on the palate.

1992 Cabernet Sauvignon, Columbia Valley: All that a Cabernet should be: herbaceous, concentrated, tobaccolike aromas, with raspberry fruit.

1991 Cabernet Sauvignon, Cold Creek Vineyard: This wine was assertive and big. Soft, ripe flavors were balanced with a tannic quality, probably a result of the cold winter in 1990 that reduced the crop.

1992 Cabernet Sauvignon, Cold Creek Vineyard: Concentrated. Long, rich flavors of tobacco and raspberry fruit. A lush wine from a great Washington vintage. Contained 13 percent Cabernet Franc, which added color and complexity.

Dessert wines next.
1991 Late Harvest Riesling: Honeyed. Melon, ripe peach, and apple. And floral. A great wine; like a *beeranauslese* from Germany, it was incredibly sweet but balanced with natural acids; 11 percent residual sweetness. *Beeranauslese* wines are made from selected clusters of grapes that have been affected by the mold *Botrytis cinerea,* and the grape sugars are quite elevated.

1992 Late Harvest Semillon: Honeyed *Botrytis* nose. This wine was richer, more viscous, than the late harvest Riesling. Made in the style of a French Sauternes, it had 13 percent alcohol and just under 10 percent residual sweetness. The wine had a great depth of flavor because it was barrel-fermented and barrel-aged. Winner of the Enological Society of the Pacific Northwest's Grand Prize in 1994.

As we tasted, we talked about the winery. Chateau Ste. Michelle wines are evolving into crafted wines with the same kind of hands-on approach as some of the smaller wineries: evidence is the vineyard-designated wines. Most of those wines are produced in relatively small quantities, under 1,500 cases. These are Januik's pride and joy. It also signals a directional change for Chateau Ste. Michelle and Stimson Lane. The Chateau Ste. Michelle label has become the premium (and expensive) brand, leaving room, I presume, for Columbia Crest to fill the void.

Over the years the winery has matured, as has its customer base. Jennings told me that they now have a Vintage Reserve Club that has 600 members who receive a newsletter and special opportunities to taste rare wines, both from the cellar and current releases. Chateau Ste. Michelle no longer has to be all things to all people. I could tell that Januik was pleased. I asked him what his favorite vineyard sites were. He listed them in order: Indian Wells, Canoe Ridge, and Cold Creek.

He added, "But I also like Weinbau Vineyard and Black Rock Vineyard." Black Rock Vineyard is his name for Airport Ranch Vineyard near Sunnyside. This has been a source for particularly good Chardonnay grapes and was used in the Reserve blend. Weinbau Vineyard, like Indian Wells Vineyard, is on the Wahluke Slope and is similar to the first grapes Januik used to make wines when he started at Stewart Vineyards.

After tasting these wines, I requested that I taste these opened wines at our arranged lunch. We gathered up a few wines that I particularly liked, or that I was interested in seeing how they would complement food: 1993 Dry Riesling; 1993 Chardonnay, Cold Creek; 1992 Merlot, Indian Wells Vineyard; 1992 Late Harvest Semillon.

We were seated in the former retail room near the entrance to the winery, just off the lobby. I had had breakfast in the same room a couple of years earlier when I attended an "old-timer's breakfast" arranged by Jack Kelly for former employees of the various companies that have comprised Stimson Lane over the years, including Pommerelle and Nawico. There I met Joe Molz and Carl Kroll, both of whom I later interviewed. Joe Molz was a founding partner of Pommerelle and Carl Kroll was a cellar worker in that winery.

Jennings and I were seated in the middle of the same long, darkly finished table. At one end of the table were the large, heavy wooden doors leading to the lobby. At the other end was a small seating area with lush sofa and chairs. We were served from a door just off this seating area. I marveled at the rich textures and the luxuriant setting.

I had asked if I could taste the current release of Semillon, which turned out to be the '93 vintage. It was crisp and fresh with strawlike flavors and delicate acids. The winery no longer produces the Semillon Blanc, which used to be a little sweeter, evidence again that the winery is becoming more sophisicated, more upscale. I tasted the Semillon and the Dry Riesling with the first course, a bed of bitter salad greens topped with seared scallops wrapped with bacon. Delicious. Eating food in a winery is such a great pleasure. The vinous aromas set your palate on red alert and your whole being craves food. Wine, and its suggestions, put your being on titillating desire; there is an aching need to feed that desire. Is it the smell of the yeast in the air, the chill in the cellar, the acid in the wine, the complex flavors suggestive of fruits and berries, or is it all of this in a complex reflex mechanism that when wine is served one should expect food? I don't know, but I was ravenous.

The next course was rack of lamb served with asparagus, grilled peppers, and delightful silver dollar–size potato pancakes. I drank the 1992 Indian Wells Merlot with this and savored the symphony of flavors between the sweet, rich lamb flavors and the incredibly concentrated berrylike flavors in the Merlot.

This reminded me of the dinner put on in 1901 by John Durieux in Wenatchee. His menu as printed in *The Wenatchee Advance:* Hors D'oeuvre—Sweet Butter, Radishes, Mexican Queen Olives; Entrees— Laitues, French Dressing, Chicken marengo; Fish—Fresh Soles au Gratin, Champaignons; Vegetables—Potatoes en puri, Spinach, Asparagus; Roti—Spring Lamb Leg, Washington sauce; Dessert— Imported Roquefort and Swiss Cheese. Plain, Chocolate Cake, Fruits; Wines—Wenatchee White Claret, California Burgundy, Champagne; Cafe Noir, Cognac, Cigars, Havana. What an amazing meal. John Durieux, an immigrant from the Macon district of France, was excited to show his new countrymen a traditional French meal. I noted that his menu was almost exactly the same as a meal prepared by local chefs for Julia Child during a recent visit. It would be interesting to know what the Wenatchee White Claret was made of. I would guess that it possibly was made of Zinfandel, as that is one of the grapes recorded as being planted in the Wenatchee area.

I went back to my lunch and stuck my nose into the wineglass of Cold Creek Chardonnay. I loved its incredibly fresh and mouth-filling fruit. Being from one of Walt's favorite vineyard sites, the wine gave me added pleasure in tasting.

Dessert was a thin, flaky apple torte, the size of a large pancake, shaped like an apple with a sprig of mint as its leaf. It was framed on the plate in a lightly warmed raspberry and cream (or was it white chocolate?) sauce. A stunning accompaniment to the Late-Harvest Semillon.

Throughout the meal, Jennings outlined the boycott of Chateau Ste. Michelle products by the United Farm Workers. Begun in 1987, the boycott had become a public relations annoyance to the winery, though there was little evidence that the boycott had been effective. Jennings reported that 1994 was the best year yet for sales at Stimson Lane.

However, Stimson Lane took the boycott seriously because it prided itself in the work conditions of its farm laborers. It was very annoying to Stimson Lane that it was being singled out by the United Farm Workers because it was a good media target, as Washington's only nationally renowned brand. Stimson Lane employed about 100 full-time field workers and regularly added 80 temporaries to help through the harvest. It generally paid by the hour, between $6.75 and $10.30 per hour; the average was $7.49 per hour. Some of the workers had been with the company for over twenty years.

There are close to 115,000 farm workers in Washington state. These are the workers who do all the critical grunt work of orchards, vineyards, and fields. A vast majority of these workers are Mexican, by birth or heritage. They have swelled the populations of many of the small towns in the Yakima Valley. Their culture is beginning to dominate some communities. This has brought resentment by some long-time residents. They blame some of the more recent crimes to these people, noting an increase in drug trafficking.

But they also value these people as an inexpensive labor force, and also as a reliable labor pool. Farmers and industry have always depended on inexpensive temporary labor to bring in the harvest. Les Fleming told me that he relied on housewives in the early years. For the housewife it was an opportunity to maybe earn enough money to buy a new sofa or refrigerator. During the second world war, labor shortages began to occur. And agriculture became bigger. More farm workers were desperately needed, opening the door for laborers from Mexico. Since the '50s, Mexican farm labor has dominated agriculture in eastern Washington.

Having grown up in Seattle, I find it at once curious and offensive. I have a difficult time when I visit eastern Washington seeing the poverty of the farm workers, knowing that they are doing much of the hard, demanding work required on most of the farms, yet they receive the worst pay. I am most offended, however, by the seeming disregard shown these people. They appear treated as second-class citizens; sometimes it is as if they don't exist. I know that I am speaking generally, and also without direct experience, and I don't mean to judge. I have also seen these people given the respect they deserve. Walt informs me that Prosser annually provides $30,000 for food and clothing for migrant workers. Additionally, nearly $40,000 is raised for United Good Neighbors. I also realize that Walt Clore, and other eastside residents, are equally appalled by the poverty of aimless drifters and homeless people who congregate on downtown Seattle streets, ignored by the human hustle of urban life.

I did a quick calculation using figures provided by Jennings. Assuming that a full-time worker is employed ten months of the year (usually with December and January off) and the work week averages about 45 hours, at $7.49 an hour that works out to an annual salary of $13,482. Only slightly better than my mother's retirement income. And that is one of the better wages. It is grossly unfair.

But so are the demands of agriculture. It is a high-risk poker game, the outcome dependent on the weather, the market, and costs. The first is an act of God, the second an act of man, and the third is the only factor that seems within the control of the farmer. Increasingly, farmers are turning to mechanized labor in the wine grape vineyards to control their labor costs.

The wine grape grower has tremendous upfront costs in establishing a vineyard. It runs to nearly $10,000 an acre in eastern Washington. A moderate vineyard size of 10 acres requires $100,000 in financing. The first crop won't come off the vines until at least the third year. During this time, labor must be hired to plant, then train and prune the young vines. Finally, by year four, the vineyard's first nearly full crop, the farmer may not see payment until January.

That vineyard will produce about 50 tons of grapes, enough for a 7,500-gallon winery, or about 3,200 cases. If the vineyard is attached to the winery, those costs will not be recovered until the wine is sold. A white wine might make it to market in a year. With luck the wine might get sold in six months. A red wine could get to market in eighteen months, and possibly sell out in six months. Meanwhile the producer must purchase labels, corks, and bottles while absorbing the costs of the winery. At the earliest, the producer-farmer might begin to get a return by year six, during that entire time battling cash flow difficulties or, more realistically, like a leaking barrel, the cash drips, drips, drips.

That is why the business of wine is conducive to corporate investment; fat wallets can cover these costs. It is also why a seemingly successful winery can hemorrhage to near death, sometimes unbeknownst to the owner. It is also why UST's investment was so critical to the industry, not just to cover the costs of production but to cover the even greater costs of marketing and selling the product outside of Washington state, a cost beyond most wineries.

Most agribusiness is run on cheap labor. Enlightened management tries to find a way to scuttle cash-flow problems by paying its workers with bonuses after the company has realized a profit. In this sense the worker becomes a partner in the business.

I have no doubt that Stimson Lane values its workers. Besides the farm laborers, Stimson Lane today employs an additional 350 employees, the cellar workers being represented by the Teamsters. Stimson Lane has shown a willingness to address the concerns of its workers.

I savored the last sip of my Late Harvest Semillon. Ah, how sweet it was.

—LABOR AGREEMENT SIGNED—

On October 31, 1995, the United Farm Workers and Stimson Lane Vineyards and Estate signed the first union contract between a farming operation and field workers, ending an eight-year battle.

Mark Jennings was quoted in the *Tri-Cities Herald,* "We believe it is a fair contract."

In the same article Rosalinda Guillen, the United Farm Workers state regional director, said, "This is a good thing for the agricultural community. The taxpayers and members of the community should be rejoicing with us because it means a fair wage for agricultural workers."

The eighteen-month agreement was signed after both sides agreed to go to mediation on October 16. There were two issues dividing them: wages, and the right of the union to insist on a closed shop, one in which all winery workers would be required to enroll in the union.

The winery and union agreed on the closed shop issue.

The contract gave the full-time workers an average 5.5 percent raise, and seasonal workers an average 6.5 percent. Seasonal workers will earn from $5.40 an hour to $5.75, and full-time workers will earn $7.10 to $9.80, placing these workers in the top wage scale of other Washington farm workers and in some instances higher than farm workers in California, particularly in the upper level of pay.

Besides these nominal pay increases, workers will receive new dental coverage, a pension plan, and a continuation of existing medical coverage as well as eleven paid holidays a year and paid vacations. Seasonal workers who have logged over 500 hours with the company will be eligible for benefits.

For the winery's part, the contract protects the winery against strikes, slow-downs, and any other adverse activities by the farm workers. Additionally, the winery retained the ability to buy grapes from non-union vineyards.

This was the UFW's first contract outside California since 1972. This contract has put the rest of the wine industry on alert; pressure may build for other farm workers to request organizing help from the UFW, although without a state law or the benefit of the National Labor Relations Act, which doesn't cover farm workers, it will be difficult to make inroads against other vineyard owners.

Dr. Raymond Folwell, professor of agricultural economics at Washington State University, who had helped shape the Washington wine industry in the '70s with his marketing analysis, was quoted in the *Tri-Cities Herald*, "About 90 percent of the wine grapes in this state are harvested mechanically already, and this could speed the purchase of mechanized pruning equipment."

After lunch, Erick Olsen came by the dining hall. I had met Erick at Canoe Ridge when I tasted wines with Mike Januik and him. I had asked Jennings if I could taste some wines out of barrel.

Olsen led me down the stairs past the fifty-foot bottling line, *clankity, clank, clank,* to the white wine barrel area. On the far side of the room (I had no sense of direction because there are no windows to give you your bearings), there was a wall made up of cases of Johannisberg Riesling. Cases were stacked 18 high, slightly over 18 feet high, and 140 cases wide (nearly 150 feet wide). Truly, Chateau Ste. Michelle's Johannisberg Riesling remains a foundation of this winery's business.

Olsen brought along his glass wine thief and sought out some young Chardonnay wines from barrel. Barrels are stacked 6 high, and rows of barrels ran the length of the Riesling wall, save an area of about thirty feet wide in the middle to get at the barrels by forklift. Each set of barrels was tagged. The tag showed the vintage, the type of wine, the vineyard source, and the portion of the vineyard. Olsen crawled among the barrels and handed me various samples. First the '94 Canoe Ridge, Block 3. It was delicate and crisp. Then the '94 Cold Creek; biting, rich, and concentrated. The '94 Airport Ranch (or Black Rock) Vineyard; earthy with notable grape flavors. The '94 Weinbau; lighter and similar to Canoe Ridge.

This is how Olsen and Januik will eventually assemble their wines—barrel by barrel, tasting and comparing the component parts. Not too different from the approach used by small wineries.

Yet I was impressed. Here was one of Washington's largest wineries, fretting about individual vineyards and, ironically, Stimson Lane Vineyards and Estate answers to Gerard Bentryn's definition of owner-owned and owner-produced in much of its wines. Forget for a moment that it is owned and operated by one of America's largest corporations, UST.

Stimson Lane Vineyards and Estate owns 3,200 acres in wine grapes in eastern Washington. It also contracts for additional grapes from numerous growers throughout the Columbia Valley and the Yakima Valley. Its production level is over 2 million cases, employing nearly 450 people. It is a mammoth operation with over 210,000 gallons in stainless steel tanks and 90,000 barrels. This total includes wineries that Stimson Lane operates in California such as Conn Creek and Villa Mount Eden.

The strategy has been to spin off each winery to develop its own personality and identity. Thus the various winemakers at Stimson Lane's Washington wineries have considerable control over the direction of their wineries. Clearly, this showed as Januik presented his vineyard-designated wines to me. These really were his creations and he was obviously pleased that Stimson Lane allowed him the ability to express himself through the wines. Doug Gore, at Columbia Crest, probably feels the same way. Together with the other winemakers at Stimson Lane, they are producing exciting wines.

When talking about the Washington wine industry, one is confronted by the schizophrenic character of the industry. Today, in 1996, there are about 90 bonded wineries. Together these wineries are estimated to produce just over 7 million gallons of wine from 44,000 tons of grapes. Total sales of Washington wines is estimated to be slightly over 6 million cases, with close to 60 percent of the sales now going out of state.

Of this wine produced in Washington state, 65 percent of the wine is made by Stimson Lane wineries. Its size dwarfs its nearest competitor, which would be Hogue Cellars, Coventry Vale Winery, Columbia Winery, or Washington Hills; all produce about 250,000 cases of wines a year. The remainder of the wines produced in Washington come from tiny, independently owned wineries. That is why the Bentryns of Bainbridge Island Winery, or Mike Wallace of Hinzerling Winery, or Joan and Linc Wolverton of Salishan Winery, are so at odds with the marketplace. They are tiny players in the same game dominated by a giant.

It is also a great frustration for Stimson Lane. Allen Shoup recalled the first meeting of the Washington Wine Institute in 1981. He had called a number of people together because he was having difficulties with the Washington State Tourism Department. The tourism department wanted to help promote Washington wines but suggested it would be easier if the industry had its own organization made up of all the wineries in the state. Shoup recalled that Mike Wallace was there, as was Bill Preston, Paul Thomas, and, he thought, Jeff Gordon. (Quite a contentious group, I thought to myself.) Allen Shoup laughed as he recalled that first meeting; I'm sure he was thinking the same thing.

Shoup remembered asking the group, "Why don't we have an industry, why don't we work together? And they all turned and attacked me, 'Because your company dominates everything.' The comment was, 'Your company has always prevented it, you've never wanted it. You have always wanted to work in isolation.' I said, 'It has all changed, I don't think it's true; I'm here, Wally knows I am here.'

"'Your company doesn't help us. Your company hasn't been a very nice company.' They were saying, 'You've got a lot of very nice people in your company, don't get us wrong...but you are not a very nice company.' I said, 'But who is the company? The company is these people. The fact that it has a president, rather than an owner, because it is a corporation, is the problem that you folks have. In our instance we are a collection of people.' In effect, I had to work hard to build their trust. I said, 'We will finance this thing if you folks support it.'

"We had the first meeting at Columbia Winery, and Paul Thomas, as the first president, kind of ramrodded the whole thing through."

—Simon Siegl—

The Washington Wine Institute is one of two organizations set up to assist the Washington wine industry. The Wine Institute's role is to lobby for the business interests of this group. The other organization, the Washington Wine Commission, was set up with help from the Department of Agriculture. Its purpose is to promote the wines of Washington state. The Washington Wine Commission was set up in 1983, two years after the institute.

Until recently both organizations were headed up by Simon Siegl. It was a difficult position, as he tried to represent the views of such disparate wine companies. The Wine Institute has forty-eight members. Each member winery has one vote and pays dues on a sliding scale based on its gallonage production.

The Washington Wine Commission is funded through the sales of all wines in Washington state, including wines imported into the state. The Wine Commission is funded in three ways: 25 cents per liter on all wine sold in Washington, 2 cents per liter on all sales of Washington wines, and $3 per ton on all sales of Washington wine grapes.

Simon Siegl sat at his cluttered desk the afternoon that I interviewed him at his office in the Terminal Sales Building in Seattle. Simon Siegl, a suave, comfortable person, was slender and neat, wearing a wide-lapel suit, and distinguished with his cropped mustache peppered with gray hairs. He would be comfortable in New York or Chicago, as well as in Seattle. Siegl has performed well as director for both the institute and the commission. He is sympathetic to the complaints of the small wineries, but pragmatic with the larger needs of the whole industry and to the specific needs of Stimson Lane.

Siegl came on line in 1985, a critical turning point for Washington wines. The industry had matured at home and it needed to explore markets outside of the state. Siegl was the third executive of the Wine Institute. Before him, Ron Holden had helped inaugurate the institute on a contractual basis, doing various promotional activities. A year later Noel Bourasaw took over. Noel, a colorful man, also edited and published the *Northwest Wine Almanac,* a wine periodical with a focus on the Washington wine industry.

It was in the *Northwest Wine Almanac* that Bourasaw first published a chronological history of the Washington wine industry. This history had begun as a presentation by Howard Somers. Bourasaw continued to add to it, calling on Dr. Clore to complete much of it. As director of the Wine Institute, Bourasaw helped the fledgling institute through its difficult years as wineries during the early '80s sprang up overnight.

Bourasaw was the perfect setup man for Siegl. Siegl, with his expert organizing skills learned in the arts industry as general manager of Intiman Theatre in Seattle, was positioned to lead the industry during a particularly fast growth pace. He understood exactly that if Washington wines were to succeed, they needed to go beyond their borders.

Siegl recalled that he learned of the job through Lila Gault. Gault, an attractive and assertive woman, had become familar with Siegl at the Intiman Theatre, working as a publicist for the theater. She had left to take a job with the Washington State Department of Agriculture where she helped set up the Wine Commission at the prodding of the Wine Institute.

The Wine Commission was eventually authorized as a commodity commission in 1987. With the Wine Commission set up, Siegl could better separate his duties of the two different bodies. Through Siegl's leadership, the Wine Institute became the political arm of the industry, concerned with the business of wine, and the Wine Commission focused on marketing Washington wine.

—NATIONAL ATTENTION—

All of this coalesced at an optimal time. Washington wines were beginning to be discovered outside of Washington. A major turn occurred in 1983 when *Time* magazine ran a short but impressive article on Washington wines. Featured in the article was Mike Wallace of Hinzerling Vineyards. Wine interest was at an all-time high; California wines, with Washington wines in tow, were challenging the supremacy of European wines.

In 1985 Hogue Cellars captured the attention of the wine media when it won Best of Show for its 1983 Cabernet Sauvignon in Atlanta. It was a stunning wine, one of Hogue Cellars' first wines, from a phenomenally great vintage. Other wineries also made great red wines that year, including Woodward Canyon, Leonetti Cellars, Quilceda Creek Vintners, Columbia Winery (with its vineyard-designated wines), and Chateau Ste. Michelle.

Red wines were beginning to impress. It helped that Washington state could produce equally well both the Merlot and the Cabernet Sauvignon. The weather also helped. The latter '80s produced terrific red wine vintages. They were generally warm to hot vintages. Especially noteworthy were the '87, '88, and '89 vintages. A remarkable string of vintages, remarkable by any standard. But in Washington, where every vintage is a vintage year, the concept of a particularly good vintage loses meaning—until first the vintners, then the critics, and finally the consumers taste, evaluate, and declare the wine noteworthy or not.

Winemaking in the '80s really brought Washington wines into the international arena. Improvements were made in grape selection, both in terms of where the grapes came from and the winemakers' ability to blend different grape sources to achieve a higher quality level. Winemakers also began to understand a phenomenon somewhat unique to Washington wines: Washington wines can be both high in pH (the binding quality of the wine's acids) and high in acidity, believed to be a result of irrigation practices and the higher presence of potassium in the harvested grapes. By carefully adding tartaric acid at the beginning of fermentation, or near the beginning of the winemaking process, they found they could reduce the total acidity in the finished wine, especially in combination with refrigeration. Also the winemakers began to thoroughly understand the role of malolactic fermentation in reducing the acids harmonizing the flavors in the wine. Winemakers watched the way that they fermented their wines, increasingly opting to remove the young red wine off the skins earlier to highlight the naturally abundant fruit flavors in the wine.

The use of oak became the focus of many of those wines in the '80s. French oak, American oak. French oak is such a masterpiece of manipulation. The wood used is narrow grained. Then the split wood is often air dried. Finally, it is assembled typically over a flame, which helps the cooper bend the wood and toast the inside of the eventual barrel. This toasting process adds a sweetness to the wood as it carmelizes the natural wood sugars.

Vintners can buy barrels made from specific forests, such as Nevers or Allier, or they may purchase a specific cooper's barrel that may be a blend of woods. And the vintner can choose the amount of toast on the inside of the barrel: light toast, medium toast, or heavy toast.

The vintner then chooses the amount of oak that his or her wine will see. The use of new oak has become almost absolute in the wine industry, especially for wineries making the most expensive wines. A wine made in brand-new French oak, or even new American oak, will smell and taste better than a wine aged in older, more neutral oak. For the most part the taster is tasting and smelling wonderful wood flavors and aromatics. But how about the wine?

I am reminded of the wine tasting I participated in at Pike and Western Wine Shop's back room. Most of the older wines, wines from great Washington vintages in the '80s, were generally disappointing. For comparison we tasted the current release of Woodward Canyon, the

1992 vintage Cabernet Sauvignon. It tasted truly magnificent, but I would be very reluctant to buy more than I could drink over the next year.

This also reminded me of tastings that I used to do when I was with Pike and Western. We did a series of vertical tastings, tasting different vintages of the same winery. We tasted a number of Cabernet Sauvignon–based wines from quality-conscious wineries, including Woodward Canyon, Leonetti Cellars, and Quilceda Creek. By far the most outstanding wines were the wines from Quilceda Creek. As a group the Quilceda Creek wines definitely aged the best. In fact, the wines improved with age, developing a roundness and complexity of flavor often associated with outstanding Bordeaux.

But until recently Quilceda Creek wines were ignored. Alex Golitzen must have been very jealous of the awards and recognition given to Woodward Canyon and Leonetti Cellars. But that has changed. He has abandoned his use of neutral American oak and now uses new French oak.

I visited his winery a couple of years ago. I met his son, Paul, who is increasingly making most of the wine. We tasted a couple of wines from barrel, the '88 and '89 vintage reserve wines. They were absolutely perfect wines. They struck me as being beautifully made with just the right amount of everything: they were concentrated but not heavy. They had wonderful berry and wood smells, layered impressions of complex qualities. They were as good as any young Bordeaux Grand-Cru Classe wine I have tasted, and as good as any of the best from California.

But in their beauty I suspected their shortcomings. Alex and Paul had abandoned their former style to meet the demands of the market and I am not sure when (or if) the wines will show the shortsightedness of their efforts. I may be proven wrong, and I hope these wines will age gloriously.

Winemakers are increasingly learning new techniques to alter the flavor of the wines—to make them more market-acceptable. Not all of these new techniques will be improvements, but most will, and the winemakers will continue to explore new methods to improve their wines.

On the one hand, I have argued that the industry needs to be more market-driven, this idea being the cornerstone of the old American Wine Growers and even the highly sophisticated marketing expert Allen Shoup; on the other hand, I have argued that the industry needs

Dr. Walter J. Clore, André Tchelistcheff, and Leon Adams, recipients of the
Washington Wine Commission's 1988 Governor's Award.
—*Photo by John Imre. Courtesy of Walter J. Clore.*

to adhere to established tradition. The greatness of this region will be
defined by established criteria used to judge the best wines of Bordeaux
and Napa and Sonoma. One measure has always been the ability to age
a wine for a long time, ten, twenty, thirty or more years.

This has definitely been a hallmark of Bordeaux. It is the great
expectation of California wines, especially those wines cellared in the
'70s. California wines will be judged by these wines. The '70 vintage,
the '73, '74, '75 vintages, are now reaching their age of redemption. I
have not tasted a lot of these wines now that they are aged. Generally I
have been disappointed with many aged wines, especially after such
great expectations. And generally the wines of the cooler '73 and '75
vintages have showed better than their more famous counterparts, the
'70 and '74 vintaged wines. Having said that, I have also tasted some
great wines from all of these vintages and I have been impressed. Years
ago I remember tasting the '74 Heitz "Martha's Vineyard" Cabernet
Sauvignon and it delivered all that was promised of it.

We know that California wines are capable of aging gracefully. I
wouldn't stock a cellar on that statement, especially at the prices asked
for some of the top wines. Nor would I stock a cellar full of Washington
red wines. I would be leery of aging an expensive wine without some
track record of its performance in the cellar. I would drink it. Age it? No.

That is one frontier that Washington red wines will have to contend with. That is the area on which the Robert Parkers, the Bob Thompsons, and the Hugh Johnsons will judge Washington's red wines.

—Judging the Wines—

There are other ways to judge a region.

For the sake of argument, let's look at another area in France that is very successful: the Loire Valley. The Loire Valley is home to some of France's most appealing wines, not necessarily profound, but consumer-approachable, in cost and in style. That is where one finds glorius lemony Chenin Blanc wines, such as Vouvray and Saumur; or brisk and bright Sauvignon Blanc wines, Sancerre and Puilly-Fume. The Loire Valley is also home to crisp, pungent reds made from Cabernet Franc and Gamay; some of the best are rosé wines. Or the biting, searing Muscadet made from the Melon de Bourgogne. Taken as a group these are remarkable wines; few of them, however, are known as wines to remain in the cellar.

Actually, of all the regions of France, eastern Washington most closely resembles the Loire Valley. Eastern Washington would fit very neatly in France, somewhere between the Loire Valley, dominated as it is by the meandering Loire River, and Bordeaux, dominated by the Gironde River. From the city of Saumur in the Loire Valley to the Medoc district in Bordeaux it is about 140 miles. Eastern Washington, because of its unique situation, hiding as it does behind the Cascade Mountains, synthesizes these two vastly different areas. It is why eastern Washington can produce such normally profoundly different kinds of wines in one geographic region: Chenin Blanc can be grown next to Merlot, Riesling next to Cabernet Sauvignon, Semillon alongside Chardonnay. If you add to this diversity the potential for cool-climate grapes in western Washington, the range of styles is staggering.

And acidity. Julio Gallo once called it "acid country." It is the one thing that runs through all of the wines from Washington state. It is the backbone of the wines, and the industry. It is sharp and refreshing, never bitter.

It is diversity that will eventually make this region famous, the ability to fuse the profound with the mundane. The future is so exciting. Allen Shoup has said we have touched, perhaps, only 10 percent of our knowledge about this region's wine potential. We have so much to learn about site selection and varietal selection, matching specific varieties to their site. We have yet to work specifically with varietal clones, finding clonal differences that will be specific to conditions here in Washington.

Walt Clore told me once as we drove through the Yakima Valley, "This is still a young man's country." Meaning, without a drop of sexism, that there is still so much to learn, and the opportunity is there for the right person to prosper with the right combination of vision and luck, with commercial savvy, hard work, and a responsive market. I find that a remarkable statement from a man who today is eighty-five years old. He still exudes the same optimism and enthusiasm as when he arrived in Prosser in 1937.

—In the End—

I must relate something that Walt told me. We had just finished a long day together, in the fall of 1994, in the Puget Sound area visiting vineyards. We had intended to visit Bainbridge Island Winery to taste together its 1992 Pinot Noir, but ran out of time. Instead we jumped on a ferry at Bremerton and went into Seattle where Walt was to take the Greyhound Bus back to Prosser.

Walt bought us each coffee and a donut and we sat on the ferry at a table next to the window and watched the beautiful fall afternoon unfold in spectacular shades of blue and white. The sun shone through the window and bathed our table in warm yellow sunlight. Walt, with his baby blue hat on and a thin white jacket, looked at me and said, "Ron, I don't want this book to be about me. Sometimes you make it sound like I have done everything. There have been so many other people involved in this industry."

I told him, "Walt, I appreciate that, and I promise that I won't write this as your history. You must understand, however, that you are so central to the story; through you, I can tell the rest of the story."

He nodded. We both looked out the window, in a moment of appreciative silence, as the blueness of the sky and water drifted by.

TENDING THE VINES

"'It's been a real joy working with wine grapes,'" (Clore) said. "Besides, sippin' wine beats licking stamps.'"

The Seattle Times, May 1982

—*EASTERN WASHINGTON, JUNE 1996*—

Dennis Carter's vineyard lies about five miles north of Prosser and a stone's throw from the research center. Dennis Carter, George Carter's third-oldest son, and his family now live in the modest home at the Carter farm. Behind the home is the wine grape vineyard of 8 acres.

Three dogs were running excitedly at our heels as George Carter, Walt Clore, and I headed out into the vineyard looking for Dennis. This was our first stop in our tour of vineyards throughout eastern Washington to assess the winter damage caused by this year's late freeze.

I had asked Walt if I could join George and him in their annual spring tour of the vineyards. I had wanted to tour the vineyards in April, thinking that we could get a jump on figuring out how severe the damage was going to be, but Walt counseled waiting until late June when there would be more growth and fruit on the vines.

Dennis Carter, wearing a long-sleeved blue denim shirt, blue jeans, and a straw hat with a red bandanna tucked underneath, leaned on a weeding hoe as George, Walt, and I gathered around his Merlot grapevines.

"Most of the Merlot was killed to the ground," he said matter-of-factly.

The grapevines were bare wood, thick gnarled vines trained with cordons to either side. The vines were dead. At the base of the vine were raised green shoots, called suckers, that ran straight up. The dead vine will be removed and these suckers will be next year's trunk—and, if they survive the coming winter, can bear some fruit in 1997.

This reminded me of Walt's testimony at the legislative hearing held in Yakima in 1968. There he stated that because Washington's grapevines are own-rooted, they can gain production the next year. Graft vines would have to be regrafted or replanted with grafted rootstock.

At -14º F the cold was too much for too long. Walt said that the cold air remained below zero for five days starting January 30 and ending February 3. Usually, cold air is more likely to remain only a couple of days. Luckily, six inches of snow on the ground protected the base of the grapevines and roots, by providing insulation from the bitter cold.

Dennis Carter lost probably 95 percent of his Merlot production, much of which he sells to Chinook Winery. His Chardonnay grapes were also badly injured and he figured he might get 20 percent of a normal crop. Other varieties fared better, especially his Cabernet Sauvignon, most of which was planted in 1975.

I asked Dennis how deep the vines had been planted. He said fourteen to sixteen inches. That is one of the things that growers have learned over the years in their efforts to protect the roots from winter damage. Also the notion of hardening off the wood on the vine, by reducing the irrigation earlier, to get the grapevine into dormancy sooner. And location—learning to put the more tender varieties up higher in the vineyard. I wondered how bad it would have been had Dennis Carter and other growers not had the benefit of Walt's counsel over the years.

I told Dennis, "Just think what would have happened if you hadn't learned from these guys. You are their son."

He laughed and said, "Yeah, they're pretty powerful, but not that powerful."

From Carter's vineyard we drove north past Harold Pleasant's vineyard. We stopped and looked briefly at Mike Hogue's Genesis Vineyard. Planted to Cabernet Sauvignon, Merlot, and Cabernet Franc, it looked in good shape except for damage to the Merlot. Early assessments by the research center indicated that Cabernet Franc vines survived the cold best, while Cabernet Sauvignon vines were moderately damaged.

We then stopped in at John Salvini's vineyard. Salvini is one of Walt's clients. Salvini sells his crop to Stimson Lane Vineyards and Estate. Salvini takes great pride in his vineyard. It showed in the cultivation between the rows; weeds were at a minimum and the cover crop was typically cropped low to the ground. The soil around the vines' base had been cultivated recently.

We stopped to look at one grapevine that Walt calls his pet vine. It was astonishing. This one Chardonnay vine at the bottom of a north slope appeared to be thriving among a sea of dead wood. Walt showed how he had trained the double-trunked vine unilaterally on the cordon wire; then, by taking up two additional canes from the cordon and training each in opposite directions on the above two catch wires, he provided for two additional cordons. The cordons bear shoots, which mature into canes bearing the fruiting buds for the next year's crop. This Chardonnay vine had survived with a light crop after being subjected to a low of -21.5° F.

Other nearby vines were damaged. At their base new shoots stuck out and up. Most of the nearby vines had some growth along their cordons but Walt said the grapevines run the risk of collapsing once the vineyards see a couple of hot, 90° to 100° F days. Then the vine's growth won't be able to transport enough moisture up through the vine. And, literally, the vine collapses; the leaves wilt and crumple and the grapevine dies. Hopefully, the vineyardist will have trained up some of the suckers from down below.

The southern slope of Salvini's vineyard recorded low temperatures of -14° to -16° F. This was enough to wipe out three-quarters of his Chenin Blanc crop and to severely damage his Merlot, Sauvignon Blanc, and Chardonnay crop.

—RED WILLOW VINEYARD—

From Salvini's we got into Walt's new silver Chevrolet truck. I took over the driving as we were heading west to Red Willow Vineyard, owned by Mike Sauer, located about an hour's drive away. To get there Walt instructed me to get back on Interstate 82, and we drove past Grandview, then Sunnyside, and then left the interstate at Granger to take the back way to Sauer's vineyard, twelve and a half miles west of Wapato.

Mike Sauer's son Jonathan greeted us upon our arrival. He is a student at Washington State University where he is studying until he comes back to the ranch to help out. Mike Sauer pulled up in his big pickup. He was genuinely happy to see Walt and George. I could tell that he has great respect for them. I think the respect is mutual. Walt is greatly pleased by Sauer's success.

We drove up into the vineyards. Much of Red Willow Vineyards is on steep sloping benchland hills of the Ahtanum Ridge. There was very little evidence of damage in his vineyards except for his Pinot Noir block and a portion of Merlot planted at a lower elevation. The Pinot Noir block was a bald spot in the vineyard. Located on the western slope, it was severely damaged. Mike had a mind to tear it out but said Columbia Winery wants him to continue growing it. He mused that maybe a different clone would have fared better, such as the Clevner Mariafeld, recommended to him by Porter Lombard at Oregon State University. At the base of the hills, temperatures were -18° F, while higher up they ranged between -11° and -13° F.

His Cabernet Sauvignon vines were lush. Mike reported that the live primary buds had a survival rate of between 80 to 90 percent, far greater than the 50 percent expected back in February. Mike's vineyard rises to 1,300 feet elevation. Most of his plantings are between 1,150 to 1,250 feet.

Walt said, "I have found, for this year, that for every 100 feet in elevation gain, it gets 1° F warmer."

Mike noted that there was also eight inches of snowfall on the ground, which helped to insulate and reflect light back up to the vine.

We continued up the hill, its peak dominated by the rock chapel, which Mike calls the Monsignor chapel, a twenty-by-fifteen-foot monument he built in honor of the local priest. Below is the Syrah vineyard, which Mike calls Monsignor Vineyard. Along the way we stopped to look at the Nebbiolo and the Sangiovese; both looked strong and healthy. The Sangiovese suffered some bud injury but the trunks did well. Mike had new plantings of both Sangiovese Grosso and Sangiovese Piccolo; the latter variety he obtained by swapping Syrah for Sangiovese Piccolo with Gary Figgins in Walla Walla.

Syrah may be Red Willow's best success story. The Syrah vineyard's survival of the cold reinforced Mike's decision to have planted more Syrah. Mike said, "I think Syrah is going to be the next grape, don't you?"

From high atop Monsignor Vineyard, I marveled at the three hundred sixty–degree view, especially to the west. Less than a mile away is Mike's Olney Springs Vineyard, set on a slight mound, planted to Gewurztraminer and Riesling. It is nestled up against Ahtanum Ridge to the north. About ten miles southwest is Fort Simcoe at the base of the Simcoe Mountains and Toppenish Ridge. This is the path early settlers took to Yakima, some carrying grape cuttings.

Mike insisted that we have lunch with him. Jonathan had been grilling chicken back at Mike's workshed at the bottom of the vineyard. Mike brought out some wines for us: 1994 Graciano (or Morestal), an experimental wine made by Porter Lombard; a 1993 Sangiovese, Molly's Cuvee, made by Peter Dow of Cavatappi Winery; a 1992 Syrah by Columbia Winery; and a 1991 Thurston-Wolfe Lemberger. The Graciano was tart and full, much like a cross between a Lemberger and a hybrid grape. Mike said he served it because he thought George and Walt might find it interesting. The Sangiovese was very good. It was cherrylike with a pleasing tealike quality in the finish, dry and lingering. Its lighter weight was refreshing and true to type. Next, the 1992 Syrah was quite spectacular, brimming with rich fruit aromas, primarily of cherry with a hint of cherry stone, which carries through on the palate; it was round and full with just the right amount of flavor tartness. It was easy to understand Mike's and Columbia Winery's excitement for this grape. Our last wine was the 1991 Lemberger, which was very smooth and full, with hints of blueberry fruit.

Mike served this last wine with Walt and George in mind, knowing that it was one of their preferred grapes. George told how it always made the most consistent wine. Both were slightly disappointed that wineries and consumers have not embraced it more. But they laughed it off. Walt even took an unusual poke at Stimson Lane and recalled that President Allen Shoup made a stabbing comment about Lemberger at last year's World Vinifera Conference by questioning its value as a premium variety.

Mike would like to see more efforts made toward producing a classy Lemberger, treating the grape more like a Cabernet Sauvignon in the cellar; he said this in deference to Walt and George.

Mike said, "I thought I always owed you guys."

Walt laughed and replied, "You're our pride and joy!"

To which George added, "We've gotten you hooked."

At that Mike sat back, chuckled, turned to Jonathan at his elbow, and said, "Well, it sure beats baling hay."

—PAUL PORTTEUS WINERY—

Our next stop was in Zillah to visit the Paul Portteus Winery and vineyards located high on the Roza, on the slope of the Rattlesnake Hills. I had heard that the Portteus vineyard had been hard hit by the January cold weather but I wasn't prepared for what I saw. After the luxurious growth at Red Willow Vineyards, it looked as if someone had just dropped a bomb on the Portteus vineyard.

Paul's home sits right next to his winery, separated only by the driveway. Paul answered the door and was happy to see Walt and George, and walked us out to his vineyard that surrounds the house and winery. He has about 45 acres planted to grapevines. Much of Paul's vineyard is newly planted to Merlot but it also has Zinfandel, Syrah, Cabernet Sauvignon, and Chardonnay as well as a bit of Cabernet Franc. Hardest hit were his Merlot, Chardonnay, and Zinfandel, nearly wiping out his total production and killing the vines back to their roots.

Suckers were in evidence on the vines. Paul had been busy tying the suckers up alongside the dead trunks. In the Chardonnay vineyard Paul snapped off a dead shoot from last year. *Snap, snap, snap...*was heard while Paul broke off shoots and told how his vineyard got up to 65° F in mid-January just prior to the cold weather coming in. He thought that the warm solar temperatures may have prematurely pulled the Chardonnay and Merlot vines out of dormancy and made them susceptible to winter damage. Paul told how his vineyard tends to get a bit warmer and it is one of the reasons his grapes are sought out by wineries, as they show ripe, full flavors.

I noticed that the soils were full of rocks; some of them reminded me of the smooth, red, river rocks around Maryhill and Goldendale along the Columbia. Paul said his vineyard is dominated by caliche soils, consisting of calcified rock. The vineyard is located at between 1,350 feet and 1,400 feet, one of the highest vineyards in eastern Washington. That suggests that the soil types are probably quite ancient.

Unfortunately this premier site's warmer climate helped cause the extensive damage we were witnessing. Paul said that temperatures at his house showed a low of -10° F, enough to decimate his Chardonnay, Merlot, and Zinfandel.

In the winery I tasted Paul's 1994 Paul Portteus Winery Merlot. It is wonderfully rich and smooth with a suggestion of blueberries and blackberries. I could taste the ripe flavors and the softer acids from the '94 vintage. Paul told us the wine just got a Gold Medal at the Western Washington Fair in Puyallup, Washington.

—COLD CREEK VINEYARD—

On Wednesday we decided to travel north to Cold Creek Vineyard, located on the back side of the Rattlesnake Hills and the Yakima Ridge. To get there we drove north out of Grandview. Walt wanted me to drive past the new winery facility for Paul Thomas Cellars, built by Associated Vintners. The $2.2 million winery is set among a large vineyard of 220 acres that originally had been planted by Cascade Crest Estates and called Jolona Vineyard. A drive-by glance at the vineyard showed extensive damage to the Chardonnay grapes.

It is ironic that Chardonnay has become a leading varietal for the Paul Thomas brand. Recently I had lunch with Paul Thomas at his lovely log-cabin home outside of Woodinville. I wondered if there was any misgivings that his name, and his winery, were now showing up in the grocery stores as a ubiquitous brand. Paul seemed nonchalant.

He laughed, throwing back his head, bespectacled in his thick, round wire-rimmed glasses. He recalled how he and Brian Carter, his winemaker, cautiously made their first Chardonnay in 1986. He says, "We were afraid of it."

Paul didn't want to make Chardonnay like everyone else. To his knowledge his would be the only un-oaked Chardonnay in America. Paul was afraid that it would fail. He may have been afraid of its success as well. At the time everyone was making Chardonnay and he felt that he wanted to concentrate on his dry fruit wines and his lighter styled Cabernet Sauvingon.

As a precaution they sold the wine under a differnt name, Rush Cutter Bay Chardonnay, and bottled 900 cases in 1.5 liter bottles and sold it to Anthony's Homeport restaurant. It sold out fast. Paul and Brian couldn't believe how easy it sold. And how easy it was to make. They were use to pitting cherries or dealing with oxalic acid precipitates in Rhubarb. They bought their first Chardonnay grapes from the Indian Wells vineyard on the Wahluke Slope and had no idea what kind of wines they were going to make. Consumers wanted more.

Paul Thomas relented. They then began selling a non-oak aged Chardonnay. Crisp and fresh—a style that became the Paul Thomas signature. And now it is the signature style for Associated Vintners, as owners of the brand. Paul sold the winery in 1990 to his later winemaker, Mark Cave. Today, Mark helps direct the winemaking of the Paul Thomas brand for the Associated Vintners. Paul ruefully notes that today Paul Thomas Cellars produces up to 150,000 cases of wine, much of that lightly oaked Chardonnay.

Nearby, just north of Sunnyside, is one of the largest vineyards in Hogue Cellars' stable. It is located northeast of Snipes Mountain, which I could see in the distance. It is called Sunnyside Vineyard and its 200 acres are planted to Merlot, Cabernet Sauvignon, Chenin Blanc, Sauvignon Blanc, Gewurztraminer, Semillon, Riesling, and Chardonnay. Again, extensive damage was obvious. Along the roadway we found a huge mound of dead grapevines piled about ten feet high and maybe twenty feet long. I stopped my van and pulled one of the vines off the pile. It was big and heavy; the size of the vine's trunk, about the size of my arm, indicated that it was nearly fifteen years old. I snapped a picture of Walt and George, each holding a cordon on either side in their hands; the trunk of the vine was nearly their height. It is a wonderful picture; the grapevine's cordons appear to be arms around its buddies. It is a good example of a grapevine with a broad root system. Walt has said that the root system of the grapevine will equal the growth of the plant above ground, and often be slightly larger; leaf and shoot thinning may make the vine look smaller. The root system looked like an upside-down apple tree, full of branches.

From Sunnyside Vineyard we got onto State Highway 241, which took us over the Rattlesnake Hills. Driving through the lush summer growth of the surrounding farmlands, I recalled flying over this area four years ago. Driving through it, I was struck by how varied the land was, with gentle mounds and hills, slopes and canyons, creeks and canals. I reflected on all that I have come to learn about grape and wine history, about viticulture, and about the people and institutions that make up this industry. It is as varied as the landscape.

Beyond Sunnyside the surroundings changed dramatically as we climbed the final slope of the Rattlesnake Hills and began to descend into Cold Creek Canyon, wedged between Yakima Ridge and Umtanum Ridge. From Highway 24, Cold Creek Vineyard appeared to the north, sloping in a south to southeasterly direction. The lush growth was spectacular among the bordering sagebrush and dried prairie grass.

The entrance to the vineyard announced that Cold Creek Vineyard is dedicated to André Tchelistcheff. Cold Creek is set at about 1,100 to 1,200 feet elevation. It is easy to see why Walt still favors this vineyard; it is unmatched in its nearly uniform slope and orientation to the sun. At the trailer we met Jim Herrmann, a tall, lanky man who manages the vineyard. Jim Herrmann told us that his father, his brother, and he planted the first 100 acres back in 1973. I guessed that Jim must have been in high school then. Herrmann told us that they have lost about two-thirds of the Chardonnay.

Walt, George, and I headed out into the vineyard. It is 660 acres, a vast sea of green, yellow, and brown. The Grenache vineyard was noticeably browner, lots of dead wood. While we were looking at the vines, Jesse Sandoval, the production supervisor, drove up in his all-terrain buggy. With temperatures in the mid-'70s and a beautiful clear blue sky, he appeared overdressed to me. Under his jean jacket was a dark blue hooded sweatshirt, capped by his round white helmet. I assumed that he had probably been out here since early morning. It was about ten o'clock and plenty warm for me. Jesse nodded and said, "Grenache is crazy." They plan on tearing it out and replanting to Syrah.

He gave us directions to the Chardonnay blocks, Blocks E10 and E12, and pointed out how the two blocks, each about 20 acres planted at the same time, are contiguous to each other, the one block below the other and divided by a twenty-foot roadway. He said that last year the blocks had different growth patterns. The northerly and upper block seemed more vigorous and productive. The lower vineyard seemed weaker. This year they have reversed themselves. The upper block, Block E10, was devastated by the cold air, while the lower block was almost unaffected.

Jesse shook his round brown face and said, "It doesn't make any sense."

Walt chuckled and said, "Maybe we are not supposed to understand it."

This struck me as an odd thing for Walt to say. It didn't sound like the scientist, but the Methodist, speaking.

—WAHLUKE SLOPE—

From Cold Creek we got back on the highway and headed north to the Wahluke Slope. Driving along the river, now on Highway 243, we could see Sentinel Gap, a gap in the Saddle Mountains that allows the Columbia River to flow south. Past the tiny hamlet of Desert Aire we turned up into the 300-acre Indian Wells Vineyard. It is a broad vineyard that slopes southwesterly toward the Columbia River. I was awestruck at how large the vineyard was. And how lush it was. There was little evidence of much damage, although there were considerable suckers shooting up from the base of many of the grapevines. The grapevines looked like shaved French poodles with hairy feet, ears, and tops. The vineyard looked like it was in need of some shearing. On either side of a road that runs through the middle of the vineyard, the rows of vines ran against the slope of the vineyard and were oriented north and south. The rows of vines ran a half mile in each direction. At the south end of the rows was a line of large poplar trees, as wind breaks.

This vastness contrasted sharply with the more developed Yakima Valley. Cold Creek and Indian Wells warmed us up to this scale, but I was still immensely impressed as we drove to the top of the Wahluke Slope. On the highway driving east out of Mattawa, there was a series of orchards and vineyards set against the hillside of the Saddle Mountains. Each block was about 40 acres, set apart from one another by wind breaks. Below on the flats were fields of potatoes, alfalfa, mint, and corn. It was dazzling and inspiring, that land can be so productive and plentiful.

We stopped to visit the Rosebud Ranches, owned by Don and Norma Toci. In a letter to Walt, they had recalled how they first came to grow grapes on the Wahluke Slope. They had become interested in wines when touring Preston Wine Cellars in the mid-'70s. Bill and JoAnn Preston weren't there at the time, but their son Mark inspired the Tocis with his enthusiasm for the vineyard and the wines they produced. Norma Toci wrote, "In the fall of 1978 we contracted enough grape cuttings to plant 40 acres. (I wanted to plant 160 but Don had a fit!) We did not have a farm yet but we were looking. The realtor we were dealing with was an old man by the name of George Calvert who had been the justice of the peace in years past in Moses Lake. He knew this country very well and had been an astute 'old-timer' who knew soils. He showed us the Wahluke Slope and said in all seriousness, 'This is a wonderful country, a long way from market, harsh sometimes and hell on horses and women, but a good country.' He was right about all that!"

The Tocis uprooted from Arizona with this enthusiasm, their Arizona farm being a victim of suburban sprawl. Their initial 40-acre planting, in 1979, consisted of 20 acres of White Riesling and 20 acres of Chenin Blanc, which has blossomed to 253 acres of wine grapes. Don Toci, with a degree in agronomy at the University of Arizona, epitomizes one large element of the Washington wine industry: he is an independent, well-to-do farmer turned grape grower with the wonderful but risky innocence of not being wine knowledgeable or wine sophisticated but, rather, a thoroughbred farmer.

Down the slope was Weinbau Vineyard, now managed by Sagemoor Farms. It is a sprawling 364-acre vineyard planted mostly to

Chardonnay. We chose not to stop, but from the van it looked surprisingly good. There was very little evidence of damage. We were getting pretty good at drive-by sightings; George and Walt could identify from the van the varieties according to the color of the vines or by their growth characteristics. Semillon leaves, for instance, are a lighter green. Next to Weinbau Vineyard is the former Langguth Winery, looking rather abandoned and isolated in this land of wide-open space.

From Weinbau we headed south and crossed the Columbia again at the Vernita Bridge. This time we drove southeast on Highway 240, skirting the Hanford Site, along the backside of the Rattlesnake Hills. It was early afternoon and I was getting a bit tired, and also a little perturbed at myself that I couldn't keep up with these men in their mid-eighties. The warm sun and the monotony of the brown hills was lulling me into a drowsy state.

Abruptly Walt broke the silence: "One explanation for why those Chardonnay blocks at Cold Creek are different may have to do with the shade from the hills to the south," pointing to Yakima Ridge just southwest of us.

I knew that Walt wasn't going to leave that puzzle alone. Continuing, he added, "Remember how Paul Portteus suggested that the 65° F January days may have activated his Chardonnay vines? Well, the same thing probably happened at Cold Creek, except at Cold Creek part of the vineyard may be in the shadow of the Yakima Ridge in January when the sun is so low. It may be that the top block, Block E10, may have been in the sun while the lower block wasn't, thus remaining cool and dormant."

I smiled. This man is incredible.

—RED MOUNTAIN—

We arrived at Red Mountain in the afternoon. The temperatures were reaching the low '80s, hot enough for me. Our first stop was Klipsun Vineyards. We entered the vineyard from the road that runs along the Yakima River. The vineyard looked its normal perfect self: clean-cut grass between the rows and manicured vines. We got out of the car and looked closer. There were a few scattered dead vines amongst the Semillon vines and those vines that looked healthy were devoid of fruit clusters. It was going to be a thin harvest.

A check on the Merlot and Sauvignon Blanc also showed a minimum of fruit. These vines had been severely pruned after the winter damage. It appeared to be a case of over-management. Fred Artz may have erred on the conservative side in his effort to save the grapevines. It is not necessarily a bad strategy because next year the grapevines will be in good shape to produce a healthy crop, but he sacrificed this year's harvest for next year's.

We then drove through Kiona Vineyard directly east of Klipsun. There was more evidence of vineyard damage here, especially to Merlot, Chardonnay, and Chenin Blanc. The Chenin Blanc was almost completely gone.

Across the road was Ciel du Cheval Vineyard. We drove into the entrance, where we saw Richard Holmes talking with Chris Camarda of Andrew Will Winery on Vashon Island. Holmes told us that his Merlot was hit hard. "It's gone," he said, rather wistfully. He told us the Cabernet Sauvignon looked good, and part of the Chenin Blanc was saved because it was under the sole wind machine in the vineyard.

Holmes indicated that they may go completely to a fan system of pruning, training the vines in a fan arrangement up from the crown at ground level. This would allow them to lay the canes and trunks down and cover them with soil, something that the industry stopped doing back in 1972. It is a lot of labor and requires retraining new canes up when the trunks get too hard to bend down, which occurs after about four years. While the spurs and canes are producing fruit on the upper portion of the trunk, new canes are trained up when needed to provide fruiting wood for the following year.

Chris Camarda looked sad. He produces an excellent Merlot but he was finding it difficult to find any grapes for his wine. One of his cherished vineyards in Walla Walla, Pepper Bridge Vineyard, had been almost completely frozen to the ground. He was not happy to see his sources on Red Mountain also badly hit. Even though Andrew Will Winery has an excellent reputation, and thus would be a fine candidate for receiving grapes, he is in tough competition with local wineries, and other reputable wineries such as Quilceda Creek and Leonetti Cellars that have been buying grapes from these vineyards for nearly two decades.

Up the road from Klipsun was the new winery for Hedges Cellars. It was spectacular in the afternoon sun. Walt and I have literally watched the vineyards and winery sprout up over the last three years. We were taking a picture of the look-alike French chateau when Scott Williams of Kiona Vineyards and Winery stopped on his way to his cherry farm up the slope. Williams confirmed that he lost most of his Chardonnay, Chenin Blanc, and Merlot. He said he saw the recorded temperatures for his vineyard go down to -14.5° F. From our viewpoint at Hedges Vineyard, it was clear that Kiona Vineyards was partially in a pocket, a dangerous situation for pooling of cold air.

In contrast, the Hedges vineyard looked almost unscathed, the green growth a seeming carpet for the chateau against the backdrop of the brown hills behind. We drove up to Scott's in-laws' house, at one of the highest points on Red Mountain, to take a picture. Scott Williams has said that he has a picture taken during the mid-'80s from a similar spot, and there was only one square of green in the picture, Kiona Vineyard. Today, green dominates the landscape.

—*SAGEMOOR FARMS AND CANOE RIDGE*—

On Thursday, we headed to Sagemoor Farms and Canoe Ridge, a broad circle encompassing the Columbia Basin and the Horse Heaven Hills. Walt had me drive by Gordon Brothers Winery. It is a new facility just off of Interstate 182, at Road 68, the road we will take to Sagemoor Farms to the north. Gordon Brothers Winery has just located between Richland and Pasco in a new industrial area and nearby housing development. Currently the winery stands by itself. Its architectural design is kind of a modern tudor brick. It is designed to attract wine tasters from the nearby freeway, and its homelike appeal can accommodate wine events or banquets. Its immediate neighbor is a new baseball stadium for the local Tri-Cities Posses baseball team. It is all so new, so California in its approach—wide-open and car-dependent.

Driving on Road 68, one can easily distinguish the bluffs where Sagemoor Farms is located from about four miles away. Near the entrance to the farm were Cabernet Sauvignon vines planted in '72. One vine, dead, stood among the others. Most of the other vines seemed little affected, and it appeared that they will get a decent crop. Across the driveway is a vineyard with Pinot Noir. Walt and George estimated that Sagemoor might get about 25 percent of crop.

We then drove up to the other vineyards, Bacchus and Dionysus, five miles further north. This magnificent setting never ceases to astonish me. From on top of the vineyards it is a carpet of green, sloping southwest, looking west at the blue Columbia and the brown basin of the Hanford Site. This time, however, there were patches of brown among the green. Large patches. Chardonnay: obliterated.

The Merlot vineyard appeared to have been abandoned. The grass between the rows grew tall, suckers shot out of the grapevines, dead vines were set among the uncontrolled growth. Nature in its natural state was not at all beautiful. It was rough and chaotic. Walt said under his breath, "It's a nightmare." He said to George that he thought maybe the southwest slope may have allowed the trunks to get exposed to too much sunshine during the cold.

Walt and George both know how conscientious Erick Hanson is. They assumed that the vineyard had been abandoned for economic reasons. There was no point at this stage in putting money into the vineyard; better to wait to see if the entire vineyard will be replanted. These Merlot vines were the same ones that David Lake, of Columbia Winery, had walked through.

Further down the vineyard there was a large block that was blue and brown. The blue was the result of a plastic wrap that was rolled around each newly planted grapevine in that block. The wrap extended from the ground up about thirty inches and was used to facilitate the growth of the vine. Additionally it protected the tender vine from wind and any predators. Walt said the wrap will help the vine produce a small crop the second year and a near-normal crop in its third year. It looked like a cemetery memorializing soldiers lost in war. It was kind of a reverse cemetery; vines had been replanted to replace the dead vines. I suspected that next year this may be the look of the Merlot block.

The damage to the Chardonnay and the Merlot compared to the damage we witnessed at Paul Portteus's vineyard. We had been told that nearby vineyards, Moreman Vineyards, Balcom and Moe Vineyards, and Preston Vineyards, suffered some comparable damage. We had seen enough.

We then drove through Kennewick and got on Interstate 82 heading south to Umatilla. We lunched at a tavern in Plymouth, then drove the short distance to Paterson on Highway 14. Along the way we found a modest vineyard along the flat land bordering the Columbia River. Walt and George couldn't recall who owned the vineyard, but Walt knew he had a record advising the person against planting in that location. The vines looked healthy, however. It appeared planted to Chardonnay and Riesling. I am always surprised how many of these small, lesser-known vineyards there are. Usually they are small personal investments by professionals: doctors, dentists, lawyers.

Nearby, across the railroad tracks, are a number of orchards that sit on rather level ground. As I drove, Walt and George talked about the owners of the property. It dawned on me that they were talking about

Vere Brummund's original Veredon Vineyard. This was where Brummund had planted his dream. I was struck that it is such a difficult site. The railroad track, at the bottom of the south slope, creates a barrier so that the cold air has nowhere to drain off the rather flat site.

Our next stop was at the Columbia Crest vineyard, just north of Paterson. We entered through the service entrance. The lower portion of the vineyard was spectacular in its gentle but noticeable slope toward the Columbia River. One of the first vineyard blocks that we viewed was the Grenache. It had been badly hit, though they may get some kind of a crop. The Semillon, which is another sensitive variety, seemed to have fared quite well, even from a recent May frost.

Mark Shepherd, one of the vineyard managers, drove up when he saw our van. He told us that the temperatures dipped down to about -9° to -10° F here at Caliche Vineyard, but it got slightly colder, as low as -12° F, higher up in the vineyard. Shepherd told us that he expected the damage to be far greater. He said their vineyards were saved by a fog that covered the ridge, settling at the bottom of the vineyard but spreading up and over to the north side. It is hard to know if the fog saved the vineyards by protecting the vines from the cold air or by protecting the vines from getting warmed up by the sun. It was impressive how lucky they were.

We drove to the top of the vineyard. Each block and vineyard was clearly marked. At Raven's Butte Vineyard, we stopped and admired the fruitfulness of the Cabernet Franc vines. George said admiringly, "We haven't seen any grapes like these." Chardonnay vines in one of the blocks appeared unhurt.

We then stopped at the Clore Vineyard. Without guidance, we couldn't remember the irrigation scheme for the four different color-coded sections. I'm sure that this cold damage will provide Wample with more ammunition in getting growers to reduce their late and early watering.

Next stop was Canoe Ridge Vineyard, owned by the Chalone Group and investors from Walla Walla. We drove up to vineyard manager Bob Brown's home, set next to the vineyard. Brown told us that temperatures dropped down to -7° F. He told us that there was very little damage in their vineyard. Merlot was damaged slightly, while Chardonnay and Cabernet Sauvignon were hardly damaged at all. Brown said their damage came mainly from spring frosts in May. He confirmed that during the winter cold, fog had played a role in protecting the vines.

Brown shook his head, laughed gently, and said, "The fog may not be here next time." He looked out over the 100-acre vineyard and seemed quite pleased. He also told us that there are plans to increase the vineyard by 25 or 30 acres next year. I was impressed with their optimism.

Recently, I visited the new Canoe Ridge Winery in Walla Walla. It is a distinctive old brick building that was used to store railroad cars. The facility was restored in 1994 with slight improvements and additions to make a functional and attractive winery ready to accept grapes from the '94 vintage.

My winery guide was Matt Woodward, son of Phil Woodward, the managing partner of the Chalone Group. Phil Woodward, when an accountant in San Francisco, had begun in the wine business through his association with Chalone Winery. Matt grew up in the vineyards and wineries of California. He is twenty-five years old. He attended school in Portland at Lewis and Clark University. He recalled his first exposure to Canoe Ridge wines: He had first tasted the wines at a Chalone Group shareholder event. With 1,500 shareholders in attendance, he was attracted to a commotion in the back of the room. People were tasting and getting excited about the new wines made from Canoe Ridge. Those first wines were made at Hyatt Vineyards Winery in Zillah.

The Canoe Ridge Winery labels are quite stunning with a cream-colored background and a pen-and-ink drawing of a canoe lying alongside the Columbia River. A wonderful blend of old and new. And the wines have been a critical success since their initial release. In 1996 the winery intends to bottle 18,000 cases of wine; by 1997 it will bottle 22,000 cases. I was staggered by that amount, by its ability to sell that much wine in such a short time. The wines have been well received by the media and by consumers. I am sure it helps to have the marketing savvy of the Chalone Group as well.

The winemaker, John Abbott, was the former winemaker at Acacia Winery in California. It was not the intent of Canoe Ridge Winery to produce much Chardonnay, but the wine has been enormously successful and Chardonnay sales represent nearly half of its current sales. It was easy to see why upon tasting the '95 Chardonnay. It was a buttery and fresh rendition of a Washington Chardonnay. It was really a beautifully made wine without too much oak or heavy fruit.

Matt allowed me to taste some of the wines out of barrel from both the '94 and '95 vintages. The wines were impressive. They were well made and captured the right proportion of oak and berrylike fruit. It seemed to me that the flavors of the wines tended to be less heavy, a tendency that I now associate with wines from the Canoe Ridge area. I was particularly impressed with the '95 Merlot with its remarkably soft texture and underlying concentration of berrylike fruit flavors.

Back at the vineyard, with those flavor memories, I stood up on a little knoll above Canoe Ridge Vineyards and looked down at the vineyard while Walt took a picture of George in the vineyard. I could almost smell the lightness of the wine standing in the wind above the vineyard.

Right next door is Canoe Ridge Estate. We stopped in at the vineyard trailer-office to get a map and to give notice that we were going out into the vineyard. Our first stop was the Merlot vineyard, planted in 1992. The vines looked perfectly content. It was difficult to see any damage.

We then drove to the top of the ridge where we could view most of the vineyard. It is a sprawling vineyard of 740 acres, set along the top and southern slope of the ridge. It is not so much one solid block but rather a broad swath of the slope. The young growth and the pattern of the rows of vines created a corduroy texture to the hillside. In a few places it was easy to see worn patches, presumably where cold air had settled.

Overall, the vineyard was almost unscathed. I was really dumbfounded. I was prepared to see much worse. I had heard that the Walla Walla Valley was near totally frozen back to the ground. We have since learned that only 45 percent of 1995's crop is expected for the 1996 harvest. Walt has provided me with data from other recent winter-damaged harvests: The worst winter affecting wine grapes was '78–'79; '79 production was 28 percent of '78. In 1990–'91, a more recent winter-damaged harvest, production in '91 was 68 percent of '90.

Nearly all of the damage that we witnessed was specific to Chardonnay, Chenin Blanc, Merlot, Grenache, and Semillon. Other varieties seemed hardly or moderately affected and, once again, some varieties showed remarkable resilience, such as the Cabernet Franc, Pinot Gris, and Syrah, three promising new varieties.

These varieties show the versatile growing conditions of eastern Washington. In France the Cabernet Franc is grown extensively along the banks of the Loire River. There, it rarely reaches full color and is often turned into beautiful rosé wines. In St. Emilion, on the eastern edges of the Bordeaux district, Cabernet Franc plays a major supporting role. Although Merlot dominates in this area, Cabernet

Franc represents 20 percent of the vines. Its noblest expression is found in the wines of Chateau Cheval Blanc, where it is the predominant grape. In visits to St. Emilion I remember the broad open plains and the sandy soil types similar to the soils in eastern Washington.

Jancis Robinson, in *Vines, Grapes and Wines,* wrote, "Cabernet Franc wines are rather more herbaceous than Cabernet Sauvignon, lower in tannins, acids and extract and therefore more approachable, with a distinctive aroma that reminds some of raspberries, others of violets and me of pencil shavings. When blended with Merlot as in St. Emilion, the Merlot fills in the holes of Cabernet Franc's rather lean structure and the blend magically makes a lush mouth-filler." She then adds in an interesting aside, "Cabernet Franc wines never taste like Cabernet Sauvignon, but Cabernet Sauvignon can taste very like Cabernet Franc when made in too cool a climate. This is demonstrated particularly in Washington State, curiously mirroring the phenomenon concerning Bordeaux's two most important white grapes whereby cool-climate Semillon takes on a grassiness very like Sauvignon Blanc."

Syrah is the stellar grape of the Rhone Valley and produces spectacularly muscular wines from the hilltop vineyards of Hermitage and Cote Rotie. And although these vineyards are actually located north of Bordeaux, they are often associated with wines from the warmer, more southerly climate of the Rhone Valley. Syrah's hardiness to winter conditions and its love of radiant sun attest to the potential for this grape in eastern Washington. Eastern Washington, in its vastness, might even duplicate the micro-setting of the Rhone hills: warm summer months with cool nighttime temperatures and lingering, ideal harvest conditions.

We took a shortcut by turning north off of Highway 14, along the Columbia River, on a private road that cuts through the Mercer family farms. Walt chirped in, "I know where there is some really good vineyard land if you want to buy it." My interest piqued, I envisioned putting together an investment group to put in a 100-acre vineyard similar to Canoe Ridge Vineyard. Driving through the vineyards primes the fantasies. Then Walt added, while pointing at a nearby ridge, "If you have eight to nine million dollars, there is a terrific site with the potential for nearly a thousand acres." With that, my dream vanished in a poof.

Walt had pointed to a site on a broad hillside that faces east and stretches from the south to the north. Later I looked it up in my *Washington Atlas and Gazetteer,* and it appeared to be Golgotha Butte, not as aesthetically pleasing a name as Canoe Ridge. My dictionary says that Golgotha is a place of suffering and sacrifice; Christ hung from his cross there. Although I no longer fantasized planting a vineyard on that site, I was struck by Wally Opdycke's earlier vision for Columbia Crest, then later UST's vision for Canoe Ridge. Who would be next?

We drove past Mercer Vineyards. From the road the vineyard seemed little damaged, although I confess that by this time I was pretty well done for the day. We rolled past beautiful and bountiful fields of winter wheat due for harvest, their golden yellows and exuberant greens vibrant in the afternoon sun. We turned onto Ward Gap Road to make our descent into the Yakima Valley. Walt, clearly nervous with my driving near the edge of the road, asked me if I was familiar with driving on fresh gravel as I took the sharp turns down into the valley. I could feel his anxiety of being so close to the road's edge, especially from the perspective of the front seat in my big van. I smiled.

The Yakima Valley was absolutely stunning in the late afternoon; the sun, which was on our left, sent horizontal yellowed sunrays shooting across the valley. I'm sure it was an optical illusion caused by my van's windshield, but in that moment it was dramatic and poignant: In that giving, golden yellow light, I clearly saw the purpose of this book, of passing on the knowledge from Dr. Clore's generation to my own, like propagated cuttings from one vineyard to the next.

CHRONOLOGY

Bold type indicates a significant historical event.

<u>15 million–12 million B.C.</u> Series of extraordinary and catastrophic magma flows covered much of central and eastern Washington with a thick basalt layer.

<u>14,000–11,000 B.C.</u> Series of enormous glacial-water floods, known as Bretz or Spokane Floods, originated from collapsing ice dams at Lake Missoula, in Montana. They roared across a vast area of central-eastern Washington along much of the route of Columbia River, ending up in Willamette Valley in Oregon. Some flows equalled ten times the flow of all the world's rivers.

<u>13,500–11,500 B.C.</u> Existence of Vashon Stade, last glacier that upon receding helped form the Puget Sound Basin.

<u>1805–1806 A.D.</u> Lewis and Clark explored and mapped Snake and Columbia Rivers to Pacific Ocean at request of President Thomas Jefferson.

<u>1810</u> Spokane House established as first trading post center on Columbia River.

<u>1814</u> "Columbia Valley" shown on approved edition of Lewis and Clark's map.

<u>1818</u> Fort Nez Perce (Fort Walla Walla), established near Wallula, had gardens and fruit trees.

<u>1824–25</u> **Hudson's Bay Company established Fort Vancouver (now Vancouver, Washington). First grapes grown were from seed brought from England.**

<u>1825</u> Fort Colvile (later spelled Colville) established as an outfitting post near Kettle Falls on the Columbia by Hudson's Bay Company. Ten years later grapes were found growing there.

<u>1833</u> Columbia Country existed prior to Oregon Territory. Oregon Territory declared in 1833.

<u>1836</u> Narcissa Whitman, while visiting Fort Vancouver, wrote in her journal, "The grapes are just ripe and I am feasting on them finely."

<u>1838</u> William Bruce, gardener at Fort Vancouver for Hudson's Bay Company, spent two weeks visiting Joseph Paxton, famed botanist of Chisick Gardens. Brought cuttings, likely Black Hamburg, for planting at McLoughlin's new house.

<u>1839</u> At Fort Vancouver, "along fluted pillars a grape vine trailed and tangled;" reported to have been from Mission cuttings.

<u>1847</u> **First grape variety planted in Oregon was Isabella, an American hybrid variety, from Luelling and Meek Nursery in Milwaukie, in Willamette Valley.**

<u>1853–55</u> European and California wines available through numerous outlets in Puget Sound communities such as Olympia, Seattle, and Steilacoom.

<u>1854</u> **Three nurseries in Puget Sound area listed American and European grape varieties for sale.**

<u>1859</u> William Meek awarded medal at California State Fair for his white Isabella wine.

<u>1859–60</u> **Frank Orselli and A. B. Roberts were probably the first to plant grapes in Walla Walla area.**
A. P. Shipley, of Willamette Valley, imported "during the 1860s" from eastern United States 45 varieties of different grapes, American and European. Later he discarded all but Concord.

<u>1861–62</u> **Severest winter in Klickitat and Yakima Counties—all rivers froze solid except the Columbia, which froze fifteen feet deep.**

<u>1863</u> **Numerous grape plantings made in Walla Walla Valley: 80 varieties by A. B. Roberts and 21 varieties by Philip Ritz.**

<u>1865</u> **Frank Orselli, an Italian immigrant, retailed wine and grew grapes, as did H. P. Isaacs, in the Walla Walla area.**

<u>1869</u> Thomas B. Welch developed a method for preserving grape juice and marketed the juice as "unfermented wine."

<u>1869–71</u> Joseph Schannoand his sons, Charles and Emil, planted grapes near Union Gap, taking water out of Yakima River and Ahtanum Creek.

<u>1871</u> Herke family, German immigrants, planted grapes near Tampico west of Union Gap that still persist without care.

<u>1872</u> Lambert Evans, from Florida, planted American grapes on Stretch Island in Puget Sound area.

Philip Miller, a German, settled in Wenatchee, ending up twenty years later with 25 acres of orchard and 8 acres of grapes and making 1,400 to 1,500 gallons of wine annually. Noted to have used cuttings from Schanno vineyard.

Louis Delsol, a French immigrant, planted European grapes in Lewiston-Clarkston area.

<u>1873</u> John Galler, a German, planted fruit trees and grapes in Wenatchee area and made "sour German wines."

<u>1874–75</u> Oregon nurseries in Portland and Salem were sources of American and European grape varieties.

<u>1875</u> Temperature of -29° F in January recorded by Captain Isaac Stevens in Walla Walla.

<u>1876</u> *The Walla Walla Statesman* reported "that Frank Orselli—is cultivating the grape—successfully and has been experimenting in making wine." Also, Jean Marie Abadie of Walla Walla produced 400 gallons of white wine and 150 gallons of red wine.

<u>1880</u> The Moxee Company, owned by Gardiner Hubbard and Alexander Bell, planted cuttings of Johannisberg Riesling and Mission grapes from California in Moxee, east of Yakima. The company failed during the financial panic of 1893.

Robert Schleicher planted a vineyard three miles east of Lewiston, Idaho, along Clearwater River after filing a pre-emptive claim on 416 acres.

In early 1880s, Jewitt family planted American grape varieties on slopes below White Salmon.

<u>1882</u> Mr. Terrill, located at Juniper Springs (above Vernita), grew grapes and other fruits.

James Foster listed as grape grower in Walla Walla.

<u>1883</u> *The Walla Walla Statesman* reported that 22,000 vines, or about 30 acres, were planted in Walla Walla Valley.

Temperatures in February reached -20° F in Walla Walla.

<u>1889</u> State of Washington admitted to the union.

Adam Eckert moved to Stretch Island from Chautauqua, New York, and established a grape nursery in 1890.

Wine Creek Winery, owned by Louis Jaffe family, existed in Seattle's Pioneer Square from 1889 to 1915.

H. S. Simmons, in Wenatchee Valley, planted Zinfandel grapevines and made wine from the grapes when vines were four years old.

<u>1890</u> Washington State College (WSC) chartered as a land-grant College at Pullman.

John Brice, a homesteader, planted Sweetwater grape for home use near White Bluffs along the Columbia.

<u>1893</u> Washington State Board of Horticulture in its first report listed Concord, Moore's Early, Isabella, Black Prince, Royal Muscadine, Black Hamburg, Sweetwater, Worden, and Flame Tokay grape varieties. Ritz Nursery of Walla Walla listed Catawba, Pockington, Niagara, Diamond, Black Spanish, Black July, Red Riesling, Chasselas Rose, Delaware, and White Muscat.

<u>1894</u> George W. Wade shipped 4,000 crates of grapes grown along the Columbia at Columbus to Spokane and Portland.

Grapes planted and irrigated at Kennewick, but project failed because of an irrigation ditch failure and the economic panic of 1893.

Phylloxera found on *vinifera* vine roots in Kennewick by Harry Fisk, first horticultural inspector.

1896　Jacob Schaefer planted 60 acres of grapes in Agatha, just north of Clearwater River near Lewiston.

1899　*The Kennewick Reporter* noted the Stuibles grew Concord grapes without irrigation.

1902　**William B. Bridgman, from Ontario, Canada, arrived in Sunnyside and promoted irrigation.**
Idaho Sauternes made by Robert Schleicher evaluated in California by USDA agent George C. Hussman as "equal to the best wines made in Napa County, California."

1903　Northwest Improvement Company of Northern Pacific Railroad developed a successful irrigation project in Kennewick. Grapes planted.
Jacob Schaefer planted grapes for wine in Vineland at Clarkston.

1904　**First known Concord grapes planted in Yakima Valley by E. P. Dopps at Outlook.**

1905　Concord grapes planted at White Bluffs.
Winthrop Presby loaned $10,000 by Lucy Palmer Maddock to obtain grape varieties from Europe for planting at Columbus. Possible varieties imported: Muscat of Alexandria, Black Hamburg, Black Muscat, Malvoisie, Alicante Bouschet, Chardonnay, and Sultana.
W. E. Haxton of Kennewick claimed he got a $400 return on grapes from 300 vines of Flame Tokay, Black Muscat, and Sweetwater.
Turner Davis of Finley had 1.8 acres of Semillon.
E. F. Blaine, a Seattle attorney, grew grapes and operated Stone House Winery near Grandview, making wine out of Concord, White Diamond, Zinfandel, and Black Prince—shipping wines in 50-gallon barrels to Cle Elum and Roslyn. Also, wines made and shipped by Paul Charvet, Blaine's winemaker, at his own winery.
Gillenwaters, from a farm at Columbus, displayed 21 varieties of grapes at fruit fair in Goldendale.
Adam Eckert, writing in August 1905 edition of *The Mason County Journal*, stated that Lambert Evans arrived at Stretch Island in 1878: "Mr. Evans obtained cuttings of Concord, Hartford, Prolific [sic; should be Hartford Prolific, one variety], and an unknown variety of grapes; these fruited in, or about, 1883, and were a complete success."

1906　Delsol, Schleicher, and Schaefer had wineries producing and selling wine in the Lewiston-Clarkston area.
B. Rollins, of Richland, had 10 acres of Sweetwater grapes which returned a profit of $840 per acre.

1907　Sam Hill, noted road builder, began acquiring land at Columbus.
The Dalles Nurseries in Oregon was an early supplier of grapes for Pacific Northwest.

1908　"The Grape in Washington," by F. A. Hundtley, stated successfully established grape varieties were: (American varieties) Concord, Worden, Moore's Early, Campbell Early, Brighton, Delaware, Niagara, and Diamond; (*vinifera* varieties) Flame Tokay, Rose of Peru, Emperor, Black Cornichon, Black Hamburg, and Malaga. Best grapes for juice were Concord, Weston, and Campbell Early. Best grape areas were Columbus and Kennewick.

1909　Frank Cole planted 2 Italian wine varieties and 1 German variety at Finley, southeast of Kennewick.

Dr. F. S. Hedger, of Kiona, said "that any man without previous experience can net $300 per acre from a vineyard of a standard European variety."

Stark Brothers Nurseries and Orchard Company ad in the Kennewick paper listed these grape varieties: Mission, Worden, Niagara, Campbell, Flame Tokay, Stark Eclipse, Moore's Early, White Muscat, Stark E. Philip, Black Cornichon, and Thompson Seedless.

1910 Adam Eckert published *Grape Growing in the Pacific Northwest.* Out of 75 varieties tested, he listed the following varieties grown on Stretch Island as desirable: Green Mountain, Wyoming Red, Moore's Early, Vergennes, Delaware, Brighton, Campbell Early, Cottage, Worden, Niagara, Concord, Isabella, Catawba, Eaton, and Diamond.

In the text is first mention of the selection he called "Island Belle" (a controversial synonym for Campbell Early), which likely had been planted at least four years earlier.

1911 Jacob Schaefer's Vineland near Lewiston purchased by J. E. Moore of Rothschild Corporation of Portland, Oregon. He intended to sell 30,000 gallons of wine through developing markets.

Largest crop of grapes expected—25,000 crates, or 62.5 tons, to be shipped from Kennewick.

First Columbia River Valley Grape Carnival held, in Kennewick—over 40 entries of grape varieties.

1913 Robert Schleicher published in Idaho Manual of Horticulture that *vinifera* varieties were being tested in Snake and Clearwater River Valleys.

Reverend W. T. Jordan, who acquired Tokay Ranch from Maddock, grew Muscat of Alexandria grapes at Maryhill and shipped fresh each day, in season, by train.

Church Grape Juice Company of Kennewick processed first unsweetened Concord grape juice in the west—about 22,000 gallons.

1914 W. B. Bridgman planted Black Prince, Flame Tokay, and Ribier grapes on Harrison Hill in Sunnyside.

Valleygreen Farm near White Bluffs had vineyard of Flame Tokay and Black Hamburg.

1915 Gravity irrigation system of Sunnyside Canal completed.

Eckert Juice Company founded (and continued until 1943).

1916 First carload of Concord grapes shipped from Kennewick in 3,370 five-pound baskets; growers realized $45 per ton.

1917 Bridgman bought grape cuttings from Europe and California for planting on Snipes Mountain: Black Malvoisie, Carignane, Csaba, Ribier, Sauvignon Blanc, Semillon, Thompson Seedless (Sultana), Tokay, and Zinfandel.

WSC established Irrigation Experiment Station (IES) near Prosser, with approval of state legislature.

Estimated grape shipments from Yakima and Benton Counties: ten railroad cars at $600 each.

1918 Church Grape Juice Company of Kennewick processed 40,000 gallons of Concord and Worden grape juice and 135,000 gallons of apple juice, marketed from Victoria, B.C., to Los Angeles.

Rudolph Werberger planted 1,000 Island Belle and White Diamond (Chasselas) grapevines at Pickering Passage (northeast of Shelton), supplied by Adam Eckert.

1919 Washington State Legislature unanimously ratified 18th Amendment, known as Prohibition, to the U.S. Constitution.

Legislature funded $35,000 for WSC-IES near Prosser.

1920 The 18th amendment went into effect January 16. Prohibition laws permitted a head of household to make 200 gallons of wine each year for personal use.

Yakima County's grape yield of 992.6 tons was 55 percent of the total for state. Bridgman planted Alicante Bouschet, Black Malvoisie, Carignane, Csaba, Muscat of Alexandria, Sauvignon Blanc, Semillon, Sultana Rosea, Thompson Seedless, Tokay, and Ribier grapes in Sunnyside.

1921 R. E. Carpenter had 1 acre of Thompson Seedless, located three miles above Kennewick. Frank Friermood and G. C. Lawrence both had Flame Tokay and Muscat of Alexandria grapes along Columbia River north of Richland.

E. W. Loveland Ranch, in Priest Rapids Valley, sold 850 crates of Tokay grapes at $2.00 per crate from 1 1/8 acres.

1922 Harry R. Locklin, horticulturist, WSC, recommended the following grape varieties for commercial planting in western Washington: Campbell Early (considered the same as Island Belle) and Moore's Early, and for home use, Vergennes, Delaware, and Niagara. There were 147 half cars of grapes brought into the state; 140 half cars used in western Washington, 7 in eastern Washington—of these amounts, 62.8 percent went into by-products.

Frank Subucco had 36-acre vineyard in Attalia area along Columbia River and grew grapes for "home use" and winemaking, including varieties such as Black Prince, Muscat of Alexandria, Sweetwater (Palomino), and Concord.

1923 Yakima Valley Grape Growers Union organized in Grandview.

1929 Sixteen hundred acres of grapevines, mainly Concords, produced 6,200 tons of grapes. Major part of grape crop went to Church's Grape Juice plant. Church also sold grapes in baskets.

1930 Grape production in Yakima County was 3,755 tons, approximately 75 percent of the state's production.

Severe January weather: Hanford averaged -13.6° F for nine days; Sunnyside registered a minimum of -26° F.

1933 **Washington became 24th state to repeal 18th ammendment.**

Quarantine law invoked against importation of phylloxera-infested vines.

Fred Pardini had 30 acres of *vinifera* grapes—15 of Zinfandel, 10 of Muscat of Alexandria, and a mix of 5 acres of Tokay and Black Malvosie—at Richland "Y" near Kennewick.

St. Charles Winery, U.S. Bonded Winery No.1, established by Charles Somers on Stretch Island. Erich Steenborg, a Geisenheim, Germany, trained winemaker, assisted in making 3,000 gallons of wine.

Frank Subucco supplied National Wine Company, of Seattle, with grapes.

Melvin F. Tucker sharecropped table and wine grapes for Bridgman.

1934 Yakima Valley Grape Growers Association (YVGGA) incorporated. It recorded total harvest of 203 tons of Early Campbell and 943 tons of Concord grapes.

Erich Steenborg, Dr. Henry Benson, Edgar J. Wright, and W. R. Reeves of Grapeview, and H. E. Drew of Shelton, incorporated to form Stretch Island Winery.

Bridgman made first commercial planting of Riesling, near Sunnyside, which later was identified as Scheurrebe. Upland Winery was bonded No. 13 and opened in November; it made 7,000 gallons of wine from its own 90 acres of vineyard.

Washington State Liquor Control Board (WSLCB) created by state legislature through Steele Act (also known as Washington State Liquor Act).

1935 Steele Act amended to permit "domestic wineries," using state-grown fruit exclusively, to sell direct to wholesalers and taverns. Out-of-state wines had to be sold only through WSLCB.

Washington Wine Producers Association established on January 14: founding members were St. Charles Winery, Davis Winery, Rudolph Werberger Winery, Wright Winery and Distillery, and Pommerelle Winery.

Washington wineries sold 22,374 gallons of wine valued at approximately $40,000.

<u>1937</u>   State wine consumption was 1,988,057 gallons—1.2 gallons per capita—sixth highest in U.S.

An all-time high of 42 wineries operated in the state.

Walter J. Clore appointed assistant horticulturist at WSC-IES near Prosser. Clore initiated trial plantings of tree and small fruits, including American, European, and French hybrid grape varieties.

<u>1938</u>   Bridgman imported premium wine varieties from Europe and California for planting in Sunnyside area. Julian Steenbergen became winemaker for Upland Winery.

WSLCB began sampling all wines in process of being manufactured as well as finished wines, and confiscated thousands of gallons of spoiled or contaminated wine.

American and European hybrid varieties planted at Maryhill Museum by Zola O. Brooks, as advised by Bridgman.

Leading wineries (in production figures) were St. Charles, Pommerelle, National Wine Company, Wright Winery (Everett), Washington Distilleries, Connoisseur Winery, Upland Winery, Stretch Island Winery, and Interstate Winery.

Total wine production was 1,872,989 gallons.

Pommerelle Winery acquired shares in National Wine Company.

WSLCB required wineries to submit labels for approval, together with copies of their "winemaking formulas."

<u>1939</u>   YVGGA harvested 800 tons of Concord and Campbell Early; marketed fresh, for juice and for wine.

Washington Wine Producers Association reorganized as Washington Wine Council (WWC).

State wineries exported record 300,950 gallons of wine.

WSLCB confiscated over 60,000 gallons of wine.

<u>1940</u>   Herman Wente and Leon Adams, representing California wineries, visited Washington wineries.

Total state grape production was 12,200 tons.

First year that Washington state wines and brandy made from grapes outsold wines made from other fruits.

Bridgman provided WSC-IES with *vinifera* varieties for testing.

WSLCB required wineries to post wholesale prices to control price fluctuations.

<u>1941–45</u>   Rapid growth in wine production by wineries able to surmount wartime regulations, especially in obtaining sugar and glass.

<u>1941</u>   **At WSC-IES, Clore planted premium wine grapes supplied by Specialties Nursery of Vernon, B.C., which included Limberger.**

Upland Farms expanded grape plantings with Alicante Bouschet, Campbell Early, Csaba, Fredonia, Grey Riesling, Zinfandel, Carignane, Pinot Noir, and Sultana.

State-produced wines sold record high of 65.7 percent of all wines sold in the state.

<u>1942</u>   Twenty-six licensed wineries in the state.

Industry estimate listed use of 15,000 tons of fruit in production of wine.

Church Grape Juice Company expanded acreage of grapes to 683 acres, becoming nation's largest owner of Concord vineyards, to supply its juice plant in Kennewick and Upland Winery in Sunnyside and other wineries in the state.

WSLCB issued ration cards to liquor and spirits purchasers.

WSLCB began testing wine by UW College of Pharmacy.

<u>1943</u>   State Department of Agriculture (WSDA) issued Quarantine Order No. 25, "Grape Phylloxera in Other States." Phylloxera found in Vashon Island

vineyard by entomologist from WSC-Western Washington Experiment Station, Puyallup.

WSLCB authorized to set winemaking standards for sanitation, ingredients, quality, and identity, and to conduct studies relating to alcoholic beverages and their use and effect.

UW College of Pharmacy, at request and financing of WSLCB, chemically analyzed Washington wines "to establish or disprove, if possible by chemical means, the alleged toxic qualities of certain types of wines and to set standards of identity and purity for Washington wines." No toxicity found.

Office of Price Administration (OPA) during World War II controlled grape prices: for juices, $32.10 per ton, for wine, $30.30 per ton.

Clore and Bridgman co-authored "Grape Culture in Irrigated Eastern Washington," in March issue of *Arboretum Bulletin* of UW.

Professor Henry K. Benson of UW wrote "Grape Growing in the Puget Sound Region," in *Arboretum Bulletin.*

1944 William Barnard became manager of Upland Farms. Grape varieties grown were Thompson Seedless, Black Monukka, Perlette, Delight, Palomino, Muscat of Alexandria, Carignane, Mataro, Concord, Campbell Early, Ruby Red, Black Hamburg, Csaba, Red Malaga, Semillon, Alicante Bouschet, and Malvoisie.

WSLCB officially began testing all wines at UW's College of Pharmacy.

1945 Melvin Tucker, from east of Sunnyside, contracted with Upland Winery to grow and deliver Chasselas Rose, Brilliant, Diana, Golden Muscat, Malvoisie, and Riesling grapes, and currants, to Upland Winery.

Census of all grapevines by counties showed that 93 percent of all grapevines in the state were grown in eastern Washington.

Postwar slump caused many wineries to go out of business. OPA controls taken off of wine grapes.

Wineries produced 2,769,442 gallons, a record that stood until 1987.

1947 WSLCB regulated and set minimum retail prices on out-of-state wines.

Yakima Valley and Tri-Cities region had 6,629 acres of grapes.

Seventy-two American varieties and American hybrids and 54 European grape varieties grown on trial at WSC-IES.

1948 U.S. table wine consumption was 25 million gallons.

Operating wineries in Washington reduced to 21.

Initiative 171 passed, legalizing sale of spiritous liquor by the drink in restaurants and hotels.

1948–49 **Sustained low winter temperatures without snow cover resulted in loss of American grape varieties on shallow and gravelly soils, and severe loss of all European varieties (-8° F in January at WSC-IES).**

Fifty-five hundred acres of grapes in 1948 produced 24,000 tons. Six thousand acres in 1949 produced 20,300 tons.

1949 **E. & J. Gallo Winery made its first purchase of Concord grape juice from Washington state, of approximately 4,000 tons, supplied by YVGGA.**

1949–50 **Lowest temperature recorded at WSC-IES occurred in February, -20° F. Killing subzero temperatures in successive years discouraged planting of European grape varieties.**

1950 Dr. Nelson J. Shaulis, viticulturist, from New York Agricultural Experiment Station at Geneva, New York, spent six-month sabbatical at Prosser studying Concord grape culture. He identified beginning of 2,4-D herbicide drift problem on grapes.

Total grape production was 22,500 tons from 6,000 to 8,000 acres. Total state wine sales were 2,212,000 gallons; sales of state-produced wine were 1,006,423 gallons.

California grape growers and wineries pressured California Department of Agriculture to threaten boycott of Washington apples if restrictive out-of-state wine sales measures not removed in Washington state.

1951   Bridgman sold his controlling interest in Upland Winery.

Heavy loss of grape shoots due to frost on April 21.

Mealy bugs found on grapevines.

1952   Total acres of grapes in the state: 7,000, with 21.3 percent non-bearing. Grape crop of 36,300 tons exceeded previous high of 24,000 tons in 1948.

WSLCB sold 1,500 cases of Almaden Rosé from California, which became a popular table wine produced by Washington wineries.

1953   Research by Clore and Vic Bruns found Concord grape extremely sensitive to minute quantities of 2,4-D. Drs. Huber, Blodgett, and Clore surveyed 2,4-D injury on grapes in Yakima Valley and Pasco-Kennewick area. Church Grape Juice Company, of Kennewick, lost injunction suit to stop aerial spraying of 2,4-D by wheat growers on grain in nearby Horse Heaven Hills.

E. & J. Gallo Winery of California contracted with YVGGA of Grandview for 300,000 gallons of Concord grape juice.

Estele Elmer of Walking Horse Ranch, in east Wenatchee, had 10.4 acres nearly equally divided in plantings of Alicante Bouschet, Muscat, and Zinfandel.

1954   Federal wine laws liberalized; flavored wine permitted.

Dessert wine sales decreased for first time.

Pommerelle and National Wine Company (Nawico) merged to form American Wine Growers (AWG), and marketed Grenache Rosé in corked bottles under Granada brand name.

There were 7,500 acres of grapes in Washington, with 3 percent of acreage in western Washington. Yakima, Benton, and Franklin Counties were grape areas in eastern Washington, while Mason County was most important in western Washington.

1955   **A disastrous freeze, Black November, occurred in Pacific Northwest November 11–14, damaging many crops, shrubs, and trees. Temperature suddenly dropped to 0° F at WSC-IES near Prosser and to -8° F at Kennewick. Freeze was so damaging because of its early occurrence and lack of plant maturity.** Grape production reduced by 39 percent the following year.

Washington wineries sold 1,207,936 gallons of wine worth approximately $4 million. Value of grape crop to growers amounted to $3 million. Wineries of the state had invested over $5 million in plants and equipment.

1956   WWC named trustees: Lowell Quinn, president; Howard Somers, vice-president; Victor Allison, treasurer; Ivan Kearns, executive secretary.

AWG purchased one of Bridgman's vineyards north of Grandview, which contained Alicante Bouschet, Black Monukka, Carignane, Chardonnay, Campbell Early, Csaba, Pinot Noir, Sultana, and Zinfandel.

1957   **Alhambra Winery planted in its vineyard, near Grandview, first heat-treated certified Cabernet Sauvignon and Pinot Noir vines in the state, obtained from Foundation Plant Materials Service of UC Davis, California.**

AWG planted Grenache, Pinot Noir, and Semillon in its Vineyard No.6 north of Grandview.

Vere Brummund employed as an aide in horticultural program at WSC-IES.

WSC-IES supplied grape varieties to Agriculture Extension Service for home trials with eastern Washington growers.

1958   **Amateur winemakers in Seattle organized as Associated Vintners (AV) and began buying *vinifera* grapes from Yakima Valley growers.**

Only 9 licensed wineries in the state.

WSLCB reported 51 percent of all wine sales were Washington wines, a noted decrease.

U.S. Supreme Court refused to rule on a suit brought by state of California against protective wine laws in Washington state.

WWC named Keith Hall, president; Howard Somers, vice-president; Victor Allison, treasurer; Ivan Kearns, executive secretary; Angelo Pellegrini, consultant. Council comprised of 59 growers and 6 wineries, producing 1,500,000 gallons of wine from 8,000 tons of grapes.

Angelo Pellegrini hired as public relations consultant to wine industry, including advisory role to wineries and growers.

1959   WSC became Washington State University (WSU).

Frank A. Anderson, horticulturist, became Area Extension Agent for Benton and Franklin Counties.

Washington State Department of Commerce and Economic Development (H. Dewayne Kreager, director) published a paper, "The Grape Industry in the State of Washington."

Bridgman listed Black Muscat, Csaba, and Italia as some of the cold-hardy European grapes.

Initial request from WWC asking for help from WSU-IES to research grape problems.

1960   Total state grape production: 38,400 tons.

WWC reorganized as Washington Wine and Grape Growers Council (WWGGC).

Dr. Clore, horticulturist, and associates of WSU began wine grape field research at WSU-IES.

Dr. Charles Nagel joined WSU faculty.

George Thomas bought Upland Winery and changed name to Santa Rosa Winery; Tom Hoenish became superintendent and Marie Christensen became first female winemaker in Washington state.

Washington's per capita wine consumption was 0.9 gallon.

1961   State legislature authorized inauguration of plant propagation and certification program, which included grapes.

WSU-IES obtained *vinifera* wine varieties from Foundation Plant Materials Service of UC Davis.

Dr. Clore took a year's sabbatical in Japan studying Japanese fruit culture, including grapes.

Brummund, aide at WSU-IES, encouraged WWGGC to plant only premium *vinifera* varieties.

1962   **AV incorporated and bonded, and purchased 5.5-acre vineyard site on Harrison Hill in Sunnyside from Bridgman.**

Total of all grapes was 11,000 acres. Total production was 51,800 tons.

Wine grape production of Santa Rosa Winery was 596 tons; of Upland Farm, 77.2 percent were European and 22.8 percent were American varieties.

AWG at Grandview crushed 2,758 tons.

WSLCB noted increase in table wine sales.

1963   **AWG planted its first Cabernet Sauvignon, west of Benton City.**

AV joined WWGGC and planted its Harrison Hill vineyard to Riesling, Gewurztraminer, Grenache, Chardonnay, Semillon, and Cabernet Sauvignon with UC Davis–certified vines and Pinot Noir from AWG.

Yakima Valley Grape Producers, Inc. (YVGP) received order from E. & J. Gallo Winery for 8,209 tons of Concord grapes primarily for production of Cold Duck wine in California.

Tom Walters grew Malvoisie and Alicante Bouschet southeast of Kennewick toward Finley.

1964   **Dr. Charles Nagel, of WSU at Pullman, began winemaking research using grapes from vineyards at WSU-IES with annual funding of $1,250 from WWGGC.**

Seneca Grape Juice Company established juice processing plant at Prosser.
Grape acreage for wine consisted of 54 percent American varieties, 45 percent
European, and 1 percent French hybrid.
**WSDA established grape certification program for virus-free vine planting
stock.**
Powdery mildew became problem on European grapes.

1965   **Table wines outsold dessert wines within the state; dessert wines went from
40 percent of state sales to 27 percent, and 95 percent of Washington wines
were sold within the state.**
WSU-IES became WSU-Irrigated Agriculture Research and Extension
Center (IAREC). Seventeen grape varieties from WSU-IAREC made into
wine at WSU in Pullman by Dr. Nagel, and evaluated by tasting group of
forty people.
AWG renamed Ste. Michelle Vintners. Howard Somers became the enologist,
and began making premium wines.
St. Charles Winery sold trademarks and wine inventory to Alhambra Winery.
WSU-IAREC received indexed virus-free cuttings from USDA at Davis,
California, and established a 1.5-acre varietal test block for propagation and
wine grape studies.
In Finley, several growers had wine grape plantings: Clarence V. Rush, Doc
Mercer, Jack Blankenship, Turner Davis, Bob Cunningham, and Kirkendahl.

1966   Member wineries of WWGGC were Alhambra Winery, Ste. Michelle
Vintners, Associated Vintners, Old West Winery, Santa Rosa Winery, and
Werberger Winery and Distilling.
**George Carter, chemist, became winemaker at WSU-IAREC, sending fin-
ished wines to Dr. Nagel at WSU for taste evaluation.**
**Leon Adams, wine expert and writer, visited wineries and vineyards in
Washington and encouraged increased plantings of premium wine grapes.**
Grape varieties grown for winemaking by WWGGC were Golden Chasselas
(syn. Palomino), Chardonnay, Grenache, Portugese Blue, Semillon, Alicante
Bouschet, Muscat of Alexandria, Pinot Noir, Zinfandel, Delaware, Campbell
Early, and White Diamond.
Cooperatively with WSU-IAREC, Dorothy Prior of Prior Land Company
contributed a site behind Paterson well for testing grape varieties on Horse
Heaven Hills slope.
WSLCB reported purchases for 985 cases of Chardonnay in 1965–66.

1967   California Wine Institute lost an appeal in U.S. Supreme Court against
Washington state's protective and restrictive wine laws.
**André Tchelistcheff, Beaulieu Vineyards' winemaker, tasted Gewurztraminer
made by Phil Church, an AV partner, and proclaimed it the best he had tasted
in U.S.**
**Ste. Michelle Vintners retained Tchelistcheff as consultant and adopted Ste.
Michelle Vineyards as brand name.**
First prototype grape harvester tested experimentally by WSU-IAREC.
Robert Fay, aide, started work in grape research program at WSU-IAREC.
**Consumption of table wines exceeded that of dessert wines nationally for first
time since Repeal.**
Prior to 1968 there were an estimated 212.8 acres of premium wine grapes.

1968   Bridgman died at ninety years old. George Thomas, owner and manager of
Santa Rosa Winery, died ten days later.
**First grapes picked commercially in Washington by machine were 900 tons of
Concords by Frederic P. Kellian of Outlook with Chisholm-Ryder machine.**
**Charles Henderson planted wine grapes above White Salmon. Don Graves
planted wine grapes at Dallesport and Dr. George Stewart bought and
planted wine grapes on former portion of Upland Farm.**

Estimated grape acreage: Concord, 9,458 acres; American hybrids, 491 acres; European, 431 acres; and French hybrids, 35 acres.

Drs. Raymond Folwell and Richard Dailey joined WSU faculty for agricultural economic research, which included grapes.

1969 Grape stock certification program, established by WSDA, initiated cooperatively with WSU for providing true-to-name, productive, and disease-free propagating material. First cuttings released to Washington nurserymen from Foundation Block at WSU-IAREC.

Operating wineries were Ste. Michelle Vintners, Alhambra Winery, Associated Vintners, Old West Winery, Santa Rosa Winery, Columbia Winery, Auburn Winery, and Werberger Winery.

State legislature passed House Bill 100, called California Wine Bill, which allowed out-of-state wineries to sell their wines the same as in-state wineries, devastating state wineries.

WWGGC disbanded as result of economic effect of HB 100. Werberger Winery and Auburn Wineries closed.

Wine offerings by wine wholesalers and retailers expanded dramatically. Retail wine stores licensed.

Total Washington state consumption of wine was 4,338,813 gallons; 41.9 percent of total was state-produced wines. Washington state per capita consumption of wines was 1.27 gallons.

Thirteen mechanical picking machines harvested 31 percent of grape crop.

California researchers and winemakers responded favorably to Washington's experimental wines.

Veredon Vineyard established European varietals near Plymouth.

With release of AV's 1967 Riesling and Gewurztraminer, Stan Reed, columnist for *Seattle Post-Intelligencer*, wrote, "A new industry has been born in Washington. Its name is Associated Vintners, Inc."

1970 Wine distribution increased 53.5 percent to 6,659,720 gallons in the state, resulting from stocking shelves with out-of-state wines; 18.6 percent of wines sold in 1970 were state-produced wines, compared to 41.9 percent in 1969. There were 431.3 acres of premium wine grapes.

Bon-Vin, of Houston, Texas (Charles Finkel and Robert Conley), became U.S. agent for Ste. Michelle Vineyards brand.

Bob Moreman planted wine grapes north of Pasco. Dr. Don Merkley planted wine grapes on the Royal Slope.

After tasting Washington state wines, San Francisco Wine Sampling Club declared Washington's wines posed "a serious challenge" to California's best.

Ste. Michelle Vintners was first to harvest wine grapes by machine, picking Csaba grapes into 1-ton plastic-lined bins with a Chisholm-Ryder.

Twenty-seven thousand tons of Concords harvested by twenty-two machines, 49.5 percent of 1970 crop.

E. & J. Gallo Wine Company signed ten-year contract with YVGP for 1.5 to 2 million gallons annually of Concord juice.

Table wine sales increased dramatically, to 70.7 percent of all wines sold in the state.

1971 Washington State Grape Society (WSGS) formed.

Seneca Grape Juice Company built 250,000-gallon winery at Prosser and employed Andy Tudor as winemaker.

Julio Gallo visited WSU-IAREC, tasted experimental wines, and recognized Washington's potential for producing premium wines.

USDA Western Regional Research Laboratory, at Albany, California, partially funded WSU wine research for three years at $25,000 per year.

Snake River Vineyards, east of Pasco, planted 500 acres of Concords and 70 acres of European wine grapes.

Joan and Lincoln Wolverton planted wine grape vineyard in southwest Washington near La Center.

Maury Balcom planted 106 acres of *vinifera* grapes for Balcom and Moe northeast of Pasco.

Grape Diseases Quarantine retained by WSDA, and Registration Certification Order established with Foundation Block funded by WSU-IAREC under Dr. Gaylord Mink, plant pathologist.

A total of 79,400 tons of grapes crushed from 12,000 bearing acres; 96.7 percent were Concords.

Per capita wine consumption in Washington state rose from 1.44 gallons in 1957 to 2.43 in 1971.

1972 **Numerous new wine grape plantings made, all on own-rooted grapevines. Vineyard Management Company's Sagemoor Farms, northwest of Pasco, planted largest acreage of certified vines, managed by John Pringle.**

Total of 1,155 acres of wine grapes. Between 1968 and 1972, greatest percentage increase of wine grape plantings occurred.

Bill Preston made initial plantings of 8 wine varieties five miles north of Pasco. Other *vinifera* plantings made by David Gallant, west of Burbank; Charles Henderson, above White Salmon; Hinzerling Vineyards by Mike Wallace, north of Prosser; Don and Linda Mercer near Alderdale; Bill Timmons, north of Grandview; and Dr. William McAndrews, above Underwood.

During WSLCB fiscal year ending in June, 1,646,535 gallons of wine produced.

WSGS sponsored first annual Grape School and Trade Show, held February 1, and published proceedings.

Seneca Company introduced Boordy wines, labeled Yakima Red, Yakima White, and Yakima Rosé.

Keiichiro Yagasaki, president of The Alps Company of Japan, purchased Concord jelly and converted it back into juice in Japan because of its restrictive import measures.

Covering of cold-sensitive wine grapes by Ste. Michelle Vintners discontinued, because of expense, covering and uncovering problems, and improved cultural practices that promoted vine maturity.

Early December, -7° F caused severe loss of young grapevines.

Olivier Laporte, graduate of Bordeaux University's Institute of Enology, and whose family owns Chateau Croix Beau Séjour in St. Emilion, evaluated WSU experimental wines and was impressed with Merlot.

Alfred Newhouse bought 200-acre vineyard and orchard of Upland Farms.

AV bought 80-acre Stout property north of Sunnyside, expanding its plantings.

Of all states, Washington ranked eighth in wine entering distribution channels.

Ste. Michelle Vintners marketed 5 varietal wines under Ste. Michelle Vineyards label in twelve western states.

1973 Because of subzero '72 cold, nearly all young vineyards replanted. Older vines not affected.

Variety wine grape project initiated by Robert Wing, a Lewiston, Idaho, meteorological technician, included in Washington Wine Project studies.

DDT, used to control cutworms and leafhoppers in vineyards, banned January 1.

Pete Christensen, farm advisor and grape specialist, UC Agriculture Extension Service, Fresno, California, spent six-month sabbatical at WSU-IAREC studying Washington grape problems.

Ste. Michelle Vinters sold to investor group and changed name to Ste. Michelle Vineyards. Purchased 500 acres in Cold Creek area and planted 100 acres each to Riesling and Cabernet Sauvignon.

VMC investors planted Dionysus vineyard of 180 acres sixteen miles northwest of Pasco.

Mike Sauer established 120 acres of vineyards north of White Swan on south bench of Ahtanum Ridge.

Jed Steele planted small trial vineyard about twenty miles northeast of Spokane at 2,400 feet elevation, which proved unsuitable for premium wine grapes.

YVGP contracted to supply E. & J. Gallo Winery with Concord grapes for seven more years.

2,4-D air monitoring studies in south-central Washington conducted by WSU College of Engineering.

First Pacific Northwest Grape and Wine Seminar held, November 7 and 8, in Yakima.

1974   WSU's grape and wine research received $43,270 funding by Economic Development Administration for three additional years.

Ste. Michelle Vineyards purchased by United States Tobacco Company (UST) of Greenwich, Connecticut; 334 more acres planted at Cold Creek Vineyard. Its 1972 Johannisberg Riesling won first place in blind tasting sponsored by *Los Angeles Times.*

Ste. Michelle Vineyards accounted for 75 percent of state's production. Joel Klein became winemaker for Ste. Michelle Vineyards in August.

Dr. Raymond Folwell, WSU agricultural economist, stated that "as much as 20 percent of the state's Concord crop has been going to California to make 'pop wines.'"

Dr. George Stewart planted first premium wine grapes on Wahluke Slope southeast of Mattawa.

Charles Henderson opened Bingen Winery, in Bingen on north shore of Columbia River.

Washington Wine Society (WWS) founded and held first annual seminar, in December.

Stu Bledsoe, director of WSDA, temporarily banned high-volatile 2,4-D in Washington state.

Max Benitz, Prosser legislator, sponsored and helped pass tax on wine for grape research.

1975   Ste. Michelle Vineyards acquired Bon Vin. Japanese Emperor Hirohito served Ste. Michelle Vineyards' 1973 Semillon at White House dinner in Washington, D.C.

Enological Society of Pacific Northwest (ESPN), founded by Washington wine enthusiasts, held its first wine festival at Pacific Science Center in Seattle.

John A. Williams and James J. Holmes planted wine grapes in Red Mountain area east of Benton City.

Pascal Ribereau-Gayon, professor at Bordeaux University's Institute of Enology, visited and tasted experimental wines at WSU-IAREC.

Regional researchers from Oregon, Idaho, and Washington met at WSU-IAREC to review wine grape project funded by EDA.

1976   **Chateau Ste. Michelle's new winery and corporate offices opened in September at former site of Hollywood Farms in Woodinville.**

ESPN attained a membership of 2,300 members. Chapters eventually formed in Yakima, Prosser, Tri-Cities, Wenatchee, Vancouver, Spokane, Moses Lake, and Moscow, Idaho. Wine judges in ESPN's second festival headed by Dr. Helmut Becker, Geisenheim, Germany; Leon Adams, California wine writer; Philip Hiaring, editor of *Wines and Vines;* Tom Stockley, *Seattle Times;* Dr. Charles Nagel, WSU food scientist; and Barney Watson, OSU food scientist.

Hinzerling Winery, first modern family winery, opened in Yakima Valley

at Prosser.

Preston Wine Cellars, near Pasco, licensed and opened.

Manfred Vierthaler Winery founded, and European wine grapes planted near Puyallup in western Washington.

WSU experimental Limberger wine recognized as European red of considerable promise in tasting by San Francisco Bay Area Wine Writers.

Andy Tudor, winemaker, field man, and fruit buyer for Seneca Foods, died.

Dr. Walter J. Clore, horticulturist at WSU-IAREC, retired after thirty-nine and a half years of research, and became grape industry consultant.

Leo J. Dion, director of YVGP, wrote history of YVGP and of grape growing in Grandview area.

AV's wine production was 9,000 gallons. It released a '72 Cabernet Sauvignon and a '72 Pinot noir.

Chateau Ste. Michelle crushed its first Pinot Noir for making Blanc de Noir sparkling wine.

Salishan Vineyards, at La Center in southwestern Washington, produced its first wine under its label.

WSU published Bulletin 823, "Ten Years of Grape Variety Responses and Wine-Making Trials in Central Washington," by W. J. Clore, C. W. Nagel, and G. H. Carter (basis of Wine Project).

First sizable acreage of European grapes mechanically harvested and crushed in same operation were Cabernet Sauvignon and Riesling in Chateau Ste. Michelle's Cold Creek Vineyard.

1977   Victor Allison, vice president of production at Chateau Ste. Michelle, died September 30.

Dr. Walter J. Clore received first "Man of the Year Award" by WSGS. Subsequent awards established in Clore's name.

George Carter, chemist and wine researcher, retired from WSU-IAREC.

Operating wineries: Alhambra Winery (last year of operation), Associated Vintners, Bingen Wine Cellars, Hinzerling Winery, Preston Wine Cellars, Puyallup Valley Winery, Chateau Ste. Michelle, Leonetti Cellars, Salishan Vineyards, and Snohomish Valley Winery.

Richard L. Small planted 6 acres of Chardonnay north of Lowden in Walla Walla Valley.

Kay Simon became assistant winemaker at Chateau Ste. Michelle in Woodinville.

Washington wines represented 7 percent of all wines sold in Washington.

Dr. Nagel, WSU food scientist, said, "Washington's best white wines include White Riesling, Gewurztraminer, Chardonnay, Semillon, and Muller-Thurgau; reds are Merlot, Cabernet Sauvignon, Pinot Noir, and Grenache."

Gerard and JoAnn Bentryn planted 1.2 acres of Muller-Thurgau on Bainbridge Island, west of Seattle.

1978   Chateau Ste. Michelle planted vineyards at Paterson, first grown under circle irrigation.

Dr. Wade Wolfe, graduate of UC Davis, became viticulturist for Chateau Ste. Michelle.

Kay Simon became red wine enologist at Chateau Ste. Michelle-Grandview Winery.

Les Fleming, vineyard manager at Chateau Ste. Michelle, retired after forty-one years. He had been winery manager, winemaker, and vineyard manager.

Variety trial plots established with Colville and Spokane Indian tribes, at Kettle Falls and at Rice.

Washington state had 19,000 acres of grapes including: 15,501 acres of Concord, 822 acres of American hybrids, 2,600 acres of European varieties, and 77 acres of French hybrids.

Don and Norma Toci, farmers from Arizona, planted premium wine grapes on Wahluke Slope east of Mattawa.

David and Harold Mielke had 7.5 acres in Spokane area, but found it preferable to plant acreage on Wahluke Slope.

Wine Library was established at Prosser Public Library by Roza Chapter of Enological Society of Pacific Northwest.

Approval by WSDA, Order No. 1583, certified quality of Washington state grapevines as true to varietal type and free from known viruses.

Grape trials conducted for Puget Sound area from plantings made in 1973 by Al W. Stratton, winemaker; Dr. Robert A. Norton, horticulturist; and W. E. Bratz, research technologist, at WSU Northwestern Washington Research and Extension Unit, at Mount Vernon.

Al Stratton, near Everson, established Mount Baker Vineyards.

Dean Tucker, of Sunnyside, established vineyard for starting winery.

Gary and Nancy Figgins of Walla Walla planted Merlot.

Scott Pontin planted premium varieties for developing winery four miles north of Prosser.

Dr. M. Ahmedullah, assistant horticulturist, appointed to WSU-IAREC to conduct grape research studies.

1979 A dry, severe 1978–'79 winter damaged hundreds of acres of wine and juice grapes. Most losses due to shallow planting.

Chateau Ste. Michelle removed 324 acres of vines at Cold Creek because of cold-damaged roots. Vineyard replanted after sub-soiling and adding soil amendments.

VMC sold cuttings from its California-certified, virus-free vines, providing good planting stock for new plantings or replantings.

Preston Wine Cellars won ESPN's first Grand Prize for its 1977 Chardonnay, made by Rob Griffin.

Charles Hooper family planted wine grapes near Husum.

Eugene and Maria Neuharth planted an experimental vineyard of 33 varieties at Sequim.

Michael A. Hogue planted 110 acres on Roza Irrigation Project northeast of Sunnyside.

Frank Anderson, area horticultural agent in tree fruits and grapes in Benton County, retired.

Robert Fay, research technician in grapes at WSU-IAREC, retired.

Widespread 2,4-D contamination of grapes in lower Yakima Valley and Tri-Cities area.

Stan Clarke, viticulturist, became fieldman for Chateau Ste. Michelle.

David Lake, Master of Wine, became AV's winemaker.

First Tri-Cities Northwest Wine Festival held, in Pasco.

Total wine consumption in-state was 11,547,000 gallons, with per capita of 2.94 gallons.

1980 Second Washington Wine Symposium, sponsored and directed by Diana Comini, held at Towne Plaza in Yakima.

Seven-year research study, "Changes in Low Temperature Resistance of Grape Buds," showed survival of 50 percent dormant primary buds of Concord at -14.8° F, Riesling and Cabernet Sauvignon at -9.4° F, by E. L. Proebsting, horticulturist, M. Ahmedullah, horticulturist, and V. P. Brummund, technologist, of WSU-IAREC. Published in *American Journal of Enology and Viticulture*, Vol. 31, No. 4.

Allen Shoup named vice-president of marketing for Chateau Ste. Michelle.

Quail Run Vineyards (later renamed Covey Run Winery) planted 178 acres of 7 wine grape varieties north of Zillah.

Gail and Shirley Puryear planted small acreage of 3 premium varieties northwest of Zillah.

Jeff and Bill Gordon planted 80 acres of premium varieties east of Pasco on
north shore of Snake River above Ice Harbor Dam.

Vere Brummund retired from WSU-IAREC.

Contamination of 2,4-D severe on grapes in lower Yakima Valley, Cold Creek,
and Paterson areas.

AV's wine production increased to 25,000 gallons.

Dr. Sara Spayd, food technologist, joined WSU-IAREC faculty in August.

Total state wine consumption was 13,072,000 gallons with a per capita of
3.17 gallons.

1981   **Chateau Ste. Michelle started construction of $25 million winery at Paterson.**
         Peter Bachman became vice-president of winemaking and Greg Loeffler
         became new assistant viticulturist.

         John W. Watson, extension agent and area viticulturist, appointed as tree fruit
         horticulturist for Yakima, Benton, and Franklin Counties.

         Washington Certified Grape Nurserymen's Association provided WSU with
         $1,000 grant in support of research.

         VMC established 230 acres of premium wine grapes on Wahluke Slope, four-
         teen miles east of Mattawa, under management of Tom Thorsen, master's
         graduate in viticulture at UC Fresno.

         State total of European grape acreage was 7,742, with 55.4 percent non-bearing.
         **Substitute Senate Bill 3408 appropriated funding to departments at WSU,
         one-fourth cent per liter of wine sold, solely for research programs in viticul-
         ture, enology, and agricultural economics.**

         Ray E. Hunter, horticulturist for Grant and Adams Counties in tree fruits and
         grapes, retired.

         Art Byron, an airline pilot, planted 25 acres of Riesling on east end of Royal
         Slope at Hunter Hill Vineyards.

         Total wine consumption in-state was 13,992,000 gallons with per capita of
         3.32 gallons.

1982   Bill Powers planted 80 acres of premium grapes on Badger Mountain near
         Kennewick.

         Paul Portteus planted wine grapes northeast of Zillah.

         David Staton established three unique trellises for wine grapes just below "The
         Gap," south of Yakima.

         Michael Taggares planted wine grapes on Radar Hill at east end of Wahluke
         Slope.

         Mike and Debbie Hanson planted wine grapes in east Wenatchee.

         Leland and Lynda Hyatt planted 73 acres to wine grapes northwest of Zillah.
         First Wine and Food Fair held in Prosser August 14.

         Washington Wine Institute (WWI) formed; Paul Thomas elected president.
         Wine consumption was 13,697,000 gallons with per capita consumption of
         3.23 from 22 operating wineries in the state.

         Dr. Raymond Folwell of WSU reported 7,906 acres of wine grapes in
         Washington; 1,111 planted this year.

         Chateau Ste. Michelle-Paterson winery crushed its first grapes. Kay Simon
         became winemaker.

         John M. Anderson and John M. Salvini, in a joint operation but separate
         investments, each developed 80 acres of wine grapes. Anderson later became a
         very effective director for WAWGG and chairman of WWC.

1983   Bureau of Alcohol, Tobacco, and Firearms (BATF), on January 1, increased
         minimum varietal content of wine to be used with a varietal name, from
         51 percent to 75 percent.

Pacific Northwest Grape short course held in August.

First Tacoma Wine Festival.

Vancouver Chapter of Enological Society of Pacific Northwest sponsored Cabernet Sauvignon seminar in Vancouver.

Society of Wine Educators, at its national wine meeting in Seattle, honored André Tchelistcheff, Leon Adams, and Dr. Walter Clore for contributions made to the Washington state wine industry.

Yakima Valley appellation established by BATF on March 23.

Jack Durham, near Waitsburg, planted wine grapes.

WSDA's Wine Marketing Advisory Council formed for promotion of Washington wines out of state with $300,000, under direction of Lila Gault, funded by the legislature.

Ronald Holden became public affairs director for Washington Wine Institute (WWI). Noel Bourasaw became director later that year; remained until 1985.

Washington Association of Wine Grape Growers (WAWGG) formed.

Yakima Valley (Appellation) Wine Growers Association formed.

Hogue Cellars located its winery in Development Building in Prosser. Won two gold medals for their first two wines at ESPN's Wine Festival.

AV changed its name to Columbia Winery.

Erick Hanson, WSU horticultural graduate, became resident manager of VMC, and replaced Jerry Bookwalter.

The Wine Almanac of the Pacific Northwest first published by Noel V. Bourasaw in December.

Central Washington Wine Technical Group formed, of trained and experienced winemakers.

Total state wine consumption was 14,210,000 gallons with per capita of 3.3 gallons.

1984   **Walla Walla appellation established by BATF on January 12.**

Columbia Valley appellation approved by BATF on October 24, and included both Yakima and Walla Walla viticultural areas.

Allen Shoup became executive vice-president of Chateau Ste. Michelle.

Widespread 2,4-D injury on grapes.

Cold damage of -14° F in December 1983 and frost of 22° F in October 1984 resulted in several growers installing wind machines for freeze and frost protection.

Serious crown gall problem occurred mostly on two- and three-year-old immature vines.

Total wine production was 17,800 tons from 9,712 acres.

Forty-five wineries produced 2,988,400 gallons of wine.

Washington state became second-largest producer of premium wines in U.S.

Total state consumption of wine was 15,183,000 gallons with per capita of 3.49 gallons.

1985   Leon Adams visited Yakima Valley wineries revising his book *The Wines of America.*

Spokane Community College established a two-year vocational curriculum to train students to enter the grape industry.

Wine Grape Seminar held in May combined meetings of members of WWI and WAWGG, held at Pasco.

Chateau Ste. Michelle celebrated fifty years of grape growing and twenty-five years of making varietal wines.

Frost of 24° F on April 21 damaged vines and reduced crop.

Bob Skelton and Evelyn McLain established 5-acre vineyard of wine grapes east of Benton City on Demoss Road.

Tom Campbell and Hema Shah established a vineyard east of Zillah.

Michael and Patricia Manz planted 1 acre to Pinot Noir and Chardonnay near Spokane for producing champagne-styled wine.

First Spokane Wine Festival.

Hogue Cellars won Best of Show at Atlanta International Wine Festival for its 1983 Cabernet Sauvignon Reserve. Latah Creek won a gold for its Muscat Canelli. 1983 Latah Creek Wine Cellars' Merlot awarded gold medal at 16th International Wine and Spirits Competition in Bristol, England; 1976 Chateau Ste. Michelle Cabernet Sauvignon also awarded gold medal.

Wine and Spirits Buying Guide awards 1978 Leonetti Cellars' Cabernet Sauvignon as Best American Red Wine.

Columbia Winery released vineyard-designated wines.

Fifty-one operating wineries.

Legislature funded promotional programs for the wine grape industry at $140,000 per year until July 1987.

Dr. Wade Wolfe and Stan Clarke were instructors of viticulture and enology at Yakima Valley College (YVC).

Pacific Northwest Grape Short Course, "Canopy Management," a three-day course, held in August.

Grape Crown Gall Symposium held in Kennewick.

Washington Wine Writers' Association held its first annual dinner and selected Woodward Canyon Winery's 1984 Cabernet Sauvignon, Dedication Series, as top wine.

Total state wine consumption was 16,194,000 gallons with per capita of 3.67 gallons.

1986   **Washington Wine Commission legislation signed by Governor Booth Gardner.**

Douglas Gore became winemaker at Chateau Ste. Michelle-Columbia Crest at Paterson.

Dr. Robert Wample, plant physiologist, transferred from WSU to WSU-IAREC to conduct grape research.

First annual Western Washington Wine Fair, in Puyallup.

Snoqualmie Falls Holding Company bought controlling interest of Langguth Winery.

Total wine consumption in Washington state was 16,760,000 gallons (ranked tenth in U.S.) and 3.76 gallons per capita.

1987   WWC funded by combination of dedicated tax and direct industry assessments for promoting and marketing Washington state wines.

The Moderation Reader published by Gene Ford.

WSLCB reported Washington wine sales increased 11 percent over previous fiscal year.

First year that Washington wineries produced more wine (4,539,133 gallons) than previous record high of 1946–47 (2,769,447 gallons).

Sixty-nine wineries in operation.

Langguth Winery filed for bankruptcy re-organization.

Washington produced oversupply of wine grapes, producing 40,500 tons—largest crop to date.

Wineries shipping wine to Pacific Rim countries were Chateau Ste. Michelle, Staton Hills, Mount Baker Vineyards, Arbor Crest/Washington Cellars, Hoodsport Winery, Latah Creek Wine Cellars, Worden Washington, and Preston Premium Wines.

Hogue Cellars of Prosser shipped 150 tons of fresh wine grapes to Japan.

Total Washington wine sales: 2,698,576 gallons.

1988   **WAWGG voted to support WWC equivalent assessment.**

Simon Siegl became executive director of both WWI and WWC with office merger of these two wine organizations.

Washington wine grape growers, as of June, numbered 182.

Phylloxera found in 8 locations out of 109 sites and only one was a *vinifera* vineyard, which was destroyed.

Yakima Valley confronted with severe irrigation water shortage.

Total Washington wine sales: 3,244,457 gallons, 24 percent increase over 1987.

Largest wine grape crop produced to date: 37,100 tons of white and 8,900 tons of red grapes.

Hogue Cellars shipped 700 tons of fresh grapes to Japan.

Wine Country Magazine named Chateau Ste. Michelle Best American Winery for 1988.

Leon Adams, André Tchelistcheff, and Dr. Walter Clore presented The Governor's Award by WWC at inaugural Northwest Wine Auction at Chateau Ste. Michelle in Woodinville.

Vicki Chiechi appointed as WWI's government affairs representative.

Senator Max Benitz obtained appropriation fund of $100,000 for WSU for faculty and equipment for wine industry research.

1989   **Five Washington wines from different wineries made top 100 wines listed in December 31 *Wine Spectator* magazine: Hogue Cellars, Johnannisberg Riesling; Woodward Canyon Winery, Cabernet Sauvignon; Kiona Vineyards Winery, Chardonnay; Latah Creek Wine Cellars, Merlot; and Columbia Winery, Cabernet Sauvignon.**

Chalone Group of San Francisco and Walla Walla investors established Canoe Ridge Vineyards on east end of Canoe Ridge about nine miles downriver from Paterson.

Charles Hossom became manager of all Chateau Ste. Michelle vineyards.

Chateau Ste. Michelle named Winery of the Year by *Wine & Spirits* magazine and Taster's Guild.

Eric and Janet Rindal of Waterbrook Winery in Lowden established their vineyard five years after their winery was bonded.

Corbin Houchins became legal counsel to WWI.

First World *Vinifera* Conference held, July 17–19, in Seattle; featured Riesling grape.

Badger Mountain Winery made its first wine shipment of 4,000 gallons to The Alps Company, in Nagano, Japan.

Total sales of Washington-produced wines: 4,032,294 gallons, 24 percent increase over 1988.

1990   Jeff Gordon, former president of WAWGG, honored for his work as winegrower and dedication to WAWGG and wine industry.

Senator Max Benitz died August 29.

Hogue Cellars shipped about 1,700 cases of Johannisberg Riesling Blush and Merlot to Japan.

Washington growers harvested 38,000 tons of wine grapes.

Total state wine consumption was 15,124,000 gallons; per capita was 3.11 gallons.

Total Washington-produced wine sales: 5,029,057 gallons, 25 percent increase over '89.

1991   Mike Sauer of Red Willow Vineyards named by WAWGG as Outstanding Grower of 1990.

Stimson Lane Vineyards and Estates purchased large acreage on Canoe Ridge, downriver ten miles below Paterson, and planted 100 acres to Merlot and Chardonnay.

Chateau Ste. Michelle's '87 Cabernet Sauvignon awarded only gold medal for American red wine at Vin Expo, Bordeaux, France.

Eight Washington wines named to *Wine Spectator*'s top wines in the world.

In November, CBS's "60 Minutes" presented a program that explored the "French Paradox," which suggested that drinking red wine reduces incidence of heart disease.

Alec Bayless, Sagemoor and VMC partner and highly respected Seattle attorney and community leader, passed away.

Second World *Vinifera* Conference held, July 11–13, in Seattle; featured Cabernet Sauvignon and Merlot.

Badger Mountain Winery shipped first wine made from organically grown grapes to Japan.

Washington harvested 26,000 tons of wine grapes.

Washington wine sold in state was 2,447,615 gallons, 3 percent increase over '90. Total sales of Washington-made wines was 5,306,985 gallons, increase of 6 percent over '90.

Total state wine consumption was 14,634,000 gallons; per capita of 2.92 gallons.

1992 Jane and Vernon Brown of Fairacre Farm and Nursery named by WAWGG as outstanding growers of 1991.

Enology Scholarship Fund set up in Dr. Charles Nagel's name to be awarded to WSU food science student interested in science of wines and winemaking.

Dr. Lloyd Woodburne, one of main founders of AV (later Columbia Winery and now AV), died June 20.

April 15 issue of *Wine Spectator* recognized Rick and Darcey Small of Woodward Canyon Winery and others as producing Washington wines of world-class quality, and more affordable.

Wine Spectator, in May 15 issue, lauded Allen Shoup, president of Stimson Lane Vineyards and Estates (U.S. Tobacco's subsidiary and umbrella for wineries formerly and collectively known as Chateau Ste. Michelle), as "Washington Wine's Gentle Giant." Then in October 31 issue, featured him again in article entitled "The Force Behind Washington Wine."

Julio R. Gallo, of E. & J. Gallo Winery, in letter to Walter Clore on May 7, wrote, "We have never bought any wine from Washington state, but have bought Concord grape juice and concentrate from Yakima Valley grape growers since 1949." He further wrote, "I am impressed with the quality of the wines that are being produced in Washington at this time."

July re-broadcast of CBS's "French Paradox" influenced 39 percent increase in red wine sales nationally.

In honor of Alec Bayless, first recipients of The Alec Bayless Foundation Award were Dr. Walter J. Clore, WSU retired horticulturist, and Dr. Charles Nagel, professor of food science and human nutrition at WSU.

Washington state ranked eighth among all states in wine entering distribution channels.

Fifty thousand tons of grapes harvested.

Washington wine sold in state was 2,362,885 gallons.

State wine consumption was 14,628,000 gallons; per capita was 2.85 gallons.

Total Washington wine sales: 4,997,276 gallons, decrease of 5.8 percent from 1991.

WWC initiated publication of *Latitude 46º*, quarterly newsletter about wines and winemakers of Columbia Valley.

1993 Erick Hanson, manager of VMC vineyards and orchards, was named by WAWGG as Outstanding Grower for 1992.

State legislature passed portion of funding for WWC of one-fourth cent per liter, from dedicated portion of excise tax on wine sales.

Julio Gallo of E. & J. Gallo Winery killed in accident on his family ranch, May 2.

In May, Alec Bayless Prize Foundation Award presented to Dr. Wade Wolfe, viticulturist and manager for Hogue Cellars, and David Lake, Master of Wine and winemaker for Columbia Winery.

Third World *Vinifera* Conference held, July 14–17; featured Sauvignon and Semillon.

Chateau Ste. Michelle built Canoe Ridge Estate Winery for production of red wines.

AV purchased Paul Thomas Wines.

Record crop of 62,000 tons of wine grapes crushed.

Washington wine sold in Washington was 2,402,291 gallons, increase of 1.7 percent over '92.

Total Washington state wine sales was 5,605,344 gallons, increase of 12.2 percent over '92.

1994 Mike Hogue, of Hogue Cellars and Vineyards, elected by WAWGG as Outstanding Grower of '93.

André Tchelistcheff, dean of California winemakers and wine consultant to Chateau Ste. Michelle, died; 1901–94.

Alec Bayless Foundation Prize awarded to Mike Sauer of Red Willow Vineyards; Allen Shoup, president of Stimson Lane Vineyards and Estates; Victor Rosellini, Seattle restaurateur; and Mark Takagi, Queen Anne Thriftway's wine manager.

Yakima Valley growers faced severest water shortage in history of irrigation.

Interstate wine shipments permitted to reciprocal shipping states.

Wine Spectator **in September 30 issue recognized "Washington's Contenders," highlighting Merlot, Chardonnay, and other wines.**

WWC reported record 6,162,727 gallons of Washington wine sold in fiscal year ending June 30, increase of 10 percent over '93. Sold in-state: 41.1 percent; out-of-state: 58.9 percent.

Record 8,750,051 gallons of wine from 85 wineries produced from 1993 harvest of 62,000 tons.

Washington State Agricultural Statistics Office reported 44,000 tons of *vinifera* grapes produced from nearly 13,000 acres.

Eighty-five bonded wineries in state; 48 of them members of WWI and represent over 90 percent of state's production.

Tom Hedges of Hedges Cellars, in Issaquah, exported 12,000 cases of wine to Sweden.

According to November 15 *Wine Spectator*, Gary Figgins, of Leonetti Cellars, makes country's best Merlot, and classic Cabernet, too.

Wine Spectator **reported in December 31 issue that Washington averaged five wines in top ten wines of the world 1988–1994.**

DNA tests by Dr. Don McKenzie, pathologist at Plant Quarantine Station, Vancouver Island, B.C., found no difference in Campbell Early and Island Belle grape tissues tested.

1995 Columbia Crest Winery at Paterson added 78,000 square feet of underground storage space for 27,000 59-gallon barrels at estimated cost of $3.4 million.

Tom Hedges built million-dollar, 15,000-square-foot winery next to his 39-acre vineyard on Red Mountain, east of Benton City.

AV built new 18,000-square-foot winery for its Paul Thomas Wines, with 400,000-gallon tank capacity, north of Sunnyside.

Leading markets for Washington wines, by size, in U.S.: California, New York, Illinois, Florida, Massachusetts, Oregon, Colorado, Texas, Pennsylvania, Michigan, Virginia, and Maryland; international: Canada, U.K., Sweden, and Japan.

April 30 *Wine Spectator* lists top fifty Washington wineries that sell Chardonnay at $10 or less per bottle.

Dr. Walter Clore and Dr. Charles Nagel received 1995 Merit Awards from American Society for Enology and Viticulture.

Fourth World *Vinifera* Conference held, in Seattle, July 13–15; discussed defining world-class wines and related general subjects.

Washington Wine Honors (formerly Alec Bayless Foundation Awards) annual celebration held August 13, at WSU-IAREC. Those receiving Washington Wine Honors: Erick Hanson, viticulturist and VMC manager; Mike Hogue, of Hogue Cellars, for winery development; Christopher Figgins, for student fellowship; Lane Hoss, for Victor Rosellini Restaurateur of the year; and Bob Broderick of Associated Grocers, as Washington's retailer of the year.

Stimson Lane Vineyards and Estates provided WSU $250,000 for future wine grape research. This fund endowed professorship for Dr. Robert Wample to enhance wine grape program.

BATF approved Puget Sound appellation, effective October 4.

Gordon Brothers Cellars built new $500,000 winery off of Interstate 182 and Road 68 in Pasco.

Chalone Group opened Canoe Ridge Winery in remodeled Walla Walla Railroad building, on National Historic Register.

Sales of Washington wine totaled 7,000,000 gallons for year ending June 30.

WWC reported 89 wineries and 145 independent vineyards producing *vinifera* wine varieties on 14,000 acres.

State wine grape yield was 60,000 tons.

1996   *The Washington Post,* on January 10, stated, "Washington's Merlots and Cabernets present an unusual case, rising from obscurity to stardom on the strength of the classic virtues of balance and consistency."

Gerard and JoAnn Bentryn of Bainbridge Island Winery released their first Bainbridge Island-grown Pinot Noir.

Five days of subzero weather prevailed January 30, 3l, February 1, 2, and 3 with minimums from -5° F to -27° F in eastern Washington. Main grape sites exposed to -12° F to -16° F with six-inch covering of snow. Most devastating cold weather for grapes in forty-six years.

Annual WAWGG meeting, February 13, well attended and addressed many facets of cold problem.

American Vintners Association published Bulletin (Feb. 8): "ATF Issues Final Rules on Permitted Varietal Names." Allowed use of Island Belle name and recognized it as synonym of Campbell Early.

Last year's "unfunded mandate" acted on by legislature, requiring WSU to undertake $525,000 of activity in wine grape research.

AV purchased Covey Run Winery at Zillah.

Washington wineries and growers voted to continue supporting WWC.

Hogue Cellars in Prosser doubled its tank storage.

New winery developments: McCrea Cellars moved to Rainier; Andrew Will Winery moved to Vashon Island; Thurston-Wolfe Winery moved from Yakima to Port of Benton in Prosser.

Columbia Winery at Woodinville completed $3 million remodel of production space, retail, and tasting room.

Silver Lake Winery of Bothell moved to former site of French Creek Winery in Woodinville.

Simon Siegl resigned as executive director of WWC and WWI to become president of American Vintners Association in Washington, D.C. His replacement was Steve Burns, former international market manager for California Wine Institute.

Washington Wine Honors recipients: for viticulture, Charles Hossom, director of vineyard operations, Stimson Lane Vineyards and Estates; for enology,

Brian Carter, vice-president and winemaker at Washington Hills Cellars; for retailer of the year, Michael Teer, owner of Pike and Western Wine Shop; scholarship for Cliff Marr, in wine microbiology, WSU department of food science.

John Anderson resigned from WWC. Replacement was Norm McKibbon of Walla Walla.

Dick Boushey, WWC board member, presented to Governor-elect Gary Locke's transition team:

1) International reputation increasing, with exports to over twenty-five countries.
2) In 1995, 6,936,000 gallons produced, which had doubled in four years.
3) Fourteen thousand acres planted capable of producing 60,000 tons.
4) Producers: 225 growers, 91 wineries.
5) Over 500,000 visitors tour state's wineries annually.
6) Capital investments valued at over $250 million for vineyards and wineries; retail product value over $175 million annually; impacted state economy by more than $40 million annually; each acre of vineyard generated $4,000 in federal, state, and local tax revenue.

WINERIES

The following list includes all known wineries that have operated, or are operating, in Washington state. Change of name, or ownership, is indicated by a slash mark (/). Years of operation are listed only if known, or if clear from historical records. A dash (–) indicates that it is assumed the winery is still in operation.

Year Founded	Winery Name	Location	Known Years of Operation
1874	John Galler	East Wenatchee	1874–1910
1875	Philip Miller	Wenatchee	1875
1876	Frank Orselli	Walla Walla	1876
	Jean Marie Abadie	Walla Walla	1876
1889	Wine Creek Winery	Seattle	1889–1914
1906	Jacob Schaefer	Clarkston	1906–1911
1910	Paul Charvet	Grandview	1910
	Stone House Winery	Grandview	1910–1914
1933	St. Charles Winery/ Alhambra	Grapeview	1933–1965
	Werberger Winery	Shelton	1933–1971
1934	Davis Winery	Grapeview	1934
	Morton's Winery	Montesano	1934
	National Wine Company (Nawico)/ American Wine Growers/ Stimson LaneVineyards & Estates	Seattle/ Grandview	1934–
	Pommerelle/American Wine Growers/ Stimson Lane Vineyards & Estates	Seattle	1934–
	Upland Winery/Santa Rosa Winery	Sunnyside	1934–1972
	Washington Distil- leries/Alhambra	Seattle/Selah	1934–1977
1935	Columbia Wineries	Vancouver	1935
	Connoisser Wineries	Seattle	1935
	Muehr's Winery	Vaughn	1935
	Stretch Island Winery	Grapeview	1935–1947
	Summit Winery	Bellevue	1935
	Sunny Slope Winery	Lake Stevens	1935
	Wright Winery	Everett/Grandview	1935
1936	Fred Woermer	Edmonds	1936
	Harley Hake	Dockton (Vashon Island)	1936
	Henry Oldfield	Lake Stevens (Everett)	1936
	Italian Wineries	Seattle	1936

Year Founded	Winery Name	Location	Known Years of Operation
	Old Mill	Seattle	1936
	Rasmussen Winery	Sultan	1936
	Sennet de Louiselle	Clarkston	1936
	Smith Winery	Burlington	1936
	Stock's Winery	Gig Harbor	1936
	Union Wines/Old West Winery	Seattle/Renton	1936–1971
	Young's West Winery	Olympia	1936
1937	Mortensen & W. Reed Winery	Seattle	1937
1938	Auburn Wineries	Seattle	1938
	Berryland Wineries	Tacoma	1938
	Bert Dana's Winery	Hanford	1938
	Bert Kellett	Yakima	1938
	Claire Keene	Auburn	1938
	De Groote Winery	Cape Horn	1938
	Interstate Winery	Tacoma	1938
	L. R. Autry	Vancouver	1938
	Mary C. Borg	Bellevue	1938
	Walter Hemrich	Seattle	1938
	Washington Wineries	Tacoma	1938
	Wenatchee Winery	Wenatchee	1938
1954	American Wine Growers: merger of Pommerelle & Nawico/Stimson Lane Vineyards & Estates	Seattle/ Grandview	1954–
1962	Associated Vintners/ Columbia Winery	Redmond	1962–
1971	Seneca Foods Corp./ Boordy Vineyards	Prosser	1971–1976
1974	Bingen/Mont Elise	Bingen	1974–
	Puyallup Valley Winery/ Mount Rainier Vintners	Puyallup	1974
1976	Hinzerling Winery	Prosser	1976–
	Manfred Viertaler Winery	East Sumner	1976–
	Preston Wine Cellars	Pasco	1976–
1977	Leonetti Cellars	Walla Walla	1977–
1978	E. B. Foote Winery	Seattle	1978–
	Quilceda Creek Vintners	Snohomish	1978–
	Yakima River Winery	Prosser	1978–
1979	Paul Thomas Wines/ Associated Vintners	Bellevue/Woodinville & Sunnyside	1979–
	Kiona Vineyards Winery	West Richland	1979–
	Neuharth Winery	Sequim	1979–
1980	Hoodsport Winery	Hoodsport	1980–
	Worden's Washington Winery	Spokane	1980–

Year Founded	Winery Name	Location	Known Years of Operation
1981	Daquila Wines	Seattle	1981
	Haviland Vintners	Woodinville	1981–1987
	Lost Mountain Winery	Sequim	1981–
	Tucker Cellars	Sunnyside	1981–
	Vernier Wines/Salmon Bay Winery	Seattle	1981
	Woodward Canyon Winery	Walla Walla	1981–
1982	Arbor Crest Winery/ Washington Cellars	Spokane	1982–
	Bainbridge Island Vineyards & Winery	Bainbridge Island	1982–
	Barnard Griffin Winery	Kennewick	1982–
	Chateau Ste. Michelle–Paterson/Columbia Crest/ Stimson Lane Vineyards & Estates	Paterson	1982–
	Franz Wilhelm Langguth Winery	Mattawa	1982
	Hogue Cellars	Prosser	1982–
	Latah Creek Wine Cellars	Prosser/Spokane	1982–
	Mount Baker Vineyards	Deming	1982–
	Noel Wine Cellars	?	?
	Quail Run Winery/ Covey Run Vintners/ Associated Vintners	Zillah	1982–
	Saddle Mountain Winery/ Stimsom Lane Vineyards & Estates	Mattawa	1982–
	Salishan Vineyards	La Center	1982–
	Snoqualmie Winery/ Stimson Lane Vineyards & Estates	Snoqualmie	1982–
1983	Blackwood Canyon Vintners	Benton City	1983–
	Bookwalter Winery	Pasco/Richland	1983–
	Cloud Orchard	Vashon Island	1983
	Coventry Vale Winery	Grandview	1983–
	French Creek Cellars	Woodinville	1983
	Gordon Brothers Cellars	Pasco	1983–
	L'Ecole No. 41	Lowden	1983–
	Stewart Vineyards	Sunnyside	1983–
1984	Cavatappi Winery	Kirkland	1984–
	Champs de Brionne Winery	Quincy	1984
	Hunter Hill Vineyards	Othello	1984–
	Johnson Creek Winery	Tenino	1984–
	Mountain Dome Winery	Spokane	1984–
	Newton & Newton Winery/ Domaine Whittlesey Mark/Di Stefano Wines	Seattle	1984–

Year Founded	Winery Name	Location	Known Years of Operation
	Pontin Del Roza	Prosser	1984–
	Staton Hills Winery	Wapato	1984–
	Waterbrook Winery	Lowden	1984–
	West Valley Winery	Kent	1984
1985	Biscuit Ridge Winery	Dixie	1985
	Bonair Winery	Zillah	1985–
	Charles Hooper Family Winery	Husum	1985–
	Chinook Wines	Prosser	1985–
	Horizon's Edge Winery	Zillah	1985–
	Mercer Ranch Vineyards	Prosser	1985–
	Pacific Crest Wine Cellars	Marysville	1985
	Quarry Lake Vintners/ Balcom & Moe Winery	Pasco	1985–
	Redford Cellars	Seattle	1985
1986	Coolen Wine Cellar	South Colby	1986
	Fidalgo Island Winery	Anacortes	1986
	Oakwood Cellars	Benton City	1986–
	Seth Ryan Winery	Richland	1986–
1987	Badger Mountain Vineyard/ Powers Winery	Kennewick	1987–
	Cascade Mountain Cellars	Ellensburg	1987
	Chateau Gallant Winery Company	Burbank	1987–
	Domaine Ste. Michelle/ Stimson Lane Vineyards & Estates	Grandview	1987–
	Hyatt Vineyards Winery	Zillah	1987–
	M. W. Whidbeys/Stimson Lane Vineyards & Estates	Greenbank	1987–
	Portteus Vineyard and Winery	Zillah	1987–
	Tagaris Winery	Othello	1987–
	Vashon Winery	Vashon Island	1987–
	Wenatchee Valley Vintners	Wenatchee	1987
	Zillah Oakes Winery/ Associated Vintners	Zillah	1987–
1988	Cascade Estates Winery	Sunnyside	1988
	Eaton Hill Winery	Granger	1988–
	Facelli Winery	Woodinville	1988–
	McCrea Cellars	Rainier	1988–
	Neeley & Son Winery	Kennewick	1988
	Patrick M. Paul Winery	Walla Walla	1988–
	Steven Thomas Livingston Winery/Catarina Winery	Spokane	1988–
1989	Cuneo Cellars	Seattle/Eola Hills, Ore.	1989
	Rich Passage Winery	Bainbridge Island	1989–

Year Founded	Winery Name	Location	Known Years of Operation
	Silver Lake Winery	Woodinville	1989–
	Soos Creek Wine Cellars	Renton	1989–
	Washington Hills Cellars/ Apex Winery	Sunnyside	1989–
1990	Columbia Cliffs	Wishram	1990–
	Eaton Hills Winery	Granger	1990–
	Hedges Cellars	Benton City/Richland	1990–
	Thurston-Wolfe Winery	Yakima/Prosser	1990–
	Vin De L'Quest	Toppenish	1990
	Whidbey Island Vineyard & Winery	Langley	1990–
	White Heron Cellars	George	1990–
1991	Andrew Will Cellars	Seattle/Vashon Island	1991–
	Lopez Island Vineyards	Lopez	1991–
	Sunnyside Five	Sunnyside	1991–
	Tefft Cellars	Outlook	1991–
1992	Camaraderie	Port Angeles	1992–
	DeLille Cellars	Woodinville	1992–
	Knipprath Cellars	Spokane	1992–
1993	Canoe Ridge Estate Winery/Stimson Lane Vineyards & Estates	Paterson	1993–
	Canoe Ridge Vineyard	Walla Walla	1993–
	China Bend Vinyards	Kettle Falls	1993–
	Fairwinds Winery	Port Townsend	1993–
	Terra Blanca Vineyards	Benton City	1993–
	Wilridge Winery	Seattle	1993–
1994	Wineglass Cellars	Zillah	1994–
1995	Kestrel Vintners	Olympia	1995–
	RL Wine/Randall Harris Wines	Sunnyside	1995–
1996	Birchfield Winery	Onalaska	Recent
	Blue Mountain Cellars/ Glen Fiona	Walla Walla	1996–
	Klickitat Canyon Winery	Lyle	Recent
	Lewis & Clark Cellars	Seattle	Recent
	Pasek Cellars	Burlington	Recent
	St. Paulia Vintners	Snohomish	Recent
	Samish Island Winery	Bow	Recent
	Walla Walla Vintners	Walla Walla	Recent
	Widgeon Hill Winery	Chehalis	Recent
	Willow Crest	Prosser	Recent

GRAPE VARIETIES GROWN IN WASHINGTON STATE

Grape varieties are listed alphabetically in the first column. Some varieties are also listed by their synonym if it was equally known or used, or provides some insightful information.

In the second column, varieties are categorized broadly into three types: V symbolizes *Vitis vinifera*; AH symbolizes either *Vitis labrusca* or an American hybrid; FH symbolizes French hybrid.

In the third column, the date indicates when the variety was planted at, or in conjunction with, the Irrigated Agriculture Research and Extension Center (IAREC) in Prosser, Washington. A question mark indicates that the planting year is unknown. A blank entry indicates the variety was not at IAREC. After the date, the source is listed, if known (source key is listed at the end of the varietal list).

The fourth column indicates the period when the grape variety was grown, abbreviated into four periods: 1 = 1825–1899; 2 = 1900–1933; 3 = 1934–1969; 4 = 1970–1996.

The fifth column shows the year the variety was introduced into Washington state. The origin is also shown, if known (source key is listed at the end of the varietal list).

The sixth column lists any notes regarding the use of the variety in Washington state.

The seventh column indicates synonyms that might have been used, especially interchangeably. A synonym is also listed when it is a more commonly used name.

Grape Variety	Type	IAREC Date Planted/ Source	Period Grown	Year Introduced/ Origin	Comments	Synonym
Agawam	AH	'37/USA	1,2,3	1861		
Alicante Bouschet	V	'38/C&O	3,4	OW-F		
Aligoté	V		3,4	OW-F		
Allen's Hybrid	AH		1,2			
America	AH	'38/Mun	1,2,3	1892	Planted at Maryhill	
Aurora (Aurore)	FH	'41/BC	3,4			Seibel, 5279
Auxerrois	V		3,4	OW-F		Malbec
Baco Noir	FH	'63/NYF	3,4			
Barbera	V	'41/LF	3,4	OW-I		
Black Cornichon	V	'42/CA	1,2,3	OW		

Grape Variety	Type	IAREC Date Planted/ Source	Period Grown	Year Intro- duced/ Origin	Comments	Synonym
Black Hamburg	V	'40/CA	1,2,3	OW-AU		Trollinger (GR), Shiava Grossa (IT)
Black July	AH		1	1874(?)		
Black Malvoisie	V	'44/CA	1,2,3	OW		Cinsaut (CA)
Black Monukka	V	'40/CA	1,2,3,4	OW-P		
Black Muscat	V	'42/LF	2,3,4	OW		Muscat Hamburg
Black Prince	V		1,2,3,4	OW		Cinsaut
Black Spanish	V		1	OW-S		Lenoir
Blauer Portugieser	V	'42/USA	2,3,4	OW		Blue Portugese
Brighton	AH	'39/CAR	1,2,3,4	1870	In Eckert's Nursery	
Brilliant	AH	'52/MUN	2,3,4	1887	Planted at Maryhill	
Buffalo	AH	'48/NYF	3,4	1938		
Burger	V		3	OW-F		Monbadon
Cabernet Franc	V		3,4	OW-F		Breton (Loire), Bouchet (Bordeaux)
Cabernet Sauvignon	V	'41/LF	3,4	OW-F		Cabernet
Calzin	V	'60/DAV	3,4	1958		
Campbell Early	AH	'37/STA	1,2,3,4	1882	In Eckert's Nursery	Island Belle
Canada	AH		1,2	1800		
Carignane	V	?	2,3,4	OW-S		Carignan
Cascade	FH	'63/NYF	3,4			Seibel 13053
Catawba	AH	'37/MAY	1,2,3	1879	In Eckert's Nursery	
Charbono	V	'69/DAV	3	OW-F		
Chardonnay	V	'64/DAV	3,4	OW-F		Pinot Chardonnay
Chardonnet	V	'41/BC	3,4	OW-H		Chardonnay
Chasselas	V	'48/NYF	1,2,3,4	OW-SW		Chasselas Doré
Chasselas Doré	V	'42/USA	2,3,4	OW		
Chasselas Rosé	V	'40/WB	1,2,3	OW		Pirovano
Chasselas Rouge	V		1	OW		Gutedel
Chasselas Victoria	V		1,2	OW		
Chenin Blanc	V	'48/DAV	3,4	OWF		Pineau de la Loire
Clevner Mariafeld	V	'71/USB	3,4	OW	Pinot Noir clone	

Grape Variety	Type	IAREC Date Planted/ Source	Period Grown	Year Intro- duced/ Origin	Comments	Synonym
Clinton	AH	'41 /MAY	1,2,3	1840		
Concord	AH	'37/CAR	1,2,3,4	1849	In Eckert's Nursery	
Cornichon	V		2	1911	Grown in Kennewick	
Cornucopia	AH		1,2	1864(?)		
Cottage	AH		1,2	1809	In Eckert's Nursery	
Creveling	AH		1,2	1857		
Csaba	V	'40/WB	2,3,4	OW		Perle de Csaba
Cunningham	AH		1,2	1812		
Delaware	AH	'40/MAY	1,2,3,4	1849	In Eckert's Nursery	
Diamond	AH	'42/MAY	1,2,3,4	1870	In Eckert's Nursery	White Diamond
Diana	AH	'48/NYF	1,2	1834		
Early Burgundy	V	'41/BC	3,4			Abouriou
Ehrenfelser	V	'73/BC	4	OW-G		
Emerald Riesling	V	?/DAV	3	1948		
Eumelan	AH	'48/NYF	1,2,3,4	1847		
Feher Szagos	V	'65/USF	3,4	OW-H		
Flame Tokay	V	'37,/CA	1,2,3	OW-AL		
Foch	FH	'64/BC	3,4			Maréchal Foch
Franken Riesling	V	'40/WB	3,4	OW-G		Sylvaner
French Colombard	V	'58/CAL	3,4	OW-F		Colombard
Furmint	V	'70/DAV	2,3	OW-H		
Gamay	V	'67/DAV	3	OW-F		
Gamay Beaujolais	V	'63/DAV	3,4	OW-F	Pinot Noir clone	
Gewurztraminer	V	'42/USA	1,2,3,4	OW-G		Traminer
Green Hungarian	V	'42/LF	3,4	OW		
Green Mountain	AH		1,2	1850	In Eckert's Nursery	Winchell
Grenache	V	'63/DAV	3,4	OW-S		Garnache
Grey Riesling	V	'40/WB	1,2,3,4	OW-F		Chauche Gris
Grignolino	V	'68/DAV	3	OW-I		
Gutedel	V		1,2,3	OW		Chasselas Rouge
Hartford Prolific	AH		1,2	1849		
Himrod	AH	'56/NYF	3,4	1952		
Interlaken Seedless	AH	'48/NYF	3,4	1947		
Iona	AH	'39/MOY	1,2,3	1885		

Grape Variety	Type	IAREC Date Planted/ Source	Period Grown	Year Intro- duced/ Origin	Comments	Synonym
Isabella	AH	'37/ARM	1,2,3	1816	In Eckert's Nursery	
Island Belle	AH		2,3,4	1910(?)	In Eckert's Nursery	Campbell Early
Ives	AH	'46	1,2,3	1840		
Jefferson	AH		1,2,3	1874		
Johannisberg Riesling	V	'40/WB	1,2,3,4	OW-G		Riesling
Leon Millot	FH		4			
Limberger (Lemberger)	V	'41/BC	3,4	OW-H		Blue Burgunder, Kekfrankos (HUNG), Lemberger (GR,WA), Blaufrankisch (AUS)
Lucie Kuhlmann	FH	'68/USB	3,4			Kuhlmann 149.3
Madeleine Angevine	V	'74/USB	4	OW-F		
Madeleine Sylvaner	V		4	OW-F		
Malaga	V	'40/CA	1,2,3,4	OW-F		Semillon Blanc
Malbec	V	'62/DAV	3,4	OW-F		
Malvasia Bianca	V		?	OW-I		
Malvoisie	V	'40/WB	3,4	OW		Malvasia
Mataro	V	'42/LF	3,4	OW-S		Mourvédre
Melon (de Bourgogne)	V	'37/CAR	3,4	OW-F		Muscadet, Pinot Blanc (CA)
Mericadel	AH	'38/MUN	3		Planted at Maryhill	
Merlot	V	'65/DAV	3,4	OW-F		
Meunier	V	'42/LF	2,3,4	OW-F	Pinot Noir clone	Pinot Meunier
Mission	V	'42/LF	1,2,3,4	Chile(?)		
Moore's Early	AH	'37/CAR	1,2,3	1868	In Eckert's Nursery	
Morio Muscat	V		4	OW-G		Sylvaner- Pinot Blanc
Muller-Thurgau	V	'69/DAV	3,4	OW-G		Riesling- Sylvaner
Muscadine	AH		1,2			
Muscat of Alexandria	V	'40/WB	1,2,3,4	OW		Moscatel (SP)

Grape Variety	Type	IAREC Date Planted/ Source	Period Grown	Year Intro- duced/ Origin	Comments	Synonym
Muscat Canelli	V	'69/DAV	1,2,3,4	OW		Muscat Blanc
Muscat de Ferdinand de Lesseps	V	'41/BC	2,3	OW-F		
Muscat de Frontignan	V		3	OW-F		Muscat Blanc
Muscat Hamburg	V	'38/C&O	3,4	OW		Black Muscat (AUS)
Muscat Ottonel	V	'41/BC	3,4	OW-F		
Nebbiolo	V	'48/NYF	3,4	OW-I		
Niagara	AH	'37/CAR	1,2,3,4	1868	In Eckert's Nursery	
Norton	AH	'46/?	1,3	1830		Cynthiana
Okanagan Riesling	AH		3,4			Missouri Riesling(?)
Othello	AH		1,2,3	1859		
Palomino	V	'42/CA	1,2,3,4	OW-S		Sweetwater
Perlette	V	'51/DAV	3,4	1948		
Petite Sirah	V	'41/LF	3,4	OW-F		Durif (FR), Petite Syrah (CA)
Petite Verdot	V	'42/USF	3,4	OW		
Pinot Blanc	V	'44/?	3,4	OW		Clevener (GR)
Pinot Gris	V	'48/DAV	3,4	OW-F		Tokay d'Alsace
Pinot Noir	V	'41/LF,BC	1,3,4	OW-F		
Pinot St. George	V	?	?	OW		Negrette
Pirovano	V	'41/BC	3,4	OW		Chasselas Rosé
Pockington	AH		1,2	1870		
Queen	V	?	3,4			
Red Malaga	V	'40/CA	3,4	OW		Molinera
Red Riesling	V		1	OW		
Refosco	V	'37/LF	3	OW-I		Momdease
Ribier	V	'40/CA	2,3,4	OW		
Rkatsiteli	V	'71/USA	4	OW-R		
Rose of Peru	V	'40/WB	1,2,3,4	OW		Black Prince
Royalty	V	'61/DAV	3,4	1958		
Rubired	V	'61/DAV	3,4	1958		
Salem	AH		1,2	1867		
Salvador	AH	?/DAV	3,4			
Sangiovese	V		4	OW-I		
Sangiovese Grosso	V		4	OW-I		
Sangiovese Piccolo	V		4	OW-I		
Sauvignon Blanc	V	'42/LF	2,3,4	OW-F		Fumé Blanc

Grape Variety	Type	IAREC Date Planted/ Source	Period Grown	Year Intro- duced/ Origin	Comments	Synonym
Sauvignon Vert	V	'41/LF	3,4	OW		Muscadelle
Scheurrebe	V	'40/WB	3,4	OWG		Sylvaner-Riesling
Semillon	V	'40/WB	2,3,4	OW-F		Semillon Blanc, Chevrier
Seneca	AH	'37/NYF	2,3,4	1930		
Sheridan	AH	'44/NYF	3	1921		
Siegerrebe	V	'74/DAV	4	OW-G		
Sultana Rosea	V	'40/WB	3			
Sweetwater	V	'46/C&O	1,2,3,4			Palomino
Sylvaner	V	'41/BC	1,2,3,4	OW-G		Silvaner, Franken Riesling
Syrah	V		4	OW-F		Shiraz (AUS), Sirah, Petite Syrah (FR)
Tempranillo	V		4	OW-S		Valdepenas
Thompson Seedless	V	'40/CA	1,2,3,4	OW-P		Sultanina
Tokay	V	'37/CAR	1,2,3	OW-A		
Trousseau	V	'65/DAV	3,4			Bastardo
Up-to-Date	AH	'68/USB	4			
Valdepenas	V		4	OW-S		Tempranillo
Verdelet	FH	'62/NYF	3,4			Seibel 9110
Vergennes	AH	'48/NYF	1,2,3,4	1874	In Eckert's Nursery	
Viognier	V		4			Vionnier
Walter	AH		1,2	1850		
White Chasselas	V	'41/BC	3,4	OW		
White Riesling	V	'61/CA	1,2,3,4	OW-G		Riesling
Wilder	AH		1,2	1858		
Winchell	AH	'38/NYF	1,2	1850		
Worden	AH	'37/MAY	1,2,3	1863	In Eckert's Nursery	
Wyoming Red	AH		1,2	1910	In Eckert's Nursery	
Zinfandel	V	'37/CA	1,2,3,4	OW-I		Primitivo

Source key for grape varieties obtained by IAREC (as shown in the third column in the variety list above):

ARM	Armstrong Nursery; Ontario, California
AUE	T. Auestad; Seattle, Washington
BC	Tunbridge Nursery; Vernon, British Columbia
DAV	Plant Foundation Block, University of California Davis; Davis, California
CA	California Nursery Company; Niles, California
CAR	Carlton Nursery Company; Carlton, Oregon
C&O	Columbia & Okanogan Nursery; Wenatchee, Washington
LF	La Fata Brothers; St. Helena, California
MAY	May Nursery Company; Yakima, Washington
MIL	Milton-Freewater Nursery; Milton-Freewater, Oregon
NYF	New York State Fruit Testing Cooperative Association; Geneva, New York
USB	Bureau of Plant Industry, U.S. Department of Agriculture; Beltsville, Maryland
USF	United States Horticultural Station; Fresno, California
STA	Stark Brothers' Nursery; Louisiana, Missouri
STR	Stranahan Nursery; Lewiston, Idaho
WB	William B. Bridgman, Upland Farms; Sunnyside, Washington
MUN	T. V. Munson; Denison, Texas
MOY	C. E. Moyer; Roseburg, Oregon
OD	O. Dickerson's Nursery; Salem, Oregon

Source key for the origin of a variety (as shown in the fifth column in the variety list above):

OW	Old World
-A	Africa
-AL	Algeria
-F	France
-G	Germany
-H	Hungary
-I	Italy
-P	Iran
-PO	Portugal
-R	Russia
-S	Spain
-SW	Switzerland

SELECTED BIBLIOGRAPHY
AND REFERENCES

Listed are works that have been used directly in the making of this book. This list is by no means a complete record of all the works and sources consulted by Ronald Irvine or Dr. Walter J. Clore. It indicates the substance and breadth of material used to help formulate ideas found in this book. It is also intended as a guide to readers who wish to further explore grape growing and winemaking history in Washington state.

The authors have relied extensively on personal interviews and recorded interviews.

BOOKS

Adams, Leon D. *The Wines of America.* 4th ed. New York: McGraw-Hill, 1978.

Amerine, Maynard A., ed. *Wine Production Technology in the United States.* Washington, D.C.: American Chemical Society, 1981.

Baily, L. H. *Cyclopedia of American Horticulture.* London: McMillan, 1910.

Bancroft, Hubert Howe. History of Oregon. 2 vols. San Francisco: History Company, 1886.

————. *History of Washington, Idaho, and Montana.* San Francisco: History Co., 1890.

Bancroft, Hubert Howe. *The Works of Hubert Howe Bancroft.* Vol 27. History of the Northwest Coast. San Francisco: A. L. Bancroft, 1884.

Baxevanis, John L. *The Wine Regions of America: Geographical Reflections and Appraisals.* Stroudsburg, Penn.: Vinifera Wine Growers Journal, 1992.

Bennett, Robert Allen. *Walla Walla: A Nice Place to Raise a Family; 1920-1949.* Walla Walla: Pioneer Press, 1980.

————. *Walla Walla: Portrait of a Western Town; 1804-1899.* Walla Walla: Pioneer Press, 1980.

————. *Walla Walla: A Town Built to Be a City; 1900-1919.* Walla Walla: Pioneer Press, 1982.

Berry Parker, Martha. *Tales of Richland, White Bluffs and Hanford.* Fairfield, Wash.: Ye Galleon Press, 1986.

Board of State Viticultural Commissioners of California. *Directory of the Grape Growers, Wine Makers and Distillers of California.* Sacramento: Board of State Viticultural Commissioners of California, 1891.

British and American Joint Commission for the Final Settlement of the Claims of the Hudson's Bay and Puget's Sound Agricultural Companies. 14 vols. Washington, D.C.: Government Printing Office, and Montreal: J. Lovell, 1865-1869.

Chazanof, William. *Welch's Grape Juice—From Corporation to Cooperative.* New York: Syracuse University Press, 1977.

Church, Phil E. *Climates of the Pacific Northwest.* Seattle: Otis W. Freeman and Howard H. Martin, 1942.

Clark, Corbett. *Wines of the Northwest.* New York: William Morrow Co., 1989.

Clark, Norman H. *The Dry Years: Prohibition and Social Changes in Washington.* Seattle: University of Washington Press, 1988.

Crawford, Jeanne R. *As the Valley Was.* Yakima: Federal Savings and Loan Assoc., 1968.

DeLorme Mapping Company. *Washington Atlas & Gazetteer.* Freeport, Maine: DeLorme Mapping Co., 1988.

Dietrich, William. *Northwest Passage: The Great Columbia River.* Seattle: University of Washington Press, 1995.

Drury, Clifford M. *Marcus and Narcissa Whitman and the Opening of the Old Oregon.* Glendale, Calif.: A. H. Clark Co., 1973.

Eckert, Adam. *Grape Growing in the Pacific Northwest.* Detroit, Wash.: Eckert, 1910.

Folwell, Raymond J., and John L. Baritelle. *The U.S. Wine Market.* Washington, D.C.: U.S. Department of Agriculture, 1978.

Franchere, Gabriel. *Narrative of a Voyage to the Northwest Coast in the Years 1811, 1812, 1813 and 1814.* Ed. and Trans. J. V. Hungington. New York: Redfield, 1854.

Galet, Pierre. *A Practical Ampelography: Grapevine Identification.* Ithaca: Cornell University Press, 1979.

Gibson, James R. *Farming the Frontier: The Agricultural Opening of the Oregon Country; 1786-1846.* Seattle: University of Washington Press, 1985.

Gilbert, Frank T. *Historic Sketches of Walla Walla, Whitman, Columbia and Garfield Counties, Washington Territory.* Portland: A. G. Walling, 1882.

Gregutt, Paul, and Jeff Prather. *Northwest Wines: A Pocket Guide to the Wines of Washington, Oregon & Idaho.* Seattle: Sasquatch Books, 1994.

Hedrick, U. P. *Manual of American Grape Growing.* New York: MacMillan Co., 1917.

———. *Grapes and Wines.* New York: Oxford University Press, 1945.

Henry, Bernard Stauffer. *Studies of Yeasts and the Fermentation of Fruits, and Berries of Washington.* Seattle: University of Washington Press, 1936.

Highsmith, Richard M., and Jon Kimerling. *Atlas of the Pacific Northwest.* Corvallis: Oregon State University Press, 1979.

Hill, Chuck. *Northwest Wines & Wineries.* Seattle: Speed Graphics, 1993.

Himes, George H. "Farms of the Pioneers. Tillers of the Soil in Hudson's Bay Company Days. No General Market for Products Until the Discovery of Gold in California." *Scrapbook, Number 21.* 1910.

Holbrook, Stewart. *The Columbia.* New York: Rhinehart & Co., 1956.

Holden, Ronald, and Glenda. *Touring the Wine Country of Washington.* Seattle: Holden Pacific, 1983.

Hull, Linley M., ed. *A History of Central Washington, Including the Famous Wenatchee, Entiat, Chelan and the columbia Valleys.* Spokane: Shaw & Borden, 1929.

Hussy, John A. *The History of Fort Vancouver and Its Physical Structure.* Portland: National Park Service and Washington State Historical Society, 1957.

———. *Champoeg: Place of Transition.* Portland: Oregon Historical Society, 1967.

Interstate Publishing Company. *An Illustrated History of Klickitat, Yakima and Kittitas Counties.* Chicago: Interstate Publishing Co., 1904.

Jackson, Gary L. *Remembering Yakima by Those Who Were There.* Yakima: Golden West Publishing Co., 1975.

Janick, Jules, and James N. Moore. Advances in Fruit Breeding. West Lafayette, Ind.: Purdue University Press, 1975.

Johnson, Hugh. *The World Atlas of Wine.* New York: Simon and Schuster, 1985.

———. *Vintage: The Story of Wine.* New York: Simon and Schuster, 1989.

Kirk, Ruth, and Alexander, Carmela. *Exploring Washington's Past: A Road Guide to History.* Seattle: University of Washington Press, 1990.

Lee, D., and J. H. Frost. *Ten Years in Oregon.* New York: J. Collard, 1844.

Locati, Joe J. *The Horticultural Heritage of Walla Walla Country: 1918-1977.* College Place, Wash.: The Color Press, 1977.

Lyman, W. D. *An Illustrated History of Walla Walla Country.* San Fransisco: W. H. Lever, 1901.

———. *Lyman's History of Old Walla Walla Country.* Vol 1. Chicago: S. J. Clarke Publishing Co., 1918.

———. *History of the Yakima Valley.* Chicago: S. J. Clarke Publishing Co., 1919.

McKee, Bates. *Cascadia—The Geologic Evolution of the Pacific Northwest.* New York: McGraw-Hill, 1972.

Meeker, Ezra. *Pioneer Reminiscenses of Puget Sound.* Seattle: Lowman and Hanford, 1905.

Meinig, Donald W. *The Great Columbian Plain: A Historical Geography, 1805-1910.* Seattle: University of Washington Press, 1973.

Meredith, Ted Jordan. *Northwest Wine.* Kirkland, Wash.: Nexus Press, 1980.

———. *Northwest Wine: Winegrowing Alchemy Along the Pacific Ring of Fire.* Kirkland, Wash.: Nexus Press, 1990.

Miller, D. A. *1880 Walla Walla Directory.* [?]:Statesman Book and Job Presses, 1880.

Moulton, Gary E., ed. *The Journals of the Lewis & Clark Expedition.* Vol 5. Lincoln, Neb.: University of Nebraska Press, 1989.

Nisbet, Jack. *Sources of the River: Tracking David Thompson Across Western North America.* Seattle: Sasquatch Books, 1994.

Parker, Martha Berry. *Kin-I-Wak, Kennewick, Tehe, Kennewick.* Fairfield, Wash.: Ye Galleon Press, 1986.

Parker, Samuel. *Exploring Tour Beyond the Rocky Mountains, 1835-1837.* New York: Wiley and Putnam, 1844.

———. *Journal of an Exploring Tour: Beyond the Rocky Mountains.* Moscow, Idaho: University of Idaho Press, 1990.

Pellegrini, Angelo M. *Wine and the Good Life.* New York: Knopf, 1972.

Pellett, Kent. *Pioneers in Iowa Horticulture.* Des Moines, Iowa: Iowa State Horticultural Society, 1941.

Peterson, Ruth Jordan. *This Land of Gold and Toil.* Caldwell, Idaho: Caxton Printers, 1982.

Phillips, James W. *Washington State Place Names.* Seattle: University of Washington Press, 1982.

Pinney, Thomas. *A History of Wine in America From the Beginnings to Prohibition.* Berkeley: University of California Press, 1989.

Pitt, R. D. *Directory of the City of Seattle.* Seattle: Hanford & McClaire Printers, 1879.

Purser, J. Elizabeth, and Lawrence Allen. *The Winemakers: Of the Pacific Northwest.* Vashon Island, Wash: Harbor House Publishing, 1977.

Rittich, Virgil J., and Dr. Eugene A. Rittich Burgess. *European Grape Growing.* Minneapolis, Minn.: Publishing Co., 1941.

Robinson, Jancis. *Vines, Grapes and Wines.* New York: Knopf, 1986.

Sagerson, Mary, and Duane Robinson. *Grapeview, the Detroit of the West: A Narrative History of the Early Years, 1872-1923.* Shelton, Wash.: Mason County Historical Society, 1992.

Schoonmaker, Frank, and Tom Marvel. *American Wines.* New York: Duell, Sloan & Pearce, 1941.

Sheller, Roscoe. *Courage and Water: A Story of Yakima Valley's Sunnyside.* Portland: Binfords and Mort, 1952.

———. *Blowsand.* Portland: Metropolitan Press, 1963.

Shideler, John. *Coal Towns in the Cascades: A Centennial History of Roslyn and Cle Elum.* Spokane, Wash.: Melior Publications, 1986.

Smith, Leta May. *The End of the Trail.* Hickesville, N.Y.: Exposition Press, 1976.

Snowden, Clinton. *History of Washington: The Rise and Progress of an American State.* Vol. 5. New York: Century History Co., 1911.

Splawn, A. J. *Ka-mi-akin: Last Hero of the Yakimas.* Portland: Binfords and Mort, 1944.

Stockley, Tom. *Winery Tours in Oregon, Washington, Idaho and British Columbia.* Vancouver, B.C.: Gordon Soules Book Publishers, 1978.

Taylor, Terri A., and Patricia C. Erigero. *Cultural Landscape Report: Fort Vancouver National Historic Site.* U.S. National Park Service, vol 1. (Seattle, 1992).

Townsend, John Kirk. *Narrative of a Journey: Across the Rocky Mountains to the Columbia River.* Lincoln, Neb.: University of Nebraska Press, 1978.

Toupin, Alice M. *Moxee, The Enchanting Moxee Valley: Its History and Development.* [N.P.],1974.

Tuhy, John E. *Sam Hill: The Prince of Castle Nowhere.* Portland: Timber Press, 1985.

United States Senate, Twenty-fifth Congress, Dec. 1837. *Memorial of William A. Slacum.* Fairfield, Wash.: Ye Galleon Press, 1972.

Wagner, Philip M. *American Wines and Wine-making.* New York: Knopf, 1956.

———. *Grapes into Wine.* New York: Knopf, 1976.

Washington State Historical Society. *The New Washington: A Guide to the Evergreen State.* Rev. ed. Portland: Binfords and Mort, 1950.

Whitman, Narcissa. *The Letters of Narcissa Whitman.* Fairfield, Wash.: Ye Galleon Press, 1986.

Winkler, A. J. *General Viticulture.* Berkeley: University of California Press, 1962.

Winkler. A. J., J. A. Cook, W. M. Kliewer, and L. A. Lider. *General Viticulture.* Rev. ed. Berkeley: University of California Press, 1974.

Wirsing, Dale R. *Builders, Brewers and Burghers: Germans of Washington State.* [Olympia?]: The Washington State American Revolution Bicentennial Commission, 1977.

Wyeth, Nathaniel J. *The Journals of Captain Nathaniel J. Wyeth's Expeditions to the Oregon Country, 1831-1836.* Ed. Dr. Don Johnson. Fairfield, Wash.: Ye Galleon Press, 1984.

ARTICLES, UNPUBLISHED WORKS, PAPERS, BRIEFS, PAMPHLETS, AND THESES

Asher, Gerald. "Washington State Reds." *Gourmet,* November 1993.

Adams, Leon D. "The Wines of Washington." Brochure, Bon-Vin, 1975.

American Wine Growers. "Record of Grapes Used by Type." 1954, 1955, 1962.

Bell, Elizabeth Rose. "Seventy-two Years an Islander." Unpublished personal notes. Grapeview, [unknown date].

Benson, H. K. "Grape Growing in the Puget Sound Region." *Arboretum Bulletin.* No. 5, September 1942: 26-28,

Boddewyn, Jean Jules. *The Protection of Washington Wines: A Case Study in the State Regulation of Business.* Doctural Thesis, University of Washington, 1964.

Bridgman, W. B. "Memo to Prospective Grape Growers." Personal collection, Walter Clore. 1937.

———. "Correspondence to Zola O. Brooks of the Maryhill Museum." 1938-39. Personal collection, Walter Clore.

———. "The Pruning of Grapevines." Memo. 1946. Personal collection, Walter Clore.

———. "Notes on Life and Upland Winery." Briefing papers. 1946.

———. "Brief Relative to the Development and Condition of the Grape Wine Industry of Washington State." Briefing papers. 1948.

———. "Wine Industry Letter to WSLCB." 1950.

———. "Letter to American Wine Growers." 1956.

———. "The Wine Industry of Washington State." Briefing papers. 1965.

Cardwell, J. R. "The First Fruits of the Land: A Brief History of Early Horticulture in Oregon." *The Quarterly of the Oregon Historical Society* 7, March 1906.

Chesshire, R. H. "Fort Vancouver: Address Given at Dedication Ceremonies of the Fort Vancouver National Site, March 18, 1962." Vol III, Clark County History. Fort Vancouver Historical Society.

Choir, M. *Choir's Pioneer Directory of the City of Seattle, King County, W. T.* (Pottsville, Penn., 1878-1908).

Christiansen, P., Cyril Woodbridge, W. J. Clore, and A. I. Dow. "Boron Deficiency Occurrence and Symptoms in Washington Vineyards." *Proceedings of the Washington State Grape Society,* 1973.

Churchill, Creighton. "Wines of the Northwest." Promotional brochure, Bon-Vin. [unknown date].

Clarke, Stan. "From Berry to Bottle." *Yakima Herald-Republic.* Continuous weekly column, 1982-1996.

Clore, W. J., C. W. Nagel, G. H. Carter, V. P. Brummund, and R. D. Fay. "Wine Grape Production Studies in Washington." *American Journal of Enology and Viticulture* 23 (1972).

Clore, W. J., C. W. Nagel, and G. H. Carter. "Ten Years of Grape Variety Responses and Wine Making Trials in Central Washington." WSU Bul. 823 (1976).

Clore, W. J., and W. B. Bridgman. "Grape Culture in Irrigated Eastern Washington." *Arboretum Bulletin.* Vol.VI, No.3, March 1943.

Clore, W. J., and C. W. Nagel. "Is There a Potential in Washington for Growing *Vinifera* Grapes to Make Fine Table and Varietal Wines?" *Proceedings of the Washington State Horticulture Association.* December 1969.

Clore, W. J., and V. F. Bruns. "The Sensitivity of the Concord Grape to 2,4-D." *Proceedings of the American Society of Horticultural Science.* 1953.

Davison, Casey, ed. "Food Dealers Enjoy Washington Grapes, Wine Tour." *Washington Food Dealer.* 61, No.10, October 1966.

Davidson, Nancy. "October Is a Good Time to Explore the NW Wine Country." *Sunset Magazine.* October 1974.

Department of the Treasury. "Formula and Process for Formula Wines." Washington, D.C.: Internal Revenue Service, 1945.

———. Bureau of Alcohol, Tobacco and Firearms. Appellations (Viticultural Areas): Yakima Valley Viticultural Area, Federal Register 48, No. 65 (4 April 1983).

———. Walla Walla Viticultural Area, Federal Register 49, No. 25 (6 February 1984).

———. Columbia Valley Viticultural Area, Federal Register 49, No. 220 (13 November 1984).

DeTurk, I., Board of Viticultural Commissioners. "The Vineyards in Sonoma County;

Being the Report of I. DeTurk, Commissioner for the Sonoma District." Sacramento, 1893.

Eckert, Adam. "Grape Culture in Mason County." *The Mason County Journal.* Special Edition,August 1905.

Eckert, W. O. "Grapes in the Sound Country." *Better Fruit.* 17. November 1922: 7–8

Edwards, G. Thomas. "Irrigation in Eastern Washington, 1906-1911: The Promotional Photos of Asahel Curtis." *Pacific NW Quarterly* 72. No.3, July 1981.

Fessler, Jules H. "Sterile Filtration of Wines." *The Wine Review* 17. No.5, May 1949.

Folwell, Raymond J., Charles Nagel, and Daniel J. Kirpes. "Size and Distribution of Washington Grape Acreage". WSU Irrigated Agriculture Research Extension Center. Research Circular XCO648. Pullman, 1983.

Ford, Gene. Video Interviews of Washington Wine Pioneers. Washington Wine Commission. 1993–94.

Furgason, R. D., ed. "A Feasibility Study of the Economic Potential for the Developing Vineyards and a Wine Industry in Idaho." University of Idaho, 1973.

Gibson, James R. "Food for the Fur Traders; 1805-1846." *Journal of the West* 7:1, 18 (January 1968).

Goldwyn, Craig. "Northwest Wines Come of Age." *Pacific Search.* December-January 1979–80.

Hagood, Pat. "Columbia Basin Termed Ideal for Grape Growing." *The Goodfruit Grower* 15. April 18, 1981.

———. "Fleming Reflects on Grape Industry." *Prosser Record-Bulletin* (27 June 1985).

Hussman, George. "Grape, Raisin, and Wine Production in the United States." *Yearbook of the United States. Department of Agriculture.* Washington: Government Printing Office, 1903.

Klickitat County Historical Society. "Columbus: Located in 1852 by Amos Stark, It Was Discovered by Sam Hill in 1907." Klickitat County Historical Society 5, 1979. (Goldendale, WA).

Klickitat Heritage. "Columbus: Discovered by Sam Hill in 1907." Klickitat County Historical Society 5, No.2, 1975 (Goldendale, WA).

Knapp, Anna Sloan. "The History of the Liquor Laws of the State of Washington." *The Washington Historical Quarterly* 5, 1914 (Seattle).

Kreager, Dewayne. "The Grape Industry in the State of Washington." Working paper produced by the Department of Commerce and Economic Development. 1959 (Olympia, WA).

Laporte, Olivier. "A Frenchman Takes a Look at Washington State Wines." *Wines and Vines* (February 1972).

Ledwitz, M. W. "Technical and Economic Assistance in Fostering the Economic Development of the Wine Grape Industry of Washington." WSU College of Agriculture Research Center. 1976 (Pullman, WA).

Lewelling, Seth. Diaries. Oregon Historical Society, Portland, Ore.

Lippincott, James S. "Climatology of American Grape Vines." Report of the Commissioner of Agriculture for the Year 1862. Washington, D.C., 1863.

Locklin, Harry D. "Grapes in Western Washington." *Western Washington Experiment Station Bulletin.* 1922.

Luce, W. A. "Washington State Fruit Industry: A Brief History." *The Goodfruit Grower.* 1972 (Yakima, WA).

Mawe, Thomas, and John Abercrombie. *Every Man His Own Gardener* London: 1839.

Miller, D. A. *1880 Walla Walla Directory.* Statesman Book and Job Presses, 1880.

446 *The Wine Project*

"Mr. Abadie of Walla Walla." *Washington Standard,* 13 January 1877.
Nesbit, Robert, and Charles Gates. "Agriculture in Eastern Washington, 1906-1911." *Pacific NW Quarterly.* 37, October 1946: 279–302
North Pacific History Company. *"History of the Pacific Northwest: Oregon and Washington* 1 (Portland, 1889).
Northern Pacific Irrigation Company. *Kennewick and the Highlands.* Kennewick, WA: Northern Pacific Irrigation Company. [1910?].
Olsen, Michael Leon. *The Beginnings of Agriculture in Western Oregon and Western Washington.* Doctural Thesis, University of Washington (Seattle, 1970).
Pattison, Hugh. "Nursery Account Records; 1854-." Washington State Historical Society, Tacoma.
Peterson, W. H. "Washington State Varietal Wines." *San Francisco Wine Sampling Club.* Newsletter. (September 1970).
Roberts, A. B. "The Empire Builders." *Up-to-the-Times Magazine.* Third Year, No.27 (January 1909).
Ross, Lester A. *Hudson's Bay Company Suppliers: 1821-1852.* Internal papers shelved at Ft. Vancouver National Historic Site. Vol 1. 1979.
Schleicher, Robert. *Grape Culture in Lewiston-Clarkston Valley.* Pamphlet. Lewiston, Idaho, and Clarkston, Washington, 1906.
Scribner, B. H. "A Matter of Opinion: A Wine Smuggler Spills All." *Seattle Magazine.* Vol.5, No.56 (November 1968).
Sisters of Providence. "Journal of Expenses of the Sister of Providence of Holy Angels of Vancouver." Sacred Heart Province, 1856. Located in the Sisters of Providence Archives (Seattle, WA).
Smith, Steven B. "Valley's First White Settler." *The Wenatchee World,* 30 August 1992.
Somers, Harley. "History of Grapeview." Unpublished report held by Bob Eacrett, 1956 (Grapeview, WA).
Steenborg, Erich. "The Wines of Yakima Valley." *The Wine Review.* Vol.17,No.5 (May 1949).
Steiman, Harvey. "Washington's Contenders." *Wine Spectator* (30 September 1994).
Sullivan, Ed. "These Wines Are Good, Very Good . . ." *Seattle Business* 57, No.31 (July 1972).
"Sunnyside Pioneer Built First Winery." *Tri-Cities Herald,* 12 March 1972.
Tukey, Ronald B., and W. J. Clore. "Grapes—The Suitability for Production in Washington." Washington State University, Bul.635 (Pullman, 1973).
"Two Revolutions in Progress in Washington Grape Industry." *California Grape Growers Magazine* (April 1971).
U.S. Department of Agriculture. *Yearbook of the United States Department of Agriculture-1898.* Washington, D.C., 1899.
U.S. Department of Agriculture and Washington State Department of Agriculture. "Washington Grape Report." Washington Agricultural Statistics Service.
Walker, Anna Sloan. "History of the Liquor Laws of the State of Washington." *Washington Historical Quarterly* 5. (April 1914).
Walling, G. W., and Son. "Fruits and Ornamental Trees." Catalog of the Willamette Nursery. Oswego, Ore., 1875.
Wample, Robert L. "Evaluation of the Effect of Drought Stress on Wine and Juice Grapevine Yield, Quality, Cold Hardiness and Survival." Pamphlet. WSU Irrigated Agriculture Research and Extension Center (Pullman, January 1991).
———. "1992 Annual Report: Circle 100 (Walter Clore Vineyard) Irrigation Study; Columbia Crest." WSU (Pullman, 1992).

———. "1992 Annual Report: Circle 100 Irrigation Study Columbia Crest Winery." Washington State University (Pullman, September 1992).

"Washington's Oldest Vineyard." *NW Grape Grower/Winemaker,* March 1985.

Washington State Department of Commerce and Economic Development. "New Directions for Washington's Wine Industry." *Progress* (Spring 1970).

Washington State Legislature. *Joint Committee Hearing.* Commerce and Agricultural Committees of the Legislative Council. Yakima, June 7, 1968.

Washington State Liquor Control Board. "Annual Reports of the Washington State Liquor Control Board; 1934-1975." Washington State Liquor Control Board (Olympia, Wash.)

Washington State University. "Growing Grapes in Washington." WSU Extension Service Bul. 271 (Pullman, 1961).

———. "Economic Development Impact of an Expanded Wine-grape Industry in Washington." Washington State University, Department of Agriculture (Pullman, 1974).

———. "Data on Weather from 1924-1976." Irrigated Agriculture Research and Experiment Center Bul. 858 (Prosser, 1977).

Washington Wine Commission. *Touring the Washington Wine Country.* Brochure (Seattle, 1995).

"The Washington Wine Market." *Wines and Vines,* August 1938.

"Washington Wines on Way to Be Famous." *Seattle Post-Intelligencer,* 15 August 1938.

"Wenatchee's Resources." *The Wenatchee Advance,* 26 May 1894.

"Werbergers Look Back on 45 Years of Grapes." *Tacoma News Tribune,* 7 October 1965.

Wetmore, A. K. "Twenty Years Progress in the Vineyards and Wineries of Washington." *Tavern Topics.* (October 1956).

Willard, Helen. "Seneca to Introduce Boordy Label Red, White, Rosé Wines." *The Goodgrape Grower* (15 July 1972).

———. "Wine Grape Production Challenges Snipes Mountain Grower." *The Goodgrape Grower* (15 July 1973).

"Wined and Dined." *The Wenatchee Advance,* 23 March 1901.

"Wine Industry to Boom Without Santa Rosa Winery." *Yakima Herald-Republic,* 14 December 1971.

Wing, Robert N. "History of Wine in Lewiston." *The Journal* (Nez Perce County Historical Society) 10, No.1, 1990.

Woehler, Robert. "WWII Prison Camps Revisited: Italian POWs Sent to Work in Fields of Mid-Columbia." *Tri-City Herald,* 22 August 1993.

———. "Great Grapes: Washington Wineries Enjoy an Explosion of Growth, Expansion." *Tri-City Herald,* 23 September 1993.

Woodburne, Dr. Lloyd. Assorted papers, notes, slides, minutes: Woodburne Archives. Manuscripts and University Archives, University of Washington, Seattle.

Woodburne, Dr. Lloyd. "Associated Vintners: The First Twenty Years." Report,Seattle, 1992. Mimeographed.

Yakima Commercial Club. *The Yakima Valley.* Promotional pamplet. North Yakima. [1910?]

ARCHIVES, HISTORICAL SOCIETIES, MUSEUMS, COLLECTIONS, LIBRARIES

Archives, Sisters of Providence, Seattle.
Benton County Historical Society and Museum, Prosser.
Cle Elum Historical Society, Cle Elum.
Eastern Washington State Historical Society, Cheney-Cowles Museum, Spokane.
Eells Northwest Archive. Lawrence Dodd, Archivist. Penrose Memorial Library, Whitman College, Walla Walla.
Fort Vancouver National Historic Site, Vancouver.
Goldendale Public Library, Goldendale.
Kennewick Museum, Kennewick.
Kitsap County Historical Society and Museum, Silverdale.
Manuscripts and University Archives. University of Washington, Seattle
Maryhill Museum of Art, Goldendale.
Mason County Historical Society, Shelton.
Northwest Room. Gary Fuller Reese, Librarian. Tacoma Public Library.
Olde St. Charles Winery, Grapeview.
Oregon Historical Society, Portland.
R. E. Powell Museum, Grandview.
Roslyn Historical Museum, Roslyn.
Seattle Public Library, Seattle.
Special Collections and Preservation Division. University of Washington, Seattle.
Sunnyside Historical Society and Museum, Sunnyside.
Vashon Branch, King County Library. Vashon Island.
Washington State Historical Society, Tacoma.
Wine Library, Prosser Public Library, Prosser.
Yakima Geneological Society, Yakima.
Yakima Historical Society and Musuem, Yakima.
Yakima Valley Regional Library, Yakima.

NEWSPAPERS, PERIODICALS

The Argus (Seattle)
The Daily American Journal (Bellevue)
The Goodfruit Grower (Yakima)
The Goodgrape Grower (Yakima)
The Goldendale Sentinel
Lewiston Tribune
Los Angeles Times
The North Pacific Rural (Seattle)
NW Grape Grower (Othello)
NW Palate Magazine (Portland)
Northwest Wine Almanac (Seattle)
Olympia Pioneer and Democrat
Practical Winery and Vineyards (San Rafael, CA)
Prosser Record-Bulletin

Puget Sound Courier (Steilacoom)
Puget Soundings (Seattle)
Seattle Post-Intelligencer
The Seattle Times
The Shelton-Mason County Journal
Sunnyside Daily Newscast
Tacoma News Tribune
Tavern Topics (Seattle)
Tri-City Herald
Up-to-the-Times Magazine (Walla Walla)
The Vashon Island Press
Walla Walla Statesman
Walla Walla Union
The Wall Street Journal
Washington Democrat (Olympia)
Washington Farmer (Veradale, WA)
Washington Standard (Olympia)
The Wenatchee Advance
The Wenatchee Daily World
The Wenatchee World
The Wine Review (Los Angeles and San Fransisco)
Wine Spectator (New York)
Wines and Vines (San Rafael, CA)
Yakima Herald

INDEX